International
Public Opinion
and the Bosnia Crisis

International Public Opinion and the Bosnia Crisis

Edited by
Richard Sobel and Eric Shiraev

LEXINGTON BOOKS
Lanham • *Boulder* • *New York* • *Oxford*

LEXINGTON BOOKS

Published in the United States of America
by Lexington Books
A Member of the Rowman & Littlefield Publishing Group
4720 Boston Way, Lanham, Maryland 20706

PO Box 317
Oxford
OX2 9RU, UK

British Library Cataloguing in Publication Information Available

Library of Congress Cataloging-in-Publication Data

International public opinion and the Bosnia crisis / edited by Richard Sobel and
   Eric Shiraev.
      p. cm.
   ISBN 0-7391-0479-9 (hardcover : alk. paper)
   1. Yugoslav War, 1991–1995—Public opinion. 2. Yugoslav War,
   1991–1995—Bosnia and Hercegovina. I. Shiraev, Eric, 1960– II. Sobel,
   Richard, 1949–
DR1313.7.P83 158 2002

                                                           2002009873

Printed in the United States of America

♾™ The paper used in this publication meets the minimum requirements of
American National Standard for Information Sciences—Permanence of Paper
for Printed Library Materials, ANSI/NISO Z39.48-1992.

For Ole Holsti and Cheryl Koopman,
who inspired this work.

Contents

Introduction

Eric Shiraev and Richard Sobel

The last two decades of the twentieth century dramatically changed the international situation. The Berlin Wall fell, marking the rapid disintegration and collapse of the communist system in Eastern Europe. As a result of this transformation, the world in the early 1990s no longer appeared divided into two hostile camps. Under the assumption that democracies do not wage wars against each other, many anticipated the beginning of a unique period of human history without military confrontations. In addition, many believed that path-breaking technologies and communication would bring nations and people together. However, these rapid geopolitical, ideological, and technological metamorphoses did not create lasting peace in the world. Terrorist acts, wars for sovereignty, and violent ethnic conflicts continued to destabilize the world after the end of the Cold War.

On the territory of former Yugoslavia, at the heart of Europe, the bloodiest conflict in European history since World War II took many thousands of lives and caused pain and suffering to millions. The conflict smashed hopes for a continuous peace and sparked renewed discussions of the nature of ethnic and religious conflicts, questioning the involvement of the international community in resolving them. Moreover, the events in Kosovo in 1999 and the military intervention of NATO in Yugoslavia caused confrontations between western governments and Russia and China—two large nuclear powers. The Balkan tragedy also showed the world that despite public awareness about the conflict and desire to stop bloodshed and ethnic cleansing, their leaders' views on how to bring the conflict to an end differed substantially.

This cross-national study explores some effects of domestic public opinion on cooperative action during an earlier phase of the larger Balkan

tragedy—the war in Bosnia in the 1990s. The chapters in this volume describe how democratic governments responded to the political opinions of
their citizenry—reflected in the political debates and media assessments of
the conflict—on the conduct of foreign policy regarding interventionist measures in the former Yugoslavia.

In the context of the conflict in Bosnia-Herzegovina, the book attempts to
answer several major questions about the relationship between policy and
opinion. For example, did foreign policymakers ignore public attitudes
when the war began because the public was generally disinterested in the
conflict? Did foreign policymakers ignore public opinion because it was seen
as being too volatile to take it seriously? Or, did policymakers—in their effort
to educate the public—seek to lead public opinion and media coverage of
the conflict? All in all, did policymakers follow public opinion on international issues including the Bosnian conflict in their quest for reelection?

Overall, the authors of the volume pursued several objectives. The first
was to investigate whether public opinion matters in international conflict
resolution in general and in the Bosnia crisis in particular. Democratic theory
contends that elected leaders must be responsive to the views of their electorate. Official policy then must reflect public opinion, or political leaders
will be turned out of office. However, it was generally believed that mass
opinion about international affairs was inconsistent and inarticulate and,
therefore, had little or no impact on official policy. Have more recent events,
particularly those in former Yugoslavia, changed this relative independence
of foreign polices from public opinion? Was the international intervention in
Bosnia a predictable government's response to the demanding public opinion and the powerful media in various countries? If yes, to what extent was
the intervention based on opinions and, if not, what other factors have influenced the decision to intervene? When, how, and under what circumstances can public opinion influence elite decision making?

The second objective was to examine the links among media, public opinion, and governmental policies. If, in democracy, media help inform public
opinion by reporting on events and issues that confront government and act
as a mediating force between elites and publics, transmitting information in
both directions, media coverage should resemble public opinion in the selected countries. The book addresses the issue on whether the worldwide array of print and broadcast media capable of instantaneous coverage of
breaking events contributes to a loss of policy control for government elites
and policymakers in general. The authors also examine whether the deter-
mination to intervene in the Balkan conflict was the result of diplomatic and
bureaucratic operations, with news coverage and subsequent public opinion
responding to those decisions.

Each national case addresses at least three key issues. First, the authors
identify major national events and policies related to the conflict. Second,

they provide an overview of public opinion and media coverage of the war. Third, they investigate the links between public opinion and decision-making regarding the crisis. Each case presents and summarizes the available public opinion data about attitudes in the country toward participation in the resolution of the conflict. It also discusses how the media and political debates represented public opinion and whether the levels of support and opposition were accurately reported. Each chapter analyzes and discusses the evidence of the influence of public opinion and the media on the country's policy. This derives, when possible, from interviews with public officials in participating countries regarding their assessment of public opinion toward the intervention and how opinion affected political calculations in their nations about intervention in Bosnia.

The volume includes cases about the major participants in the Bosnia intervention, the contributors of troops to the UN or NATO forces and providers of substantial logistical and financial support to the international mission: the United States, Great Britain, France, Germany, Canada, Russia, the Netherlands, and Italy.

Chapter 1 by Erin Carrière, Marc O'Reilly, and Richard Vengroff explores Canadian public opinion and foreign policy and examines existing approaches to opinion-policy links. Based on the analysis of opinion polls, media, and elite debates, the authors then show that, to a large extent, Canadian policy has reflected public opinion about Bosnia. The authors suggest that Canadians' strong support for involvement in Bosnia is closely tied up with their self-image as a middle-power that is particularly adept at peacekeeping. The role of peacekeeping is intrinsic to Canadian political culture and thus helps some Canadians in differentiating their country from the United States. Despite the threats to the lives of Canadian troops, lack of clarity about their role in Bosnia, and significant budget cuts for the Canadian armed forces, Canadians persistently considered their country as a world leader in international peacekeeping. In general, the attitudes of elites and masses toward peacekeeping had a common source and thus naturally converged in providing ongoing support for Canadian involvement in Bosnia.

Chapter 2 by Robert J. Wybrow investigates the interrelationship among government decisions, the media, and British public opinion. It examines opinion polls conducted by Gallup and other major survey organizations in Great Britain. At the beginning of the conflict, even though members of the government were shocked at the images being transmitted by the media, the civil war in the former Yugoslavia hardly affected the government's policy in the region. With recollections of the Gulf War still fresh in their minds, and fear of repeating America's mistakes in Vietnam, there was a reluctance to get involved in Bosnia's problems. This policy of non-intervention, though, was unpopular with the general public. A majority of people were dissatisfied with the government's handling of the situation and favored the use of

British troops to protect food and medical aid convoys, as well as to help keep the warring factions apart. Even in the event of British troops suffering serious casualties in protecting aid convoys, many favored reinforcing the troops rather than pulling them out. Moreover, as media attention heightened and the violence increased, there was little shrinking in the public's support for Britain's involvement, particularly as part of an international force. The media coverage raised the public's concern about the military situation in Bosnia, thereby pressuring the government to alter its initial reactions. Throughout this period dozens of opinion polls were published, informing the government on the mood of the public. By the middle of 1996 the public were actually supportive of the way John Major was handling the situation. Thus the media had informed the general population about Bosnia's problems, and the public opinion was strong enough to force the government to follow policies that they initially had rejected.

Chapter 3 by Steven Kull and Clay Ramsay demonstrates that since 1992 the American public was inclined to favor U.S. involvement in Bosnia and generally rejected arguments against such involvement on the basis of isolationism. Arguments in favor of involvement on the basis of both humanitarian concern and national interest received strong support. Nevertheless, Americans felt they had the latitude to impose conditions on their support. The majority of Americans have only been supportive of U.S. participation in Bosnia if the operation is clearly multilateral, the United States is contributing no more than its fair share, and the operation is likely to succeed. Support has also been complicated by overestimations of how much the United States is contributing relative to other countries and by underestimations of the success of the operation. However, decision makers in Washington did not have a very accurate image of the public's attitudes, and that was influential. Initially, policymakers perceived themselves as partly constrained by the public's supposed reluctance to intervene. Later, once intervention occurred without strong opposition, they assumed that it was due to their efforts in communicating the policy and the absence of casualties. Support consolidated, not because there had not been fatalities (most Americans thought there had been) but because there was an increase in the perception that the operation in Bosnia was succeeding.

Emphasizing that a majority of the French public has consistently supported a French peacekeeping presence in Bosnia even at the expense of French casualties, Marc Morjé Howard and Lise Morjé Howard in chapter 4 illuminate the relationship between mass public opinion and elite policymaking in French policies in the Bosnia conflict. At the outset of the Yugoslav tragedy, there was a disjuncture between the French state's historical ties of affinity with Yugoslavia and Serbia, on one hand, and public opinion's outrage in response to the reports of Serb aggression, on the other. Initially, France's policy promoted the continuation of a united Yugoslavia; neutrality toward the conflicting sides; advocacy for humanitarian, rather than military intervention; and a desire to have France as a leader in efforts to end the conflict. Over time, the first three policy elements transformed, reflecting the wishes of the majority of the French public, while the desire to be a leader was consistent with public opinion since the beginning of the conflict. Over time, this gap between policy and public opinion closed. Throughout the conflict, public opinion remained fairly stable, while foreign policy changed slowly toward public opinion. Public opinion appears to have been influential, by means of its general pressure over time, along with intense pressure from the media. The chapter shows that the combined forces of public opinion polls, opinion leaders, and the media influenced significantly the direction and content of French foreign policy on intervention in Bosnia.

As Eric Shiraev and Deone Terrio imply in chapter 5, Russian elites were not careful followers of public opinion in shaping policy on Bosnia. Instead they made decisions motivated primarily by the desire to gain political capital in the country's continuous power struggle. The vast majority of Russians cared little about Russian policy in Bosnia, as was revealed in the few public opinion polls that touched on the subject. However, the "concerned minority," including opinion leaders and opposition elites, did voice opinions critical of Russia's policy on the Balkans. Gradually, in the early 1990s, Russian officially "balanced" policy toward former Yugoslavia began to change to a pro-Serbian and anti-NATO position. These policies were tactical maneuvers designed mainly to improve the government's position in elections. Similarly, the changes were presumably motivated by the rational desire to reduce tensions with opposition legislators and regional officials as domestic policies in many areas remained bogged down after the 1993 and 1995 parliamentary elections. The decision to send troops to Bosnia was stimulated by "moderate" anti-western sentiment supported by the overall public frustration over the economic collapse, loss of national identity, and diminishing of the country's superpower status.

Using a two-level game approach, content analyses of a prestige newspaper, and the political debates on Bosnia in the Italian Parliament, Paolo Bellucci and Pierangelo Isernia in chapter 6 assess the weight and role of public opinion in decision makers' calculations toward the Italian intervention in Bosnia. The Italian case found, on one hand, a strong and steady public support for a more active armed involvement of Italian troops in Bosnia and, on the other hand, an extreme reluctance of the Italian government to consider such an involvement. In order to examine the role of public opinion on the Italian policymaking process, one needs to enlarge the view to a wider set of actors and roles: the Italian foreign policymaking process as the result of the interplay among four set of actors: parties, government, bureaucracies, and public opinion, with the media as a channel of communication among parties, government, and public opinion. The remarkable stability in public

opinion support for an Italian armed intervention over the entire period between 1993 and 1996 is in sharp contrast with the irregular trends of attention to the conflict by the Parliament and the media.

Analyzing the "body bag" and "free rider" syndromes of public opinion in
the Netherlands, Philip Everts in chapter 7 discusses the role of mass opinion and media in the foreign policy process both influenced by perceived effectiveness of military actions and by the degree of persuasiveness and unanimity at the level of political decision making. Everts bases his analysis on
various sources including political debates in parliament and in the media,
the daily press cuttings by the Dutch Ministry of Defense, and opinion polls.
Over the years, the government, elites, and the mass public have shared the
same assessment of the conflicts in the former Yugoslavia. Divisions of opinion existed, but they did not crystallize into opposition to government policy among organized public opinion or in parliament. As the conflict in
Bosnia continued, support for intervention diminished, confirming the casualty hypothesis that predicts a drop in support for military operations proportional to the number of casualties. However, the support for military action rapidly recovered and there was no notable opposition to continued
involvement of the Netherlands in the conflict. Yet both government and
parties seemed generally to anticipate an unwillingness of the public to support casualties, and thus diminishing support can be seen as the result of the
government's self-fulfilling prophecy.

Karin Johnston in chapter 8 shows that Germany faced growing pressure
to extend its international responsibilities, including considerations for using
military force in international conflicts. After unification, Germans gradually
accepted the realities of the post-Cold War environment and a larger role in
the world. They were supportive of humanitarian aid efforts, showing a
strong preference for this as well as other soft power tasks. However, the
German public found it just as difficult as their political leadership to come
to some kind of resolution on the acceptability of intermediate international
roles. Overall, Germans were supportive of peacekeeping missions in principle, but when faced with a specific scenario requiring German participation, public support declined dramatically. In the Bosnian case, some government officials wanted Germany to assume more international
responsibilities and assume an expanded military role in the world. But
while there had been external pressure, particularly from the United States,
for Germany to take on a greater military role, there was stiff opposition from
a variety of political forces. As a consequence, Chancellor Kohl concluded
that the most appropriate strategy was to deploy very small contingents of
German military personnel in out-of-area missions conducted within a multilateral framework. However, cultural and political factors continued to restrain public opinion in its support of a new German role in the world.

The analytical conclusions in chapter 9 by Eric Shiraev and Richard Sobel
summarize the evidence in the book according to an approach for comparative

study of opinion-policy links. According to this approach, each country's particular policy climate—as a frame of reference for foreign policy—is originated by and linked to a set of testable variables. These diverse variables may be examined from several dimensions that refer to specific socioeconomic, political, cultural, and psychological conditions of each of the examined countries. This approach facilitates a more comprehensive evaluation of the relations between public opinion and foreign policy from a comparative perspective and directs attention to conditions that may be overlooked in national cases.

Overall, the book shows that, in the Bosnia case, the countries' policies were shifted generally in the direction chosen by the public. From the very beginning of the conflict, public opinion in many of the examined countries supported intervention in Bosnia with relative consistency. The governments, however, with the exception of Canada and the Netherlands, started with a non-interventionist stance during the earlier years of the conflict, then gradually moved in the direction of public opinion: non-intervention soon gave way to humanitarian intervention, which eventually turned into military intervention.

The findings suggest that the opinion-policy connection is more likely to be interactive and reciprocal. Moreover, people's opinions and decisions that politicians make about the participation of their country in an international military operation do not occur under identical conditions. Internal political considerations, the relationship between executive and legislative branches, religious, ethnic, and other values, the role of opinion leaders, and overall perception of public opinion, these and many other factors can determine why governments pay attention to public opinion in some countries and remain uninterested in other cases.

One of the central issues in the book's investigation was a question about why the decision to intervene in Bosnia was finally made and why it took the nations such a long time. The controversy in the decision-making process about the use of international military action in conflict resolution is based on opposite tendencies. On one hand, there was considerable reluctance of some people to commit troops to risky military operations for causes obviously beyond immediate and clear self-interest. The public's indifference, doubts in the likelihood of ethnic antagonisms ending, and disappointing calculations of potential gains and losses in the conflict, all contribute to the disbelief in the possibilities of successful international military actions. On the other hand, there is a strong public commitment to international peace and stability, to human rights, and against killing and genocide.

The book also considers the future of the relationship between public opinion and peacekeeping operations. Few countries want their government to play a single and exclusive role in settling ethnic conflicts. Most publics wait for others to move first, or expect a consensus-based agreement that would specify a "reasonable share" in the collective burden of the peacekeeping mission. Three possibilities may develop in future conflicts. First, the role of the leader may remain to be traditionally assigned—and supported by the public—to the United States. (Military actions against terrorist groups in 2001 provide evidence in support of this assumption.) Second, other countries such as Great Britain, Canada, or Germany may claim their leadership by using numbers of opinion polls and becoming actively engaged in peace-keeping missions. However, as the third option, some countries—among them China and Russia, as the events in Kosovo in 1999 partly confirm—may challenge the leadership role of the United States and their allies in international military operations; this may create worrisome developments and conflicts.

In sum, the book suggests that whether or not allied policies and peace-keeping will lead to regional and international stability will depend, in part, on how strongly publics around the world, abetted by the media, support the continuing pursuit of peace, and how carefully governments and leaders pay attention.

1

"In the Service of Peace": Reflexive Multilateralism and the Canadian Experience in Bosnia

Erin Carrière, Marc O'Reilly, and Richard Vengroff

Prominently located in Ottawa, near the Parliament Buildings and the National Museum of Fine Arts, stands an impressive granite and bronze monument dedicated to Canada's "blue helmeted" UN peacekeeping troops. Engraved on it are the words "In the Service of Peace." This monument, which so eloquently characterizes Canadians' view of their most important role in world politics, highlights a self-image that has become an integral part of Canadian political culture. It permeates the thinking of both elites and the general citizenry, the printed and electronic media, school social studies texts, the foreign and defense policy statements of most political parties and even traverses the broad cultural divide between English and French Canada.

In polls conducted in 1992 and again in 1997, Canadians in overwhelming numbers (90 percent and 94 percent respectively) proudly identified their country as a world leader in international peacekeeping (Angus Reid 1997). As noted by Denis Stairs (1982), "those in Canada who reflect on the broadly distinguishing characteristics of our involvement in world affairs have tended to think primarily of Canadian contributions to the resolution of international conflict." It is little wonder, then, that Canadian troops were among the first to touch down in the former Yugoslavia in 1992. It is equally unsurprising to find Canadian peacekeepers still involved in the region today. This in spite of some early humiliations, the thanklessness of the operation, threats to the lives of Canadian troops, lack of clarity regarding their role, and significant budget cuts for the Canadian armed forces.

To what can we attribute Canada's ongoing involvement in peacekeeping in Bosnia? Is this the role that the international community in the post-Cold War era has assigned to Canada? Is Canadian participation in these activities simply that of a client state acting as a proxy for the United States, its more

1

powerful neighbor? Is this a convenient role for a cynical middle power seeking to promote an international image consistent with its needs in terms of expanded world trade in the context of an increasingly global economy? Or does Canada's foreign policy simply reflect the "will of the people" as expressed in public opinion polls?

Directly related to these questions is the impact of public opinion on Canadian involvement in peacekeeping in Bosnia. Is this an instance of elite manipulation of mass attitudes through the use of the media (winter 1992), elite-mass consistency in their opinions, elite responsiveness to mass opinion, or a convenient confluence of the two? How have changes in the situation in Bosnia influenced elite-mass opinion? Finally, have events in the region effected changes in policy?

These central questions will be explored in this chapter's three sections. Section one discusses the theoretical literature regarding foreign policy and public opinion. The objective of the section is to highlight the debates within this field and to generate hypotheses applicable to the Canadian case. Section two examines the history of Canadian foreign policy in the twentieth century, in particular the development of Ottawa's peacekeeping policy after 1945. The section serves to contextualize the Canadian government's decisions on Bosnia. The final section spotlights Canadian public opinion and political culture vis-à-vis international peacekeeping. This section also offers an overview of elite thinking at the policymaking level and within the Canadian Parliament.

PUBLIC OPINION AND FOREIGN POLICY: THEORETICAL PERSPECTIVES

An extensive literature has developed regarding the relationship between public opinion and foreign policy, with much of the research coming out of and/or focusing on American public opinion. The general consensus of the post-World War II period regarding the relationship between public opinion and foreign policy is referred to as the "Almond-Lippmann consensus." This consensus view characterized public opinion as volatile and incoherent and, as a result, having little impact on policy outputs (Almond 1950; Lippmann 1955; Cohen 1973; Morgenthau 1973). Those works in the tradition of the Almond-Lippmann consensus see a direct correlation between the informed nature of public opinion and whether such opinion could have an effect on policy. During and following the Vietnam War scholars began to question the validity of this conception (Page and Shapiro 1984, 1988, 1992; Hurwitz and Peffley 1987; Wittkopf 1990; Monroe 1979; Hartley and Russett 1992; Bartels 1991; Powlick 1991; Graham 1986; Beal and Hinckley 1984; Hinckley 1992). Indeed, in many of these works, the authors argue for a more positive view of public opinion and suggest that there is a role for it in understanding the policymaking process.

In recent studies, we do not see a direct correlation between the informed or uninformed nature of opinion and its ability to impact policy outputs. The relationship between opinion and foreign policy is viewed as a more complex and variable one than that identified in those studies in the Almond-Lippmann tradition. Relying on quantitative analyses, interviews with decision makers, and case studies, this latter body of literature presents varying results. The quantitative studies (e.g., Hartley and Russett 1992; Page and Shapiro 1992; Bartels 1991; Jentleson 1992) tend to show significant correlations between polling data and policy outcomes. Works that rely on case studies (Graham 1986; Powlick 1991) demonstrate a mixed relationship between opinion and policy. The most important function of public opinion is shown to be as a constraint on policy. However, those works do not show a direct connection between opinion and policy. They also emphasize the importance of contingent factors.

What, if any, role does public opinion play in the formation of policy? The literature associated with the Almond-Lippmann school of thought portrayed such opinion to be largely uninformed, inattentive, and acquiescent. Further, these authors argued that the relationship between opinion and policy was one in which the opinion of the public was manipulated and/or was not dealt with seriously by policymakers in any way (Almond 1950; Lippmann 1955; Cohen 1973; Morgenthau 1973). In the American case, for example, the notion of the president as the "bully" in the "bully pulpit" was the consensus. The conclusion that the public had little to no impact on policy was logically inferred from this evidence.

These ideas have been challenged in recent years by a number of studies (Page and Shapiro 1994; Bartels 1991; Monroe 1979; Jentleson 1992; Aldrich, Sullivan, and Borgida 1989). Jentleson (1992) and Page and Shapiro (1994), for example, offer evidence that suggests that public opinion on foreign policy is quite consistent, linked to a stable belief system, and not easily manipulated. Jentleson canvassed eight cases of limited military force in the 1980s and the 1990–1991 Persian Gulf War, and attempted to discover whether a "pattern" of public support for the use of military force existed. He argued that while there existed a general lack of knowledge regarding the eight cases involved, there also existed a pattern of support determined by the "principal policy objective" for which force was used. That is, the public tended to support actions involving the use of force that are perceived to be aimed at restraining an aggressor state as opposed to those that have as an objective imposing internal political change within another state.

Jentleson qualifies his argument by noting two factors that limit/inhibit this tendency. First, the public tends to support initiatives that involve the quick and successful use of force, even if such force has been employed to secure internal political change. Second, he notes that "public support will not necessarily just be there; [but] must be cultivated and evoked through effective presidential leadership." The significance of such evidence is that despite general public ignorance of specifics regarding foreign policy issues, a stable pattern of public support for certain policies exists. This support is linked to a more general belief system.

Page and Shapiro (1988) also provide evidence to suggest that public opinion is not necessarily acquiescent, manipulable, and unstable. They examined more than four hundred foreign policy items that had been repeated in national surveys at various times over a fifty-year period. They found that slightly over half of those items showed no statistically significant change in opinion at all, that half of those that did change showed shifts of fewer than ten percentage points, and that there was very little fluctuation in the direction of change in opinions about foreign policy. The authors concluded that "collective opinion tends to be rather stable; it sometimes changes abruptly, but usually only by small amounts; and it rarely fluctuates" (Page and Shapiro 1988, 243). They also found changes in opinion "to be reasonable, or sensible," and largely a response to "the contents of the mass media—especially reports from experts and commentators" (Page and Shapiro, 1988, 243).

A number of scholars (Page and Shapiro 1983, 1992; Bartels 1991; Monroe 1979; Aldrich, Sullivan, and Borgida 1989) look more closely at the relationship between the stability of opinion and policy. In a study of presidential campaigns between 1952 and 1984, Aldrich, Sullivan, and Borgida (1989) discovered that, in five of the nine elections, foreign policy issues had significant effects on the outcomes. Bartels (1991) found in an analysis of voting on the Reagan administration's defense buildup that public opinion, as expressed through Congress, played a significant role in the area of defense spending.

Several more works (e.g., Monroe 1979; Page and Shapiro 1983) study the congruence between public preferences and policies over the course of extended periods. Monroe's work examines the years between 1960 and 1974, while Page and Shapiro studied the period of 1935–1979. In both studies, significant congruence was observed between mass policy preferences and policy outcomes in relation to both domestic and foreign policy. Monroe found that 92 percent of the time there was congruence between public preferences and policy outcomes, while Page and Shapiro showed this to be the case 62 percent of the time. Page and Shapiro argued that government policy was more likely to change in response to a shift in public opinion than vice versa and to shift in the direction preferred by the public.

Case study analyses by scholars such as Graham (1986) and Powlick (1991) challenge the notion of an inattentive public without a role in the opinion-policy relationship. Graham's work employed four case studies, five hundred public opinion surveys, and other primary source materials to investigate whether the apparent relationship between opinion and policy was causal or spurious. The analysis demonstrated that public opinion had a significant impact on policy outcomes during all stages of the policy process. Graham also noted that the impact of the opinion was directly related to the amount of public support for the policy. That is, the more public support a policy maintained (majority, consensus, preponderant, or virtually unanimous), the greater the impact of public opinion on policy decisions. Graham argues that the level of public support and stage of the policy process are but two of four conditions that affect the influence of opinion on foreign policy. The remaining two conditions are the effectiveness of elite communication and elite awareness of the varying components of opinion.

Powlick also sought to determine whether the relationship between opinion and policy was causal or spurious. He investigated the relationship between public opinion and the Reagan administration's decisions regarding the Lebanon intervention. Based on interviews with numerous government officials, he concluded that public opinion had an impact on mid-level officials but little impact on the higher-level decision makers including Reagan. According to Powlick, the higher-level officials tended to consider congressional attitudes the voice of the people and hence did not look much further. Public opinion failed to have a direct impact at the highest levels. It may have an indirect impact through the Congress, and a more direct effect on implementation through mid-level policymakers.

The works by these authors suggest that public opinion acts as a constraint on foreign policy just as Jentleson proposed. Such evidence indicates that opinion has a role in the development of policy, and a significant one given that these constraints may be imbedded in the belief systems of the people and the government. However, views on the particular nature of the relationships posited vary considerably. That is, while Page and Shapiro (1983), Bartels (1991), Monroe (1979), and Aldrich, Sullivan, and Borgida (1989) see that relationship in terms of a "consistency/congruence" model, Jentleson (1992), Graham (1986), and Powlick (1991) see opinion as a constraint on policy. In a general sense, these studies challenge the notion of a lack of public input into policy.

These studies that challenge the Almond-Lippmann consensus also suggest factors that may influence the effect of opinion on policy. Among the most prominent are: (1) the nature of the issue under consideration (crisis vs. non-crisis); (2) the nature of the policy being proposed (one that shows restraint or one that does not); (3) the nature of the communication between elites (effective or ineffective); (4) elite awareness of the full range of opinions held and their various components; (5) the level of public support for a policy; (6) decision-making issues involving both structure and timing; and (7) specifically contextual issues.

CANADIAN PUBLIC OPINION
AND PEACEKEEPING POLICY

An examination of Canadian public opinion on foreign policy issues suggests that opinion stability, as delineated by Page and Shapiro (1988), Jentleson (1987), and others for the American case, also applies to Canada. Martin
and Fortmann (1995) investigate the coherence and stability of Canadian
public opinion regarding peacekeeping and in so doing also challenge the
Almond-Lippmann consensus. Although the question of whether opinion
leads policy or policymakers lead opinion is not central to their analysis, they
do address this issue. In order to show that Canadian opinion regarding
peacekeeping is coherent and stable, they examine polling data and policy
over time to see whether and when the two diverge. Looking at the drop in
support for peacekeeping in the early 1990s and the subsequent increase in
support in the mid-1990s, Martin and Fortmann try to determine whether
such drops indicate that the traditional Canadian support for peacekeeping
and internationalism is eroding. These authors conclude that while the Canadian public is sensitive to the costs and risks of peacekeeping operations, the
general support for them will continue.

Applied to the Canadian case, Martin and Fortmann's challenge to the
Almond-Lippmann consensus is convincing. The authors show through
the use of polling data and an examination of events surrounding the polls
that Canadian opinion on peacekeeping is both coherent and stable. When
changes occur, they are "reasonable responses to changes in the circumstances of Canadian participation in United Nations peacekeeping operations" (Martin and Fortmann 1995, 371). They qualify their position by arguing that, while such opinion is coherent and stable, it is not necessarily
perfectly informed about international events. Furthermore, they note that
opinions of individual citizens do not change in the same "rational" way.

Martin and Fortmann's conclusion is strikingly similar to that of Jentleson. Recall that the latter author argues that publics maintain imperfect information/
knowledge levels while primarily relying on belief systems as the source of
their foreign policy attitudes. Martin and Fortmann (1995) conclude that the
Canadian public acquires information from the media and opinion leaders but
primarily relies on a core set of beliefs to form an opinion about international
events. They also state that such beliefs are more sophisticated than merely
supportive or unsupportive of peacekeeping operations and an internationalist position. Thus, while these authors accept that the Canadian public is less
informed than would seem ideal in terms of participating in the formation of
policy, they believe that it maintains consistent, coherent belief systems that
guide it when making choices among alternative government policies.

Given the nature of public opinion formation and the context of the Canadian parliamentary system, "how in principle might public opinion come to

affect the conduct of foreign policy?" (Stairs 1977–1978). In Canada, this may take the form of (1) agenda setting, (2) parameter setting, (3) policy setting, and (4) administration setting or implementation (Stairs 1977–1978). Stairs argues that in Canada the influence is there in all four areas. As he notes, "its [public opinion] presence as a significant factor in the policy process cannot be denied" (Stairs 1977–1978, 148).

It seems to be the case that decision makers in Canada are "in tune" with public opinion in that the nation's foreign policy continues to ensure a place of primacy for peacekeeping/common security operations (Martin and Fortmann, 398). However, with no clear differences in attitudes separating elite and mass opinion, how do we determine the direction of the influence when it comes to the case of Bosnia, for example?

Defining the Nature of the Relationship between Opinion and Policy

Many issues exist with regard to the conduct of research on the relationship between opinion and policy. First, there is often a lack of continuity in the kinds of questions pollsters use in surveys on defense issues. It is difficult to measure opinion and changes in opinion when such a lack of continuity exists. Second, Holsti (1992) found that the complexity of many foreign policy issues forces individuals to structure their opinions according to contrasting core dimensions of isolationism or internationalism.

Several difficulties arise with regard to the proclivity of publics to form opinions around these contrasting core dimensions. However, such opinions may also embody other subtle and more sophisticated tendencies. That is, opinions may be sensitive to the costs and risks associated with certain policies and, hence, categorized as internationalist in one instance and more isolationist in another. For example, Canadian public opinion is generally very supportive of the continuation of Canadian peacekeeping operations and, hence, can be argued to be internationalist in its proclivities. The Canadian public is not as supportive of a continuation of peacekeeping operations when higher costs and risks are perceived. The relationship between opinion and policy may thus be context-bound. In other words, to understand the relationship, we must fully understand the context in which it played out. Hence, broad generalizations may be inappropriate (Foyle 1997).

When considering the context and the importance of it, it is useful to remember that public opinion can only have an impact in political systems that provide for the transmission of those ideas into the policy process. And, that if the structure of the decision-making process, and, hence, the mechanisms through which opinion is transmitted, is altered, determining the relationship between opinion and policy can be made more difficult. It would seem that an evaluation of the relationship between opinion and policy regarding peacekeeping in Canada over time is made more difficult by the fact that the

Canadian government attempted to make the policymaking process more open and transparent in the 1990s, thus changing the dynamic.

"Framing," whereby elites define foreign policy issues for the public, must also be considered. According to framing theory, elites use the media to generate support for policy decisions by defining (framing) the issue in a manner designed to elicit maximum sympathy and support. As Payerhin and Hubert note, "In terms of political communications, frames are designed to define for the public the nature of an issue and a range of appropriate responses" (Payerhin and Hubert 1998, 2; see also Gamson 1989; Iyengar 1997; Nelson, Oxley, and Clawson 1997; Zaller and Chui 1996; for the case of Canada, see Winter 1992). Thus, since the Canadian public is known to be very sympathetic to and supportive of peacekeeping operations, elites can "frame" other policy options (defense spending, for example) in these terms. The public may believe that it is endorsing one type of policy when in fact it is providing succor for another and thereby strengthening the hand of elites in getting their way on policy.

The existence of a consistent set of beliefs, despite low information levels on the part of the public, certainly makes for a stronger case in terms of the impact of public opinion on the policymaking process. However, just because the public maintains a stable belief system, this does not necessarily translate into influence in the policymaking process. The public's beliefs have to be communicated to the policymakers and have an impact on them in order for the public's wishes to be translated into policy outputs. Whether or not such influence can be determined is unclear.

Yeric and Todd (1983) present three models of the public opinion-policy relationship: (1) the majority rule model; (2) the consistency model; and (3) the satisfying model. The majority rule model is "based on the idea that public officials should enact policies that reflect the wishes of a majority of the citizens" (Yeric and Todd 1983, 162). Hence, if the public wishes a new policy to be enacted regarding health care and the public wishes for that policy to be "x," then the government should respond by passing and implementing policy "x."

Their consistency model "utilizes the consistency or congruence concept and is concerned not with a fixed percent of respondents for or against a policy but rather with the relationship between public opinion and public policy over a period of time" (Yeric and Todd 1983, 163). The idea is that there needs to be congruence between opinion and policy as a result of patterns of opinion as they change over time. This model does not assume majority rule and, hence, may be more reflective of the real world of politics (Yeric and Todd 1983, 64).

The third model of the opinion-policy relationship is that of the satisfying model. According to Yeric and Todd, "the importance of this concept is that it takes into account situations in which public opinion and public policy appear to be moving in opposite directions. The key to understanding this relationship is to note that once government reacts to the public's demands,

public demand for governmental action decreases, even though governmental support for the position in question may actually be increasing"
(Yeric and Todd 1983, 164). The essence of this model is that as the government responds to public demand, such public demand decreases but the
fundamental response of the government remains the same for some time.
Certainly, it is the nature of the process of developing and implementing policy that allows for this to occur.

The questions that arise with regard to the presentation and explication of
these models are associated with attempts to apply them. First, how is majority opinion or patterns of opinion supposed to be measured? And, second,
how can one ascertain whether the public's demands have been "satisfied"?

Much of the scholarship on this subject proposes congruence models.
That is, if opinion and policy are congruent, and opinion precedes policy
outputs, then it is said that opinion leads policymakers. If opinion and policy diverge, then it is argued that policymakers lead opinion. Martin and Fortmann, while utilizing the congruence model, also argue that it is the embedded belief systems that guide policymakers.

Hypotheses

In later sections of this chapter we examine the relationship between public
opinion in Canada and that country's involvement in the "peacekeeping" missions in Bosnia. A critical question, which needs to be addressed here, is just
what impact, if any, Canadian public opinion has on those charged with making foreign policy, especially policy regarding peacekeeping operations. Where
there is a clear divergence of opinion between foreign policy elites and the
mass public, the task of sorting out the level of influence on policy is method-
ologically much neater. We can look at temporal sequences among these
groups in adopting positions, unity within each group, strength of commitment,
relative salience of the issues, the impact of the media, and comparisons between policy decisions and the positions of various elite and mass groups.

Where elite and mass opinions seem to converge and both are highly consistent with policy outputs, the task of the analyst becomes more complex. In
which direction do we draw the arrows indicating influence or the impact of
each group. The temporal sequence is again important. However, here the emphasis must be on identifying exogenous variables that may play a key role.

There are foreign policy issues on which there has been considerable divergence of opinion between masses and elites in Canada. The whole free
trade (Free Trade Agreement [FTA] and North American Free Trade Agreement [NAFTA]) debate produced broad elite-mass disagreement, a divergence
that at times became quite conflictual (Winter 1990; Vengroff 1996). Thus we
can not argue that foreign policymaking in Canada is always characterized by
generalized consensus or even that it is only moderately conflictual.

Based on the discussion presented above, three alternative hypotheses will be considered here:

Canadian public opinion was supportive of the Bosnia peacekeeping mission(s) because it was largely guided and created by elite opinion modulated by the media.

Canadian foreign policy elites are strongly influenced by public opinion, and policy in Bosnia thus reflects this influence.

The views of both elites and masses are influenced by exogenous factors, such as core values in Canadian political culture and/or traditions in Canadian foreign policy, which produce a convergence in policy and opinion.

To test these hypotheses, however, we must first consider the historical context of international peacekeeping within Canada's foreign policy.

THE "CANADIAN WAY":
THE DOCTRINE OF PEACEKEEPING

So-called Middle Powers enjoy opportunities unavailable to other powers. Via institutions, for example, they can promote multilateral endeavors such as United Nations (UN) peacekeeping without incurring the wrath of dueling Great Powers or the criticism of Small Powers. Positioned within the U.S. sphere of influence, a country such as Canada can invoke its positive conflict-management reputation when trying to resolve some of the world's thorniest problems (Clark 1997; Axworthy 1997). For fifty or so years, Canadians have applied their diplomatic and technological skills to make a valued contribution to the United Nations' efforts at collective security. With the outbreak of war in Yugoslavia, Ottawa involved itself in the politico-military problem of the day by reflexively turning to its peacekeepers.

Peacekeeping, then, remains the "Canadian way." In Andrew Cooper's words, it "is more than an ordinary sphere of activity in Canadian foreign policy. [It] has been central to the definition of Canada's national identity, role and influence in the world" (Cooper 1997, 173). This tradition started in 1956, the year of the Suez War. Canada's foreign minister, Lester B. Pearson, sought to defuse this crisis by calling for the creation of the United Nations Emergency Force (UNEF) (O'Reilly 1997; English 1993; Pearson 1993). Pearson's diplomacy won him the Nobel Peace Prize and confirmed the *raison d'être* of his country's foreign policy: to lobby for multilateral solutions whenever conflict threatened to disturb the post-World War II peace. Such thinking conformed to previous Canadian policy, whose genesis lay in bittersweet past experiences.

Canadians fought in the Great War in the name of the British Empire, not for Canada *per se*. Fierce combat at Ypres, the Somme, Vimy Ridge, and Passchendaele sobered Canadians and buried notions that war could be glorious—even though Canada's soldiers displayed skill and courage in very difficult conditions. Impressed, the British acknowledged Canada's contribution, and "ultimately there would be the reward of full nationhood" (Dancocks 1989, 342).

Though Ottawa exercised full discretion over the country's external affairs after the 1926 Balfour Declaration and the 1931 Statute of Westminster, the United Kingdom continued to cast its shadow across its dominion's political and foreign policy landscape until the Second World War (Hillmer 1992, 8). In the interwar years, Canadian leaders such as Mackenzie King acquiesced in London's desire for a Commonwealth of Nations as a successor to the British Empire, but insisted on scrutinizing and debating imperial policies. Still, in 1939 duty called, as Canada followed Great Britain into another war with Germany. During World War II, Canada's youth found agony at Dieppe in 1942, glory at Normandy in 1944.

The Allied victory in 1945 underscored Canada's newly achieved prominence and transformed the Canadian-British relationship into a partnership. Emancipated from its "British proxy" reputation (Holmes 1970, 5), Ottawa sought to assert itself in postwar international forums. Canadian diplomats recognized, however, that their country would take its cue from the United States, whose power reverberated across the 49th parallel. Pearson stated that Canada "had to accept the reality of being a North American nation . . . and that [its] supreme foreign policy task was to influence the American government to adopt wise policies" (Thordarson 1974, 77). The creation of the North Atlantic Treaty Organization (NATO) sanctioned the militarization of the Cold War, thereby obliging Ottawa to support the American-led Atlantic Alliance unconditionally despite occasional misgivings.

Cold War tensions worried Canadian diplomats, yet the Soviet-American rivalry restricted Canadian chances to contribute to world order. In 1951, Pearson outlined Canada's predicament when he wrote that his country constituted "neither a great nor an overseas Power; and only occasionally can her voice be influential in deciding the policies of the free world" (Pearson 1951, 17). While deferring to the Americans on NATO military policy and other issues of power politics, Canadian policymakers searched for a foreign policy that could fulfill two wishes: (1) identify Canada as more than just a U.S. satellite; and (2) allow Canada to try out its "utilitarian morality" (Stairs 1989, 220). Ottawa could play a constructive role in international politics if it could discover tasks well suited to its strengths—diplomacy, economic aid, and technological expertise.

In the 1940s and 1950s, Canada acquired the title of Middle Power (Mackay 1992; Holmes 1992), not Great Power, though it actively participated in the Allied victory in World War II and contributed significantly to the establishment of the United Nations (Smith 1988; Hilliker 1990). In a January 1947 speech, then Foreign Minister Louis St. Laurent told a University of Toronto audience that "national unity," "political liberty," "[t]he rule of law," "[t]he values of a Christian civilization," and "[t]he acceptance of international responsibility in keeping with our conception of our role in world affairs" explained Canada's past reactions to international events (St. Laurent 1970, 388–99). As St. Laurent's successor, Pearson referred to this "checklist" in selecting Ottawa's foreign policy priorities (Pearson 1973, 26).

As a Middle Power, Canada devised and carried out policies based on the "functional" principle (Granatstein 1982, 132). Its decision makers spotlighted problems, such as food relief to starving war refugees, which, as a major grain producer, their country understood well and could help remedy. They raised economic and social issues at the United Nations, which Pearson considered "our sole world organization" (Pearson 1973, 40), and offered money and expertise to cope with them. The Canadian style, relying upon "Quiet Diplomacy" (Stairs 1982, 683), emphasized negotiation over confrontation, much to the satisfaction of the newly independent countries of Asia, Africa, and the Middle East. While their diplomatic handiwork won them praise, Canadian policymakers worried that global peace remained in jeopardy, especially when nuclear weapons could be delivered to enemy territory with devastating consequences for everyone. Without collective security, moreover, localized conflicts could engulf East and West in yet another world war.

Pearson epitomized the Canadian belief in the United Nations. In 1945, with the outcome of the war decided, he invested his hopes for a more peaceful world in the nascent organization (English 1989). At the San Francisco Conference, he concentrated on "the proposals that dealt with the organization of security and with measures to prevent and defeat aggression" (Pearson 1972, 272). He thought that the United Nations could improve upon the League of Nations' cumbersome enforcement mechanisms and, through the Security Council, act as a policeman and final arbiter of international disputes. After the ravages of two world wars, he extolled the importance of this newest international forum: "the growth of the United Nations into a truly effective world organization was our best, perhaps our last, hope of bringing about enduring and creative peace if mankind was to end a savage tradition that the strong do what they can and the weak suffer what they must" (Pearson 1972, 283). He believed that if the United Nations stuck to its principles, it could prevent another Ethiopia, Nanking, or Munich—critical events that undermined the League of Nations' authority and exposed collective security as empty rhetoric.

The war in Korea in 1950 allowed the United Nations to turn away the North Korean invaders, who sought to unify the Korean peninsula in defiance of the UN Charter. Ottawa wholeheartedly endorsed the Washington-sponsored resolution calling for a return to the *status quo ante bellum*. Canada offered only token troops, however, leaving the United States to contribute the bulk of soldiers to the UN operation. Canadian diplomats realized that their state could not conduct extensive military operations à la Douglas MacArthur for lack of resources. Such a setback reminded them that Canada could not consider the prosecution of wars as a national talent. Instead, Canada would await circumstances in which its skills could be applied to preserve world order.

By 1956, UN members considered Canada "one of the most international-ist countries, ready to support almost all UN initiatives. Canadian diplomats became, if not the power-brokers at the UN, some of the chief mediators and innovators whenever problems arose" (Thordarson 1974, 73). In the fall of that year, Israel invaded Egypt's Sinai Peninsula after secretly conspiring with the British and the French. When Cairo refused to surrender, London and Paris ordered their navies to join the war.

Predictably, Canada sought a UN solution with Pearson in the forefront of Canadian efforts to resolve this particularly stressful Cold War crisis (Holmes 1982, 356–57). Pearson recognized that Canada could not weather a Suez storm if it destroyed the two foreign policy structures Ottawa prized most, NATO and the Commonwealth. As a result, he floated the idea for a UNEF (Rosner 1963; Pearson 1957) with his cabinet colleagues on November 1, 1956. In his memoirs, Pearson explained UNEF's purpose: "to provide a substitute for British-French intervention, thus giving them a good reason to withdraw from their own stated objective of restoring peace before they could be for-mally condemned by the [UN General] Assembly" (Pearson 1973, 244). This "compromise" perhaps could assuage London, Paris, and Tel Aviv, as well as those opposed (particularly the Asian Commonwealth countries) to the Sèvres protocol—which called for the British, French, and Israeli invasion of Egypt.

In New York, Pearson worked assiduously to convince U.S. Secretary of State John Foster Dulles and other foreign policy elites that a UNEF could help end the Middle East war before it escalated into a superpower conflict. The Cana-dian understood that neither the General Assembly nor Egyptian President Gamal Nasser would endorse U.K. Prime Minister Anthony Eden's tokenism. Under no circumstances could British and French troops be used to separate the Israelis and Egyptians, the purported belligerents (Pritchard to Lord Home [CRO], November 3, 1956). Pearson also realized that Canada could not vote in favor of an American cease-fire draft resolution since it did not "provide for any steps to be taken by the United Nations for a peace settlement, without which a cease-fire [could] be only of temporary value at best" (Pearson 1973, 245).

To complement Washington's efforts, the Canadian foreign minister pro-posed the creation of a "truly international peace and police force," a UN force "large enough to keep [the] borders at peace while a political settle-ment is being worked out" (Pearson 1973, 245). Such a proposal, he rea-soned, could satisfy both supporters and opponents of Anglo-French military endeavors. It would also position Canada as a peace broker that could offer diplomatic integrity and solutions.

Pearson's diplomatic maneuvering proved controversial. With British and French bombs killing more Egyptian civilians, the crisis intensified.

Still, respectful of Canada's decision to criticize its two motherlands, Britain and France, most Third World states warmed to the UNEF concept (Kyle 1991). Several diplomats even asked Pearson to work out a plan whereby the United Nations could send peacekeepers to the Sinai Peninsula so that no future rerun of the events of October-November 1956 could surprise as well as polarize the international community.

In devising a plan for a UNEF, Canada could count on its solid UN reputation, the experience of its diplomats, its lack of partisan involvement in the events following Nasser's nationalization of the Suez Canal in July 1956, and NATO support (Pritchard to Lord Home [CRO], November 2, 1956). Most Canadian radio and press, as well, supported Pearson's "initiative" (Pritchard to Lord Home [CRO], November 2, 1956; CBC 1979). The *Ottawa Citizen*, for example, said that Canada "has a policy to seek a UN solution" (Pritchard to Lord Home [CRO], November 3, 1956). Though some newspapers, including the *Toronto Star* and the respected *Financial Post*, reconsidered earlier opinions with respect to the Anglo-French intervention, most counseled, as the *Montreal Star* did, that "[t]he sooner now that the whole problem is turned back to the United Nations the better" (Pritchard to Lord Home [CRO], November 2, 1956).

The General Assembly eventually voted in favor of a Canadian draft resolution (UN Document A/3276), which called upon the Secretary-General to create the first ever peacekeeping operation (PKO). Dag Hammarskjöld presented his report to the Assembly, which overwhelmingly adopted Pearson's UNEF plan (UN Resolution 1000 [ES-I]) on November 5, 1956 (Pearson 1973). Several countries, including Canada, then volunteered their soldiers for peacekeeping duty in Sinai.

With a cease-fire in place, this initial peacekeeping mission commenced in 1957. Perhaps the *Winnipeg Free Press* best summarized Canada's Suez experience and Ottawa's penchant for collective security, when it editorialized that "[t]he position taken by Mr. Pearson is exactly the right one for the Canadian Government" (Pritchard to Lord Home [CRO], November 5, 1956). The UNEF, moreover, vaulted Pearson and his country into international prominence, a position Canada welcomed.

Sending peacekeepers to trouble spots such as Lebanon, Congo, and Cyprus in the decade following Suez buoyed Canadian spirits at a time when Canada's international role waned. The hallmark of its foreign policy, peacekeeping provided Ottawa with a purpose while the Americans and the Soviets played geopolitical chess. Canadians could relate to the individuals who served as UN Blue Helmets. The latter's traits seemed so consonant with how Canadians perceived themselves: selfless, determined, committed, and caring. According to Geoffrey Hayes, "peacekeeping was something upon which all Canadians could find common ground" (Hayes 1997, 79). Yet other Middle Powers, such as Sweden and Norway, could offer the United Nations the same skills as Canada.

Ottawa's post-World War II commitment to internationalism (often referred to as "Pearsonian internationalism" [Nossal 1989, 143–48]) intensified following its Suez tour de force. World events precluded a repeat of Pearson's exploit, however. New members at the United Nations criticized Western imperialism, the United Kingdom in particular, to whom Canadians still paid respect. Finally, the United States pursued its foreign policy while mostly dismissing the advice and opinions of its allies. Whereas Canada performed a critical political task in 1956, after the crisis it would content itself with consistently answering the UN call for assistance whenever wars broke out. Even John Diefenbaker's Conservative Government (1957–1963) endorsed peacekeeping despite its vociferous criticism of St. Laurent and Pearson's pro-United States, anti-British, Suez policy.

Generally uninterested in, or unaware of, Canada's pre-Suez role in preserving truces in Palestine, the Indian Subcontinent, and Indochina and in monitoring elections in South Korea, Canadians rejoiced in Pearson's diplomatic victory and urged their leaders to send soldiers whenever the United Nations asked for peacekeepers. In 1960, Prime Minister Diefenbaker and his cabinet hesitated when the world body intervened in an imploding Congo and asked for contributions to a multilateral "peacemaking" force. The Canadian press, including staunchly Conservative newspapers, and the Opposition Liberals chastised Ottawa for shirking its international duty. Under pressure, Diefenbaker sent the requested signalers and pilots to central Africa. More Canadian personnel traveled to obscure countries, such as Yemen, in the early 1960s. As Jack Granatstein noted, "Peacekeeping was the Canadian role, and the Canadian people demanded the right to play it. The national self-image required it" (Granatstein 1974, 16).

After their victory in the national election of 1963, the Pearson-led Liberals turned to peacekeeping in dramatic fashion the following year. Foreign Minister Paul Martin fostered an arrangement whereby UN troops inserted themselves between warring Greek and Turkish factions on the island of Cyprus—much to the relief of American policymakers, who dreaded yet another NATO rift (Granatstein 1974).

Unfortunately, Nasser's controversial decision in 1967 to remove the UNEF from Sinai deflated the Canadian hope that peacekeeping could ensure a safer world. With the UN buffer removed, Egyptians and Israelis resumed their protracted war. The Six Day War emphatically reminded Canadians that a leader bent on conflict could dispose of peacekeepers whenever convenient despite their importance to the Canadian psyche. After the Israeli victory, Canadians soured on peacekeeping: "Suddenly Canadians began to question why peace had not followed peacekeeping. Suddenly they began to wonder why their troops should ever have been exposed to difficulty, hardship and danger in a thankless desert. The sense of futility was very sharp" (Granatstein 1974, 18). The war also jolted Ottawa, which could not avoid concluding that "[t]he cornerstone [of Canadian foreign policy] had crumbled" (Granatstein 1974, 16).

Disappointment abroad mixed with violence at home. With the Front de Libération du Québec (FLQ) exploding bombs in Montreal, wary Canadians fretted as their country coped with internal strife. Canadians expressed dismay as so-called Québec separatists sought independence for their province. Prime Minister Pearson seemed bewildered, as the Canadian federation frayed. Quickly, questions regarding Canadian unity eclipsed foreign policy concerns. Why worry about peacekeepers in the Middle East when Canada itself seemed in the throes of a serious upheaval? Such a shift in domestic politics meant that "[t]he internationalism of 1948 and the idealism of 1956 had been superseded by the neo-isolationism of 1968" (Granatstein 1974, 16).

Pearson's successor, Pierre Trudeau, zeroed in on the excesses of Québec nationalism. With respect to Canada's external policy, in which the prime minister showed only "sporadic" interest (Granatstein and Bothwell 1990, 378), he called for a reassessment of Quiet Diplomacy, the country's preferred international tactic. Unconvinced that Canadian diplomats could portray themselves as "Helpful Fixers," Trudeau sought to lower expectations in view of Canada's reduced ability to influence international outcomes (von Riekhoff 1978, 271). Yet peacekeeping survived as a core foreign policy objective, "though cautiously" (Granatstein and Bothwell 1990, 239).

The Trudeau Government supported the principle of collective security, but shied away from intervention in another country's internal affairs. Canada respected the sacrosanct notion of state sovereignty, the cornerstone of the UN system. As prime minister, Progressive Conservative Party leader Brian Mulroney reaffirmed the Canadian commitment to nonintervention until the demise of the Cold War allowed new international norms to manifest themselves (Keating and Gammer 1993).

The 1990s witnessed the emergence of "humanitarian intervention" as an accepted form of multilateralism. Foreign Minister Barbara McDougall said to the UN General Assembly that "We must not allow the principle of nonintervention to impede an effective international response . . . the concept of sovereignty must respect higher principles, including the need to preserve human life from wanton destruction" (quoted in Keating and Gammer 1993, 725). UN missions to Somalia and the former Yugoslavia called for peacemaking, a difficult proposition at best, yet Ottawa unhesitatingly volunteered its servicemen and -women. Trying to save "failed states" (Helman and Ratner 1992–1993) seemed the correct policy as well as an opportunity for Canada to contribute to world peace—a value Canadians still cherished.

In Somalia, Canadians stayed (Keating and Gammer 1993; Carment 1996) even when the Americans pulled out—after Somalis killed U.S. soldiers. Sadly, a handful of Canada's "peacemakers" behaved badly, torturing and killing some Somalis in their custody. Such brutality embarrassed Ottawa and shocked Canadians everywhere. Would such a scandal impact Canada's Balkan policy? Would it cause Canadian public opinion to waver in its traditional support for UN endeavors?

When Yugoslavia imploded in the early 1990s, Ottawa took the lead in asking the United Nations to intervene and promised to contribute personnel and equipment to any UN mission (Keating and Gammer 1993, 730). On February 21, 1992, the UN Security Council voted in favor of UNPROFOR. Unlike in the case of UNEF, no cease-fire existed when 1,300 Canadians arrived in Croatia in the midst of brutal ethnic warfare reminiscent of World War II. Instead of peacekeeping, Canada and the other countries that comprised the UN contingent would be asked to make peace—a task they could not acquit themselves of without increased firepower and a broader UN mandate (Carment 1996). Confronted with one of the nastiest civil wars of the century—a conflict that promised to tax Canadian resources and to try its leadership and patience—the country that invented peacekeeping strove to keep its soldiers alive and its public behind Canada's policy. Would Canadians endorse Ottawa's reflexive multilateralism or would they clamor for a withdrawal once the war worsened and spilled over into Bosnia?

All total, Canada contributed 2,100 soldiers to the UN force in the former Yugoslavia, including Croatia and Bosnia (Department of Foreign Affairs and International Trade, 1996). Only four countries sent more personnel. In June 1992, 750 Canadians took part in the Sarajevo airlift. In April 1993, 220 of Canada's troops traveled to Srebrenica as part of UNPROFOR. In June 1994, some sixty Canadian peacekeepers worked in Gorazde to ensure a three-kilometer "exclusion zone." Ottawa also authorized forty-five civilian police monitors from the Royal Canadian Mounted Police (RCMP) to join the UN mission in the Balkans.

One would expect Canadians to back their country's Balkan policy despite the Somali incident and the potential harm to Blue Helmets in Sarajevo and elsewhere. Past experiences and national pride called for support of UN-PROFOR. In the next section, we probe these questions by exploring Canadian public opinion and its impact on the Bosnian mission.

CANADIAN PUBLIC OPINION: POLITICAL CULTURE, SELF-IMAGE, AND INTERNATIONAL PEACEKEEPING

As suggested by Lipset (1990) in his classic comparison of the United States and Canada, two different nations with two very different views toward authority, the state, religious values, and group solidarity emerged from the American Revolution. Much subsequent research has found continued support for the basic thesis of *Continental Divide* (Alston, Morris, and Vedlitz

1996). Perhaps the most critical difference between Canadian and American political culture is in the area of attitudes toward authority.

Canadians' relatively high respect for authority has produced a very different set of heroes and conceptions of heroism than those so integral to the United States. Canadian deference to authority and the greater sense of collective responsibility as opposed to the individualism of the American frontier has made the hero in Canada the law rather than the gunslinger. The image of the RCMP courageously bringing peace, justice, and order to the Canadian West is central. This is an image that carries over into Canadians' views of the role of their armed forces in the world today. It is clearly no accident of history that many modern conceptions of international peacekeeping have their origins in Canada.

Sharing a continent with its more powerful and ten times more populous southern neighbor, much thinking north of the 49th parallel has been devoted to differentiating Canada and Canadian values from those of Americans in general and the U.S. government in particular. Canadian identity has often been characterized as an "anti" identity, heavily influenced by a constant effort to find a means to distinguish Canadians from Americans. In recent decades this has taken the form of a glorification of the differences in terms of the provision of basic social services, especially health care. Canadians see themselves as a more caring, less individualistic, and less selfish people than their neighbors. In this respect, maintaining the distinctiveness of Canadian culture in response to the onslaught of American television and printed media has become somewhat of an obsession.

In the international realm, Canada has had to work hard to overcome an entrenched image as a client state first of Great Britain and then of the United States. Clearly differentiating, or at least nuancing, its foreign policy from its closest allies has required a major effort. As can be seen in table 1.1, Canadians see it as desirable that their defense policy be closely linked to that of the United States. On trade policy, they are fairly evenly split in terms of whether or not there is a need to have a more independent national policy. Recent differences between the two countries over Iraq and trade with Cuba are revealing.

In the area of foreign policy, however, an overwhelming number of Canadians see the need to maintain their independence. Canada's role as a leader in international peacekeeping is one key area in which it is easy to distinguish its foreign policy, and the nation as a whole, from that of the only remaining "superpower." The comments by Liberal Member of Parliament (MP) Bill Graham during a House of Commons debate on Bosnia are illustrative. He urged MPs to remember that "[w]e have a moral superiority in dealing with our American colleagues at this time because of the tremendous contribution our forces are making. It establishes a credibility in dealing with the United States that we must not forget" (Hansard, March 29, 1995: 11241).

Table 1.1. Canadian Foreign Policy and the United States*

Should Canada work more closely with the United States
or be more independent with regard to:

Policy Area	% More Closely	% More Independent
Defense Policy	55	35
Trade Policy	44	47
Foreign Policy	34	56

*Source: Canadian International Development Agency (1995), "Canadians'
Opinions on Canadian Foreign Policy, Defense Policy, and International
Development Assistance." At: www.acdi-cida.gc.ca/cida_ind.nsf

Although some studies show a convergence of values in North America (Inglehart, Nevitte, and Basanez 1997), there remain some critical differentiating characteristics. Canada's political culture has been influenced not only by its historical break with the United States during and immediately after the revolution but by critical socioeconomic changes. As noted by Nevitte (1996), Canada has emerged as a major advanced industrial nation, experiencing many of the social and economic transformations occurring in Western Europe. This, in turn, has brought significant value change, including the increasing importance of postmaterialism as a political force.

The rise of postmaterialism represents a change in value priorities associated with increased levels of economic security. As a result of political socialization during a long period of relative plenty, peoples' value priorities change from issues of economic growth and national defense toward quality of life issues, such as concern for the environment and individual freedom. Postmaterialism is very closely associated with support for the human rights movement both in Canada and around the world. In the 1990 World Values Survey (Inglehart et al. 1991), for example, strong support for the human rights movement was expressed by well over two thirds (69.3 percent) of those Canadians classified as postmaterialists, but by only about half (48.1 percent) of the materialists.

Postmaterialism is also associated with a cosmopolitan worldview. As noted by Nevitte in his study of Canadian political culture, "[p]ost-materialism is the strongest predictor of cosmopolitanism" (Nevitte 1996, 70). He goes on to say, "post-materialists are about three times more likely than materialists to have these cosmopolitan identifications" (Nevitte 1996, 67). This cosmopolitanism translates into a sense of responsibility for events beyond Canada's borders. This "internationalism" contributes significantly to the commitment to an international peacekeeping role.

Furthermore, in Canada, more so than in all but two other nations included in the World Values Survey (Finland and the Netherlands), postmaterialists outnumber materialists by a wide margin (Inglehart 1997, 157), the ratio being of more than two to one (Nevitte 1996, 30–31). Generational change is increasing these numbers in favor of postmaterialist values even more. This commitment and more cosmopolitan worldview clearly contribute to Canadians' support for peacekeeping efforts around the world that involve the protection of human rights.

With the free trade agreements with the United States (e.g., FTA) and subsequently Mexico (e.g., NAFTA) and Chile, Canada's growing internationalism and its role as an active participant in globalization have impacted not only its trading patterns but also its cultural and value commitments. In addition to the outward-looking imperatives generated by increased international trade, Canada's experience as an immigrant nation has contributed to growth in value diversity and produced a more cosmopolitan outlook. All of these factors have had, and continue to have, a profound impact on how Canadians view themselves and the nature of the values at the core of the socialization process. Together, these propagated a uniquely Canadian political culture. With the development of Canada as an advanced industrial nation and the associated economic security, value change in the form of postmaterialism and greater cosmopolitanism, and the diversity of immigrants who built modern Canada, a worldview very supportive of international "altruism" emerged. These factors, in turn, have increased the need for the nation to both assert and protect its distinct foreign policy identity. Canadian support for peacekeeping "rests on a specific self-image, a coherent world view, and a set of distinctly Canadian values" (Martin and Fortmann 1995, 379). The perception of their nation playing the selfless role of peacekeeper is very consistent with Canadians' political culture and sense of identity.

By way of summary, we see a convergence of several important sets of factors in Canadian political culture that contribute to its association with international peacekeeping: (1) the clear need to differentiate Canada and its values from the United States; (2) a very positive historical experience with peacekeeping beginning after World War II; (3) the sense of cosmopolitanism, and collective responsibility, which contributes to an outward-looking perspective; and (4) the rise of postmaterialist values, which place more emphasis on quality of life issues, including those of human rights and responsibilities. Finally, it should be emphasized that, in light of the internal conflicts within Canada that threaten to tear the nation asunder, peacekeeping efforts tap a distinct set of values that potentially unite its diverse peoples.

CANADIAN FOREIGN POLICY AND PUBLIC OPINION

Recall that Canadians view their nation as a world leader in "working for peace" (Reid 1997). This is an image that Canadians and the governments of Canada have tried to promote both at home and abroad. Over four out of five

(83 percent) individuals surveyed in twenty different countries around the world regard Canada as a leader in working for peace (Reid 1997). Furthermore, when asked to identify what they are proud of about their country, its leadership role in promoting world peace is cited by overwhelming numbers of Canadians. Thus, Canadians see their country as heavily involved in peacekeeping and approve very strongly of that activity (see table 1.2).

When Canadians were asked to identify the most important foreign policy goal for their nation, "working for international peace" far outdistanced any other objective. Three quarters of those interviewed rated this as a very important goal and an additional 20 percent rated it at least somewhat important. Peacekeeping is regarded as an important source of Canada's international reputation with 70 percent rating it as a positive factor. Membership in the United Nations is rated as more important than participation in NORAD (North American Aerospace Defense Command) and NATO defense forces. Participation in UN activities such as peacekeeping, having an international peacekeeping role for the Canadian armed forces, and working to discourage human rights violations around the world all rank as important or very important activities for overwhelming numbers of the Canadian public. Remarkably, although the public considers the national defense role of the Canadian armed forces very important, the overall proportion of Canadians rating it either important or very important is about the same as for its international peacekeeping function. As noted above, having a foreign policy

Table 1.2.   Canadians' Priorities on Foreign Policy

Item—Importance of	% Very Important	% Somewhat Important
Working for International Peace	75	20
Having a Canadian Foreign Policy that is Independent from the U.S.	48	33
Participating in Activities of the UN	42	42
Work to Discourage Human Rights Violations	49	35
Importance of Membership in International Organizations—UN**	61	24
International Role of Canadian Armed Forces in Protecting Canada	57	21
International Role of Canadian Armed Forces in Peacekeeping	46	33
Sources of Canada's International Reputation*—Peacekeeping	32 very positive	38 positive

Sources: Gallup Canada Poll (1994) January 27; Gallup Canada Poll (1995) January, June, September, December; and Reid, Angus (1997) "International Views on Canada—Canada's Foreign Affairs and Policy" at: www.angusreid.com/cdnwrld/world_b/sld019.htm.
*The next highest scoring issue was trade for which only 22 percent said it had a very positive effect.
**Comparable responses for NORAD and NATO were 46 and 40 percent respectively for very important.

distinct from that of the United States is highly valued, and peacekeeping is a way to distinguish Canadian and U.S. foreign policies.

This tradition of peacekeeping has strong roots and has been manifested in a consistent set of policies over the years. For example, the leadership shown by Canada in the recently signed Anti-Personnel Land Mine Treaty (APLM) of 1997 continues this tradition. Schneider notes that the treaty "tapped a humanitarian tradition in Canadian foreign policy that dates to the 1950s" (Schneider 1997, A39).

Even during the most difficult days of Canada's involvement in the former Yugoslavia, public support for its role in UN peacekeeping efforts hovered around the 60 percent level, with less than a third wishing to decrease or eliminate such involvement. Even when the UN peacekeeping mission in Yugoslavia was undergoing considerable stress and reappraisal, pluralities of Canadians still favored continuing or even expanding their country's involvement in the operation (Gallup polls 1994, 1995).

The data presented in table 1.3 seem to indicate that the generalized support for peacekeeping carries over even into relatively difficult and unsuccessful operations such as the Bosnia mission. Martin and Fortmann argue that such support is sensitive to perceptions of significant costs and risks (Martin and Fortmann 1995). The worst periods still seemed to produce a fairly even split in public opinion on participation in the former Yugoslavia. There thus appears to be a strong base of residual support for "peacekeeping" even when conditions and results are not optimal.

One very significant question, which must be posed here, is the actual salience of the whole Bosnian involvement to the Canadian public. Martin

Table 1.3.   Public Support in Canada for UN Peacekeeping and for Bosnia Peacekeeping*

% Increase or Remain the same and (% Decrease or Eliminate)	January 1994	December 1994	June 1995	September 1995	December 1995
Canada's Peacekeeping Role in the UN	59 (32)	62 (29)	58.6 (18.9)	61.6 (30.7)	62.1 (31.8)
Canada's Peacekeeping Role in Bosnia	43 (43)	45 (43)	42.2 (47.7)	45.2 (42.8)	59.8 (31.7)**

*Source: Gallup surveys
** The question posed in December 1995 was "Should Canada contribute peacekeepers in Yugoslavia?" rather than the question posed in the other surveys as to whether the involvement should be increased, remain the same, be decreased, or be eliminated.

and Fortmann (1995) report the results of a May 1993 poll in which more than half (52 percent) of the public was able to identify Yugoslavia or Bosnia as trouble spots. However, knowledge of Canadian involvement remained "admittedly fuzzy." In 1995, when Canadians were asked to recall Canada's UN Activities (multiple responses were encouraged), the most common response was peacekeeping (56 percent). Even though the survey was conducted during a period of peak media coverage of the former Yugoslavia, the salience of the issue to them appears to be relatively low. Less than one in ten interviewees (9 percent) named Bosnia as part of Canada's UN peacekeeping activities. Although this is higher than comparable identification of the Somalia (4 percent) and Rwanda (1 percent) missions, it is still remarkably low. Thus, the low knowledge and salience of the particular cases, except for a relatively small portion of the public, lends itself to a more generalized public reaction in terms of "peacekeeping" itself.

When we track popular support for involvement in Bosnia, we notice the appearance of a rather startling disparity (see table 1.3). The data for December 1995 appear to indicate a marked rise in support for Canada's peacekeeping role in Bosnia from the previous surveys. Why do such major differences appear suddenly between surveys? The favorable responses to involvement in Bosnia in the first four surveys in the table are quite consistent, ranging from 43 to 45 percent, the differences between them being well within the margin of sampling error. In the last survey shown (December 1995), support jumps to 59.8 percent.

Two factors come into play here. The first involves the context, the second the survey instrument, particularly the question posed. Recall that the Dayton Peace accords were signed in early December 1995. A tremendous amount of publicity and media coverage was associated with this event. The issue thus became very salient, and the accord at last seemed to signal some success and a real chance for peace. When the issue was "framed" by decision makers and the media in terms of "peacekeeping," the generalized support of Canadians for such efforts transcended the specific case of Bosnia and its recent history.

It is important to note that the question posed by the Gallup organization in the December 1995 survey differed from previous questions. Canadians had been asked "Do you believe that Canada's presence in the former Yugoslavia as part of the United Nations peacekeeping forces should increase, remain the same, decrease or be eliminated altogether?" By changing the question to "Do you support sending Canadian peacekeepers to Bosnia?" in light of Dayton, a seemingly new and promising operation, rather than simply continuing to support an existing one, we obtain a different response. The resulting opinion on involvement in Yugoslavia (59.8 percent in favor of sending troops) does not significantly differ from the more general favorable response to Canada's traditional peacekeeping role in the UN (62.1 percent).

Participation in the Bosnia mission clearly is the beneficiary of more generalized public support for peacekeeping regardless of the particular country
involved. This makes it relatively easy for foreign policy decision makers to
"frame" issues, through the media, in terms designed both to generate popular support and to use the latter to reinforce their preexisting position.

Foreign Policy Elites

At times, public support for peacekeeping has reached such heights that it
threatened to dominate Canadian foreign policy and to limit thoroughly the
government's policy options and/or exceed its capabilities. As early as the
end of the 1960s, "policy makers in Ottawa had become so alarmed by public enthusiasm for the conflict-resolution role that they thought it prudent to
belittle its significance in the hope thereby of lowering the level of expectations among the most attentive constituent" (Stairs 1982). Although very supportive of peacekeeping, policymakers see public opinion as a not entirely
legitimate basis for decision making and themselves as being only marginally influenced by it.

The position of foreign policy elites in Canada, however, has also shown a
consistent pattern of strong support for peacekeeping as a key component of
foreign policy. Barbara McDougall, secretary of state for external affairs, testifying before the House of Commons Standing Committee on External Affairs
and International Trade, stated that "Canadians have always seen peacekeeping as a reflection of Canadian values, as a way of promoting our international
objectives—peace and security, respect for human rights and democratic
freedoms, and a say in decisions that shape the world" (Blanchette 1994).

Support for peacekeeping as a principal has generally been nonpartisan.
Virtually all of the leading parties support the international mediation role for
Canada's armed forces in one form or another (at times, though, members of
the Reform Party have been quite ambivalent). The center-right Tories (Progressive Conservatives) were ready to establish a rapid deployment force for
peacekeeping, while the left-of-center New Democratic Party (NDP) was in
favor of strengthening the United Nations' peacekeeping capacity. Even the
Bloc Québécois (BQ), a party seeking independence for Québec, generally
strongly supports Canadian participation in international peacekeeping missions. This is especially noteworthy in that troops from Québec are involved
in Bosnia, and Québec nationalists have traditionally opposed participation
of Québec Francophones in foreign war situations, including both world
wars. Only the Reform Party, off on the right of the political spectrum, has at
times expressed serious reservations about peacekeeping.

In seeking a critical role for itself in world affairs, while differentiating itself
from the United States, Canada has practiced a sort of "niche politics." "Niche
or value added diplomacy . . . lets Canada play a tangible role in world affairs

despite acknowledged limits on its resources" (Schneider 1997, A1). This entails "a holistic approach [that] includes a full range of political, diplomatic and military instruments" (Carment 1996, 238). Thus, an area in which Canada plays a significant role is "its continuing contribution to peacekeeping within multilateral frameworks. Multilateral operations have the distinct advantage of exemplifying the cooperative security arrangements that have been a cornerstone of Canada's foreign policy" (Carment 1996, 238).

The pride expressed in this role at the elite level is underlined by the writings of such notables as former Prime Minister (also a former foreign minister) Joe Clark, who emphasizes that Canada is "the first international country," a country that "has defined its national interest more broadly, less selfishly, than many others" (Clark 1997, 541). Current Foreign Minister Lloyd Axworthy also underlines the critical role of Canadian foreign policy as providing leadership in the quest for "human security" (Axworthy 1997). This is further highlighted by the Canadian leadership in the APLM treaty and by the development of a new core initiative known as "peacebuilding." This distinctly Canadian initiative constitutes an effort to build on Canada's peacekeeping experience to create a more proactive approach to international peace and security. Both the Ministry of Foreign Affairs and the Canadian International Development Agency are intimately involved in this new initiative (Department of Foreign Affairs and International Trade, 1996).

The position of Canadian elites is further clarified by the debates on Bosnian peacekeeping in the House of Commons. In the initial forum on the Bosnian crisis of January 25, 1994, the newly elected Liberals sought to distance themselves form their predecessors, the Conservatives, who never consulted Parliament on Canada's peacekeeping deployments to Croatia and Bosnia. The ministers of foreign affairs and of national defence criticized the Mulroney government for excluding MPs from an important debate. Though the Liberals renewed the Tory commitment to peacekeeping in the Balkans, they asked MPs to voice their concerns (Hansard, January 25, 1994). "Despite concerns about the safety of Canadian ground troops in Bosnia, [Chrétien] renewed their assignment after an inconclusive Commons debate" (Sallot 1997, D1). In spite of some reservations, a majority (52 percent) of the Canadian public supported this decision.

THE VIEW FROM PARLIAMENT

Although the executive in Canada determines foreign policy, Parliament can serve as a check on Cabinet authority, particularly when a policy involves a risk to Canadian lives. Thus, it is worth reviewing some of the key issues raised in the very extensive House of Commons debates.

In the opening debate, Foreign Minister André Ouellet outlined the Liberal position. "Canada has been closely associated in the minds of Canadians and of other countries with leadership and expertise in peacekeeping" (Hansard, January 25, 1994: 263). He added, "Canadians have always believed in the value of promoting multilateral mechanisms for security and crisis management. Peacekeeping is one of the most important of these mechanisms" (Hansard, January 25, 1994: 263).

Ouellet recognized that events in Bosnia in no way resembled those in Croatia, where "our peacekeepers are engaged in a relatively traditional UN operation" (Hansard, January 25, 1994: 265). In Bosnia, "the situation is radically different. There is no ceasefire and there are certainly no lines" (Hansard, January 25, 1994: 265). The United Nations wanted Canadian and other peacekeepers to deliver humanitarian assistance rather than patrol a buffer zone as in Croatia. The Minister for Foreign Affairs explained that "[t]he task in Bosnia is an infinitely more difficult and dangerous one than that which our peacekeepers have traditionally faced. In addition to the dangers of simply operating in a war zone, we must face the fact that some of the factions do not always want the humanitarian aid to get through" (Hansard, January 25, 1994: 265). Ouellet also reminded MPs of the diplomatic ramifications: "Beyond this humanitarian effort it is often pointed out that Canada's presence in Bosnia has served to demonstrate our continuing commitment to act with our NATO allies in the promotion of European security. It also demonstrates to the world that Canada is a nation which is prepared to carry out its international obligations under difficult circumstances, while others are merely willing to offer advice from the sidelines" (Hansard, January 25, 1994: 266).

The BQ's Lucien Bouchard, the leader of the Loyal Opposition, concurred with the foreign minister's analysis of Canada's historic role as international peacekeeper. "We pioneered this type of mission," he said (Hansard, January 25, 1994: 267). "We have acquired experience and expertise in the field that are respected by the whole world" (Hansard, January 25, 1994: 267–68). Despite praising Canada's role as defender of world peace, he declared that "what is happening in Yugoslavia is without any real precedent. The apparent futility of our efforts, the risks our soldiers are running, the astronomical figures that have circulated about the costs of the operation and the daunting complexity of the political and military situation there have shaken the support that public opinion has traditionally given this type of commitment" (Hansard, January 25, 1994: 268). While stressing that Canadian soldiers could not keep a nonexistent peace, he noted that "[t]he easy thing would be to throw our hands up, pack our bags and leave but this is not the way Canada earned its well deserved reputation abroad as a steady peacemaker willing to walk the extra mile in the name of peace" (Hansard, January 25, 1994: 270). Bouchard chastised Prime Minister Jean Chrétien's early January 1994 comment that Canada might recall its peacekeepers and argued that "[t]he peacekeepers must stay" (Hansard, January 25, 1994: 270). He concluded that Canadians "must continue, insofar as our capabilities allow it, to fulfill our fair share of the obligations that result from our allegiance to the values of democracy, peace and justice, values which, given their universality, deserve our efforts to further them abroad" (Hansard, January 25, 1994: 270).

BQ MP Jean-Marc Jacob opined that displeased Canadians thought that "governments lack the political will to authorize a military strike and that because of this, our peacekeepers should withdraw and leave these peoples to decide their own fate. And this is precisely what the United Nations and Canada must not do" (Hansard, January 25, 1994: 281). He added that "[t]he loss of confidence by the Canadian people certainly reflects the mood, the public opinion in other UN nations. That is why, given Canada's leadership in peacekeeping, if we withdrew our forces, that could trigger a similar move on the part of other UN nations, which would be unfair and fatal for the civilian populations concerned" (Hansard, January 25, 1994: 281).

Svend Robinson of the NDP questioned the appropriateness of a withdrawal and informed MPs that "[o]ur troops are profoundly opposed to the suggestion that Canada would simply give notice that we would pull out after the mandate expires at the end of March. It is their position that this would result in an incredible increase in the level of bloodshed and violence and that the very important humanitarian work they are doing in helping to bring in and escort NGOs [nongovernmental organizations] and bringing in food and medicine would be profoundly jeopardized. Many innocent people would die and would starve" (Hansard, January 25, 1994: 273).

While quick to applaud Canada's international contributions, some MPs from the Reform Party doubted the wisdom of retaining peacekeepers in Bosnia in a time of war and "ethnic cleansing." Jack Frazer mentioned that "the feedback I am now receiving from my constituents reveals their concern with the present Canadian involvement in Bosnia. They worry that Canadian lives are being put at risk in what they perceive to be a questionable cause. They wonder, if the people of Bosnia show no inclination to put aside their differences and find a peaceful resolution of their problems, is Canada helping to end or merely perpetuating this unhappy situation?" (Hansard, January 25, 1994: 272). Jan Brown stated that "[o]ur humanitarian role has been reduced to a bottomless intravenous bag sustaining a killing machine" (Hansard, January 25, 1994: 287).

Despite his party's contention that Ottawa should remove its military personnel, Reformer Bob Mills expressed a change of heart: "Initially, I said we had to get out. It is a civil war and we should be out of there the sooner the better. However, for the reasons I have given I would now say I have modified that position to say that it is only a last ditch thing to pull out" (Hansard, January 25, 1994: 275). Another Reform MP, Bob Ringma, underlined Canadian ambivalence and anxiety vis-à-vis the Bosnian mission when he remarked that "[m]y constituents have images of Canadian soldiers trying hard to help and sometimes being humiliated in the process. This is very much resented, to the point where some say: 'Let us get our personnel out of there.' Balancing this is the view that our troops do prevent many atrocities in their own sector and enable humanitarian aid to be given. Some therefore say that we must stay for humanitarian reasons alone. These views of my constituents seem to be in consonance with the views of other Canadians" (Hansard, January 25, 1994: 289). Liberal Ron MacDonald echoed these sentiments when describing constituent reaction in his riding: "They support the proud tradition of Canadian peacekeeping but in this particular instance they are asking the Government of Canada to take a lead role to ensure that there is a peace made before our people are asked to keep a peace that simply does not exist" (Hansard, January 25, 1994: 290).

In the September 21, 1994, debate on peacekeeping, MPs reiterated their positions first uttered in January of that year. Politicians continued to underline the dangers to Canada's Blue Helmets in Bosnia, yet only the Reform Party talked of Canadians exiting that war-torn country immediately. Canada's continued stay in Bosnia seemed contingent, however. Liberal Janko Peric explained that "[t]here is an uneasy peace to keep in Bosnia-Hercegovina. We are needed there. However, if the safety of Canadian peacekeepers becomes an issue, those peacekeepers must be pulled out. In particular, if the arms embargo is lifted, we must assure that the safety of our peacekeepers is first and foremost" (Hansard, September 21, 1994: 5981). Fellow Liberal Ted McWhinney acknowledged the unwise nature of the Bosnian mission, but underscored that "[o]nce committed . . . we have said we will not abandon it just because it is unpopular or the public whim is against it" (Hansard, September 21, 1994: 5983).

Reformer Jim Hart said: "I think Canadians across the country, I know in my riding, are getting a little tired of this particular conflict. They are getting worn out because there does not seem to be an end to it" (Hansard, September 21, 1994: 5985). Chuck Strahl, another Reform member, mentioned that a March 1994 poll "showed that almost 60 percent of Canadians wanted Canada to increase its involvement in peacekeeping generally. The opinions are the same in various regions of Canada. This shows there is broad support for Canada's role as a peacekeeper, but there is less support for situations where Canada gets enmeshed in an irreversible situation" (Hansard, September 21, 1994: 5994). MPs also worried that Canada had overburdened itself by participating in too many peacekeeping operations. With Canadians in Cambodia, Somalia, and Rwanda and with Parliament discussing a possible mission to Haiti, elected officials wondered if their country could shoulder the increased financial and psychological burdens that accompanied the "New World Disorder." Despite these concerns, Liberal Bill Graham asserted, "Can we not bring in a sense of Canadian values that will enable others to resolve their problems peacefully" (Hansard, September 21, 1994: 5996).

On March 29, 1995, another session on Bosnia ensued. Minister of Defence David Collenette reaffirmed the Canadian government's policy: "Canada's position is that we say to Canadians we know their feelings of pride in Canada in trying to assist in this very difficult situation in the heart of Europe. Canadians have been quite happy to do their part with their continued presence in both Croatia and Bosnia. We also understand that Canadians are becoming a little bit concerned that this deployment not be open ended and that we not continue ad infinitum. I think we were in Cyprus for about twenty-nine years. We do not plan to be in Bosnia and Croatia for twenty-nine years" (Hansard, March 29, 1995: 11227).

BQ leader Lucien Bouchard upbraided the Liberals for not divulging details with respect to Canada's presence in the Balkans. Such a strategy meant that Ottawa had no choice but to remain involved in the Bosnian nightmare. Still, Bouchard offered his party's support, but in the form of a "very conditional yes. A yes that comes with lots of questions and doubts. Not a very happy yes" (Hansard, March 29, 1995: 11230).

Reform's Jack Frazer mentioned his party's four conditions, first outlined in December 1994, for Canada to remain in Bosnia. If unmet, Ottawa should recall its soldiers. He added, "Canadian resources are stretched to the limit. We should be aware of this and we have to accept it. It can be safely said that Canada has done her share. We have now committed our troops there for three years. We have done exemplary work. I do not think that anyone can point at Canada and say that we are not pulling our weight" (Hansard, March 29, 1995: 11233). He concluded by saying that Reform "advocates that Canada tell the UN that we would like our commitment to come to an end. We will give it a three-month period of grace after which time we will effectively withdraw" (Hansard, March 29, 1995: 11233). Previously of two minds on Bosnia, Reformers now presented a united front.

BQ representative Stéphane Bergeron refuted Reform's position. "To bring back our peacekeepers in these circumstances would not only mean abdicating our responsibilities and moral obligations as human beings, it would also extinguish that flicker of hope these people still have, people who for the most part are innocent victims of man's inhumanity to man. It would also mean leaving them to face a tragic escalation in the current conflict" (Hansard, March 29, 1995: 11236).

Fred Mifflin, parliamentary secretary to the minister of national defence, claimed that "[t]he support for peacekeeping in my constituency and in those parts of Canada to which I travel . . . was very strong. I sense that today it is not as strong as it was six months ago. I suggest the reason for that is the perception that we are not making any headway." Fellow Liberal Bill Graham opined that a withdrawal would prove "extremely devastating" to Canada's

European allies. "We are making a contribution in Europe. We are helping the Europeans solve their problems. We are helping solve world peace in our own interests but in their interests as well. That makes us a force in world affairs" (Hansard, March 29, 1995: 11237–40).

In late May 1995, following NATO strikes directed at them, the Bosnian Serbs took UN peacekeepers as hostages to deter renewed attacks. These "human shields" included ten Canadians. Reformer Bob Mills exclaimed: "Canadians are rightly outraged that our soldiers are being held hostage and their lives endangered. The government has failed our peacekeepers and has failed Canadians. It renewed our mandate in Bosnia without any criteria for evaluating the mission." He noted that "Canadians are demanding action. According to a recent poll of thousands, 90 percent wanted Canada to pull out now" (Hansard, May 29, 1995: 12896–97).

Prime Minister Jean Chrétien defended his government's policy by stating that "[w]e are there [in Bosnia] to play a useful role. Thousands and thousands of lives have been saved because our troops are there." He added that "[i]t has been a tradition that when lives of Canadians are at stake in a difficult circumstance we back them up" (Hansard, May 29, 1995: 12896–97).

The leaders of the Reform Party and the BQ, Preston Manning and Lucien Bouchard, criticized the Liberals for their Bosnia policy. Reform called for a pullout and for precise guidelines that Ottawa would follow when determining future peacekeeping missions. The BQ seconded the latter point but stopped short of advocating a withdrawal. The NDP's Simon de Jong endorsed Reform's position when he argued that Canada's Blue Helmets "serve no useful purpose any more" (Hansard, May 29, 1995: 12963).

The minister of defense, David Collenette, acknowledged that "[t]he situation is grave. It is serious. " Still, he cautioned, "Let us not try to take the easy way out. As Canadians, let us try to talk this out to bring some of our tolerance and civility to that country." Then he intoned that "[t]here is a reason that the Canadian peacekeepers are the best and that the Muslim faction, the Croat faction and the Serb faction respect us the most. It is because we are a culturally pluralistic society which knows that discussion, compromise and accommodation can keep multi-ethnic, multi-religious and multi-racial societies together" (Hansard, May 29, 1995: 12939).

Reformer Bob Mills replied that "[t]he Canadian people are demanding leadership from the government. It cannot bury its head in the sand and wait for Britain and France to make a decision. The UN mandate is a flop. Our peacekeepers are extremely vulnerable and getting more vulnerable every day. With no peace in sight the only fair thing for the government to do is [to] bring our peacekeepers home" (Hansard, May 29, 1995: 12941–42). Christine Stewart, secretary of state for Latin America and Africa, then retorted that "[w]e are not prepared to retreat when pushed. We remain committed to a solution that safeguards the rights of all communities within the states of the former Yugoslavia and a more secure and stable Balkans. In the final analysis, this is in our own long term interests as a multi-ethnic trading nation and a key partner in the community of transatlantic values" (Hansard, May 29, 1995: 12943).

What inferences can be drawn from these debates? First, the high priority placed on peacekeeping as an integral part of Canadian foreign policy is clear. Second, various MPs expressed considerable pride in Canada's world leadership in this area. Third, support for peacekeeping transcends party and regional lines. Fourth, MPs express considerable sensitivity to public opinion, but clearly do not view it as the determining factor in policymaking. Fifth, as long as the role of Canadian forces is clearly defined as "peacekeeping," support is strong and consistent. When mission objectives are blurred and risks increase, however, support declines.

CONCLUSION: THE DOMESTIC
SOURCES OF CANADIAN FOREIGN POLICY

In the Canadian political system, the dominant theme is a pluralist conception of the origins of politics, a politics characterized by a perpetual give and take (Stairs 1982). As Stairs has argued, "some of the principles and practices of Canadian politics at home may also be evident in our behaviour abroad" (Stairs 1982). In other words, the spirit of compromise and negotiation that characterizes domestic politics also spills over into foreign policy.

Canada's international relations have been generally characterized as functionalist in approach. That is, there is a general "rejection of ideological criteria in foreign relations" (McNaught 1988; cited in Lipset 1990, 220–21). In this regard, "Canadians, like Europeans, are more disposed to perceive international conflict as reflections of interest difference, and therefore subject to negotiation and compromise" (Lipset 1990, 220). But these are values that are derived from Canadian political culture and permeate domestic politics as well. This pluralist conception makes it far easier for Canadians to insert themselves in a peacekeeping role from a relatively neutral and perhaps objective perspective.

The nexus between socialization and a pro-peacekeeping policy came in response to Canada's experiences in this century's world wars and in the early Cold War period. Lester Pearson's smashing triumph at Suez galvanized a country eager to perpetuate its mission as a guardian of world order. Though support for Canada's Blue Helmets wavered on occasion, peacekeeping continued to serve as one of the cornerstones of Canadian foreign policy.

This consistent belief in the moral rectitude of peacekeeping, which developed as a counter of sorts to U.S. foreign policy, drew upon Canada's political culture. Canadians perceived themselves as more compassionate than

Americans when it came to conflict resolution. While Americans emphasized geopolitics, their neighbors to the north stressed peace. This somewhat utopian vision invigorated Canadians, who considered themselves serious peacemakers. More cosmopolitan (out of necessity) than their U.S. counterparts, Canadians embraced postmaterialist values such as support for human rights.

Their exuberant internationalism resulted in repeated cases of reflexive multilateralism where Ottawa volunteered peacekeepers instinctively rather than purposefully. This occurred when the former Yugoslavia disintegrated. Once civil war raged, the Mulroney government called for UN intervention; Canadians, as usual, supported the decision. Unsurprisingly, the country's foreign policy elites endorsed Ottawa's policy—thus confirming Martin and Fortmann's contention that an embedded Canadian belief system regarding peacekeeping indeed exists. When the Liberals extended Canada's commitment to Bosnia and asked for Parliament's input, only the Reform Party doubted the wisdom of Canada's decision to remain in the Balkans once the UN mission, UNPROFOR, proved incapable of fulfilling its objectives. It is possible, then, that government elites successfully "framed" the issue of Canada's intervention in the former Yugoslavia as one of peacekeeping, knowing that the public had continuously supported such a role since the 1950s.

In this chapter, we have argued that the role of peacekeeping is integral to Canadian political culture, that this role helps Canadians meet the imperative of differentiating their country from the United States, and that Canadian values and practices in the pluralist tradition make peacekeeping a natural role for the nation to play. Finally, we find a convergence of elite and mass views on peacekeeping in general and on the Bosnian involvement in particular. The explanation for this consistency seems to lie with exogenous factors rather than with the direct influence of public opinion on foreign policy behavior. Again, as noted by a leading analyst of Canadian foreign policy, "our diplomatic praxis abroad meshes too well with our political praxis at home to admit of our dismissing out of hand the possibility of a connection between the two" (Stairs 1982, 684).

The positions on foreign policy held by both elites and masses, especially involvement in peacekeeping, may be derived from a common source, the political culture. In sum, the values of foreign policymakers originate in "political socialization from the practice of politics in their domestic environment" (Stairs 1982, 684). Hence, the attitudes of elites and masses toward peacekeeping have a common origin and, thus, naturally converge. The beneficiary in this case is the ongoing support for Canadian involvement in Bosnia.

2

British Attitudes toward the Bosnian Situation

Robert J. Wybrow

In the foreword to *The Pulse of Democracy*, written almost sixty years ago, Gallup and Rae wrote, "What is the common man thinking? The life history of democracy can be traced as an unceasing search for an answer to this vital question" (Gallup and Rae 1940). Even earlier, James Bryce made the observation, "The people who are the power entitled to say what they want are less qualified to say how, and in what form, they are to obtain it; or, in other words, public opinion can determine ends, but it is less fit to examine and select means to those ends." (Bryce 1888, 347). Winston Churchill, Britain's most popular prime minister in recent history, said on the topic, "Nothing is more dangerous than to live in the temperamental atmosphere of a Gallup Poll, always taking one's temperature. . . . There is only one duty, only one safe course, and that is to try to be right and not fear to do or say what you believe to be right" (quoted in George Gallup 1976, 4).

British forces have been engaged in three relatively "major" incidents over the last two decades: the Falklands (1982), the Gulf (1990–1991) and Bosnia (for most of the early 1990s). In each case, while the British public would rather have negotiated or let a supra-international agency—like the United Nations—take over the problem, substantial proportions approved of the use of British forces. The "Great" in Great Britain, for example, still means something to the British public: in a study (November 1996), 12 percent of the British public thought that Britain was the country with the greatest future; this was second only to the United States, with 15 percent.

The situation in Bosnia, after five bloody years, has calmed and NATO has replaced the UN as the peacekeeping or protection force. Hot on the heels of the Gulf War, British troops once again joined the firing line and took casualties. In the first part of the chapter an attempt is made to look beyond the bald opinion statements, rich and interesting though they may be, to the views of the possible end-users and what impact, if any, the data may have on their decisions and actions—that is, to what degree did the "leaders" lead public opinion or were led by it—by examining the record of debates in the House of Commons and interviewing as many government officials as possible. The interrelationship among government decisions, the media, and public will be investigated. This chapter then looks in detail at the British public's view of the conflict in that part of the Balkans once known as Yugoslavia: whether they wanted British troops employed in that far-off land, once a favored holiday site; their attitudes towards the British government, the American government, NATO, and the United Nations; and the effect on international relations. At what point would the body count become unacceptable to a majority of the public?

The chapter is based on a number of questions asked by Gallup across a number of years, many of which have been repeated over time, plus the results from questions asked by the other major survey organizations in Britain. While the Gallup database on Bosnia is not as extensive as its Gulf War counterpart, it is probably the largest in Britain on the topic.

BRITAIN'S FOREIGN POLICY
AND MILITARY INVOLVEMENT

The Foreign and Commonwealth Office, the nerve center of British diplomacy and otherwise known as the Foreign Office, was established in 1782 and is responsible for the conduct of foreign policy, representation of British interests abroad, relations with other members of the Commonwealth, and overseas aid policy and administration. Altogether there are over 8,000 permanent staff, with a ministerial team of a secretary of state, four ministers of state, and one parliamentary secretary. Although the assessment of international events and how Britain should react to them is arrived at in the Foreign Office and the Joint Intelligence Committee, differences between No. 10 and the Foreign Office have occurred, and have occasionally proved irreconcilable. Mrs. Thatcher was, for example, also advised by Sir Percy Cradock, who was her foreign policy adviser and chairman of the JIC, and before him Sir Anthony Parsons.

According to Sir Percy, "Mrs. Thatcher had acquired her first Foreign Policy Adviser at the beginning of 1983 in the light of her disenchantment with the Foreign Office as a result of the Falklands experience" (Cradock 1997, 8). At the outbreak of the Falklands War the Conservative MP Julian Amery accused the Foreign Office of being unable to tell the difference between diplomacy and foreign policy (Comfort 1995, 211). In discussing the relationship between foreign policy advisers and the Foreign Office, Sir Percy wrote, "Foreign affairs advisers at No. 10 have a bad name in the Foreign Office. They have existed rarely and usually at inauspicious times. The title conjures up the ill-omened figure of Sir Horace Wilson, translated by Baldwin from the Ministry of Labor to No. 10, there to become Neville Chamberlain's most active collaborator in the appeasement of Germany in the late 1930s. More generally, it spells divided authority and the possibility that No. 10 could rival or displace the Foreign Office in the direction of foreign policy. Prime Ministers, as they grow more experienced and confident, invariably move in on this area" (Cradock 1997, 8). He described the responsibilities of the adviser to be: "to anticipate crises and see that the Prime Minister was briefed in advance of having to take quick decisions on Foreign Office recommendation; to interpret to the Foreign Office what was in the Prime Minister's mind in the field of international relations; to offer the Prime Minister independent advice on important issues" (Cradock 1997, 10).

In an earlier book with the subtitle, *An inquiry into the Foreign Office,* Sir Percy's comments on the rift between No. 10 and the Foreign Office were confirmed: "But it has also arisen from the resistance of many prime ministers to the Foreign Office as an institution. Successive occupants of Downing Street have felt the need for independent advice. This is not in itself a new development. Most prime ministers have liked on occasions to be their own foreign secretaries—Chamberlain, Churchill, Macmillan were all notorious for circumventing and abusing the Foreign Office when it suited them. . . . However, few prime ministers have been as vehement in their private attacks on the Foreign Office as Mrs. Thatcher. From her early experiences of Common Market negotiations—when she was convinced the Foreign Office was conspiring behind her back—through to the Falklands debacle, she viewed the department with suspicion and regarded its ministers as tainted" (Jenkins and Sloman 1985, 114–15). And as the lady herself said in the House of Commons (October 26, 1989), though admittedly in the context of economic advisers, "Advisers advise and ministers decide."

In November 1990, Mrs. Thatcher, Britain's longest-serving prime minister this century but with her party unpopular with the electorate, was forced into a leadership election and was humiliated in a defeat, firstly by not winning outright against Michael Heseltine in the first ballot and then by having to withdraw from the second ballot to avoid even more humiliation. In this latter ballot none of the three hopefuls—Michael Heseltine, Douglas Hurd, and John Major—received sufficient votes to emerge as outright leader but Major secured just two votes fewer than Hurd and Heseltine between them. Following this vote the other two contenders gracefully conceded, and Mr. Major became the new Conservative leader and prime minister. Despite his victory in the leadership election and the subsequent national election in April 1992, Mr. Major was soon leading an unpopular party. On September 16, "Black Wednesday," Britain was ejected from the

Exchange Rate Mechanism and the Conservatives' popularity went into free-fall. Thus any policy, be it domestic or foreign, had to bear this unpopularity in mind.

The military advice to Mr. Major in August 1992 was that there should be a light force of some eight hundred men but, with the American experience in Vietnam still always before him, there was a reluctance to commit British forces to Yugoslavia. But neither, as an "influential" member of the United Nations, was it a viable option for Britain not to be part of a UN peacekeeping force. The first London Conference, held shortly after, was reckoned to be a diplomatic success for John Major and Boutros-Ghali when it was announced that the warring factions had agreed to virtually all demands for a swift conclusion to the fighting. As it transpired, these agreements were mere words and the war rumbled on (Seldon 1998).

Britain had no military presence in Yugoslavia in 1991–1992, but in the following year, as part of UNPROFOR, British forces in Croatia amounted to 263, consisting of three observers and a medical unit. The Croatian force in 1993–1994 remained very similar at 250, consisting of nine observers and a medical unit; but Britain also sent a force to Bosnia, again as part of UNPROFOR: 2281 in total, consisting of one mechanized infantry battalion group and one engineer squadron.

The force was enlarged in subsequent years:

1994–1995: 3,688—one armored infantry, one mechanized infantry battalion group, two armored reconnaissance squadrons, one artillery battery, nineteen observers, one engineer squadron, and four Sea Kings (UNPROFOR).

1995–1996: 4,440—element of one air-mobile brigade plus one armored infantry, one mechanized infantry brigade group, two armored reconnaissance squadrons, two artillery batteries, one logistics battalion group, thirteen observers, one armored engineer squadron, and four Sea Kings (UNPROFOR).

1996–1997: 10,500—one corps HQ, one divisional HQ with two reconnaissance squadrons, one engineer, one aviation regiment, one armored brigade with one armored infantry, one mechanized infantry battalion, two tank squadrons, four artillery batteries, one engineer regiment plus logistics and two support transport helicopters, four Sea Kings, fourteen Lynx, four Gazelles, and six Chinook (IFOR).

The United States aside, Britain played a major role in the former Yugoslavia as part of the contingents from both the United Nations and NATO. British casualties were, thankfully, very light and included, for example, vehicles running over mines.

Who would go to Yugoslavia? In January 1989 (January 6–10, n = 981) and again in March 1990 (February 28–March 5, n = 894), when Yugoslavia was a peaceful, blossoming holiday venue towards the eastern end of the Mediterranean, 51 percent of the British public felt that holidays in Yugoslavia were popular, "in" fashion. When the question was next repeated, in July 1991 (July 10–16, n = 1032), the proportion had dropped to a mere 10 percent, with eight times as many (82 percent) thinking that holidays in Yugoslavia were "out." Such was the effect in such a short time of the breakup of Yugoslavia on their potential tourist trade. Putting the figures into sharper focus, of all the countries tested, only northerly Finland obtained a lower figure, with just 8 percent thinking it an "in" place to go on holiday. Coincidentally, at the end of June around one thousand British tourists had been stranded in Slovenia.

BOSNIA AS A "PROBLEM"

The British public, like the people in many other nations, tend to be interested more in domestic problems—inflation, unemployment, their children, etc.—than in problems farther afield. They can be periodically concerned, however, when something happens either to encroach on Britain's "interests" or when their emotions are aroused. This heightened concern, though, tends to be short lived. Gallup has asked monthly for many years, "What would you say is the most urgent problem facing the country at the present time?" followed by "And what would you say is the next?'" On only three occasions did Bosnia do better than single percentage mentions in answer to the first of these questions, and taking the results to the two questions combined, Bosnia peaked at 9 percent in late May 1995. When specifically asked for "the most important foreign policy issue or international problem facing Britain" in late June 1996, only 2 percent mentioned Bosnia. To put these rather low figures into perspective, one can look at two other recent "hot spots" where British troops were involved, but there, perhaps, the comparability begins to fade. In the spring of 1982, for example, mentions of "international affairs" (otherwise known as the Falklands) as the most important problem (foreign or domestic) leapt from nowhere to 27 percent in April, peaked at 42 percent in May, and plummeted to just 2 percent in July. Similarly, mentions of the "Middle East" (otherwise known as the Gulf War) ranged from between 10 percent and 17 percent in the last few months of 1990, started 1991 at 27 percent, peaked at 37 percent in early February, then fell away to 13 percent later in the month and to just a single percent in March.

People have also been asked at the year-ends since 1957 to predict what would be true of the international situation in the coming year—"peaceful year, more or less free of international disputes" or one "troubled, with much international discord." The public's thoughts about the New Year in late 1990 were in stark contrast to how they had looked forward to 1990 in late 1989. In 1989 the public were almost evenly divided between the "optimists" (37 percent) and the "pessimists" (34 percent) in their predictions. A year later the optimists (19 percent) were outnumbered three to one by the pessimists (61 percent). In the subsequent four years, the pessimists continued to be the dominant group, achieving majorities in 1992, 1993, and 1994. The public's gloomy thoughts about the coming year, however, were not conditioned solely by what was happening in Bosnia, of course; there were other hot spots around the world.

Seen probably as "a little local affair," no polling organization asked any questions (or were asked to by their clients) on the conflict as such until August 1992. In the preceding five months Bosnia's independence had been recognized by the United States and the European Commission on April 7; Serb forces bombarded Sarajevo, Goradze, and other towns; there were systematic ethnic "cleansing" campaigns; the existence of concentration camps was confirmed; and the Serbs were reported to the UN Human Rights Commission in Geneva. The first survey on Bosnia was conducted by NOP (August 15, 1992, n = 1072) and found that only 27 percent of the public were satisfied with the way the British government was handling the situation. Twice as many, 53 percent, were dissatisfied. Naturally, analysis by political party of the interviewee showed significant differences in attitudes: 41 percent of Conservatives were satisfied with the government but only 17 percent of Labor supporters were. There was also, as might be expected, a gender gap, with more women being undecided than men were—25 percent and 14 percent respectively on this question—leading to fewer women being satisfied—23 percent and 31 percent respectively (see table 2.1).

Table 2.1.   Satisfaction with Government's Handling of the Situation

Q. Thinking about the situation in the part of Europe that used to form the country Yugoslavia, are you satisfied or dissatisfied with the way the British Government is handling the crisis?

| | | Sex | | Age | | | Voting | |
	Total	Male	Female	18–34	35–54	55+	Cons	Lab
n=	1072	515	557	364	343	365	403	369
Satisfied	27	31	23	24	22	34	41	17
Dissatisfied	53	55	52	54	61	46	41	63
Don't know	20	14	25	22	17	20	18	20

Perhaps surprisingly, for a relatively insular people, 16 percent of the British public said that they were following events in Yugoslavia very closely, with a further 52 percent saying that they were following events fairly closely. This claimed interest in events in Yugoslavia was not, however, matched by knowledge of the country: 60 percent, for example, (including 75 percent of women) did not know which of the three countries that made up Yugoslavia the United Nations had an economic embargo against. Around one in four (28 percent), however, correctly thought that it was Serbia, 7 percent mentioned Bosnia, and 6 percent Croatia. One in three could also identify Sarajevo as Bosnia's, capital. Asked who they sympathized with most in the fighting, five times as many chose Bosnia (34 percent) as chose Serbia (7 percent).

NOP finally put seven suggestions to people about possible British policies regarding Yugoslavia (see table 2.2). The full findings can be found in the following table but at one extreme 86 percent were in favor of sending British troops, under UN auspices, to protect convoys, while at the other 79 percent were opposed to sending military supplies to Bosnia. Thus it would appear that the British public, as with many other topics, were "spongy" in their attitudes towards the situation: the 86 percent supporting the use of British troops to protect convoys fell to 61 percent in an "intervention force" scenario and fell further still to 35 percent when a possible repeat of the Vietnam imbroglio was mentioned—53 percent were opposed in this latter scenario. One in two were also opposed to the idea of sending the RAF as part of an international force to bomb Serbian artillery positions.

Again, there were differences across the sexes, party supported, and the generations. On the second, "intervention force" item, for example, fewer women (55 percent) than men (68 percent) agreed to Britain sending troops to help keep the two warring factions apart. Similarly, women were more inclined to agree that Britain should not send troops if it might lead to a repeat of the Vietnam situation (the third item): 59 percent and 46 percent respectively. It was on this item that the biggest gap between the views of the generations occurred, with 40 percent of those aged under thirty-five agreeing with it, compared to 70 percent of those aged fifty-five and over. This pattern was repeated on the fourth item though not to the same degree: more women agreed than did men—56 percent and 46 percent respectively; and more of the over fifty-fives agreed than did the under thirty-fives —66 percent and 41 percent respectively. The sixth item, dealing with a possible relaxation of immigration rules, created the biggest difference of opinion between supporters of the two main political parties: while 25 percent of Conservatives agreed with a change in the rules, 40 percent of Labor supporters did so.

Table 2.2.   Possible British Policies in Yugoslavia

Q. Here are some suggestions that different people have made to what Britain should do. In each case, can you tell me how much you agree or disagree.

Britain should send troops, as part of a United Nations' force, to protect food and medical aid convoys to Bosnia

Agree	86
Disagree	11
Don't know	3

Britain should send troops, as part of an intervention force to help keep Bosnian and Serbian troops apart

Agree	61
Disagree	30
Don't know	9

Britain should not send troops to Yugoslavia as it would end up like Vietnam with the fighting going on for years

Agree	53
Disagree	35
Don't know	12

Britain should keep clear of any military action in Yugoslavia, as the situation does not justify putting British lives at risk, it is not worth it

Agree	51
Disagree	38
Don't know	11

Britain should be prepared to send the Royal Air Force, in cooperation with other Western countries, to bomb Serbian artillery positions

Agree	37
Disagree	50
Don't know	13

Britain should change its rules and allow more refugees from Yugoslavia to settle in this country

Agree	33
Disagree	60
Don't know	7

Britain should send weapons and ammunition to Bosnia to help it fight Serbia

Agree	13
Disagree	79
Don't know	8

Table 2.3.   Possible British Policies in Yugoslavia

Q. Here are some suggestions that different people have made to what Britain should do. In each case, can you tell me how much you agree or disagree.

		Sex		Age			Voting	
	Total	Male	Female	18–34	35–54	55+	Cons	Lab
n =	1072	515	557	364	343	365	403	369

Britain should send troops, as part of a United Nations' force, to protect food and medical aid convoys to Bosnia

Agree	86	86	85	87	88	81	85	88
Disagree	11	12	10	9	9	14	12	9

Britain should send troops, as part of an intervention force to help keep Bosnian and Serbian troops apart

Agree	61	68	55	63	66	55	60	63
Disagree	30	27	32	29	26	34	33	28

Britain should not send troops to Yugoslavia as it would end up like Vietnam with the fighting going on for years

Agree	53	46	59	40	47	70	52	54
Disagree	35	43	29	48	40	19	38	34

Britain should keep clear of any military action in Yugoslavia, as the situation does not justify putting British lives at risk, it is not worth it

Agree	51	46	56	41	47	66	51	54
Disagree	38	46	30	46	41	27	39	37

Britain should be prepared to send the Royal Air Force, in cooperation with other Western countries, to bomb Serbian artillery positions

Agree	37	46	29	35	40	36	41	34
Disagree	50	44	56	49	50	52	48	56

Britain should change its rules and allow more refugees from Yugoslavia to settle in this country

Agree	33	35	32	38	39	24	25	40
Disagree	60	59	60	56	55	68	69	54

Britain should send weapons and ammunition to Bosnia to help it fight Serbia

Agree	13	15	11	12	13	13	12	15
Disagree	79	77	80	80	80	76	82	76

This spread of results, and events in Yugoslavia, perhaps helps to explain the otherwise out-of-sync ICM results found a month later, when in September (September 20–27, n = 1017) ICM asked a single question about Bosnia, "Do you think we should send our troops to Bosnia in Yugoslavia?" Early in September an Italian aircraft was shot down and a UN convoy near Sarajevo airport came under heavy machine gun fire, killing two French soldiers. The ICM question found the public almost evenly divided between those in favor of sending troops to Bosnia (45 percent) and those opposed (43 percent). This parity, however, hid divisions between the sexes and the generations: whereas 53 percent of men said "send them," only 39 percent of women did so; and while 53 percent of the under thirty-fives shared this view, 35 percent of those aged sixty-five and over did.

In January 1993, ten Serb leaders were named for possible prosecution for war crimes, and in February the UN Security Council voted to create a war crimes tribunal. Also, on January 6, Yugoslav President Dobrica Cosic warned Serbs that they had to choose between capitulating in Bosnia or war with the West. An ICM question around the same time (February 5–6, n = 1365) found that one in five of the British public were opposed to the use of British troops in Bosnia. A little over one in five (22 percent) thought that they should be used in a humanitarian role, while almost twice as many (40 percent) thought they should be used "in a peace keeping role to implement a peace plan agreed by all sides." Around one in ten (9 percent) took a "hawkish" view, wanting British troops to be used "in a combat role to impose a peace settlement on all sides." Just days after a Clinton administration promise of "decisive action" to ensure relief supplies were delivered in Bosnia's most needy areas, a UN aid convoy was held up by Serbian troops twenty miles from the besieged Muslim enclave of Cerska. On February 17, Serb troops stopped another Bosnian relief convoy and the UN said it was suspending aid operations. In a Gallup study towards the end of the month (February 18–23) the British public was fairly evenly balanced in their satisfaction with both the British government's handling of the situation in Bosnia and of President Clinton's: 38 percent were satisfied with the British government, while 43 percent were dissatisfied. The relevant figures for President Clinton were 28 percent and 33 percent respectively. Given that the first of these questions asked about "the Government's handling . . . " there were significant differences in the replies from supporters of the two main parties. One in two (49 percent) of Conservatives expressed satisfaction, while 32 percent were dissatisfied. The figures were completely reversed among Labor supporters: 32 percent and 48 percent respectively.

Table 2.4. British Troops in Bosnia

Q. Do you think we should send our troops to Bosnia in Yugoslavia?

	Total	Sex		Age		
		Male	*Female*	*18–34*	*35–64*	*65+*
	1017	488	529	346	458	213
Yes, should	45	53	39	53	45	35
No, should not	43	40	45	36	43	54
Don't know	12	7	16	11	12	11

Surveys for the United States Information Agency in early 1993 (January and March) found majorities in favor of the use of military force in certain circumstances. Using the results from March (though the earlier surveys showed similar findings) 84 percent favored using military force "to protect the delivery of humanitarian aid in the former Yugoslavia." Around three in four (73 percent) favored force to "enforce a cease-fire," while two in three (66 percent) did so to "separate the warring parties." The use of military force to "impose a solution" in the former Yugoslavia also gained majority support (58 percent), with 32 percent opposed. When the question was asked separately in the January study to specify the use of British troops, only slightly lower figures were obtained: protect humanitarian aid (79 percent); enforce cease-fire (63 percent); separate warring parties (60 percent); impose solution (56 percent).

On February 25 President Clinton formally announced that the United States would start airdrops of relief supplies to areas cut off from UN-organized ground convoys and NATO foreign ministers gave their unanimous approval of the plan the following day. On March 2, the besieged Bosnian Muslim enclave of Cerska fell to Serbian attacks before the inhabitants could recover supplies dropped to them by U.S. aircraft. On the same day, the Russian foreign minister said that Russia was prepared to join the United States in flying aid missions to isolated communities in Bosnia. Five days later UN Secretary-General Boutros Boutros-Ghali said that UN member states must be ready to send ground troops to Bosnia if Bosnian Serbs refused to withdraw from occupied territory. The Serbs continued with their sieges of Bosnian enclaves.

A question asked in the spring 1993 Eurobarometer[1] survey (n = 1,073) found 60.3 percent in favor of military intervention to establish peace, with 24.2 percent opposed. In early April (April 1–6), Gallup asked many more questions on the topic and a MORI survey touched upon it for the first time. The continuing "bad press" obtained by the Serbs was apparent in the Gallup study, with only one in ten sympathizing with them. Three times as many (32 percent) sympathized with the Bosnian Muslims, while 9 percent supported both sides and 21 percent supported neither side. Almost three in four (72 percent) supported the use of British troops to protect humanitarian aid convoys, with one in five disapproving. In the event of serious British casualties, however, one in three (32 percent) wanted to pull the troops out, but 17 percent opted for the status quo (limited to fighting back only when attacked), while the biggest single proportion (43 percent) wanted the troops reinforced. While there were some differences (probably not statistically significant) across the sexes and ages in answer to the first of these two latter questions, they were much bigger in the replies to the second of the two questions. A majority (53 percent) of men opted to reinforce British troops in the event of serious casualties, but only 34 percent of women were prepared to do so. The biggest difference across the age groups was to be found in the proportions answering "pull them out": rising from 21 percent among the under thirty-fives to 51 percent among those aged sixty-five and over.

Table 2.5.   What to Do if British Suffer Casualties

Q. If the British troops protecting the aid convoys suffered serious casualties, should we pull them out, continue to limit them to fighting back only when they are attacked, or take steps to reinforce them?

		Sex		Age			
	Total	*Male*	*Female*	*18–34*	*35–44*	*45–64*	*65+*
n=	994	479	515	375	191	274	154
Pull them out	32	27	36	21	25	39	51
Limit	17	13	21	19	23	14	9
Reinforce	43	53	34	50	44	38	34
Don't know	8	7	10	9	8	9	5

Although slightly fewer than one in two (47 percent) thought that it would be possible for an international force to enforce a peace settlement in Bosnia—30 percent took a pessimistic view—61 percent thought it desirable to send such a force to try to enforce a peace settlement. A majority (58 percent) of this latter group felt that the force would still be desirable even if it was thought likely that they would have to stay in Bosnia for several years, while slightly fewer (47 percent) continued to think the force desirable if it was thought likely that it would suffer heavy casualties. Despite very similar proportions among men and women—62 percent and 61 percent respectively—thinking an international force would be desirable, women were more fragile in their views once any "problems" were brought into the equation. Whereas 67 percent of men initially supporting the idea still thought it desirable if the force had to stay in Bosnia for several years, the proportion among women was down to 51 percent. Similarly, if the force was believed likely to suffer heavy casualties, the proportions fell to 57 percent and 38 percent respectively.

In line with the earlier findings, 67 percent were in favor of British troops forming part of an international force, with almost as many, 68 percent (and increasing with age), thinking that it would have to be a very large force. Almost two in three (62 percent) took a pessimistic view of the future of the area, thinking that the civil war could lead to a wider Balkans' war—again increasing with age, from 51 percent of the under thirty-fives to 71 percent of those aged sixty-five and over—and a gloomy 46 percent felt that it posed a threat to the peace of Europe outside the Balkans. One in four even saw the situation in Bosnia as a possible threat to Britain! Despite these potential threats, or possibly because of them, 61 percent wanted Britain and other European countries to be involved in the conflict. Only 28 percent opted to stand to one side and let the antagonists fight it out among themselves. Among those aged sixty-five and over, however, opinions were more evenly divided: 49 percent and 41 percent respectively.

The MORI study in April 1993 found a marked degree of dissatisfaction with the way the situation was being handled by the British government and by the United Nations. Three times as many were dissatisfied with the government (60 percent) than were satisfied (20 percent), and the ratio was more than two to one so far as the UN was concerned (58 percent and 27 percent respectively). Even among Conservatives almost one in two (49 percent) was dissatisfied with the government, with 30 percent satisfied. As might be expected, Labor supporters were even more censorious—69 percent and 14 percent respectively. This could be partly explained by the little over one in two (52 percent) feeling that Britain was not doing enough in dealing with the war. Almost as many, however, either felt that Britain was doing all it could (35 percent) or was already too involved (9 percent). Again, while a majority of Conservatives thought that Britain was either doing all it could (44 percent) or was too involved (9 percent), only one third of Labor supporters shared these views—27 percent and 7 percent respectively. There was also a generation gap, with 59 percent of people aged eighteen to fifty-four thinking Britain was not doing enough but only 39 percent aged fifty-five and over giving this response. The public was almost evenly divided on sending British troops "in order to defend the Bosnian Muslim population": 45 percent supporting the idea but 48 percent opposing it. Opposition to the use of British troops rose to 55 percent in a scenario of the conflict lasting for several years. A similar proportion, 52 percent, were also opposed to the lifting of the embargo on the supply of arms to any side.

In May 1993, a War Crimes Tribunal for the former Yugoslavia was set up at The Hague and the UN proposed the establishment of six protected "safe areas." Bosnian Serbs, however, continued to shell Sarajevo, killing twenty people at the end of May. On June 6, the UN Security Council voted to send reinforcements to guard six Muslim enclaves in Bosnia. Four days later NATO foreign ministers agreed to allow NATO planes to protect UN soldiers from attack throughout Bosnia, and the following day Prime Minister John Major strongly backed British soldiers who fired on Croat gunmen, adding that he was prepared to send reinforcements if necessary.

A repeat of the Gallup questions in June (June 16–22) found that, in the main, little had changed over the intervening few months, though where attitudes had changed it had been for the worst. While 67 percent, for example, still approved of the use of British troops, in the event of them suffering serious casualties the biggest single group (39 percent) opted for pulling them out. The previous dominant group—those wanting reinforcements—had fallen from 43 percent to 34 percent. Similarly, the proportion thinking that an international force would be able to enforce a peace settlement in Bosnia had declined ten points to 37 percent and was outnumbered by the 43 percent no longer thinking peace would be possible. Fewer people, too, thought that it would be desirable to send an international peacekeeping force to Bosnia: down from 61 percent to 50 percent.

The drop of five percentage points between April and June—not statistically significant—in the proportion approving of the use of British troops to protect humanitarian aid convoys was due in the main to a decline, from 71 percent to 59 percent, among Labor supporters—the biggest shift in opinion of all the groups analyzed—suggesting a possible political partisanship effect in an otherwise nonpolitical issue. In contrast, the increase from 32 percent to 39 percent thinking the British troops should be pulled out if the aid convoys suffered heavy casualties was almost evenly spread among both Conservative and Labor supporters: up from 29 percent to 38 percent among Conservatives and from 31 percent to 43 percent among Labor supporters. While a majority of senior citizens (aged sixty-five and over) still thought the troops should be pulled out if attacked—up from 51 percent to 59 percent—it was at the younger end of the age scale that the biggest increases occurred: by 13 percent among the under thirty-fives and by 12 percent among those aged thirty-five to forty-four.

The shifts in opinion on the possibility of enforcing a peace settlement were due to a number of factors: first, 6 percent fewer Conservatives thought it was possible, compared to 15 percent fewer Labor supporters; secondly, a 6 percent drop among men was matched by a 13 percent decline among women; and while the proportion of people aged thirty-five to sixty-four sharing this view remained fairly stable, it fell fourteen points among the

Table 2.6. What to Do if British Suffer Casualties

Q. If the British troops protecting the aid convoys suffered serious casualties, should we pull them out, continue to limit them to fighting back only when they are attacked, or take steps to reinforce them?

April 1993	Total	Sex		Age			
		Male	*Female*	*18–34*	*35–44*	*45–64*	*65+*
n =	994	479	515	375	191	274	154
Pull them out	32	27	36	21	25	39	51
Limit	17	13	21	19	23	14	9
Reinforce	43	53	34	50	44	38	34
Don't know	8	7	10	9	8	9	5

June 1993	Total	Sex		Age			
		Male	*Female*	*18–34*	*35–44*	*45–64*	*65+*
n =	971	469	502	358	165	266	181
Pull them out	39	34	43	34	37	33	59
Limit	17	17	17	20	14	20	9
Reinforce	34	43	26	33	40	41	22
Don't know	10	6	14	12	9	6	10

under thirty-fives and twenty points among senior citizens. This pattern was repeated in the question relating to the desirability of sending an international force to try to enforce a peace settlement in Bosnia.

As might be expected, when the questions were repeated in late August (August 26–31) there were few significant changes of opinions. But the changes were in an optimistic direction, back towards the situation found in April, and on the margins of statistical significance in certain demographic groups. On the question of the use of British troops in Bosnia, for example, the biggest shifts in opinions were among Labor supporters (an increase of 12 percent approving) and the under thirty-fives (an increase of 14 percent).

Compared with February, however, the British public were more critical of how the situation was being handled by both the Major and Clinton administrations: while the net balance of opinion in February had been −5 (satisfied minus dissatisfied) for both governments, the figures had slipped to −14 for the British government and to −33 for the American. So far as the former was concerned, the net balance of opinion among Conservatives had improved from 17 to 26, while it had deteriorated from −16 to −28 among Labor supporters. In contrast, partisanship played no part in the rating of the Clinton administration—the figures for supporters of the two main parties being very similar on both occasions.

The year 1984 began with Lord Owen (January 4) issuing another in a series of warnings that UN troops would not stay beyond the spring if there was no sign of peace. On January 10 NATO heads of government warned Belgrade of their readiness to use air power at Srebrenica and Tuzla. Many of the Gallup questions were repeated in late January (January 26–31, n = 1085), with the addition of a few fresh ones, and new high points were found on some of them concerning the involvement of British troops: 74 percent approved of their use to protect humanitarian aid convoys; 75 percent wanted to see them as part of an international peace force; and 65 percent continued to feel that the rest of Europe should be involved in the conflict. Not surprisingly, in answer to one of the new questions, only 21 percent, if the fighting continued, wanted the British troops to be withdrawn at the end of winter. Slightly more (24 percent) felt that the troops should be kept there to help with the humanitarian aid program and twice as many (47 percent) wanted to "seek to impose a peace settlement as part of an international force, reinforcing our troops as necessary." Majorities felt that it would be justified to risk British lives "if it helped to bring about a peace settlement of the Bosnian problem" (68 percent) or "if this contributed to keeping large numbers of the civilian population alive" (59 percent). When the question was asked with a preface suggesting "the force would be likely to suffer heavy casualties," the figures dropped to 40 percent and 29 percent respectively. Thus, significant minorities of the British public were prepared to accept even heavy losses to bring about a peace in Bosnia. Asking people to quantify the level of acceptable losses did not lead very far, with 51 percent not being able to put a figure to the question. One in three (31 percent) said that they were not prepared to accept any British casualties and the remainder split between 1–50 (9 percent), 51–100 (3 percent), and over 100 (6 percent).

A Serb mortar attack on a Sarajevo market in February 1994 killed sixty-eight people, leading to a NATO ultimatum. A Flash Eurobarometer survey in the same month (n=506) again found around two in three (64.8 percent) favoring military intervention to establish peace—up slightly on the 60.3 percent of almost a year earlier—and with 25.6 percent opposed. The survey also included questions on the favorability of five options and these were repeated in March and again in June. The full run of figures follow but can be briefly summarized as, on the one hand, massive majorities (more than three in four) favoring fighting to get convoys through, confirming to some degree earlier findings; while on the other hand, equally substantial majorities (around two thirds or more) opposed letting things continue as they were. In between, those opposing tended to be the dominant groups, with around two in three opposed to the withdrawal of all troops, around three in five opposed to lifting the embargo, and almost one in two opposed to the launching of air attacks—though a majority was obtained in the March study.

Later in the year (November 18) Serbian jets dropped napalm and cluster bombs on a UN-proclaimed safe area, passing through a NATO-patrolled no-

Table 2.7. Attitudes toward Intervention in Bosnia

	February 25, 1994	March 25, 1994	June 29, 1994
n=	506	507	501
Let things continue			
Favor	11.5	28.4	15.7
Oppose	80.3	65.6	78.3
Don't know	8.2	6.0	5.0
Withdraw all troops			
Favor	24.7	26.7	28.3
Oppose	67.1	68.4	65.7
Don't know	8.1	4.9	5.9
Lift Bosnia embargo			
Favor	28.2	26.4	25.6
Oppose	55.5	58.9	58.1
Don't know	16.3	14.7	16.3
Fight to get convoys through			
Favor	84.4	83.5	77.6
Oppose	11.8	10.3	17.1
Don't know	3.8	6.3	5.3
Launch air attacks			
Favor	38.9	55.2	43.0
Oppose	51.7	37.3	47.3
Don't know	9.4	7.5	9.7

fly zone. On November 22, the United States warned that NATO would destroy Serb aircraft if attacks on the Bosnian enclave of Bihac continued and two days later NATO was plunged into crisis when the U.K. and France refused to back a U.S. plan to save the town.

ICM asked a single question in early December 1994 (December 2–3, n = 1450), "In view of the renewed fighting in Bosnia, do you think the UN troops should . . . ?" offering people four possibilities and coincidentally ending with four equal groups. The first of these wanted the troops "pulled out immediately" (23 percent); followed by "kept in their present humanitarian role as long as possible" (22 percent); "kept there in the hope that a new peace plan emerges" (22 percent); and "upgraded to a combat role so that they impose a peace settlement on all sides" (23 percent). Thus two in three supported the continuing presence of UN troops in Bosnia. Again the sexes differed in their response to such a question and, surprisingly, more men (29 percent) than women (18 percent) wanted to pull out immediately. This 11 percent difference was the largest across the four options given. There were also generation differences, with senior citizens, as might be expected, opting for the pullout (38 percent) as their main choice, almost double the 20 percent found among those aged under sixty-five. Analysis by social class showed two significant differences, the first of these being on the "pullout" option: with 18 percent of the ABC1s (middle class contacts) in favor compared to 28 percent among the C2DEs (working class contacts). These proportions were virtually reversed for the "humanitarian role" option: 27 percent among the ABC1s and 18 percent among the C2DEs.[2]

In late February 1995, Serbia all but rejected the latest plan put forward by the international community to end the Bosnian conflict, while on March 6 Croatia and Bosnia announced the formation of a military alliance against rebel Serbs in both countries. Gallup returned to the topic in March (March 8–13, n = 1020) with a few questions on war casualties. More than four in five (83 percent) thought that it was right for "British armed forces to be used in

Table 2.8. UN Policy in Bosnia

Q. In view of the renewed fighting in Bosnia, do you think the UN troops should be . . . ?

	Total	Sex		Age				Class	
		Male	Female	18–24	25–34	35–64	65+	ABC1	C2DE
n=	1450	696	754	187	301	660	302	681	769
Pull out	23	29	18	20	16	20	38	18	28
Humanitarian role	22	21	24	18	23	25	18	27	18
New peace plan	22	18	25	25	22	22	20	22	21
Upgraded	23	26	20	27	27	23	15	25	21
Don't know	10	7	13	9	13	9	10	8	12

the defense of British territories and territorial waters" and one in two thought that they could be used in the defense of "foreign allies and their territories," though only 31 percent opted for their use to defend "other countries and their territories." In each of these scenarios men were more likely to support the action than were women, by an average of 13 percent. Looked at from another direction, 34 percent felt that it was right to use British troops solely in the domestic situation; 20 percent felt that it was right in the domestic situation and where the defense of allies was concerned; and 29 percent supported the use of troops in all three situations. As might be expected, only on the "British only" and "none of them" did women outnumber men. Asked specifically about acceptable levels of casualties (not necessarily British) in "peacekeeping, for example, in Bosnia," 48 percent chose "10 killed" as the point at which they would withdraw the survivors. Fifteen percent were willing to accept fifty deaths, 5 percent accepted 100, and a sanguinary 11 percent were prepared for 150 or more killed. Perhaps unusually, the "don't knows" were almost identical among men and women, though women were prepared to accept fewer losses. With the Gulf War possibly still at the back of their minds, people were asked for their level of tolerance of "friendly fire" casualties in a Bosnian peacekeeping situation. Around three in four (73 percent) said (perhaps unrealistically) that no troops should be killed by their own side. Eleven percent said that they would accept five deaths through friendly fire, 4 percent accepted ten, and 6 percent accepted twenty deaths or more.

On May 24, 1995, the UN commander in Bosnia threatened both government and Serb forces with NATO air strikes the following day if they continued the artillery battles at Sarajevo—the conflict escalated. Twenty French UN peacekeepers and thirty-three U.K. soldiers were captured by Bosnian Serbs. Britain and its Western allies placed their armed forces on a war footing on May 29. In June (June 8–13, n = 976), a return was made to a number of the "tracking" questions. Reports from the War Crimes Tribunal at the same time suggested that the Serb leadership had planned acts of genocide in advance. The British public's ratings of the various "organizations" involved in the dispute was still poor, with those dissatisfied outnumbering those satisfied: the British Government being given a net balance of −11, President Clinton−32 and the United Nations −21 (asked for the first time in June 1995). Approval of the use of British troops in Bosnia had fallen since the previous year from 74 percent to 64 percent—though still a significant majority—and a majority (52 percent) continued to want the troops to protect the aid convoys even if they "suffered serious casualties." Support for the inclusion of British troops in an international peacekeeping force, while still a majority at 62 percent, fell to its lowest point in mid-1995, as did the proportion thinking that the other European countries should be involved in the conflict (54 percent). The proportion thinking they should step aside rose to 36 percent.

In July, Serb forces overran the Srebrenica "safe area" and Zepa, and by the end of the month the Tribunal indicted the Bosnian Serb leader and the military chief for crimes against humanity. A MORI survey in the second half of July (July 21, n = 1104) found a decline, compared with April 1993, in the public's satisfaction with both the British government's handling of the situation and the UN's handling. Those satisfied with the government's handling fell from 20 percent to 14 percent, while an even greater fall, from 27 percent to 15 percent, occurred for the UN dissatisfaction, which had risen to 65 percent and 67 percent respectively. Even among Conservatives one in two were dissatisfied with the government, with almost half as many (27 percent) satisfied. Labor supporters were more than nine to one dissatisfied: 75 percent and 8 percent respectively. In contrast, Conservatives were more critical of the UN than the government, while Labor supporters were less critical: a net balance among Conservatives of −23 increased to −44, while Labor's −68 improved to −58.

Almost one in two, 47 percent, felt that Britain was not doing enough in dealing with the war in Bosnia, though almost as many thought that Britain was either doing all it could (30 percent) or was already too involved (14 percent). Again, supporters of the two main parties differed in their replies to the question. While 45 percent of Conservatives felt that Britain was doing all it could and a further 13 percent thought it was too involved already, 37 percent said not enough was being done. This latter response was actually a majority opinion (56 percent) among Labor supporters, with only half as many (27 percent) thinking everything was being done. One in ten said Britain was too involved. The generations also differed in their responses, with a majority (53 percent) of the under fifty-fives thinking not enough was being done but only 36 percent of those aged fifty-five and over sharing this view.

A slight shift of opinion could be seen in the question relating to the lifting of the embargo on the supply of arms. The proportion supporting it had risen from 32 percent in April 1993 to 37 percent, while those opposed fell from 52 percent to 46 percent over the same period. While the views of women had hardly changed over the two years, those supporting ending the ban had risen from 37 percent to 47 percent among men, making this the largest single group. In 1993, the figures for men had been 35 percent and 52 percent respectively. Similarly, whereas the views of Conservatives had remained static, Labor supporters were exactly evenly divided, with 43 percent each supporting or opposing it.

On balance, the public were fairly evenly divided on the number of British troops that should be in the UN forces: 43 percent thinking the number should be increased, while almost as many either wanted fewer (17 percent) or thought there should be none at all (18 percent). One in two (52 percent) of men wanted more British troops involved, but only one in three (35 percent) women thought so. The generations were divided by a similar margin: 47 percent of the under fifty-fives thinking there should be more British troops, compared with 33 percent aged fifty-five and over. The political differences, however, were not significant, matching the national divisions fairly closely. This was partly reflected in the social class analyses, with almost one in two

(48 percent) ABC1s thinking there should be more British troops, compared to 37 percent among the C2DEs. At the other extreme, while 12 percent of the ABC1s wanted no British troops at all, twice as many C2DEs did so.

One in two (52 percent) supported British soldiers being involved in armed conflict in order to defend the Bosnian Muslim population, though significantly fewer wanted them to be involved in armed conflict if they had to stay in the area for a long period (39 percent) or if many were likely to die (36 percent).

Men were the more militant sex, with almost two in three (63 percent) supporting the use of British troops to defend the Bosnian Muslims, compared with only 42 percent among women. This spread of support was replicated in the age analyses, with 57 percent of the under fifty-fives and 42 percent of those aged fifty-five and over. Once again, supporters of the two main parties were in close agreement. The classes, however, tended to be less evenly divided, with a majority (57 percent) of the ABC1s in support and 35 percent opposed. Among the C2DEs the split was much closer: 48 percent and 44 percent respectively. When it was a question of the troops being in the area for several years, one in two men (51 percent) were in support but only 28 percent of women were; 44 percent aged under 55 supported the idea, while 30 percent of the remainder did so; and whereas 44 percent of ABC1s were supportive, 35 percent of C2DEs were. A similar pattern emerged if there were likely to be many British casualties, with the support levels being, men (49 percent) and women (24 percent); eighteen to fifty-four years old (40 percent) and fifty-five and over (27 percent); ABC1s (40 percent) and C2DEs (31 percent).

Table 2.9. British Involvement in Bosnia

Q. Would you support or oppose British soldiers being involved in armed conflict. . . .

	Total	Sex		Age			Class	
		Male	*Female*	*18–34*	*35–54*	*55+*	*ABC1*	*C2DE*
n=	1104	525	579	363	365	376	530	574
In order to defend the Bosnian Muslim population?								
Support	52	63	42	57	57	42	57	48
Oppose	39	31	47	34	37	47	35	44
Even if they may have to stay in the area for several years?								
Support	39	51	28	44	44	30	44	35
Oppose	51	42	58	45	47	59	45	56
Even if many were likely to die?								
Support	36	49	24	39	41	27	40	31
Oppose	53	43	63	51	48	60	46	60

Table 2.10.   Involvement of British Air Forces

Q. Would you support or oppose British forces being involved in air attacks on Serbian positions in order to protect the Bosnian Muslim population?

		Sex		Age			Class	
	Total	Male	Female	18–34	35–54	55+	ABC1	C2DE
n=	1104	525	579	363	365	376	530	574
Support	59	73	48	65	62	52	64	55
Oppose	31	22	38	26	29	37	26	35

Majorities were also supportive, in order to protect the Bosnian Muslim population, of the involvement of British forces in air attacks on Serbian positions. Around three in five (59 percent) supported air attacks—including 73 percent of men and 48 percent of women—with 31 percent opposed. Again the generation gap occurred at the age of fifty-five, with 63 percent of those younger than this in support of air attacks and 52 percent of those aged fifty-five and over also in support. The difference between the views of the classes was probably on the margin of significance, with 64 percent of ABC1s supporting air attacks, while 55 percent of the C2DEs did so.

On a question of risking British soldiers' lives in order to protect the Bosnian Muslims, one in two thought it was right but 40 percent felt it was wrong. More men (62 percent) thought it would be right than did women (39 percent), though the generation gap was less marked, with 54 percent among the under fifty-fives and 42 percent of those older thinking it was right. Here the classes were more at odds, with a majority (58 percent) of ABC1s willing to risk British lives, but only 42 percent of C2DEs willing.

By early August, July's events in Bosnia had helped to sink even further the British public's faith in their "leaders" as measured by Gallup (August 2–7, n = 963). For the first time a majority (55 percent) were dissatisfied with the

Table 2.11.   Support for Risking British Lives to Protect Bosnian Muslims

Q. Do you think it would be right or wrong to risk British soldiers' lives in order to protect the Bosnian Muslim population?

		Sex		Age			Class	
	Total	Male	Female	18–34	35–54	55+	ABC1	C2DE
n=	1104	525	579	363	365	376	530	574
Support	50	62	39	53	55	42	58	42
Oppose	40	31	47	37	34	47	32	46

British government's handling of the situation and the net balance of satisfaction fell to −33. The net balance fell to a low point of 3 percent among Conservatives and to a staggering −45 among Labor supporters (with 62 percent dissatisfied). The rating of President Clinton's handling of the situation, always highly negative apart from early 1993, obtained a net score of −45, with 59 percent dissatisfied. The same proportion, 59 percent, were dissatisfied with the UN, giving them a net score of −39.

In late August, another Serb mortar attack on Sarajevo killed forty-three people, prompting NATO air strikes against Bosnian Serb military positions. This aggressive retaliation from a previously passive, retroactive force struck a receptive chord in the British public's psyche. Almost as many in mid-October (October 12–17, n = 987) were satisfied (35 percent) with the government's handling of the situation as were dissatisfied (40 percent). The government's standing among Conservatives improved by 28 points, while among Labor supporters it improved by even more, 32 points. Their rating of President Clinton's handling, too, improved, to 27 percent and 43 percent respectively, while the UN's handling obtained virtually the same figures, 29 percent and 45 percent. Approval of the use of British troops to protect aid convoys rose eight points to 72 percent and those wanting to reinforce the British troops even if they "suffered serious casualties" equaled the all-time high of 43 percent. On the other hand, those wanting the troops to be pulled out fell to 30 percent, a new all-time low.

Another Gallup study, in January 1996 (January 17–22, n = 987), showed a stabilized attitude towards the "leaders" but a possible touch of "war-weariness" in the results. The net satisfaction, for example, for the British government stood at −1, President Clinton's at −5, and the UN's at −14. In contrast, satisfaction with NATO's handling of the situation, asked for the first time in January, was +10. Fewer people, however, 65 percent, were in favor of the use of British troops "for peacekeeping purposes"—a slight wording change in the question previously talking about "to protect humanitarian aid convoys," when a figure of 72 percent had been obtained. Similarly, the proportion wanting to pull the troops out if they suffered serious casualties was the single biggest group at 43 percent—an all-time high—and the "reinforcers" had fallen to 35 percent. Belief in pulling out troops rose with age, from 33 percent among those aged under thirty-five to 52 percent among senior citizens. Similarly, this belief increased as one went down the social scale: from 35 percent among ABC1s, to 45 percent among C2s, and to 53 percent among the DEs. This was set against a background where a majority (54 percent) felt that there had been "very few" British casualties in Bosnia so far. One percent thought there had been "very many," while a further 16 percent thought there had been "a fair number." Asked to look into the future, as the situation continued, the public took a gloomier view of potential casualties: 6 percent thought that there might be "'very many," and 26 percent forecast "a fair number." One in two prophesied (or possibly hoped for) "very few."

The most recent Gallup survey on the topic (June 27–July 1, 1996, n = 1010) took an overview of the relatively peaceful situation in Bosnia. Around nine in ten (87 percent) said that they had "seen, heard or read about the events in Bosnia," though only half as many claimed to either understand the events "very well" (5 percent) or "fairly well" (37 percent). Seven in ten did not see the situation in Bosnia as a threat to Britain's security, with a mere 2 percent thinking it was a major threat. Again, on balance, the public approved of the way Mr. Major was handling the situation in Bosnia: 45 percent approving against 23 percent disapproving—a perception possibly more bedded in domestic politics than in a view of international affairs: the net balance nationally of 22 percent can be compared with 60 among Conservatives but just 6 among Labor supporters. Approval was more forthcoming to Mr. Major's decision to send troops to Bosnia: 59 percent against 28 percent. Again, a net balance of 60 among Conservatives could be measured against 18 among Labor supporters. Three in ten thought that "the British military effort in Bosnia" had at best been "mostly successful"; 44 percent took the view that the saw had been "only somewhat successful"; while one in ten saw it as being "not at all successful." While 44 percent of Conservatives thought that the effort had been at least mostly successful, 26 percent of Labor supporters shared this view.

Gallup asked the "troops in Bosnia" question seven times between April 1993 and January 1996, with the proportion approving ranging from 64 percent to 74 percent, with an average shift in opinion of 6 percent among the general public (summing the shifts of opinion from each occasion to the next and dividing by six). But the longitudinal study of the replies within the demographic groups shows significant differences in the levels of shifts of opinion over the (almost) three-year period. Labor supporters, for example, were liable to greater shifts than were Conservatives, with average changes of 9 percent and 4 percent respectively. Women also tended to be more volatile in their opinions than men—9 percent and 3 percent respectively—while young adults (average 8 percent) were more volatile than senior citizens (average 5 percent).

THE "WIDER WORLD"

Mention has already been made of the public's ratings of the UN and of the Clinton administration in relation to the situation in Bosnia. Other questions, with no specific "Bosnia link" but related, were asked over the same period. Asked in February 1993 (February 17–22), for example, "In general, do you feel the United Nations is doing a good job or a poor job in trying to solve the problems it has had to face?" a majority (53 percent) felt that the UN was doing a "good job," while 32 percent considered they were doing a "poor job." When the question was next repeated in August 1995 (August 2–7, n = 963), the figures were 43 percent and 46 per respectively—a positive net balance of opinion going negative: from +21 to –3. Asked also in 1993 (February 17–22), but not, unfortunately, any later, "Do you think that the United Nations does a better job at keeping peace or does it do a better job at helping poor countries to develop their economies?" 36 percent chose solely "helping poor countries," while 26 percent felt that the UN was better at "keeping peace." One in ten thought that they did both equally well and 11 percent thought that they did neither particularly well.

Between early 1991 and mid-1996, Gallup asked a series of trend questions on nine separate occasions dealing with the public's attitudes towards the United States and President Clinton. The first of the questions asked, "How much confidence do you have in the ability of the United States to deal wisely with present world problems—very great, considerable, little or very little?" and the respondents were allowed to spontaneously reply "none at all." On the three times the question was asked in 1991, the proportion saying they had at least "considerable" confidence averaged 50 percent—ranging from 44 percent to 53 percent. Across the subsequent six repeats, the average had almost halved: 28 percent. Similarly, when asked, "Has your confidence in the ability of America to deal with world problems tended to go up lately, go down, or remain about the same?" there was a significant difference between the replies obtained throughout 1991 and those obtained in later years. In 1991 those saying that their confidence had gone up outnumbered those saying it had gone down by an average of 6 percent. After 1991, the reverse was true, by a negative average of 23 percent.

In 1942, Gallup asked the British people whether they agreed or disagreed with four statements made about "the Americans." One of the series repeated earlier in 1996 (March 20–25, 1996, n = 1001)—"The Americans are too willing to let other people fight for them"—is perhaps apposite for this paper. In 1942, 28 percent of the British public agreed with the sentiment; 55 percent disagreed. Over fifty years later the proportion agreeing had risen to 41 percent, with slightly more, 47 percent, disagreeing. This mistrust of the militancy of the American people, however, is not completely a recent event. A decade ago, in 1984, the figures were 43 percent and 44 percent respectively.

For many years Gallup has been asking a question about Britain's relationship with a number of countries. Perhaps not surprisingly, the shift of opinion relating to the United States was one of the most significant of the eight countries contained in the study. Between June 1991 and November 1995 (November 16–21, n=974)—no intervening data—the proportion saying that the Anglo/U.S. relationship was "too close" fell from 31 percent to 26 percent, while those saying it was "not close enough" rose from 8 percent to 12 percent—a shift in the net balance of nine points, towards a closer relationship. In contrast, the public's attitude towards the "Entente Cordiale" had shifted in the opposite direction, to an even greater degree: from a net balance of 9 points ("too close" minus "not close enough") to 26 points. The 40 percent thinking that Britain's relationship with France was too close was the highest in almost thirty years of asking the question.

Where do the British see themselves in the world? The replies to two other questions (November 9–14, 1995, n = 972) would seem to suggest a perception of declining British power but one that they would like repaired. Asked "Do you think that Britain's influence in the world has increased, decreased or remained the same over the past two years?" 61 percent—the highest for more than a decade—answered "decreased." Less than one in ten (9 percent) said "increased." When asked, however, "Do you think it is important for this country to try to be a leading world power, or would you like to see us more like Sweden or Switzerland?" 41 percent—the highest in more than a decade—wanted more of a world role for Britain, while as many, 42 percent, opted for a lesser role. Around seven in ten (69 percent) in late June 1996 (June 27 to July 1, n = 1010) thought that it would "be best for the future of this country if we take an active part in world affairs," with just 21 percent wanting to stay out of world affairs.

The most recent questions (November 6–13, 1996, n=959) were first asked in November 1978 and repeated a further five times in all. It asked people to pick a description to rate the power in the world of four nations: Russia, America, China, and Britain. Although the data for the first three of the four is interesting, only so far as it relates to Britain will be dealt with here. The six times the question has been asked divide neatly into two in the late 1970s, two in the post-Falklands period and two in the 1990s. The descriptions employed, five in all, run through "the most powerful country in the world," "one of the most powerful countries in the world," "as powerful as other countries in the world," "one of the least powerful countries in the world" to "not at all powerful." Let us look at the addition of the first two descriptions where Britain is concerned: whether it is at least one of the most powerful countries in the world. In the first two surveys (November 1978 and November 1979) the proportion rating Britain as one of the most powerful countries in the world stood at 8 percent. In the next two (March 1984 and March 1986), after Falklands and Mrs. Thatcher's second election victory, the proportion had doubled to 16 percent; and the in latest studies (November 1990 and November 1996) had risen to 27 percent. To help to put these figures in perspective, apart from their dramatic rise, the latest relevant figure for the United States was 89 percent (with 48 percent seeing America as the most powerful country in the world). One is tempted to suggest that the significant increase in the perception of Britain as a world power stems from two main possible causes: the first, the "Thatcher era," when the "Iron Lady" demonstrated Britain's power by generally "handbagging" friends and foes alike and, in particular, the Argentineans over the Falklands dispute; and the second, Britain's not inconsequential military effort in both the Gulf War and the long-running Bosnian conflict.

PUBLIC OPINION, THE MEDIA, AND THE GOVERNMENT

In a press conference, broadcast by Otkrytoye Radio, with Michael Martin Stenton and Serge Trifkovic from the Lord Byron Foundation for Balkan Studies, Mr. Stenton summarized British public opinion as being not very well informed and not very interested in the Yugoslav civil wars (Official Kremlin International News Broadcast, October 6, 1995). Almost certainly true but equally certainly an elitist and dismissive view of public opinion when it doesn't exactly coincide with someone else's views. When public opinion is thought to be "wrong," the public's lack of information is one of the first things commented upon. Even earlier, in January 1992, the leaders of the Serbian community in the UK accused the British media of being guilty of a "nearly universal anti-Serbian bias" in its reporting of the war in Yugoslavia (*Guardian*, January 25, 1992).

It is impossible to disentangle the individual effects of public opinion and the media on foreign policy. In the commercial world—where a great deal of time and money has been spent in answering a question—this would be analogous to trying to separate the cumulative effects of advertising into its various component parts: television, newspapers, magazines, radio, posters, etc. There can be little doubt, however, to state the obvious, that the media has a significant initial effect, given that without the media the public would be considerably less well informed than they might otherwise be. Then with some information, enabling them to form attitudes and opinions, pressure from the public begins to build up, particularly for unpopular administrations who either propose unpopular policies or fail to implement the policies preferred by the public.

I had hoped to be able to discuss with potential users/clients of opinion surveys—apart from media clients—how they saw such surveys, what were their uses, and whether any of the results were actionable or purely informative. In this apparently simple task I failed. Starting with the Ministry of Defense's Directorate General Development and Doctrine, nobody there was prepared to say anything about the use of polling data. Telephone calls and a subsequent letter to the director of public relations (Army) at the MoD also failed to elicit any comments (or even a reply). Similarly, a letter to the Defense Research Agency at Farnborough (accompanying some data that they had requested for an academic paper) also struck the bureaucratic wall of silence. (God save us from the Official Secrets Act!) I have, therefore, had to rely on the cornucopia of interviews and other comments from my predecessors on this track, especially Nik Gowing at ITN. A long-term acquaintance who once, many years before, had been at the Foreign Office suggested that ministerial interest would probably be along one line only—"body-bags." In other words, to what degree would casualties be tolerated before support for any military action began to fade? Possibly a rather "black or white" approach, though as Mark Almond was to write, "a lexicon of timidity could easily be composed from the statements of Her Majesty's ministers expressing deepest concern about the risks of military involvement. As early as June 1992, John Major had assured the House of Commons, 'It would take only one ground-launched missile to cause serious loss of life.' A year later, his defense secretary insisted that 'Every single UN soldier in Bosnia is within range of Serb artillery. If there were attacks on Serb positions, it is entirely within the power of the Serbs to retaliate by shelling the British forces. . . . They are, I repeat, all within range of Serb artillery'" (Almond 1994, 296–97).

Mr. Major specifically likened the situation to that faced by the French at Dienbienphu (*Times*, June 26, 1992). As one British official speaking about media coverage put it, "saving lives by UN convoys made less headlines than dead bodies" (quoted in Gowing 1994, 83). Conor Cruise O'Brien writing in the *Times* under the headline "Blundering into Bosnia," confirmed this view when he wrote, "as the body-bags continued to stream home, domestic pressure on the contributing countries to withdraw their forces would become irresistible," though one could argue that his interpretation of the effect on public opinion was not wholly correct (*Times*, December 15, 1992). Another critical article in the same newspaper—"The Janus Faces of Hurd"—drew together the three strands of this paper, "Yet he seems to accept this duty almost as one forced on British diplomacy by a public opinion with high, and in his view unrealistic, expectations fed 'by a media whose instinct is to dramatize and simplify.' He urges his officials to bring home to the public that the human and material cost of securing a new world order will be 'far greater' than it is now prepared to contemplate" (*Times*, January 2, 1993).

The polling companies, too, have taken this concept of casualties on board in designing their studies. During the Vietnam War, for example, more than thirty years ago, Gallup asked questions about what Britain's policy should be—to send troops or to send war materials only. More recently, towards the end of the Gulf War, questions have been asked about British casualties and similar questions have been asked about the situation in Northern Ireland.

Another problem was Britain's decision to send peacekeepers to Bosnia in addition to stationing troops in Northern Ireland. As Michael Evans wrote in the *Times*, "With an election looming, ministers may try to play down the strain on manpower by talking of Yugoslavia as a short-term commitment. It is widely recognized, however, that once UN peacekeepers have arrived in Yugoslavia, they will be there for a long time" (*Times*, February 14, 1992).

Martin Ivens, writing later in the same newspaper in an article entitled "Whitehall at war," proposed that "British foreign policy in the Balkans has at best been inept." He began, "If war is too important to be left to the generals then it is too important by far to be left to the journalists. The uproar caused by the harrowing television coverage of the ethnic cleansing camps in Bosnia prompted the government's original dispatch of 2,400 troops to conduct humanitarian relief without forethought for the political or military consequences. Film footage from the siege of Sarajevo is likely to galvanize public opinion in similar fashion." He commented upon the contrast between the Major government and his predecessor's, when "The cabinet would be cajoled, the press squared and the British public told to do its patriotic duty" (*Times*, December 30, 1992).

In discussing the breakup of Yugoslavia a defense writer suggested that "Nobody should take the suggestion (now frequently made) that governments did not expect the war in Yugoslavia. . . . Yet nothing was done, mainly because of the traditional inertia which always surrounds the formulation of foreign policy: as long as violence did not erupt, no foreign ministry thought it appropriate to intervene and, once the bloodshed accelerated, everyone claimed that any intervention was too late" (ISR 1993, 232–33).

Sir Percy Cradock, in an appreciation of the situation produced for John Major in September 1991, "came to the unsatisfactory conclusion that while we were ready to concede that the federation was irretrievably fragmented, we still recoiled from the conclusion that international aggression was occurring. This ambivalent attitude was very much the mood at the time; and, unsurprisingly, there was no general clearing of minds.

"The underlying reason was that we did not want to get too deeply involved. As we saw it, Britain's interests were not seriously threatened. A decision to try to restore order would mean peacemaking rather than peacekeeping: there was manifestly no peace to keep. It would also mean deployment of massive forces in very difficult terrain for an indefinite period. There would be no domestic tolerance for engaging British troops in a Balkan equivalent of Northern Ireland. John Major was clear on the point and the military experts were even more wary" (Cradock 1997, 187).

On the surface, there is little to indicate any significant availability of polling data to the powers-to-be, though in the past it was obvious that staff at the Office of Population Censuses and Surveys were photocopying extracts from Gallup's monthly publication, the Gallup Political and Economic Index, and circulating them to interested government bodies. This would include access to all of Gallup's political, social, economic, and international survey data. There is no reason to believe that, given that much of this data did not appear anywhere else, copies of the Bosnia material were not passed to the Ministry of Defense. However, a search of the Parliamentary publication, Hansard, gives few clues as to how much information government ministers might have had at their finger tips. Between November 7, 1990 and October 22, 1991, for example, opinion polls were raised forty-four times in the debates in the House of Commons, mainly commenting on the expenditure of public money to measure such things as the effectiveness of advertising material. In the next three years, opinion polls figured just sixty-five times in all in the debates, but with literally hundreds of mentions of Yugoslavia, Bosnia-Herzegovina, or Croatia—though with just one tantalizing cross-reference: Bosnia-Herzegovina and opinion polls. But when Mr. Kirkwood asked the secretary of state for foreign affairs whether he would place a copy of the results of a Gallup survey in the library, he received the reply, "No. The survey was commissioned on a private basis and was not intended to be made public" (Volume 248, November 3, 1994, 1386).

On the other hand, in a letter to David Owen in the summer of 1991 John Major wrote, "Nor do I detect any support in Parliament or in public opinion for operations which would tie down large numbers of British forces in difficult and dangerous terrain for a long period" (Owen 1995, 18). The prime minister, of course, gave no indication of what his 'detection methods' were and David Owen expanded on Mr. Major's letter, "In fairness, John Major's letter kept the door slightly ajar in case public opinion demanded more action" (Owen 1995, 19). Ex-Premier, Sir Edward Heath, echoed Mr. Major's sentiments when he too wrote to Owen in 1993, "The people in this country don't want us to go to war. They don't want planes bringing back dead bodies" (Owen 1995, 147). Peter Riddell, writing in the *Times*, quoted Mr. Major's letter to David Owen and said of the prime minister, "John Major prides himself that like one of his political heroes Stanley Baldwin he has an almost intuitive understanding of the British public's mood. He reckons that the public are outraged by the pictures from Bosnia like the atrocities in detention centers shown on television last night and in this morning's papers. So they want 'something done.' This means humanitarian help and pressure on the participants to stop fighting. But the public does not back large-scale British military intervention" (*Times*, August 7, 1992).

And David Owen, himself, employed the concept of "public opinion" when he wrote, about NATO's non-intervention in the autumn of 1992, "nor, when public opinion was outraged by the shelling of the historic port of Dubrovnik" (Owen 1995, 342). That there must have been some measure of "public opinion" was recognized by writers in the *Times* when, discussing Malcolm Rifkind and the UN's mandate in Bosnia, they wrote, "Although ministers are willing to support fresh military pressure on the Serbs, they fear it could prove a slippery slope towards the more direct engagement of British forces in the conflict. But their doubts may be countered by public opinion in Britain. Ministers expect that their cautious policy towards the Balkan conflict will be questioned over the Christmas holiday if television broadcasts fill the customary news vacuum with harrowing footage of Bosnian women and children dying from hypothermia" (*Times*, December 9, 1992). Even at the first London Conference, John Major had said, "The people who we represent have been appalled by the destruction, the killing, the maiming, the sheer cruelty which has disfigured Yugoslavia" (*Times*, August 3, 1992).

In August 1992 the *Times* conducted a straw poll among a number of British political thinkers on whether the West should intervene militarily to end the conflict: Michael Foot, Roger Scruton, Julia Neuberger, Hugh Montefiore, Paddy Ashdown, E. P. Thompson, Lord Hailsham, David Howell, Sir Stephen Spender, and Sir Anthony Parsons. Only the latter, former ambassador to the UN, however, said anything apposite for this chapter, "Public opinion is beginning to build up and governments will have to take notice. . . . If there hadn't been such media coverage we wouldn't have seen the rescue of the Kurds from the mountains" (*Times*, August 3, 1992).

On the third dimension of the equation, the media, opinion surveys have suggested that television is the dominant opinion-former, or that at least is the view of the public. This extends, too, to the commercial arena, where majorities of the public, for example, have claimed to have seen an advertisement that had deliberately only appeared in the press. This conflicts with the views of one former British official quoted by Nik Gowing, "Papers have more clout than TV. There are no summaries of broadcast news, so there has to be a fuss in the papers first" (Gowing 1994, 26). When it came to the broadcasting of the horrors of the prison camps at Omarska and Trnopolje, Ed Vulliamy of the *Guardian* is quoted as believing that "his newspaper story would never have made the same impact had it not been reenforced by the simultaneous transmission of the vivid and emotive ITN pictures" (Gowing 1994, 40). Channel 4 announced that it was to devote fifteen hours of prime-time television to heighten public awareness of the war in Bosnia and the suffering it had caused (*Times*, July 20, 1993).

It has been estimated that around one in three of the population watch one of the two main evening news programs. On the "small screen," and from a very unscientific sample of one (the author), come a few abiding memories of television images over the long coverage of the conflict: artillery shells raining down on unprotected civilian targets, such as Vukovar and the ancient coastal town of Dubrovnik; devastated towns with their inhabitants "living" in abject poverty and appalling conditions; concentration camps and scenes of ethnic cleansing; captured, helpless "peacekeepers" and, mercifully few, casualties; low-flying jets fighting "fire with fire."

Looking solely at the coverage of Bosnia by the ITN (the BBC's would be very similar), their archive shows just thirty-four "documents"—presumably news stories—in the first quarter of 1992, that is, roughly one story every three days. This increased sharply in the second quarter to a little over two stories per day and to more than three a day in the third quarter. In the third quarter of 1995, there was a peak of roughly 800 stories, with a tally of around 2,100 for the year as a whole. Thus, it would have been almost impossible for a majority of the public not to have seen many items about the Bosnian conflict over a lengthy period of time.

In an abstract to a recent paper on the television coverage of the situation in Bosnia, Nik Gowing (1994, 24) wrote: "Television journalists must not delude themselves about the impact of their images on foreign policy. On a few occasions it can be great, especially when it comes to responding with humanitarian aid. Routinely, however, there is little or no impact when the pictures cry out for a determined, pro-active foreign policy response to end a conflict."

In a leader article in the *Times*, comparisons were made with World War II, "But night after night the pictures of civilians shot as they search for food, or blown up by mortars in their homes, have begun to change perceptions. Are the people of Sarajevo, like the Jews of the Warsaw ghetto, to be starved and shelled into submission while armed troops go from house to house in their chilling 'ethnic cleansing' operation?" (*Times*, June 29, 1992). This was echoed by Edward Bickham, former special adviser to the foreign secretary: "The power of television in foreign policy is a mixed blessing. As a medium it plays too much to the heart, and too little to the head. It presents powerful, emotive images, which conjure strong reactions.

"Anecdotes about individual suffering make compelling television, but they rarely form a good basis to make policy. . . . Foreign policy should be made by democratic governments, accountable to Parliament, not in reaction to which trouble spots the news gathering organizations can afford to cover from time to time. . . . Reactions to the priorities of the news room are unlikely to yield a coherent or a sustainable foreign policy" (Gowing 1994, 4).

David Owen, in Balkan Odyssey (1995, 119), made a similar comment about media coverage: "Reuters, Agence France Presse and the BBC kept a fair balance, but much of the reporting out of Bosnia took place with shells landing around the cameraman, and was bound to be emotive. It is no use politicians and diplomats bewailing the so-called CNN effect. It is here to stay and in that it means millions of people know more about the world we live in politicians and diplomats will have to learn the skills to counter instant emotions and to present facts and complexities with better skills than those who distort or slant information."

The impact of television was not confined solely to the general public; even sometimes hard-headed officials—including John Major—and their families were said to be visibly upset. It had to be, however, "business as usual" and this meant amending the way policies were presented, including "often vaguely-defined but frequently-cited concepts of either 'public opinion' or 'national interest'" (Gowing 1994, 8). On the one hand, it was said, about Yugoslavia, that on the basis of regular opinion polls and the light post bags relating to the former Yugoslavia, ministers decided that public pressure was not really significant. Commenting, however, on a selective oil embargo following the attacks on Sarajevo, Douglas Hurd said, "that these had swayed many people into believing, as he did, that measures should differentiate between those factions willing to negotiate and those who were not" (*Times*, November 2, 1991). According to a senior Red Cross official, "On one side there are pictures on television, but on the other hand people are people are bored by it. They are not motivated" (Gowing 1994, 28).

In the *Times* of August 21, 1992 under the title "Television's superficial war" Peter Millar argued against the fleeting emotive images shown on television, "that pictures of conflict can never replace a thousand words of reasoned print." Eschewing sour grapes he wrote, "Those of us lacking such technological paraphernalia [microphone booms and video cameras], armed only with notebooks and chewed ballpoint pens, are shunted to the sidelines, to be poked in the eye or clunked on the head." And to finish his article, "The old-fashioned art of listening and distilling the facts behind the flannel has been superseded by gladiatorial on-screen pyrotechnics. But then, that's show business."

One of Nik Gowing's conclusions was that "ultimately, journalistic voices of anger on Bosnia did not weigh as heavily on government thinking as many have assumed. Neither did public opinion. By and large the aim of governments was to maintain within limits a well-defined, low-risk, low-cost policy line" (Gowing 1994, 28). In Misha Glenny's view, Britain's interest in Europe was limited (Glenny 1992), while Mark Almond's acerbic comment was, "The denizens of the FCO [Foreign and Commonwealth Office] in King Charles Street have always expressed disdain for little countries ever since the stable map began to break up with the First World War. . . . To the mind trained in the Foreign Office, the desire of small nations for independence and their own identity was synonymous with petty and unworthy squabbling" (Almond 1994, 56).

David Rieff, in *Slaughterhouse*, wrote, "To a very large extent, the diplomats acted as they did because from the start they knew, even if we in the press did not, that there would be no intervention. When governments have made up their collective minds, the influence of the media, the so-called 'CNN effect,' is greatly overrated" (Rieff 1995, 14). Further on in his book, he pulls together the three strands—the media, the public, and the authorities: "The hope of the Western press was that an informed citizenry back home would demand that their governments would not allow the Bosnian Muslims to go on being massacred, raped or forced from their homes. Instead, the sound bites and 'visual bites' culled from the fighting bred casuistry and indifference far more regularly than it succeeded in mobilizing people to act or even to be indignant.

"In retrospect, those of us who believed the result could have been otherwise were naive. There was a 'CNN effect,' in the broad sense that without CNN, the BBC, and others showing it all the time, the Bosnian tragedy would have faded from people's minds after the first few months of fighting. . . . And, in a narrower sense, it really was the television cameras and not NATO, let alone the United Nations, that saved Sarajevo after the massacre in the Central Market in early February 1994. . . . They [the authorities] had insisted that the mandate did not permit it [the use of force], that the risk to the humanitarian effort was too great, that in the end military threats would be counterproductive. But in the wake of the market massacre, they realized that there was real anger back home, for once, anger that would not be dissipated as easily as it had in the wake of past atrocities" (Rieff 1995, 216–17). Stewart Purvis, editor-in-chief of ITN, summed up television's role, "We influenced events, but not the outcome" (Gowing 1994, 19).

Looking at the British national newspapers, the *Times*, a quality broadsheet, has been chosen as the starting point for coverage of Bosnia in print. In 1990, Yugoslavia was a single reference—though taking up almost seven columns (three columns to a page) in an A4-sized volume—with subreferences covering among other things Bosnia-Herzegovina, Croatia, Serbia, and Slovenia. The following year the same pattern applied but now the coverage had extended to twenty-one columns. With the disintegration of Yugoslavia, the indices for 1992–1995 contained separate references for Yugoslavia as well as the former republics, with "civil war" an extensive subcategory, on almost a daily basis: coverage of the news, editorial comment, and major articles by such people as Edward Heath, Bernard Levin, Woodrow Wyatt, and Conor Cruise O'Brien.

The *Guardian* too had an extensive coverage of events in the former Yugoslavia over the same period and it too favored an A4-sized volume with triple columns. By giving more detail in its index, eighteen pages were thus employed dealing with 1991 and this increased to thirty pages for the following year. Almost certainly, while the popular tabloid newspapers' coverage might not have been to the same depth as the qualities, it would have been comparable in terms of the number of days on which the international problem was discussed.

All the media would have had some indications as to the state of public opinion during this unhappy period: through the published opinion surveys, through the letters from interested readers or viewers, and from their own feel for what the public was thinking. The Parliamentary lobby system in Britain, where government officials fed information and lines to the media would also have given the media some insight (be it one-sided) as to the views of the authorities.

CONCLUSION

More than a decade ago, Joel Brooks began an article with, "Few issues in the comparative analysis of democracy and elitism have been more debated and less tested empirically than the relationship between mass public opinion and public policy" (Brooks 1985, 250). It was true when he wrote it in 1985 and is only slightly less true today. It is analogous for the author with the debate in the commercial field over the specific impact of advertisements in newspapers for a product or brand where similar advertisements are appearing on television and in the other media. It is relatively simple to measure the impact at the gross level but to disentangle the individual components to arrive at their net effect is a much more difficult issue. So it is for public opinion, the media, and government actions.

There can be little doubt that, depending on the situation posed to them, the British public were in favor of British troops being used in Bosnia, particularly when they appeared to be doing "something useful," such as protecting the aid convoys or in a peacekeeping role. The first question asked on the subject, by NOP in August 1992, found majorities supporting sending British troops to Bosnia, though a month later ICM found only slightly more supporting the idea than opposed it. From then on, as can be seen in the table below, never fewer than 62 percent, and peaking at 74 percent, approved of the use of British troops. Substantial majorities, in 1994, were opposed to just "letting things continue." Mrs. Thatcher too added her own none-too-placid voice for a call for military intervention in 1993.

During the 1990–1991 Gulf War, similar proportions were found supporting the use of British troops across a number of different situations:

defending Israel if attacked (47–61 percent)
toppling Saddam Hussein's regime (62–70 percent)

Table 2.12. British Troops in Bosnia

Q. Do you approve or disapprove of the use of British troops in Bosnia to protect humanitarian aid convoys? (Results to Gallup question unless otherwise noted.)

	Approve	*Disapprove*	*Don't know*
Aug 1992*	86	11	3
Sep 1992**	45	43	12
Apr 1993	72	20	8
Jun 1993	67	25	7
Aug 1993	73	21	7
Jan 1994	74	21	6
Jun 1995	62	27	11
Jun 1995	64	26	10
Oct 1995	72	20	9
Jan 1996***	65	28	8

* NOP: "Britain should send troops, as part of a United Nations' force, to protect food and medical aid convoys to Bosnia"
** ICM "Do you think we should send our troops to Bosnia in Yugoslavia?"
*** Gallup "Do you approve or disapprove of the use of British troops in Bosnia for peacekeeping purposes?"

defending Saudi Arabia and the Gulf States (66–75 percent
protecting the West's oil supplies (67–78 percent)
restoring Kuwait's independence (68–82 percent)

It is equally apparent that government officials, some quoted above, felt
that they were being pressured by the media into actions that they felt were,
at best, premature and risky. Added to this were the results of public opinion surveys both published in the media and privately commissioned.
Though the surveys might have been dismissed, they were in the public domain; and while public opinion might often be ill-informed, volatile and
shallow, Abraham Lincoln recognized that "public sentiment is everything.
With it, nothing can fail; against it, nothing can succeed. Whoever moulds
public sentiment goes deeper than he who enacts statutes, or pronounces judicial decisions."

It would appear from the above that the media led in this case, informing
and influencing public opinion, and pressure from both "forced" the government to act earlier, or in different ways, than they might otherwise have
wished. To begin with, as has been seen, there was a disinclination on the
part of some of those both in the military and the diplomatic services to get
involved in Bosnia in any way at all, reminiscent of Bismarck's comment on
the relative values of the Balkans and a Pomeranian grenadier. Then the media informed the public and, it would appear, even some of those in government. The public could not, did not want to, stand by while the tragedy of Yugoslavia unfolded. While obviously not preferring military action with its
accompanying casualties, they were fully prepared to support the use of
British forces to protect the humanitarian convoys and, if necessary, to use "a
big stick rather than a carrot" in both peacemaking and peacekeeping roles.

The broader conclusions of this chapter are mirrored by other studies. In
discussing the relationship between public opinion and foreign policy in a
four-country study, for example, one of Thomas Risse-Kappen's (1991) main
conclusions, echoing Lincoln, was that mass public opinion mattered in each
of the four countries (the United States, France, the Federal Republic of Germany, and Japan), albeit to very different degree. Policymakers in liberal
democracies do not decide against an overwhelming public consensus.

In discussing the horrendous floods of early 2000 that struck Mozambique,
ITN's Mark Austin wrote, "When our television footage was broadcast, it had
an immediate impact. Finally, the world took notice of the scale of the disaster. Aid agencies issued appeals and western governments were forced to
respond, albeit slowly" (*Guardian*, March 5, 2000). All other things being
equal, it is almost as though he was talking about Yugoslavia. And such is the
implied impact of the media on the public that ITN film in a detention camp
is now (March 2000) at the center of a court case amid claims that the footage
had been fabricated.

NOTES

1. The results of the USIA and Eurobarometer surveys are quoted from Richard Sobel's "U.S. and European Attitudes toward Intervention in the Former Yugoslavia: Mourir pour la Bosnie?" in *The World and Yugoslavia's Wars*, ed. Richard H. Ullman (Council on Foreign Relations, 1996). The figures from the Eurobarometer surveys have been reproduced to the first place of decimals but it goes without saying that this is a case of "spurious accuracy" given sample sizes of little more than 500. The sampling error (95 percent) on a figure of 50 percent is in excess of four percentage points.

2. The socioeconomic groupings peculiar to Britain date back more than forty years and despite attempts at harmonization with our European neighbors—probably for as long—some explanation should be given as to their meaning. They are the market research industry-accepted definitions, based on the occupation of the chief wage earner or head of the household. The proportions of each group fluctuate over time and, therefore, only a rough indication will be given. The ABs are upper middle class and middle class respectively, the first part (As) defined as higher managerial, administrative or professional, the second (Bs) as intermediate managerial, administrative or professional and together they represent a little over 20 percent of the adult population. The C1s make up the remainder of the non-manual group—just over one in four of the population—and consist of supervisory or clerical, and junior managerial, administrative, or professional. The C2s are skilled manual workers (a little under one in four) and the DEs are the working class (semi- and unskilled manual workers) or those at the lowest level of subsistence—a little over one in four. The latter group (the Es) is highly correlated with age—consisting, as it does, of a high proportion of senior citizens.

3

U.S. Public Opinion on Intervention in Bosnia

Steven Kull and Clay Ramsay[1]

Has the American public supported U.S. intervention in Bosnia? There is no simple answer to this question. An abundance of poll questions on this issue has elicited a wide range of responses. However, we shall see that a close examination of the wording of these various questions reveals a complex—but nonetheless coherent—majority position.

With such a wide array of results, it has been easy for pundits and policymakers to focus only on poll results that are consistent with simple and preestablished assumptions about public attitudes. Richard Sobel has detailed how the U.S. media persisted in asserting that the public was overwhelmingly opposed to U.S. intervention in Bosnia while ignoring abundant evidence to the contrary (Sobel 1998). This view of the public as simply opposed to intervention is also consistent with a widely held view within the media and the policymaking community that the public in the wake of the Cold War is going through a phase of isolationism. However, as the authors of this paper have demonstrated elsewhere, this general view of the public—while widespread—is a profound misperception (see Kull, Destler, and Ramsay 1997; Kull and Destler 1999). And, as we shall see, it cannot be sustained by a thorough reading of polling data on U.S. intervention in Bosnia.

Taking a comprehensive view of existing polling data, we will argue that the majority of Americans, from the beginning of the war in 1992 through to the present, have shown a desire to take some action in Bosnia. This has been prompted largely by humanitarian and other normative considerations, but also by a view that doing so would serve U.S. interests broadly defined, by ensuring that war did not spread.

At the same time, Americans have shown a strong desire not to act in a fashion typical of U.S. conduct during the Cold War. This means, first of all, that a U.S. response would not be reflexive and imperative. The struggle against communism was frequently portrayed as seamless—requiring sustained effort on all fronts. However, Americans have viewed intervention in Bosnia as important, but nonetheless optional. This means that a substantial number of Americans feel that they can place conditions on their support. Thus, only when these conditions are met does a majority coalesce around a course of action.

One of these conditions has been that in a Bosnia operation the United States would not act as the hegemonic power. As we shall see, the only poll questions that have elicited majority support spell out that the United States would be participating in a *multilateral* intervention.

A closely related condition is that the United States should not contribute more than its fair share of troops as compared to other countries. Americans feel that during the Cold War they did—and to a great extent still do—carry a disproportionate share of the burden of maintaining order in the world and they have been wary of repeating this pattern in Bosnia.

A third condition is that the operation must have a reasonable likelihood of success. Finally, a fourth closely related condition is that the operation be assertive and not simply passive.

As we shall see, given the conditions that many Americans place on their support, Americans are very sensitive to how poll questions are worded. By paying close attention to the variations in responses to different wordings, it becomes possible to ascertain the complex and conditional message that Americans are trying to send through the limited response options of most poll questions.

Another element that can complicate the analysis of polling data is the fact that most Americans pay little attention to events in Bosnia. Thus, as we shall see, Americans have had numerous misperceptions of what has occurred in Bosnia and what the United States and other countries are doing there. Analysts can easily misinterpret the significance of poll findings when they do not factor out the role of such misperceptions in poll responses.

The first section of this chapter examines a number of the complex dynamics that have generated the wide array of poll results on the question of U.S. intervention in Bosnia. It begins with a review of the basic sources of support for intervention. It then reviews findings that highlight the conditions that the majority of Americans wanted fulfilled for such an intervention to receive their support and identifies how a number of key misperceptions on the part of the public generated results that create the appearance of lower support than actually existed. In particular, it draws on a number of innovative poll questions developed by the Program on International Policy Attitudes (PIPA) designed to differentiate these various factors.

Secondly, the chapter presents a comprehensive chronological review of polls from a wide variety of sources through the various stages of the Bosnian conflict, up to the present. At each stage, the combination of conditional public support, the changing political situation, and public misperceptions produced a wide range of poll responses, but this range is understandable when all these factors are taken into account.

THE DYNAMICS OF PUBLIC ATTITUDES ON INTERVENTION IN BOSNIA

Overall, there is an abundance of evidence that at the level of fundamental values, Americans have had a strong underlying predisposition in favor of intervention in Bosnia. Beginning in May 1993, PIPA has regularly presented respondents with series of strongly stated arguments both in favor and in opposition to intervention in Bosnia that are reflective of the current debate. Asked to evaluate each one in terms of how convincing it is, respondents have repeatedly found the arguments in favor of intervention more convincing than those against it. Pro arguments nearly always receive majority support, while con arguments most often do not.

The most popular arguments in favor of intervention are ones that emphasize the humanitarian dimension. In April 1994, 69 percent found convincing the argument:

> Over 200,000 people have died in the war in Bosnia, over a million people have been made refugees and countless atrocities have been committed. For moral reasons, the U.S. should contribute some of its troops, together with other countries, to efforts to try to end the bloodshed.

In focus groups (conducted by PIPA in the first half of 1995), a recurring theme was that the UN should take military action in Bosnia because of the large-scale suffering of innocent civilians. "You can't stay back and watch and allow other people to live this way. . . . I tend to look at what has happened to their freedom, their dignity, their lives. For me it's on a personal level," said a Kalamazoo woman. Numerous participants echoed the comment of another Kalamazoo man, "Suffering is the key thing."

Other polls have also found such sentiments. In a January 1993 *Los Angeles Times* poll, 58 percent agreed that the United States "has an obligation to use military force in . . . Bosnia if there is no other way to get humanitarian aid to civilians and prevent the warring parties there from practicing atrocities" (disagree: 29 percent). This number is actually surprisingly high because, as we shall discuss below, Americans resist the idea that the United States "has an obligation" to act.

Similarly, at the height of the debate over introducing U.S. troops into Bosnia as part of a NATO peacekeeping force to enforce the Dayton accords, a December 1995 CBS/*New York Times* poll presented a number of possible reasons for contributing troops to Bosnia. "Stopping more people from being killed in this war" was the most popular, with 64 percent finding it a good enough reason to send U.S. troops. Also in November 1995, ABC found 56 percent thought that "sav[ing] the lives of Bosnian civilians" was a "good enough reason for sending 20,000 U.S. troops to Bosnia as part of an international peacekeeping force." In a February–March 1998 PIPA poll, 71 percent found convincing the argument in favor of continued U.S. participation in the NATO operation: "Before NATO went into Bosnia, many thousands of people died, many of them innocent children and bystanders. The presence of NATO has completely stopped this killing."

Especially persuasive have been arguments that emphasize the need to uphold the norm against genocide. In a March 1994 CNN/*USA Today* poll, 63 percent found "what Serbian forces are doing to other ethnic groups in Bosnia" to be very or somewhat similar to "the Holocaust which occurred in Nazi Germany during World War II." In an April 1994 PIPA poll, 62 percent agreed that "The Bosnian Serbs' effort at 'ethnic cleansing' through killing Muslims is essentially a small version of Hitler's genocide against Jews. The United Sates should be willing to risk some of its troops in an effort to stop this genocide." In the July 1994 PIPA poll, 76 percent agreed (53 percent strongly) that "the current situation in Bosnia, with Serbs carrying out ethnic cleansing of Muslims, falls into the category of genocide." Asked what should happen if a UN commission studied the situation in Bosnia and also came to this conclusion, 80 percent said "then the UN, including the U.S., should intervene to try to stop the genocide."

This conviction was strong in focus groups. "I think any reason for deciding whether someone lives or dies because of culture or race . . . or religion is wrong," said a Kalamazoo man. "If Bosnia was an issue of . . . territory, then maybe you should just let them fight it out. But . . . genocide is wrong and when that is occurring, something needs to be done to stop it."

Closely related to humanitarian concerns, but also connected to U.S. interests, has been the popular argument that, left unattended, the conflict in Bosnia may spread. In a June 1996 PIPA poll, a remarkably high 70 percent agreed with the statement:

> If the war in Bosnia had continued, there was a chance that it might have spread to other countries in the region. While this chance may have been small, the consequences could have been very grave for Europe and for U.S. interests. Therefore, contributing some U.S. troops to the peacekeeping operation in Bosnia is good insurance.

When a counter-argument was presented, only 39 percent agreed:

> Although there was some risk that the war in Bosnia might have spread to other countries in the region, it is impossible to know whether this really would have

happened. We also cannot be sure the troops there are actually going to solve the problem. Therefore, having troops in Bosnia is not worth the risk and resources.

Fifty-seven percent disagreed. Similar results were elicited when these questions were asked again in February–March 1998.[2] In the CBS/*New York Times* poll of December 1995, 63 percent said that "keeping the war in Bosnia from spreading to other parts of Europe is a good enough reason to send U.S. troops."

Another popular argument was based on the principle of collective security. In PIPA's May 1993 poll, 68 percent found convincing the argument:

> The UN was established around the principle of collective security, which says that when one nation attacks another, this is a violation of international law and UN members have an obligation to help defend the attacked nation. Since Serbia is making direct attacks on Bosnia as well as sending weapons to the Serbian rebels, members of the UN should help defend the Bosnian government.

In sharp contrast to the pro arguments, few con arguments were found convincing by a majority. None of the arguments that dealt with fundamental values received strong support. For example, an argument based on national interest did quite poorly. Asked in April 1994, 37 percent found convincing the argument: "Bosnia is far from the U.S. and we have no real interests there. Therefore it would be wrong to risk the lives of American troops in a UN peacekeeping operation in Bosnia." In February–March 1998, only 35 percent found this same argument convincing about the NATO operation.

Arguments that have directly raised the concern about the potential loss of American lives have also not fared very well. In the February–March 1998 PIPA poll, only 44 percent found convincing the argument that "Eventually the tensions in Bosnia will boil over. If we stay in the operation there, Americans are likely to be killed. Therefore we should get out now before Americans come back home in body bags."

In a May 1993 PIPA poll a bare majority of 51 percent found convincing the argument: "When there is a civil war inside a country, it is best to simply let the warring parties fight it out and not get involved." However, in April 1994 a majority did not endorse this type of argument when it was applied to Bosnia in terms then current in public discussion. Only 44 percent found convincing (52 percent unconvincing) the statement that "Ethnic groups have been fighting in Bosnia for hundreds of years. It doesn't make sense for the U.S. to contribute troops to a UN effort to try to solve a conflict that can't be solved." In February–March 1998, just 45 percent found convincing the same argument applied to the NATO operation.

The con arguments that were found the most convincing were not about the validity of intervention, but about whether the operation would succeed —reflecting how support is conditioned by the probability of success. In May

1993, 61 percent found convincing the argument: "Due to the complexity of the conflicts as well as the mountainous terrain in Bosnia, if the UN-sponsored troops try to intervene it would ultimately lead to more, not less, bloodshed." This argument may also have been found convincing because it drew in part on humanitarian considerations—concern about the bloodshed from intervention.

Also convincing were arguments that pointed to past failures. In April 1994, 59 percent found convincing the argument that "Our experience in Somalia shows that UN peacekeeping operations do not work very well and that American soldiers may be killed and humiliated. We should not take the risk that we will have a repeat of the same mess we got ourselves into in Somalia." However, contrary to the assumption that the public was possessed by a Vietnam syndrome, in May 1993 just 48 percent—and in April 1994 41 percent—found convincing the argument: "We should never commit U.S. troops to Bosnia even as part of a United Nations operation. There is too great a chance of becoming bogged down like in Vietnam."

The Optional Nature of Intervention

Despite the strong support for arguments in support of intervention, Americans have resisted the idea that it is imperative for the United States to intervene. The attitude that the United States is not obliged to intervene has appeared in several poll questions. In February 1993, 57 percent said that "The fighting in Bosnia is mainly a European problem, and the European nations have the responsibility to take the leading role in ending it" (ABC/*Washington Post*).[3] A February 1994 Gallup poll asked, "Do you think the United States has a moral obligation to stop the Serbian attacks on Sarajevo?" and only elicited 47 percent agreement. A similarly worded *Time*/CNN poll of February 10 elicited an even lower 41 percent agreement, with 50 percent disagreement.

Though, as noted earlier, most Americans reject the argument that the United States should not be involved in Bosnia because it is not in the national interest, they also reject the argument that involvement in Bosnia is essential to the national interest. When a February 1994 Gallup poll asked, "Do you think the United States needs to be involved in Bosnia in order to protect its own interests?" only 32 percent said yes, while 59 percent said no. And when asked by Yankelovich Partners in October 1993 whether "the United States has a great deal at stake in what happens in . . . Bosnia," only 38 percent said the United States does have a great deal at stake, while 52 percent said it does not.

The argument that proved so persuasive within the Clinton administration —that the United States must intervene to prove the viability of NATO—has also done poorly. In ABC's November 1995 poll, only 38 percent endorsed "maintaining the credibility of NATO, the U.S.-European military alliance" as a good enough reason to send U.S. troops; 58 percent rejected it.

Americans also reject the argument that the United States should necessarily intervene to maintain its role as a world leader. In the December 1995 *New York Times*/CBS poll, "maintaining the U.S. role as a world leader" was rejected as a good enough reason for sending troops by 66 percent (29 percent good enough), while the argument that "the U.S. helped negotiate the Bosnian peace agreement" was rejected by 60 percent (35 percent good enough).

Conditions for Majority Support

But despite the rejection of these traditional rationales for U.S. intervention, in a great many cases the majority of Americans have supported intervention. This support, though, is contingent on some conditions being met. The key conditions are that the operation be multilateral, that the United States only contribute its fair share, that the operation have a likelihood of success proportional to the risk taken, and that the operation is assertive rather than passive.

The Multilateral Condition

Not only have Americans not been persuaded by the argument that the United States should intervene in Bosnia to maintain its Cold War-era role as world leader, most Americans have wanted to make sure that the United States is only involved in Bosnia as part of a multilateral operation. Being part of a multilateral operation is a key condition for public support.

Often respondents are unclear whether a proposed or actual operation in Bosnia is multilateral or not. Therefore, the wording of the question is highly critical in determining the response. For example, between December 1992 and May 1993, six different polls simply asked about sending U.S. ground troops to Bosnia and found, on average, 43 percent support. However, when four other polls presented it as a multilateral action, average support was 60 percent. In other words, it appears that unless the question explicitly states that the operation is multilateral, a significant portion of the public responds to the question in terms of how they feel about the United States taking the action unilaterally.

This has created a substantial amount of misunderstanding about public support for U.S. intervention. As we shall see in detail below, both before and after the Dayton accords questions that do not spell out the multilateral character of the operation have been more common than those that do. Thus, many journalists and policymakers have regularly encountered polling data suggesting that the majority is opposed to U.S. intervention.

The "Fair Share" Condition

Extensive polling data show that Americans are very sensitive to the question of whether the United States is contributing its fair share to international efforts and generally tend to feel that the United States contributes more than its fair share in international efforts (Kull, Destler, and Ramsay 1997). In the February–March 1998 PIPA poll, when respondents were asked, "In the NATO operation in Bosnia—as compared to the U.S., do you think the Europeans are carrying their fair share?" Sixty-seven percent said the Europeans are carrying less than their fair share, while only 21 percent said the Europeans are carrying their fair share.

There is also evidence that these fair share concerns suppress the level of support for U.S. participation in an operation in Bosnia that is expressed in standard poll questions. Apparently, some Americans who express opposition to U.S. participation are actually expressing opposition to the assumed level of U.S. participation.

This dynamic was demonstrated in an experiment conducted by PIPA in June 1996. First, half the sample was asked a standard question about U.S. participation in the Bosnia operation, using the same question that the Pew Center asked in January 1996. Pew asked respondents whether they "approve or disapprove of President Clinton's decision to send 20,000 U.S. troops to Bosnia as part of an international peacekeeping force," without stating that other countries would be supplying the majority of the troops. Forty-eight percent said they approved, while 49 percent said they disapproved. When PIPA repeated the same question, it produced a similar result—51 percent approve, 44 percent disapprove.

The other half sample was then asked what percentage of the troops they would like to see the United States contributing, with "none" being a clearly stated option. In this context, 59 percent said the United States should contribute some troops, while only 38 percent said that the United States should contribute none. Thus it appears that some respondents in the standard "favor-oppose" question refrain from expressing their support for the operation because they disapprove of the level of U.S. participation they assume, though not necessarily participation in the operation per se.

The Success Condition

Another factor that has influenced support for the Bosnian and other peacekeeping operations is the question of whether an operation is likely to succeed, or if American soldiers might be put at risk in a losing effort. Apparently, a substantial portion of the opposition to participation has been derived from a lack in confidence in the operation, more than an opposition to contributing in principle.

Thus, support has waxed and waned according to conditions on the ground in Bosnia. In May 1993 when there was no peacekeeping operation in Bosnia, PIPA found 77 percent support for contributing U.S. troops to police a peace agreement there. By April 1995, when the UN peacekeeping operation had been in place awhile but was going very poorly, PIPA found that support for contributing troops in the event of a peace agreement had eroded to 52 percent and stayed around this level through the implementation of the Dayton Accords.

As we shall see, in the early stages of the NATO operation, questions that asked about the operation's prospect of success also showed low levels of confidence; thus, support for the operation remained divided. However, we shall see that in early 1998 after the NATO operation had been in place for some time, optimism grew that the operation would succeed and support picked up substantially.

Among respondents the perception of probable success was highly related to readiness to support U.S. participation in the operation. In a February–March 1998 PIPA poll, among those who believed that the operation was succeeding, 79 percent favored participation, as compared to 47 percent among those who thought it was not.

Dissatisfaction with the operation's performance can also mask underlying support for the operation itself. In the February–March 1998 PIPA poll, respondents were given a question that allowed them to differentiate their feelings about the operation's performance from their attitude about U.S. participation by presenting them three options. Only 26 percent chose the unequivocal option: "I am opposed to continuing participation in the operation in Bosnia." Just 26 percent chose the option: "I think the operation in Bosnia is going fairly well, and would support continuing U.S. participation." The largest number—43 percent—said: "I am not satisfied with the way the operation in Bosnia is going, but I think it would be a mistake for the U.S. to pull out its troops now." Thus an overwhelming 79 percent showed support for the operation itself, though 69 percent expressed dissatisfaction with how well the operation is going. Thus, it appears that in some poll questions when respondents are given just two options and express opposition to the operation some respondents are actually expressing their dissatisfaction with how well the operation is going, not opposition to the operation itself.

The Assertive Condition

Closely related to their concerns about the potential success of the operation in Bosnia, many Americans have indicated that they will only support an assertive operation. During the UN operation many Americans were quite unhappy about its passive nature. In an April 1995 PIPA poll, an overwhelming 79 percent agreed with the statement: "Overall, UN peacekeeping operations are not very successful because they tend to do just enough to keep the situation from getting totally out of hand, but not enough to really solve the problem." Similarly, 75 percent agreed in the same poll that "UN peacekeeping operations are often ineffective and even dangerous because they send troops into civil wars without the means to defend themselves or the ability to deter attacks . . . UN troops wind up being sitting ducks." Presented three options, only 13 percent wanted the UN to "stay the course"; 29 percent wanted it to "withdraw," while the largest number—50 percent—wanted the UN peacekeeping force to "get tougher."

As we shall see below, throughout the period leading up to the Dayton Accords, strong majorities were supportive of taking strong actions. For example, there was very strong support for making threats to bomb Serb positions if they did not comply with demands and then follow through if necessary. Strong majorities favored using force to protect aid convoys and to protect safe havens. As Richard Sobel noted, "During times of inaction or vacillation, the public has tended to disapprove more than approve. . . . When the president has threatened or participated in direct allied action in Bosnia, a larger proportion of Americans typically approved than disapproved of his handling of the situation" (Sobel 1996, 147).

Since the United States has gone into Bosnia, strong majorities have expressed frustration that NATO has not actively sought to arrest Bosnian leaders charged with war crimes. In two of PIPA's polls, respondents were presented the following:

> There is a controversy about whether the NATO force in Bosnia should seek out and arrest the two Bosnian Serb leaders who have been charged with war crimes and turn them over to the World Court. Some say that the NATO force should arrest these leaders because they are responsible for the systematic killing of thousands of civilians. Others say that such an effort might lead to armed conflict as in Somalia, and some American troops might be killed.

In February–March 1998, a very strong majority of 73 percent said they favored (45 percent strongly) "having the NATO force carry out these arrests" —up from 70 percent when the same question was asked in June 1996. Only 19 percent were opposed (down from 24 percent).

The Role of Misperceptions

As we have seen, the conditions that some Americans place on their support for U.S. intervention in Bosnia sometimes obscure the underlying support for intervention in principle. Another factor that can obscure this underlying support is widespread misperceptions about the nature of U.S. participation in the Bosnia operation. In fact, it appears that if a number of key misperceptions were corrected, support for the operation would be substantially higher than it is. In a number of dimensions the conditions Americans impose on their support for intervention are actually being fulfilled more than they realize.

Overestimation of the U.S. Share

One key example of the misperceptions regarding intervention in Bosnia is about the portion of troops the United States contributed to the operation. As discussed, Americans are quite concerned that the U.S. contributes no more than its fair share. Apparently, Americans dramatically overestimate the portion of troops the United States contributes. When asked in PIPA's February–March 1998 poll, "What is your hunch about what percentage of the troops in the peacekeeping operation are American?," the median response was 50 percent. This had risen from a median of 40 percent when PIPA asked this question in June 1996 and a mean of 45 percent when Louis Harris asked the question in October 1997. In fact, at the beginning of the operation the United States contributed one-third of the troops, but this soon dropped to 25 percent and was 21 percent as of October 1998.[4] In February–March 1998, 67 percent of respondents estimated that the U.S. contribution was above 25 percent.

Most significantly, a strong majority of Americans say they would support the actual level of U.S. participation. In June 1996, among those who favored contributing some troops, the median preference was for the United States to contribute 25 percent. In February–March 1998, PIPA asked about United States participation in an extension of the mission with the question, "If our European allies and some other countries would provide 75 percent of the troops for this extended mission, should the U.S. be willing or should the United States not be willing to contribute 25 percent?" Seventy-eight percent said the United States should be willing, while only 18 percent said it should not.

The public has a long-standing tendency to overestimate the level of United States participation in Bosnia peacekeeping. In April 1995, when the United States was only contributing 2.5 percent of the troops to the peacekeeping operation in the former Yugoslavia, PIPA asked respondents to estimate the percentage of the troops there that were American. The median estimate was 30 percent—about twelve times the actual level. A full 90 percent of respondents overestimated. When respondents were asked what an "appropriate" percentage would be, only 13 percent of respondents said the United States should not contribute any troops while a full 83 percent gave some number—far more than the number who said they favored contributing troops per se. The mean preferred level was 20 percent (median 15 percent).

In January 1996, Pew found that only 21 percent of Americans knew that the United States was providing, at that time, less than half—actually, one-third—of the NATO troops in Bosnia to enforce the Dayton agreement (29 percent thought the U.S. was providing "about half"; 31 percent thought "most"). In Pew's poll, among those who thought correctly that the U.S. contribution was less than half of the force, 54 percent approved the decision to send troops; but among those who thought that U.S. troops made up "most" of the peacekeeping force, only 45 percent approved.

Misperceptions Related to Success

PIPA's February–March 1998 poll found that a substantial portion of respondents had perceived the operation as going much more poorly than it was in fact. These perceptions significantly diminished the perception that the operation is succeeding, which in turn lowered support for U.S. participation.

A strong majority believed that American troops have been killed in Bosnia. When asked, "Is it your impression that American soldiers have or have not been killed by hostile fire in Bosnia over the last year?," almost a two-thirds majority—63 percent—said that Americans have been killed. In reality, as of this writing, no Americans have been killed by hostile fire. Only 22 percent of respondents knew this, while 15 percent could not answer the question. Among those who said American soldiers have been killed, when asked to estimate how many have been killed over the last year, the median estimate was 25 deaths. A substantial number of respondents also gave estimates in the hundreds, so that the average estimate of U.S. fatalities was 172.

Only a minority of respondents were clearly aware that the fighting in Bosnia had stopped. Asked whether "in Bosnia now the factions are actively fighting a war, or has the combat stopped?," only 42 percent said that the combat had stopped. Forty-one percent said the war is still going on, and 17 percent could not say. Thus, it appears that a majority (58 percent) was, at the least, unsure whether the NATO operation has been successful in maintaining the peace in Bosnia. Among those who said the war is still going on, when asked to estimate how many people were being killed each month, the median estimate was 100. A substantial number gave estimates in the thousands, so the mean estimate was even higher— 527 killed.

Only a minority was aware that most Bosnians support the NATO operation.[5] Asked, "Is it your impression that most Bosnians support the NATO operation or that most Bosnians want NATO to leave?," only 46 percent answered correctly that most Bosnians support the operation. A substantial minority of 35 percent believed most Bosnians want NATO to leave, while 19 percent could not give an answer. Thus, a majority (54 percent) was at least unsure of whether most Bosnians were backing NATO efforts.

All of these misperceptions have a significant impact on the perception of the success of the mission. Among those who knew that the war has stopped, the percentage saying the operation was succeeding was 15 points higher than for those who said the war was still going on or said they did not know. Among those who knew that Americans were not being killed, belief that the operation is succeeding was 17 points higher. Among those who knew that most Bosnians support the operation, belief in success was 16 points higher. And, as discussed, this perception of success was closely related to support for the operation.

The Possibility of Fatalities

According to a widespread view among policymakers and the media, public support for U.S. intervention in Bosnia is inherently frail because it is likely to collapse in the event that the United States suffers a substantial number of troop fatalities. This view is often based on the mistaken assertion that when eighteen U.S. Rangers were killed in Somalia in October 1993 it lead to an overwhelming public demand for the immediate withdrawal of U.S. troops.[6] A variety of evidence suggests that this would likely not be the case.

Perhaps the most compelling evidence is the just-mentioned finding that a majority of Americans believe that a substantial number of Americans have already been killed in the operation in Bosnia. However, even among those who had this mistaken belief the majority supported the operation.

PIPA also asked respondents how they would respond to a number of hypothetical scenarios. Respondents in the February–March 1998 poll were asked to:

> imagine that at some point NATO peacekeeping troops have a confrontation with an organized group resisting the Dayton peace agreement. Imagine that this confrontation becomes violent and some NATO troops are killed, including 20 Americans. Imagine that you saw the bodies of the Americans on television.

They were then asked what they thought they would want to do under these circumstances, and were given four choices. Only a small minority— 15 percent—said that they would want to withdraw all American troops. Sixteen percent said they would want to "stay the course." A plurality of 34 percent chose to "strike back hard at the attackers," while another 28 percent chose to bring in reinforcements—making a 61 percent majority who preferred an assertive response. When PIPA presented similar scenarios in April 1995 the responses were essentially the same.[7]

In the focus groups conducted in spring 1995, participants very rarely shifted from their initial support for an operation when the possibility of large-scale fatalities was posed. A man from Kalamazoo explained how he came to terms with the possibility of fatalities:

> If we're simply stating that our mission is to prevent these moral atrocities from developing and continuing, for me, once that decision is made that gives meaning to death. Death is never pleasant it is never nice, it's painful for all involved, it's terrible, but at least there's meaning attached. . . . To me that's how you give meaning to death in [a UN operation in] another country and why we're there . . . it's important, it's something bigger.

PUBLIC OPINION OVER THE
COURSE OF THE BOSNIAN CRISIS

We now turn to an analysis of how U.S. public opinion evolved over the course of the Bosnian crisis, from its beginning in 1992 to the present. At each stage we will see the complex interplay of the underlying support for intervention in principle interacting with the various conditions on support imposed by large portions of the public and the effect of widespread misperceptions.

When the Bosnian war broke out in the summer of 1992, a very strong majority supported an effort to handle the problem through UN peacekeeping forces. The first reports of atrocities and genocidal policies took time to be confirmed and filtered out slowly to the public, but by early 1993 a majority was ready for a major military intervention, provided that it was multilateral and authorized by the UN. Throughout this phase, a strong majority was also ready to support U.S. participation in a multilateral force to police a peace agreement, had one materialized.

In the spring of 1993 and again in the spring of 1994, the international community appeared—for a moment—to be on the verge of applying decisive force, and such action was supported by a strong majority of Americans. However, on each occasion the international community drew back, unable to resolve its internal differences. This repeated process, and the frequent humiliation of UN peacekeepers taken hostage by Bosnian Serbs, tended to lower the expectations of the public.

By spring 1995, support for participating in a force to police a hypothetical agreement had dropped to a bare majority, while support for taking a more assertive approach in Bosnia was still robust. Before the NATO bombing campaign began, just such an action (airstrikes to stop the shelling of civilians) was supported by a healthy majority, as it had been throughout the war—even though the public was now much more inclined than before to doubt that a stable peace could be brought about in Bosnia.

Expectations of success for a peace agreement took long to recover from the disappointments of 1993 through summer 1995. At the time the Dayton accords were signed, the public was divided over contributing U.S. troops to the NATO force to police the accords. However, underlying support in principle remained—alongside pessimism about success. Not until the beginning of 1998 did polls show evidence of growth in the public perception of success, along with greater approval for contributing troops that brought support to majority levels.

July 1992–April 1993: Beginning of the War and the First Public Reactions

Early polling on the Bosnia crisis showed strong majority support for international military efforts to address the problem. Support in principle for the UN peacekeeping operation in Bosnia was an overwhelming 80 percent in July 1992 (Harris), when the operation was only a few months old. Later, in December 1992, 57 percent thought "U.S. armed forces should go into Bosnia as part of a United Nations effort to deliver relief supplies there" (should not: 36 percent; Gallup), while 62 percent supported "sending United Nations troops including some U.S. troops to help the Bosnians defend themselves against the Serbs" (32 percent opposed; Harris, January 1993).[8] If the charges of massive human rights violations against Serb forces proved true, a very strong majority—68 percent—thought the United Nations should send troops, including U.S. troops, to stop the atrocities (22 percent opposed; *Time*/CNN, January 1993).

Other questions showed support for even tougher courses of action—if taken multilaterally. An August 1992 question asked what role respondents thought "the U.S. should play in efforts to stop the fighting in Bosnia." Fifty-three percent endorsed one or more very muscular approaches: participate in "UN-backed ground action against Serbian forces" (6 percent), or in "UN-backed air attacks" (13 percent), or "do both" (34 percent); only 35 percent said "do neither" (sample of registered voters, Gallup). Similarly, 68 percent supported "shooting down any Serbian planes which violate the no-fly zone over Bosnia" (24 percent opposed; Harris, January 1993).

A pair of questions from this period sharply highlights the importance that Americans attach to U.S. troops being part of a force together with other countries. When asked: "President Clinton has said the U.S. would be willing to send some ground troops to Bosnia as part of a peacekeeping force if a peace agreement is reached between the warring factions," 51 percent said they opposed this, while 41 percent supported it (NBC/*Wall Street Journal*, March 1993). But when asked in a different question about "President Clinton's proposal to send U.S. troops to Bosnia as part of an *international* [emphasis added] peacekeeping force if the groups who are currently fighting in Bosnia can agree to a settlement that would end the conflict there," only 32 percent disapproved, while 58 percent approved—a 17-point difference in support (*Time*/CNN, February 1993).

On the other hand, when asked about the United States taking action alone —without the explicit mention of forces from other countries—Americans were considerably more wary. While 67 percent favored "the use of U.S. air forces to help keep humanitarian aid flowing to the civilian population in the besieged areas of Bosnia" and only 22 percent opposed it (*Los Angeles Times*, August 1992), no more than 50 percent thought that U.S. air units "should participate in air strikes against Serbian forces in Bosnia" (Gallup/*Newsweek*, August 1992— asked to registered voters). Fifty-three percent said in the same poll that "the U.S. should take the lead in seeking United Nations-backed air strikes" if Serbian forces continued to block relief efforts. When asked about unilateral use of troops, as little as one-quarter of Americans were supportive: for example, only 24 percent thought the United States should "send troops to end the violence in Sarajevo," with 66 percent opposed (*Time*/CNN, August 1992).

In early 1993, a majority of the public was even willing to see the United States take some types of action unilaterally—though the idea of acting alone lowered support. Using U.S. military planes to drop relief supplies into Bosnia received 67 percent to 75 percent approval (CNN/*USA Today*, ABC/*Washington Post*, February 1993). Enforcing the no-fly zone in Bosnia got 63 percent approval, even in a question that implied the United States would do so without allies (Gallup/*Newsweek*, January 1993). For many Americans, reminders of the severity of the human rights situation were at times strong enough to overcome concerns about acting alone: 58 percent agreed that the United States "has an obligation to use military force in . . . Bosnia if there is no other way to get humanitarian aid to civilians and prevent the warring parties there from practicing atrocities" (disagree: 29 percent; *Los Angeles Times*, January 1993). But when the question of unilateral action was put in language that did not emphasize humanitarian issues, only 32 percent favored "the use of U.S. military force in Bosnia to help end the fighting there" (oppose: 55 percent; *Times Mirror*, January 1993).

Some of the willingness at that time to deploy force, even unilaterally, to address humanitarian issues may have come from the initial success of the Somalia operation at the same time. While only 42 percent had said they favored "sending U.S. forces to restore peace and assure humanitarian aid in Bosnia" in December 1992, 57 percent said they favored this in January 1993—a few weeks after U.S. troops landed in Somalia (Gallup/*Newsweek*).

May–June 1993: The Vance-Owen Peace Plan and the "Lift and Strike" Proposal

In May–June 1993 two different approaches to seeking a resolution in Bosnia both collapsed: the UN-backed Vance-Owen peace plan, which was refused by the Bosnian Serbs; and the "lift and strike" proposal of the Clinton administration, which was withdrawn after European allies gave it a chilly reception.

The Vance-Owen peace plan raised the prospect of a NATO peacekeeping force, one-third of it American, to police the agreement if it materialized. Support ratings varied across poll questions, with support lowest when the question provided little description of the proposed operation. For example, only 41 percent favored, and 51 percent opposed, the United States "sending some ground troops to Bosnia as part of a peacekeeping force if a peace agreement is reached" (March 1993, NBC/*Wall Street Journal*). Forty-eight percent supported, and 45 percent opposed, sending U.S. troops "if the United Nations sent a peacekeeping force to Bosnia to enforce a cease-fire agreement" (May 1993, CBS). A CNN/*USA Today* poll question stated that a peace agreement might be reached "by all the groups currently fighting in Bosnia. If so, the Clinton administration is considering contributing 20,000 troops to a United Nations peacekeeping force"; 68 percent favored doing this while 30 percent opposed it (May 1993). A PIPA question that briefly described the Vance-Owen plan and explained that the United States would contribute 20,000 of a 60,000-strong NATO peacekeeping force found 77 percent favoring U.S. participation. Factors making for higher levels of support included: the information that the operation would be multilateral; that the U.S. share of forces would be one-third of the total; and that the operation would enforce a peace agreement signed by all parties to the conflict, not just a cease-fire.

The Clinton administration's "lift and strike" proposal would have lifted the embargo on international arms sales to the ex-Yugoslavia for Sarajevo's government only—allowing it to redress its deficiencies in equipment—and launched NATO airstrikes against the Bosnian Serbs' artillery and supply lines (as ultimately would be done in September 1995). Support for lifting the arms embargo seemed to rise over early 1993 with 53 percent in January—and 61 percent in May—supporting "allowing the Bosnians to buy weapons to defend themselves against the Serbs" (Harris). PIPA's May 1993 poll found 58 percent in favor of lifting the embargo, but when respondents heard pro and con arguments about lifting the embargo, no argument on either side was found convincing by more than a bare majority, suggesting uncertainty about this step's potential to improve the situation.

As for using airstrikes, majorities generally opposed the United States conducting airstrikes on its own, but supported the United States participating in multilateral airstrikes. Fifty-six percent opposed the United States conducting airstrikes without allies, even when told in the question that the Bosnian Serbs had rejected the peace plan (CNN/USA Today, May 1993). In April and early May, seven polls asked about unilateral airstrikes; support ranged from 30 percent to 50 percent (average 39 percent; CNN/USA Today, Newsweek, Harris, Time/CNN, U.S. News & World Report). However, 53 percent supported "having U.S. forces participate in UN-approved bombing of Serbian artillery and supply lines" (PIPA, May 1993) and 65 percent supported "the United States, along with its allies in Europe, carrying out air strikes against Bosnian Serb artillery positions and supply lines" (ABC, May 1993).

After the Vance-Owen peace plan collapsed and the Clinton administration dropped the lift-and-strike option in response to opposition from European governments, support for strong measures remained in the public. Sixty percent favored the United States and its allies carrying out air strikes against "Bosnian Serb forces who are attacking the Bosnian capital of Sarajevo" (ABC, August 1993). This is virtually identical to the 59 percent who would support such airstrikes two years later in July 1995—shortly before the actual NATO bombing campaign began (CBS/New York Times)—and the 59 percent who supported the airstrikes while they were proceeding (CBS, September 1995).

Very strong majorities wanted to see UN peacekeeping forces backed up by airstrikes. An overwhelming 85 percent supported "allied air strikes if the Bosnian Serb forces were threatening United Nations peacekeeping troops" (ABC, August 1993); 61 percent even supported the United States acting alone and "using its Air Force to bomb targets" if UN forces were attacked (CBS, August 1993). (A third question asked about the United States and its allies bombing in order "to retaliate" for attacks on UN forces and found a lower 54 percent support—perhaps because the term "retaliate" suggests a proportionate, "tit-for-tat" response that would not preempt future attacks; *Time*/CNN, August 1993.)[9]

However, there were also signs that the public was beginning to lower its expectations about whether decisive action could be taken to resolve the situation. A *Time*/CNN poll question (August 1993) seeking to measure such a decline offered respondents three statements about "military intervention in Bosnia" by the United States and its allies—a phrase that implies the possibility of ground troops. One statement was "I have never supported military intervention": only 35 percent chose it. Another statement was "I support military intervention today": 44 percent subscribed to this. The last statement was "I would have supported military intervention several months ago, but not today": 13 percent subscribed to this statement. Thus, a total of 57 percent said they had supported military intervention, or still did—a number similar to those in the questions about muscular military options reviewed above. This level of 55–60 percent support for muscular options would appear again and again in questions in the years to come, at moments when opportunities for such action did arise. Thus, the 13 percent who said in 1993 they had *previously* supported military intervention were likely expressing disappointment and low expectations, not an actual change of views in principle.

In October 1993, the news of the deaths of eighteen U.S. Army Rangers in Somalia apparently caused a temporary drop in support for contributing to a future peacekeeping force to enforce an eventual agreement in Bosnia. For example, two polls conducted by NBC/*Wall Street Journal* asked whether the U.S. military should take part in "an international effort to enforce a peace agreement in Bosnia." On October 22, 1993, this question received a 48 percent favorable response (with 43 percent unfavorable), while in March the same question had received a 53 percent favorable rating.[10] However, this drop proved temporary, and did not necessarily apply to the issue of taking forceful measures in the existing situation. As events would soon show, when the international community actually seemed to be on the brink of applying decisive force in Bosnia, the support for doing so was very strong.

February 1994: The Sarajevo Market Massacre and the NATO Ultimatum

On February 7, 1994, news reports portrayed in grisly detail the shelling of the marketplace in Sarajevo in which sixty-seven civilians were killed.

Though this event is largely remembered as leading to the NATO ultimatum requiring the Bosnian Serb forces there to move back or hand over their heavy artillery, it did not elicit any surge in support for bombing the Serbs. On February 7, immediately after the reports of the bombing on the evening news, ABC repeated the exact wording of its question of August 1993 calling for bombing to end Serbian attacks on Sarajevo and registered 57 percent support—a drop of 3 points. Also on February 7, a Gallup poll found only 48 percent support for airstrikes "against Serbian military positions."

However, the Gallup poll also had a follow-on question that foreshadowed the surge of support that would come days later. It asked: "Regardless of what your current feelings are, if President Clinton and Congress do order air strikes, would you be inclined to support the air strikes, or not?" This question registered 65 percent support, a 17 percent jump in support.

On February 9, 1994 the United States together with NATO issued an ultimatum to the Bosnian Serbs demanding that they stop shelling the city of Sarajevo and pull back their artillery several miles or face NATO airstrikes. A poll conducted by PIPA over February 9–13 found an overwhelming 76 percent in favor of NATO issuing this ultimatum, and 80 percent in favor of NATO following through on its threat if the Bosnian Serbs failed to pull back.[11]

April–May 1994: The Gorazde Crisis; Bosnian Serbs Take UN Hostages

On April 5–8, 1994—that is, on the eve of the international community's next crisis in Bosnia—PIPA conducted a poll that tried to find the outer limits of public support for stronger action. The questions covered a wide range of options: changing the UN peacekeepers' rules of engagement; using the threat of airstrikes to stop Bosnian Serb attacks on cities, as NATO had done for Sarajevo; massive intervention by a multilateral force, including the United States; carrying out the "lift and strike" option; contributing U.S. troops to UN PROFOR; and contributing troops to a UN peacekeeping operation to police a future peace agreement. An overwhelming 90 percent (70 percent strongly) favored "authorizing UN peacekeepers to use force, if necessary, to protect UN convoys delivering food and aid." Eighty-one percent (54 percent strongly) favored using NATO threats of airstrikes again after the recent success in Sarajevo "to try to stop the Serbs from attacking other cities in Bosnia." Fifty-six percent favored the maximal proposal presented in the poll—"sending a very large force of ground troops from various countries, including the U.S., to occupy contested areas and forcibly stop ethnic cleansing"; 39 percent were opposed. And, "if the parties to the war in Bosnia do come to a peace agreement," 73 percent favored having the United States contribute troops, together with other countries, to a UN peacekeeping operation to enforce the agreement (25 percent opposed).

In April 1994, Bosnian Serb forces began to attack the town of Gorazde, which held large numbers of Muslim refugees and had been declared a UN "safe area." For the first time, NATO conducted limited airstrikes against Serbian positions near Gorazde. In response, the Bosnian Serbs found a tactic that would serve them effectively for the next fifteen months: they took hostage about 200 UN personnel in various parts of Bosnia—thus proving the vulnerability of the UN forces, constituted as they were for a strictly humanitarian mission.[12] This was the end of the "Sarajevo model." The Bosnian Serbs had discovered the perfect riposte for any threat of force from NATO, until such time as the United States, Britain, France, and the UN could agree on a new military policy.

Polling during April 1994 showed robust majorities in favor of the United States participating in multilateral airstrikes to protect the safe areas and the UN's efforts and personnel. This support was strongest when the question made clear that the safe areas were designated by the UN. Sixty-four percent favored airstrikes "to stop Serbian fighters from attacking Bosnian cities that the United Nations has declared to be safe havens" (NBC/*Wall Street Journal*). Sixty-five percent favored "President Clinton's decision to conduct air strikes against Serbian military positions in Bosnia to stop the Serbs from attacking United Nations observers" (CNN/*USA Today*)—a startlingly high level, given that no allied participation was mentioned in the question. However—in a question that did not mention the UN—a lower majority of 54 percent supported bombing Serbian targets around towns "which have been declared safe havens for Bosnia Muslims" and were under attack (CBS/*New York Times*). In a question that mentioned neither the UN nor the bombardments of civilian refugees, 48 percent supported airstrikes to protect Gorazde—described only as "under siege" (*Time*/CNN).

November 1994: The Bihac Crisis

In November 1994 the Bosnian army made significant progress in enlarging the "Bihac pocket," a Muslim enclave in the west. Bosnian Serb forces were reinforced by supplies, and even aerial bombing, from the Krajina—a bordering region of Croatia that was under the control of a Serb para-state, but being monitored by a UN force posted there. In response, NATO made one sortie against an airfield in the Krajina; runways and antiaircraft guns were damaged, but not the planes themselves. The Serbs, for their part, regained the territory around Bihac that they had lost, and went on in December to take hostage hundreds of UN peacekeepers, thus securing the near-cessation of NATO air activity (Brand 1994).

It was in this period that polling evidence began to indicate a drop in support for eventually contributing U.S. troops to a multilateral force that would police a future agreement. This need not be ascribed to a clear awareness in the public of what was transpiring in Bosnia at the time. As Richard Sobel has judged in his review of the polling data, "While the vast majority of Americans have paid attention to the events in Bosnia . . . until the summer of 1995 only about a third to a half have followed the situation closely" (Sobel 1996, 146). Indeed, the intricacies of a war that changed from a three-sided to a two-sided conflict, received covert assistance from other entities in the ex-Yugoslavia, and involved various organizations from the international community often eluded professional observers. Nonetheless, after over two years of the Bosnian war, much of the public had come to a judgment about the direction of events. As a woman in a Los Alamos focus group conducted by PIPA in March 1995 put it:

> Right now the world is thumbing [its] nose at the United Nations . . . UN troops have no clout. There's nothing backing them up, and you don't solve a bully by giving in to him. You have to set your foot down, [which means] you look bigger and stronger, and you act bigger and stronger, and you are bigger and stronger. . . . It's just been very frustrating watching the situation in Bosnia get worse and worse, where UN soldiers are getting shot at, and we can't even get food in to the refugees because the UN doesn't have the military strength to go in and clean out the snipers, make decisions and say, "This is going to stop."

Though poll results are scarce for this period, one question is indicative. In November 1994, only 34 percent favored "the United States sending ground troops as part of the United Nations peacekeeping force" "in order to try and end the fighting in Bosnia" (CBS). (At that time, UN peacekeepers were being taken hostage and being forced to lie on the tarmac of airfields to deter NATO planes from bombing them.)

PIPA conducted an extensive poll on Bosnia and UN peacekeeping in general a few months later, in April 1995. When respondents were asked about contributing U.S. troops to police the peace plan then on the table if it were agreed to by the warring parties, only 52 percent said they would favor doing so, with 44 percent opposed. This was a substantial drop from PIPA's April 1994 poll, when 73 percent said they would favor contributing U.S. troops to police a peace agreement. Apparently, now there was low confidence that a peace agreement would be effective. A majority of 61 percent said they believed the chances were high that there would be violations of such an agreement "if the UN were committed to just monitoring" the agreement—the position being taken by the UN at that time. (However, only 38 percent took this position "if the UN were committed to enforce compliance with the agreement, by military means if necessary.")

As in prior years, majorities supported taking a more assertive approach in Bosnia. Eighty-seven percent (65 percent strongly) said they would like to see "UN peacekeepers use force if UN convoys delivering food and aid to Bosnians are attacked or obstructed." Sixty-five percent said they would like to see the UN "actively defend civilians in the safe havens if they are attacked," while only 30 percent said they were "concerned that this would get the UN peacekeepers too involved in the war." When asked what they would like to see the UN peacekeeping forces in Bosnia do, 50 percent said that they would like to see them "get tougher," while only 29 percent said "withdraw" ("stay the course they are on," 13 percent).

The same poll even found strong support for intervening with a very large military force. Asked whether they would favor or oppose the UN threatening to intervene with a large military force of 150–300,000 troops, one-third of them American, "if the Bosnian Serbs continue to carry out ethnic cleansing," 64 percent favored this course of action, while just 26 percent were opposed. In a follow-up question, respondents were asked: "Regardless of whether you think the threat should be made, if the threat were made and the Serbs did not comply, do you think the UN should or should not follow through with the threat to intervene with a large military force to stop ethnic cleansing?" Sixty-six percent said the UN should then follow through.

This majority support for assertive approaches in Bosnia was sustained even when respondents were told to imagine scenarios in which the United States suffers a substantial number of fatalities, provided that the operation fulfills its objectives. In the poll's most extreme test, part of the sample was asked to imagine that in the course of intervening with a large military force to stop ethnic cleansing, "the Serbs put up strong resistance and in the course of the conflict, 10,000 UN troops were killed, 3,500 of them Americans," but that the effort also succeeded in pacifying the region and stopping ethnic cleansing. Sixty percent said they would feel that the UN had "done the right thing by threatening to intervene" while 29 percent said they would feel it had been a mistake.

May–June 1995: The Decision to Reconfigure UN Forces

In late May 1995, NATO conducted two bombing raids on the Bosnian Serb arms depot outside Pale, the capital of the Republika Srpska. This use of airpower—much more serious than earlier trials—was both an attempt to reverse mounting Bosnian Serb pressure on Sarajevo, and an effort to break out of the tactical hold that the Bosnian Serbs had on the immense military power of NATO. It could have been reasonably assumed that, given a real taste of NATO's capacity to inflict damage, the Bosnian Serbs would reconsider before again taking UN peacekeepers hostage. However, the Bosnian Serbs did use their hostage-taking riposte once more, and with success. Holding over 300 UN personnel, chaining some to potential airstrike targets as human shields, and breaking into UN arms collection depots to recover their equipment, the Bosnian Serbs showed themselves impervious to any "warning shot" approach. NATO did not resume airstrikes, and the Bosnian Serbs then released their hostages piecemeal.

In the aftermath the UN slowly redeployed its forces, clustering them into larger, more defensible groups while awaiting the arrival of a heavily armed force of about 10,000 troops provided by Britain, France, and the Netherlands. It was unclear whether the new force would ultimately be used to augment the UN mission or to protect its withdrawal from Bosnia—though the public preferred the former choice. A *Newsweek* poll of June 1995 asked whether "you think these UN forces should be withdrawn from Bosnia, located to safer positions in Bosnia, or reinforced with more fighting men and weapons?" Given these options, only 23 percent preferred withdrawal. The remainder chose either relocating (32 percent) and reinforcing (31 percent)—options that were probably complementary. Thus, 63 percent still felt that the UN operation should continue, despite the new blows to its credibility that it had just received.

In this setting, extensive polling by media organizations consistently suggested that there was a 60 percent base of support for contributing U.S. troops to several possible responses to the crisis.

The participation of U.S. troops to *assist redeployment* was raised by President Clinton and then dropped after a firestorm of Congressional criticism. Before Clinton spoke on the issue, several polls asked the public whether they would support such participation. While one poll found a divided response (NBC/*Wall Street Journal*), four polls taken in the first week of June that used near-identical wording found support in the 65–70 percent range for using U.S. ground troops to aid redeployment (*Newsweek, USA Today*/CNN, *Time*/CNN, and *Times Mirror*). The average of all five poll questions on aiding a UN redeployment was 62 percent in support.

At this same time, policymakers were also debating the use of American forces to *rescue UN peacekeepers who were being held hostage* and, in some cases, used as human shields by the Bosnian Serbs against airstrikes. Three polls in June 1995 asked respondents whether they would support U.S. troops being used in such rescues, and responses ranged from 57 percent (CBS) to 78 percent (*Newsweek*) in favor (*Time*/CNN: 62 percent).

Americans remained reluctant to have the United States act alone. When asked by CBS (June 4–6) whether "In order to protect the United Nations peacekeeping forces currently in Bosnia" they would "favor or oppose the United States sending in ground troops," only 43 percent were in favor with 52 percent opposed (asked again in July, 31 percent in favor with 61 percent opposed).[13]

The option of withdrawal became more vivid as the June 1995 crisis unfolded. Three polls asked respondents whether they would support the involvement of U.S. troops in *assisting a safe withdrawal of UN forces* from Bosnia. *Time*/CNN found 59 percent and 64 percent support, respectively, for sending U.S. troops to help withdraw UN peacekeeping troops.

CBS/*New York Times* asked about the *use of air power* by the United States and NATO "to bomb Serbian targets" if the Serbs "continue attacking other 'safe areas.'" In July 1995, 59 percent supported such bombing—up from April 1994, when the identically worded question found 54 percent support.

Finally, a poll question by NBC/*Wall Street Journal* posed the objectives of protecting both UN peacekeepers and Bosnian cities, asking about airstrikes by the United States with its allies "if the Serbian forces continue to attack Bosnian cities or the United Nations peacekeeping troops." Fifty-six percent supported such airstrikes (June 1995). However, when airstrikes were presented to the public with no reference to the safety of either civilians or UN peacekeeping forces—but were presented instead as military actions that could strengthen the fortunes of one side—support was much lower. A low of 35 percent was registered by a *Time*/CNN question (June 1995), which simply proposed "using U.S. planes and pilots—along with those of other countries—in an all-out bombing of Serbian positions."

August–December 1995: From NATO Bombing to NATO Peacekeeping

When the Bosnian Serbs again shelled the Sarajevo marketplace in late August 1995, killing thirty-eight civilians, NATO both needed and was able to make a full military response. UN peacekeepers had been consolidated into fewer locations, greatly reducing their exposure to hostage-taking tactics. But while redeployment had proceeded, Bosnian Serbs had flouted the West by taking two of the UN "safe areas"—Zepa and Srebenica—and in Srebenica they had conducted what was probably the largest single massacre of the war.

NATO's sixteen-day bombing campaign was undertaken to achieve the same objectives set out in February 1994: the withdrawal of the Bosnian Serbs' heavy guns from the hills around Sarajevo and an easing of the siege there. But in practice, the campaign was directed at the Bosnian Serbs' capacity to make war. On the first day, over sixty aircraft struck at radar installations, surface-to-air missile sites, communications facilities, and artillery and heavy mortar batteries (Atkinson and Pomfret 1995). For the first time, airstrikes were sustained and—as long the Bosnian Serbs chose to resist— open-ended. By September 17, the weakened Bosnian Serbs were complying with NATO's requirements. At the same time, they were losing territory rapidly to the forces of Croatia, the Bosnian government, and Bosnian Croats.

While the bombing was in progress, a CBS poll showed that 59 percent approved and 25 percent disapproved (CBS, September 5–6, 1995). This 59 percent was unchanged from the 59 percent majority that, in July 1995, had supported action by the United States and NATO "to bomb Serbian targets" if the Serbs "continue attacking other 'safe areas'" (CBS/*New York Times*).

This 59 percent support for NATO's airstrikes did not derive from any majority optimism that the Bosnian war could be settled. In a poll concluded

September 19—when NATO had paused its bombing raids against the Bosnian Serbs, who were actively withdrawing artillery from Sarajevo and losing territory elsewhere—the public remained pessimistic. Fifty-two percent thought that "current military and diplomatic efforts by the U.S. and its allies" would *not* be "successful in producing a peace settlement" (would succeed: 37 percent; NBC/*Wall Street Journal*). This pessimism—apparently the fruit of the preceding three years of war—would color public attitudes toward contributing troops to enforce the Dayton accords. As mentioned earlier, in April 1995, support for participation in a hypothetical UN force to police an agreement had fallen to 52 percent (PIPA). This was the level from which support and opposition would evolve once the Dayton peace process was under way.

The public's expectations of successful enforcement were quite low. Only 20 percent thought "the NATO peacekeepers will be able to enforce the peace agreement among the Bosnian Serbs, Muslims and Croatians," while 69 percent thought that "there will be serious fighting among these groups" (CBS, November 1995). In early December only 27 percent thought the NATO force would "be successful in establishing a long-term lasting peace in Bosnia," while 60 percent did not (*Time*/CNN); later in December 44 percent expressed confidence the effort would succeed, while 51 percent said they had little or no confidence (CNN/*USA Today*).

The majority also expected significant casualties: 53 percent thought that "If the United States sends troops as part of a peacekeeping mission . . . that is likely to lead to a long-term commitment in Bosnia involving many casualties," while 35 percent disagreed (CNN/*USA Today*, November 1995). In December, 57 percent said they were "not too" or "not at all confident" that "the U.S. will be able to accomplish its goals with very few or no American casualties" (CNN/*USA Today*).[14]

Yet the expectation of casualties did not, by itself, foreordain public opposition; more important was the question of whether success was possible. When asked in PIPA's November poll to consider a scenario in which the United States contributes troops and the operation succeeds, a fairly strong majority expressed support even when they were asked to assume that the operation would cost American lives. They were told:

> Imagine that in the course of carrying out this operation over the next year, there is an incident in which 50 American soldiers die fighting in a confrontation with a rogue band that resists the peace agreement. But overall, the operation succeeds in maintaining the peace and stopping ethnic cleansing.

In this case, 60 percent said they would feel that "in contributing U.S. troops to the operation" the United States "had done the right thing," while 32 percent said they would feel that the United States "had made a mistake." Thus, when asked to assume success—even in the context of American deaths—respondents showed underlying support in principle.

Fighting continued until the parties signed a cease-fire on October 12. By that time the territory held by the Bosnian Serbs had been reduced from three-quarters to about half of Bosnia. The presidents of Serbia, Croatia, and Bosnia were brought to Wright-Patterson Air Force Base outside Dayton, Ohio at the start of November, where they remained in negotiations for three weeks, initialing the peace agreement on November 21.

In the first phase of the Dayton process—when it was still unknown whether a peace agreement would actually be reached—two main types of poll questions about a peacekeeping force were put to the U.S. public. The first type of question stated that there was a *possibility of success in reaching an agreement:* "There is a chance a peace agreement could be reached by all the groups currently fighting in Bosnia. If so, the Clinton Administration is considering contributing U.S. troops to an international peacekeeping force." Fifty percent supported contributing troops, with 44 percent opposed (Gallup, September 1995). When this question was re-asked in October and November, it showed slight erosion in support, but only within the poll's margin of error (October: 49 percent favor, 44 percent oppose; November: 47 percent favor, 49 percent oppose). This question was also asked by Gallup in September for CNN/*USA Today*, with one difference: the force was described as "UN" instead of as "international" and garnered 52 percent support (thus matching the level of support that PIPA found for a UN force in April 1995).

The second type of question on contributing to peacekeeping did not make explicit—as the first type of question did—that a process to reach a peace agreement was under way. One such question read, "Do you approve or disapprove of President Clinton's proposal to send U.S. troops to Bosnia as part of an international peacekeeping force if the groups who are currently fighting in Bosnia can agree to a settlement that would end the conflict there?" When asked in October by *Time*/CNN, 42 percent said they approved the proposal while 50 percent disapproved. In a comparable question in November, 38 percent supported "sending 20,000 U.S. troops to Bosnia as part of an international peacekeeping force after the opposing sides there sign a peace agreement and stop fighting"—something that, as we have just seen, a majority thought unlikely.[15]

Finally, a question that described a Bosnia peacekeeping force as American, without mentioning the participation of other countries, found only 27 percent support (*Newsweek*, October 1995). From September 1995 through January 1996, there were thirteen cases in which respondents were simply asked whether respondents favored or opposed sending U.S. troops to Bosnia, with no troops from other countries mentioned; these poll questions elicited, on average, 36 percent support.

On November 21, the Dayton parties initialed a peace agreement, and the public was now asked questions about a peacekeeping force in the context of the agreement. Support varied from 30 percent to 50 percent, with much of this variation depending on whether or not it was clarified that: the fighting on the ground had stopped; an agreement had been signed; the peacekeeping force would be multilateral; and the United States would be contributing a minority of the troops.

PIPA's poll (conducted November 22–25) spelled out these conditions in the following way:

> As you may know, in Dayton, Ohio, the leaders of the conflict in Bosnia have come to a peace agreement. In addition to ending the fighting, the peace agreement includes provisions for redistributing land, stopping ethnic cleansing and holding elections. The agreement is to be enforced by 60,000 well-armed troops under an American commander and with UN approval. The U.S. has committed to contribute one-third of these troops, with the other two-thirds to come from other countries, mostly European. Some members of Congress, though, are against contributing U.S. troops. Do you favor or oppose contributing U.S. troops to this operation?

Respondents were divided, with 50 percent favored contributing troops and 47 percent opposed even though it was also specified that there was Congressional opposition.

The public also gave a divided response to other poll questions that provided information. For example, A CNN/*USA Today* question told respondents, "Now that a peace agreement has been reached by all the groups currently fighting in Bosnia, the Clinton Administration plans to contribute U.S. troops to an international peacekeeping force." Forty-six percent favored contributing troops, with 40 percent opposed and 14 percent "don't know" (November 1995).

When other questions implied a dominant U.S. share in the peacekeeping force, support was lower. A late November ABC question—"President Clinton said now that a Bosnian peace treaty has been signed, he's sending 20,000 U.S. troops there as part of an international peacekeeping force"— found 39 percent in favor and 57 percent opposed. Since 20,000 troops sounds large enough to be most of the force, this factor tended to lower support. Other questions that also implied that the force's mandate might be wider than Bosnia alone, that left unclear that the fighting had stopped, or did not state that a peace agreement had been reached, found support ranging from 30 to 40 percent.[16]

Overall, it seems clear that the public was divided over contributing U.S. troops to a multilateral force for policing the Bosnia agreement, though support could appear lower when the actual conditions were not specified. As we shall see below, it also appears that in this period, support was being dampened by the low expectations of success derived from the preceding years of disappointing results from the UN peacekeeping operation. However, a majority never settled on a rejection of U.S. participation. As Richard Sobel put it in the *New York Times* on November 22, 1995, "Though surveys have consistently shown that the public opposes the idea of the United States going it alone, nearly a majority of Americans polled over the last year have said they could back a multilateral military effort. Different survey groups, questions and timing produce varying results, but there is a distinct pattern: the American public has an open mind."

1996-1998: An Ongoing NATO Presence

In December 1995 and January 1996, NATO-led forces entered Bosnia and established their control. Americans seemed to move out of the "cold feet" immediately leading up to the decision and for the first time, there was a trace of public optimism about the potential for success of the operation: 52 percent thought that "the peace will hold in Bosnia," while 38 percent thought that "U.S. forces will become involved in a major shooting war in Bosnia" (Pew, January 1996). Approval for Clinton's handling of Bosnia showed improvement in the same month moving from an average in the low 40s before the accords to 51 percent and 55 percent in respective polls by the ABC/*Washington Post* and CBS/*New York Times*. Questions about contributing troops showed a slight upward movement —41 percent approved "of the presence of U.S. troops" (*Time*/CNN); 48 percent approved of "sending 20,000 U.S. troops . . . as part of an international peacekeeping force" (Pew).

Support was dampened by a widespread belief that the United States was providing a disproportionately large share of the forces. Pew found that only 21 percent knew that Americans made up less than half of the force, while 29 percent thought Americans were "about half," and 31 percent thought they were "most" of the operation (January 1996). In Pew's poll, among those who thought correctly that the U.S. contribution was less than half of the force, 54 percent approved the decision to send troops; but among those who thought that U.S. troops made up "most" of the peacekeeping force, only 45 percent approved.

As the peacekeeping operation consolidated its presence in Bosnia, and opposition to contributing troops lessened in the U.S. Congress, the frequency of polling on the subject dropped. The available evidence suggests that the public remained divided, and more pessimistic than optimistic, about Bosnia through 1996 and most of 1997. Questions asking about approval "of the presence of U.S. troops in Bosnia" (with no indication that the operation is multilateral) continued to show slight majority disapproval.[17] As for the public's perception of success, in October 1996 44 percent thought the Clinton administration's policies in Bosnia had been generally unsuccessful, 38 percent thought they had been generally successful, and 18 per-

cent were not sure (NBC/*Wall Street Journal*). This low perception of success persisted into the fall of 1997: in September, 61 percent felt that the
Bosnia operation had not "improved the chances of finding a way to permanently end the fighting there," while only 27 percent felt that it had (Pew).

Over the winter of 1997–1998, the public shifted toward a more positive
evaluation of the Bosnia operation. In February-March, PIPA re-asked the
Pew question just cited about whether the operation had improved the
chances of "permanently end[ing] the fighting." The number feeling the operation had not improved the chances for peace dropped 18 points to 43 percent, while the number feeling the operation had improved the chances
jumped 22 points to a 49 percent plurality.

Not surprisingly, support for the operation moved up dramatically. Even
in response to a question about "the presence of U.S. troops" which had usually received low levels of support because it did not spell out the multilateralism of the missions, in a January 1998, CNN/*USA Today* poll 53 percent
approved—the first time this question wording had ever gotten majority approval. In the February-March PIPA poll asked whether the respondents favored or opposed U.S. troops "participating in the peacekeeping operation
in Bosnia," 65 percent said they favored it while 33 percent were opposed.[18]

Particularly striking, the PIPA poll found that the perception of success was
up even though many Americans underestimated how well the operation is going. Forty-one percent said that they believed the war is still going on and an
extraordinary 63 percent mistakenly believed that American troops had been
killed in the previous year (median estimate twenty-five dead).

In 1999 support for the operation continued to hold. The question on "the
presence of U.S. troops" went up to 57 percent support in a March 1999 Pew
poll. A May 1999 PIPA poll found support for U.S. troops "participating the
peacekeeping operation" holding at 63 percent, even though 56 percent still
believed that Americans had been killed in the previous year (median estimate twenty dead). Belief in the success of the operation was also steady
with 49 percent saying that it had improved the chances for peace and 47
percent saying that it had not.

Public Opinion and U.S. Policy on Bosnia

The foregoing review of U.S. public attitudes does, of course, leave a difficult
question unresolved. What was the relationship between public opinion and
the formation of policy? This relationship—rarely easy to determine—is, in a
sense, clearer than usual in the case of Bosnia, because there was so much public discussion of public opinion in the policy discourse.

Our past research has put an emphasis on policymakers' *perceptions* of
the public as a factor in policy—a different thing from public attitudes
themselves. In the case of Bosnia, the policy community arrived at, and

largely kept to, a commonly held picture of the nature and limits of public support that was long impervious to contradictory evidence. This picture of the public was a potent factor in policy formation—much more potent than the public itself. Richard Sobel has argued similarly that relatively strong public support for multilateral intervention in Bosnia contrasted with weak government actions during most of the war. The comparatively strong approval of humanitarian aid and multilateral involvement went largely unreported in the media and political debates. Neither the press nor politicians presented much evidence for Americans who supported intervention that anyone else agreed with them, or for opponents that anyone disagreed. Reporters, citizens, and policymakers did not perceive public opinion accurately. As policymakers reflect their perceptions of public opinion, these misperceptions may have affected Bosnia policy (Sobel 1998).

The interaction between the foreign policy community's *perception* of public opinion and the formation of policy on Bosnia can be roughly divided into three phases. In the first phase, the policy community perceived opposition in the public to a more interventionist policy, and the administration largely strove to limit its involvement in Bosnia: thus the perception of the public and the direction of policy were in accord. In the second phase, the policy community still perceived few sources of support in the public for a more interventionist policy, but the administration had chosen to expand its involvement: thus, the perception of the public and the direction of policy were at odds. In the third phase, the policy community perceived a slight and fragile increase in public support, while the administration was now committed to deep and ongoing involvement: thus the perceived tension between public opinion and policy moderated.

Phase One: Summer 1992–Spring 1995

When war broke out in Bosnia in the summer of 1992, the foreign policy community was still struggling to understand the American public's reaction to the end of the Cold War. The uppermost question was whether the American public would retreat into isolationism, now that the Soviet threat no longer loomed. Thus, policymakers were unsure how the American public would react as reports of the situation in the former Yugoslavia began to surface in the press and as debate began over the appropriate American reaction.

Media coverage in the summer and fall of 1992 described public opinion as either a catalyst or a hindrance to action in the Balkans. A *New York Times* editorial saw it as a catalyst, claiming that U.S. participation in the international airlift in Bosnia was a reaction to public outcry: "President Bush, under pressure from Bill Clinton and public opinion, has quickened his response to the carnage in the Balkans" (August 7, 1992, A14). In November, an opinion piece in the *Washington Post* saw it as a hindrance, asserting that "Although the American people have expressed a desire for their national leaders to concentrate primarily on domestic affairs, President Bush will not likely be granted this luxury—not even during his last two months in office" (Weymouth 1992, 21).

Over 1992, the public was frequently characterized as needing to be restrained by policymakers. The public was supposedly eager to intervene, but with no stamina for military difficulties or casualties. An opinion piece in the *New York Times* entitled "False Humanitarianism" declared that "Mr. Bush and Mr. Major know well how atrocity stories stimulate their publics to throw caution to the wind. They also know that these enthusiasms quickly wane once troops sink into inconclusive battle" (Gelb 1992, 15). As President Bush prepared to send some air and naval support forces to the region, the *New York Times* reported (July 19, 1992):

> Military officials say that the tragic images emerging from the war-weary Sarajevo coupled with the United States' success in the Persian Gulf war have raised unrealistic public expectations that the American military should be capable of quickly ending the fighting in Bosnia.
>
> "People have been mesmerized by Desert Storm," a senior Army official said. "But the Yugoslav military and terrain is totally different. It's far more akin to the kind of fighting that's gone on in Northern Ireland, Lebanon and Vietnam."

In October 1993, the expectation that the public would not tolerate American casualties in peacekeeping missions overseas was tested when eighteen U.S. Army Rangers were killed in Somalia. Congress and the media claimed that most Americans wanted an immediate withdrawal of troops. However, public opinion polling at the time contradicted this belief. The polls showed that only a minority wanted to withdraw immediately; that a majority would support increased involvement for the short run; and that a majority did want an eventual withdrawal, whether or not Somalia was fully stabilized (Kull and Destler 1999). Nonetheless, the erroneous belief that the majority of Americans reacted to the loss of life by wanting to immediately withdraw colored the policy community's perception of public attitudes thenceforward.

The incident in Somalia clearly impacted the elite's perceptions of whether the public would support sending ground troops to Bosnia. In a *New York Times* opinion piece, Arthur Schlesinger Jr. wrote: "We have a professional army made up of men and women who volunteered for the job—and the job, alas, may include fighting, killing, and dying. But let a few soldiers get killed, and the Congressional and popular demand for withdrawal becomes almost irresistible" (Schlesinger 1995, 15).

Phase Two: July 1995–January 1996

In July and August 1995, the administration determined that a deeper level of U.S. involvement in Bosnia would be necessary—a choice that led to the bombing campaign against the Bosnian Serbs in September.

The perception of the public as unsupportive remained front and center in the fall 1995 debate over beginning the NATO-led peacekeeping operation. Speaking on "The McLaughlin Group" on December 1, 1995, Eleanor Clift said, "I think there is a strain in the American people right now that says we have problems at home, why do we want to get involved overseas?—especially now that the images of all the women and the children and the streaming refugees are off the screen." On CNN's "Late Edition" in December 1995, its anchor, Jamie McIntyre, stated regarding Bosnia, "We've seen from Somalia that the American public and American Congress have a very low tolerance for American casualties in a mission that they don't see as directly affecting U.S. vital interests." And in a hearing of the Senate Armed Services Committee, then-Senator Cohen said, "And when body bags come home, as they're likely to do, hopefully in very limited numbers, you can expect that opinion is going to solidify and put tremendous pressure upon a reluctant Congress and an administration to bring the troops home well before the nine months that they're currently planning on."[19]

Nonetheless, the tenor of the *open* debate is not sure evidence of how the inner circle of decision makers responsible for Bosnia policy viewed public opinion at the moment they were changing course. As of this writing, little evidence about the debate at the highest levels of the executive branch is yet available. However, it is possible to consult one major memoir: Richard Holbrooke's *To End A War* (1998). Holbrooke makes the following characterizations of public opinion in the fall of 1995:

> With only a year to go until the presidential election, public opinion was heavily opposed to deployments—at that time some 70 percent of the American public did not want troops in Bosnia under any circumstances. (219)
>
> While the public applauded our diplomatic efforts, opinion polls put public opposition to the deployment of American forces to Bosnia at around 70 percent. This was understandable. For almost four years, Americans had watched television pictures of United Nations troops being killed and wounded while unable to defend themselves adequately. Most Americans assumed we were sending our own troops into a similar situation, where they would suffer heavy casualties.
>
> Sending American troops to Bosnia would be the single most unpopular action of President Clinton's entire first term. Although the public was proud of the American diplomatic role in ending the war, we had to convince them that the American deployments would be different from those of the UN, that NATO would shoot first and ask questions later—and that the deployment was in our national interest. (317)[20]

Holbrooke's belief—that 70 percent of the public was opposed in fall 1995 to any deployment—does have a little evidence to support it. (Of course, it has been one of this chapter's purposes to demonstrate that only a comprehensive analysis of all the data can be a trustworthy guide to public opinion for policymakers.) Two poll questions frequently asked in fall 1995 were "Do you think that the United States should send 20,000 troops to Bosnia, or not?" (should not: 67 percent; Harris, December), and "It will be worth the loss of some American lives if sending U.S. troops brings peace to Bosnia" (disagree: 66 percent; ABC, November). But these two questions exclude most of the values that were at issue for the American public when it considered Bosnia. Most important, these questions clearly suggest a unilateral effort, which, as this article has shown, was indeed rejected by a majority from first to last.

Holbrooke is entirely right in saying it was important to the public that "American deployments would be different from those of the UN" (i.e., more assertive). It is unlikely, however, that arguing that "the deployment was in our national interest" would carry weight with more than a minority in the administration's effort to gain public support.

For both phase one and phase two, the available evidence (both the public record and Holbrooke's memoirs) suggests that the policy community's perception of public opinion bore—at most—a very weak relationship to public attitudes as shown in polling data. For phase one—the period of October 1993 through summer 1995—it might be argued that this perception of the public as refusing involvement was convenient for policymakers who were themselves seeking to limit U.S. involvement. However, in phase two— the second half of 1995—this perception was not at all convenient. For then the United States was actively planning much deeper involvement, and its policy planners—Holbrooke among them—took new and serious risks, while apparently believing that sources of public support were far shallower than in fact they were.

Phase Three: February 1996 and After

The third phase of the relation between the foreign policy community's perception of public opinion and the formation of policy on Bosnia is the hardest to substantiate. NATO entered Bosnia and consolidated its presence there; policymakers were now committed to a standing policy that had shown some success. From 1996 onward, the salience of Bosnia diminished gradually as it became clear that the war was over and would not resume. Media and congressional comments on the public's view diminished accordingly.

However, one worthwhile source on policymakers' perceptions of the public is available: comments by members of the executive branch in the interviews conducted by the Project on Foreign Policy and the Public in mid-1996. From these interviews, a coherent picture of beliefs within the executive branch about the public and Bosnia does emerge.

While members of the executive branch perceived a mild increase in public support for the Bosnia operation, they assumed that this increase was very fragile, and believed that the administration's own commitment and its efforts to persuade the public were the primary causes of increased support. Many interviewees supposed that support for the mission might collapse at once if American fatalities occurred. Executive branch members often stated that they were not familiar with actual poll findings. Instead, they were mostly aware of claims about public opinion made in Congress and the media.

The perceived tentativeness of new support came through clearly in the language of one official: "The public, certainly, initially was against Bosnia—I think that's turned around slightly now." "I'm not certain . . . they may be more confident. There is, I guess the polls reflect that, more confidence in Clinton on foreign policy, but I think that could change in a minute," said another member of the executive branch. Another official was more confident that support had risen, but assumed that support would not survive an extension of the mission: "I think their satisfaction [in] the policy as it now stands . . . wouldn't be [there] if that were somehow changed to suggest long-term occupation and that sort of thing."

Some interviewees stated very firmly that there was no prior source of support for intervening, but that government had to lead the way. As one put it: "[The administration] had to follow the Schultz line, which is to lead public opinion on the assumption that public opinion would in fact follow . . . [on] sending troops to Bosnia. . . . And I think the polling data shows this." Another commented, "I don't know what the figures are on Bosnia, but again, if leaders are willing to go out there and spend time on it, I think that's important for shaping public support."

The extent of public support was seen as resting on the absence of troop fatalities. A Defense Department official flatly declared, "By and large Americans have not been convinced with the arguments on Haiti and are very unsure whether they should buy it on Bosnia. . . . My sense is that most Americans have a real 'prove it to me' attitude . . . that . . . is never fully answered unless you complete the operation virtually casualty-free." A State Department official seemed to bank on continued absence of casualties, saying, "When the prospect of possibly going into combat is before the American people, they become extraordinarily nervous. . . . If they had known that we could simply walk in[to Haiti] and take over and put the peacekeeping force in place, I think all of a sudden, you erase a lot of those anxieties. The same thing is true in Bosnia."

In phase three, as in phases one and two, the policy community's perception of public opinion bore—at most—a very weak relationship to public attitudes as shown in polling data. Policymakers largely believed they had *raised* support through the government's own efforts; they seemed unaware that there were preexisting sources of support in the public.

In summary, the policy community had an image of the public's attitudes that was influential but was not very accurate. Initially policymakers perceived themselves as partly constrained by the public's supposed reluctance to intervene. Later, once intervention occurred, when they did not detect a strong opposition, they assumed that it was due to their efforts in communicating the policy and to the fact that there had been no fatalities. In fact it appears that there had been a base of support throughout. Support consolidated, not because there had not been fatalities (most Americans thought there had been) but because there was an increase in the perception that the operation was succeeding.

CONCLUSION

One of the challenges in interpreting polling data is differentiating between fundamental values and the effects of relatively superficial factors. In the effort to interpret public support for the operation in Bosnia, commentators have too often only focused on questions of whether the respondent approves or disapproves of the presence of U.S. troops in Bosnia. The fact that during much of the last few years a majority has not expressed approval has been interpreted as reflecting an underlying value system that is isolationist. But examining a much wider array of questions has revealed quite a different picture. Questions that ask respondents about their more fundamental values reveal that since the beginnings of the war in Bosnia in 1992 through to the present, the American public has had a strong inclination in favor of the United States being involved in trying to deal with the problem in Bosnia. Arguments against such involvement on the basis of isolationist principles have been roundly rejected. Arguments in favor of involvement on the basis of both humanitarian concern and national interest broadly interpreted have received strong support.

At the same time Americans have not felt compelled to be involved in Bosnia. Unlike during the Cold War when it was seen as imperative to address regional problems because of their implications for the struggle against communism, intervention in Bosnia is seen as optional. Thus Americans feel they have the latitude to impose conditions on their support.

As we have seen, Americans have expressed these conditions by their differential response to variations in poll questions on intervention. From these responses it becomes clear that the majority of Americans have only been supportive of U.S. participation in Bosnia if the operation is clearly multilateral, the United States is contributing no more than its fair share and the operation is likely to succeed. Support has also been complicated by overestimations of how much the United States is contributing relative to other countries and by underestimations of the success of the operation.

The conditional nature of majority support and the impact of misperceptions have thus obscured the strength of the underlying value orientation in favor of U.S. involvement in Bosnia, particularly when viewed through the lens of the assumption that the American public is going through a phase of isolationism. To the extent that Americans respond to correct information about the nature of the Bosnia operation a substantial majority does show support for U.S. involvement.

Perhaps the most salient point to be grasped—and the one most likely to be of value in other contexts that may differ widely from Bosnia—is that, once the public has been exposed to news and information for an initial period, the values and concerns that are engaged remain indefinitely as elements of the public's judgment.

NOTES

1. The research assistance of Elizabeth Detter and Timothy McDonald is gratefully acknowledged. Elizabeth Detter also contributed to the writing of the section on policy.

2. For the first argument, 74 percent agreed (23 percent disagreed); for the counter argument, 41 percent agreed (56 percent disagreed).

3. This 57 percent agreement is all the more striking since respondents were offered two other options. Twenty-two percent preferred to say that "the fighting in Bosnia is a local dispute that should be left to the countries involved," while only 16 percent chose the statement "As the world's strongest and richest country, the United States has the responsibility to take the leading role in ending the fighting in Bosnia."

4. The U.S. Defense Department stated in October 1998 that the total number of American troops in Bosnia had been reduced to below 6,800. The total of all SFOR forces then was approximately 32,000.

5. According to polls conducted by the United States Information Agency, the majority of Bosnians were supportive of the NATO operation. In USIA's poll in February 1998—the same month as PIPA began its poll of Americans—the majority of Bosnians overall (75 percent), as well as all ethnic groups (67 percent of Serbs, 73 percent of Croats, and 94 percent Muslims), said they support the Dayton peace accords—the basis of the NATO operation. When asked about the presence of the NATO-led peacekeeping force, 68 percent said they were supportive (50 percent of Serbs, 59 percent of Croats, and 96 percent of Muslims).

6. In fact, in two polls immediately following the reports of the fatalities, one poll found 37 percent support for immediate withdrawal (ABC) and another found 43 percent support (CNN/*USA Today*). Other polls taken over the next few days found similar results. See *The Foreign Policy Gap,* 91 or *Misreading the Public,* 106–8.

7. This result is similar both to earlier PIPA questions that posed hypothetical scenarios for operations in Rwanda and Haiti and to questions asked immediately after American deaths in Somalia, when (for instance) 75 percent favored retaliating against Somali warlord Mohammed Farad Aideed with a "major military attack" if

American prisoners could not be released in a timely manner through negotiations (ABC, October 1993). In July 1994 and April 1995, PIPA asked respondents to consider a variety of possible scenarios involving American deaths during UN peacekeeping missions in Rwanda and Haiti. In every case, less than 25 percent said they would want to withdraw U.S. troops, while a majority favored a vigorous response—either that of bringing in reinforcements or striking back at the attackers. For details see Kull, Destler, and Ramsay, 92–93.

8. When this question was repeated in May 1993, majority support for this forceful approach remained, but had dropped to 52 percent.

9. Richard Sobel has argued that in summer 1993 "Americans were more willing to use air power to protect UN soldiers providing aid than to save Bosnian civilians or punish the Serbian military" (Ullman, ed., 147–48). It is true that questions about using air power to bolster UN efforts often garnered the most support of all, because the legitimacy provided by the UN imprimatur, plus the public's assumption that UN action meant multilateral forces, strongly supplemented the base of support for intervening.

10. Similarly, a CNN/*USA Today* poll conducted on October 8—only three days after the Mogadishu firefight—received only 40 percent support for U.S. participation in enforcing a hypothetical peace agreement.

11. PIPA's question began by indicating that "Serbs positioned in the hills around Sarajevo have been attacking civilians." Another question, asked February 10 by *Time*/CNN, made no mention of this, described NATO's threat as being "against the Serbian military forces that surround Sarajevo if the Serbs do not withdraw their forces from around that city," and added, "the Serbs say they will do this." Given this inaccurate picture—in fact, the Bosnian Serbs were being told to withdraw the heavy artillery that targeted the civilian population, not their surrounding forces—50 percent of respondents favored NATO airstrikes if the Bosnian Serbs did not cooperate.

12. See Thomas G. Weiss, "Collective Spinelessness: UN Actions in the Former Yugoslavia," 64; Stanley Hoffman, "Yugoslavia: Implications for Europe and for European Institutions," 109; and David C. Gompert, "The United States and Yugoslavia's Wars," 138–39; all in Richard H. Ullman, ed., *The World and Yugoslavia's Wars* (New York: Council on Foreign Relations Press, 1996). Also Jonathan C. Randal, "Bosnian Serbs Seize, Harass UN Troops," *Washington Post*, April 15, 1994, A1.

13. In some questions other concerns apparently overcame this reluctance. A *Times Mirror* poll (June 1995) found 71 percent in favor of "the use of U.S. military force if United Nations peacekeepers come under attack there." Since "military force" could mean airstrikes (rather than ground troops), and the phrase "under attack" implies an urgency that is not present in the CBS question, this question found very strong majority support, even though it asked about unilateral U.S. action.

14. While the public's expectations of success were low, they did not fit the familiar image of fears that the United States would be bogged down in "another Vietnam." ABC asked about this in November and found only 33 percent who thought "the United States is heading for the same kind of involvement in Bosnia as it had in the Vietnam war," while a majority of 61 percent thought "the U.S. will avoid that kind of involvement this time." A similarly worded AP question in December found 35 percent who thought Bosnia would be like Vietnam and 55 percent who thought it would not.

15. Even less support was registered by an NBC/*Wall Street Journal* question that told respondents, "President Clinton has said the United States would be willing to send some ground troops to Bosnia as part of a peacekeeping force if a peace agreement is reached between warring factions. Do you favor or oppose using American ground troops in such an operation?" In this wording, the negotiating groups are called "warring factions," implying that the combat was ongoing. Thirty percent were in favor, with 65 percent opposed.

16. A question that implied that the United States might be sending most of the troops and that the forces mandate might be wider than Bosnia—"Do you favor or oppose sending up to 20,000 U.S. troops to Bosnia, as part of a NATO peacekeeping force, to enforce this peace agreement between Bosnia, Serbia and Croatia?"—elicited 33 percent in favor, with 58 percent opposed in November 1995 (CBS) but went up to 40 percent in favor in mid-December with 55 percent opposed. A *Time*/CNN question in early December was explicit about the proportion of the U.S. share of troops, but did not clarify whether fighting on the ground had stopped: "Do you approve or disapprove of President Clinton's decision to send 20,000 U.S. troops to Bosnia as part of a NATO peacekeeping force of 60,000 troops to enforce the peace agreement reached by the groups who have been fighting there?" Thirty-eight percent approved and 55 percent disapproved—lower than might be expected, given that both the "fair share" issue and the fact of a peace agreement were addressed—but the question left unclear whether the "groups who have been fighting" were still doing so. An early December AP question found only 30 percent support with a wording that did not mention any peace agreement or cease-fire, but spoke only of "sending 20,000 U.S. ground troops to Bosnia as part of a NATO peacekeeping force" (oppose: 58 percent).

17. Thus in May 1996 CNN/*USA Today* found 51 percent disapprove, 42 percent approve; in June 1996 *Time*/CNN found 45 percent disapprove, 44 percent approve; in February 1997 *Time*/CNN found 54 percent disapprove, 40 percent approve; and in June 1997 CNN/*USA Today* found 53 percent disapprove, 39 percent approve.

18. Why this shift in public opinion took place when it did is difficult to determine. President Clinton visited Bosnia at Christmas 1997—an event that portrayed the operation in a new and more positive light. Also, the news from Bosnia had improved: since October 1997, a number of indictees had been delivered to the war crimes tribunal at the Hague, and the Bosnian Serbs had elected a leadership more supportive of the Dayton accords.

19. These comments were collected from Federal News Service transcripts.

20. Holbrooke then proceeds to quote a *Newsweek* article, saying "*Newsweek* wryly captured the paradoxical situation." The quote characterizes the public as follows: "The foreign-policy establishment may cheer, and Balkan brigands may head for the hills, but ordinary Americans are decidedly wary of sacrifices ahead. . . . Most voters regard Bosnia as someone else's civil war. It will be up to President Clinton to convince them otherwise. . . . Baffled by Bosnia or distracted by domestic concerns, most Americans have not begun to realize the reach and depth of the U.S. commitment made last week in Dayton."

4

Raison d'état or Raison populaire? The Influence of Public Opinion on France's Bosnia Policy

Marc Morjé Howard and Lise Morjé Howard

In its long history as a unified state, France has always maintained a strict separation between the state and the people. This traditional "raison d'état" allowed the state to develop and pursue foreign policies outside and independent of public opinion. Even today, compared to other countries considered to be advanced democracies, France has a reputation of having a political elite—especially in the realm of foreign policymaking—that is largely insulated from public pressures. Elections are held regularly, and government-commissioned public opinion polls taken frequently, but it is a common assumption that French public opinion has little effect on French foreign policy.

The issue of intervention in Bosnia poses a challenge to this shared assumption about the French elite's insulation from public opinion. This chapter will summarize how, in certain crucial ways during the time period in question—from the beginning of the war to the end of 1996—France's policy on Bosnia was influenced by the pressures of public opinion. We argue that public opinion worked in two ways: first, it provided general pressures over time that gradually influenced the direction of French policy; and second, usually in response to specific events on the ground that were captured by television cameras, it exerted intense pressure that contributed to the turning points in France's Bosnia policy. We show how the gap between French policy and public opinion, initially quite wide, gradually narrowed over time, as the government's policy shifted in the direction of public opinion.

This chapter consists of three main sections. First, we provide an overview of the five distinct phases of France's foreign policy toward the former Yugoslavia. Then we turn to our three indicators of French public opinion: general public opinion surveys, the intellectuals, and media coverage. The purpose of these first two major sections is descriptive—to establish an account of the French case that is as accurate as possible. Finally, in the last section, we bring together the two previous empirical sections, by generating an analysis of the possible causal effect of public opinion on France's Bosnia policy.

OVERVIEW OF FRENCH FOREIGN POLICY ON THE FORMER YUGOSLAVIA

From the onset of the Yugoslav crisis to the present, there have been several basic changes in the French government's foreign policy regarding the conflict. In this section, we trace shifts in the political positions of the government, as demonstrated in statements, declarations, interviews, and speeches made by the president, the prime minister, and the minister of foreign affairs. We argue that French policy toward the former Yugoslavia passed through five distinct phases: (1) refusing to name an aggressor (1990–May 1992); (2) multilateral humanitarian diplomacy (June 1992–December 1994); (3) gradual turn toward the threat of force (January 1994–spring 1995); (4) Chirac's use of force (May 1995–summer 1995); and (5) France's retreat (late summer 1995–present). After describing each of these five phases, we briefly turn to the changing quantity of releases by the French Ministry of Foreign Affairs, where we assess the numbers of statements, declarations, and communiqués against our argument of the phases.

Before getting into the specifics of the case study, it is worth mentioning briefly how foreign policy is made in the French political system. France has a presidential system, in which the president, who is elected directly, appoints the prime minister, who is then ratified by the parliament (Assemblée Nationale). If the president's party also controls the legislature, then policy-making is fairly straightforward, and the president and prime minister are in close coordination. If the opposition takes control of the legislature, however, the president is then forced to appoint a prime minister from an opposing party, thus leading to what is commonly known as "cohabitation," where the president and prime pinister, however reluctantly, have to find a way to work together. During such periods of cohabitation, which have occurred three times since the 1980s, the tradition is that the president (referred to as the "head of state") oversees foreign policy, while the prime minister (the "head of government") looks after domestic issues. This distinction, however, is often blurred in reality, as the president still remains actively involved in domestic debates; moreover, since the prime minister appoints the foreign minister, the prime minister and his or her cabinet still remain closely involved with foreign affairs.

When discussing such a broad concept as foreign policy, it is important to point out that, in the contemporary political age, in which the production and control of "image" and "spin" often dominate the policymaking apparatus, it is difficult to track the implementation of policies over time. This is especially true for military policy, which sometimes operates separately from foreign policy, with its own norms, guidelines, and accountability.

In this chapter, we rely mostly on official public statements, rather than trying to monitor ground operations, for three reasons: first, actual military policy on the ground is inherently secretive and often unknowable, while the statements are public and openly available; second, even if they are laced with rhetoric that is not necessarily followed up by action on the ground, these statements are still significant, and changes in their type and quantity do represent genuine policy changes; third, since all of the French government's concrete actions (i.e., humanitarian interventions) were made through multilateral frameworks, it would be nearly impossible to disentangle French policy from those of the other intervening countries if we were to focus only on the multilateral interventions on the ground. Focusing on official policy statements made by the French government thus allows us to develop consistent categories (both qualitative and quantitative) to compare and evaluate how French policy changed over time.

Returning to the case of the former Yugoslavia, while some analysts have claimed that French foreign policy toward Bosnia has changed primarily according to changes in elected officials,[1] we suggest that elected official change does not always correspond with policy changes. Rather, in characterizing the shifts in policy, we look to both the situation in the former Yugoslavia itself and to the domestic French political climate.

Phase 1: Refusing to Name an Aggressor (1990–May 1992)

From early 1990, with the first Slovene and Croat moves toward splitting from Yugoslavia, to the summer of 1992, French foreign policy toward Yugoslavia contained three components: (1) gradually diminishing support for a united Yugoslavia; (2) unwillingness to single out the Serbs as aggressors; and (3) interest in playing a major political role, albeit multilateral and nonmilitary, in negotiating a settlement to the crisis.

First, French support for a united Yugoslavia was a continuation of traditional policies dating as far back as World War I, with France's promotion of the unification of Yugoslavia. This political relationship was strengthened during and after World War I, when France and Yugoslavia were allied against Nazi Germany. For most of this century, and especially at the outbreak of the war in the former Yugoslavia, France's friendship with Yugoslavia often overlapped, or was confused, with a French-Serb friendship. Thus, it was not surprising that before the beginning of the war in Bosnia, France sought to support the Serb-led drives to keep Yugoslavia as one country.[2] This is demonstrated, for example, in statements by François Mitterrand, who said that "I believe it was wise, in the recent past, not to reopen the issue of borders. We must push for new dialogues, and not provoke new disintegration. Peace is too fragile" (Interview in *Liberation*, November 23, 1988). Moreover, according to Mitterrand's close friend and advisor (and later French foreign minister in the Jospin government) Hubert Védrine, "Mitterrand thinks that the existence of a Yugoslav Federation is a good but fragile thing; that the ideal would be to preserve it while transforming it; that in any case, there is no good solution for replacing Yugoslavia, neither *a fortiori* for Bosnia, and especially not the breaking up into several states" (Vedrine 1966, 603). Again, in a November 19, 1990 meeting with Yugoslav Federal President Borisav Jovic, Mitterrand reaffirmed this position by stating that "We hope that Yugoslavia remains Yugoslavia. It is not desirable for existing countries to shatter into many pieces" (Vedrine 604).

As early as the summer of 1991, however, with the secession of Slovenia, it had become clear that the Yugoslav federation of six (Bosnia-Herzegovina, Croatia, Macedonia, Montenegro, Serbia, Slovenia) was no longer viable. At the same time, French policy had begun to shift from trying to keep the federation together, to facilitating its breakup. When the German government publicly announced in late November 1991 its intention to recognize Slovenia and Croatia,[3] France tried unsuccessfully to oppose it, arguing that the decision to recognize the new countries should be made by a united Europe, and that early recognition by one European country might lead to furthering conflicts both in the Balkans and among the Europe of 12.[4]

Second, while France's gradual acceptance of a splintering Yugoslavia is important to explore, the most striking element of French policy toward Yugoslavia in this first phase was its refusal to designate an aggressor. This refusal was most notably evidenced in Mitterrand's statements in a November 29, 1991 interview, which was subsequently widely criticized by the French media and intellectuals. Despite numerous reports of Bosnian Serb aggression, in this interview, Mitterrand reaffirmed the French government's refusal to specify an aggressor, reminding the French and German publics that "Croatia, not Serbia, belonged to the Nazi bloc."[5] For the next several months, Mitterrand continued to make references to this position; for example, in another interview on December 14, 1991 he stated: "You ask me who is the aggressor and who is aggressed? I am incapable of telling you" (Interview in *Frankfurter Allgemeine Zeitung*, November 29, 1991).

Finally, a third important element established in this first phase was France's interest in being a major actor in all of the humanitarian interventions and in negotiating an end to the conflict. From the summer of 1991 on, France continually offered to supply interposition forces in Croatia (through the Western European Union), and tried to help move the conflict toward non-militaristic political processes, such as sponsoring the well-intentioned but ill-fated EC-monitored elections in independent Bosnia-Herzegovina in March 1992. After this, France contributed more troops, civilian police, and military observers to the United Nation's Protection Force (UNPROFOR) than any other country; it also remained a vociferous member of all multilateral negotiating bodies.[6] This third element, France's prominent role in negotiations, in supplying ground troops to separate forces, and in delivering humanitarian aid, lasted until the end of what we call Phase 4, in the summer of 1995.

Phase 2: Multilateral Humanitarian Diplomacy (June 1992–December 1993)

During this summer, France made an abrupt about-face in its policy of impartiality, or unwillingness to designate an aggressor, marking the second phase of French foreign policy in Bosnia. Most elements, however, represent continuity with previous policies outlined above.

As the summer of 1992 progressed, reports began to emerge of Serb detention camps reminiscent of those run by the Nazis during World War II. The government's response was not to increase French humanitarian aid and troop contributions, but rather to encourage the UN to establish "safe havens" in towns such as Gorazde, Srebrenica, Tuzla, and Zepa. France, as demonstrated in Mitterrand's speeches, also stood firm on its commitments to action through international, multilateral organizations and humanitarian assistance that eschewed the use of force. Mitterrand explained that France would act only in line with its partners: "France will not wage war *alone* against Serbia" (cited by Védrine, 636); as for the use of force, "I resist the push for the use of force. . . . If a decision of the United Nations brings about a vast support and an international contribution, then things will change" (Interview in *Vendredi*, January 22, 1993).

While these two policies—multilateral action and avoidance of the use of force—were consistent with earlier French policy, the break came with France's shift away from neutrality to designating the Serbs as aggressors and the Muslims as people in need of protection. This change was initiated in late June 1992, and was manifest most distinctly in two of Mitterrand's actions: first, in his statement to the Council of Europe in Lisbon on June 27, where he declared, "Serbia is today the aggressor, even though the origins of the conflict come from much further back"; and second, in his unexpected trip to Sarajevo on June 28, where the airport was under siege by Bosnian Serbs. In a television interview on the same day, Minister of Foreign Affairs Roland Dumas summarized the goal of Mitterrand's visit: "to express solidarity in front of the suffering of these populations, to tell them 'we were with you a bit, even for a few hours—France, symbolized by the head of state, is here, present'" and moreover that "for the rest of the world, to prove that by political will and the spirit of decisiveness, we can still break this infernal circle" (Antenne 2, June 28, 1992). After one day, the French government and its partners managed to negotiate a cessation (at least temporarily) to the Sarajevo airport siege. As we develop later in the chapter, this surprising change in France's foreign policy was very well received by French public opinion, the media, and the intellectuals.

Throughout the rest of 1992 and into 1993, French policy toward the former Yugoslavia did not change in any dramatic ways.[7] While Edouard Balladur was elected to the office of prime minister on March 28, 1993, bringing with him Alain Juppé as minister of foreign affairs, this new "cohabitation" did not usher in new French policies toward intervention in the former Yugoslavia.[8] Balladur and Juppé entered office calling for active war crimes tribunals (established before they came into office, on February 22, 1993, by UN Security Council Resolution 808), and greater joint action in the former Yugoslavia.[9] All of these positions—advocating war crimes tribunals, multilateral action, and a slowly increasing French troop presence—are entirely consistent with pre-cohabitation policy toward the former Yugoslavia.

In sum, the summer of 1992 saw an about-face in the French government's stance toward the Serbs. While this signaled a significant change in French foreign policy toward the former Yugoslavia, the change in government almost one year later (in April 1993) did not usher in big policy changes as some might expect. Indeed, the next major policy change did not occur until nine months into cohabitation.

Phase 3: Gradual Turn toward the Threat of Force (January 1994–May 1995)

The insistence on multilateral action through international organizations, and reliance on diplomatic, rather than more forceful, means of negotiation, persisted until the winter of 1994. In January, before and during the NATO summit, the French began to call for a greater show of force against the Bosnian Serbs. On January 10, for example, Foreign Minister Alain Juppé declared "we are available for air-strikes." On January 10, 1994, he went on a special program called "Qui Peut Sauver Sarajevo?" ("Who Can Save Sarajevo?") to add that "we have tried, not all 16 together but at the initiative of France once again, and with our partners who have troops on the ground, to define more precisely the measures that we could take to restore the credibility of UNPROFOR."

Shortly thereafter, the tragic Sarajevo marketplace bombing in February, followed by the attack on Gorazde in March, corresponded with another change in France's foreign policy: France branched out from multilateral bargaining purely through well-established international organizations (the UN, the EU, the WEU), to actively helping to create an ad hoc "contact group."[10] Then in April, with the support of the French, the UN ordered the first NATO air strikes against Bosnian Serb ground forces. At the end of this month, France also threatened to set a date to pull its troops out of UNPROFOR unilaterally, if the latest attempt at negotiations failed. While these negotiations did fail, France's troops remained in UNPROFOR.

It is important to note that while France gradually moved toward support-ing the use of force, and toward acting outside of international organizations, its position on the UN-sponsored arms embargo on the region did not change. Throughout 1994 and early into 1995, there were many pressures on the French government—both internal to France, as discussed in the next section, and external, as manifest in U.S. congressional actions—to lift the arms embargo. Lifting the embargo was even discussed by the contact group in early September 1994, but rejected, especially at the behest of the French government.[11] For the remainder of 1994, and through the first months of 1995, France turned toward the threat of force through NATO air power, while leaving room for diplomatic maneuvering outside of the organizational framework of the UN

Phase 4: Chirac's Use of Force (May 1995–Summer 1995)

From the outset of the war up until the spring of 1995, there were gradual changes in French foreign policy toward intervention in Bosnia that did not necessarily correspond with the onset of cohabitation in 1993. That said, France's most vociferous policy shift did correspond with the election of Jacques Chirac to the presidency and his arrival at the *Elysée* in May 1995. As some scholars have explained, Chirac's foreign policy initiatives were de-signed to be "flashy" and, especially in the early months, demonstrated his "buccaneering" attempts at "neo-gaullism."[12] Chirac's ascendance to the presidency also corresponded with the third and largest UN hostage crisis. In the end of May 1995, French peacekeepers were taken hostage, handcuffed to their posts by Bosnian Serbs, and humiliated on world television for their "impotence." This led to a dramatic change in government policy, evidenced by the new Prime Minister Alain Juppé's June 6 statement: "Non-intervention was cowardly and was a stain on the original objective of the European Union that we are trying to build. We therefore intervened, France in the lead" (National Assembly debate, June 6, 1995).

Chirac's reaction was very firm and very personal, as he rapidly and single-handedly took the initiative in changing France's policy in the direction of greater use of force. In a June 27 declaration (European Council meeting in Cannes, June 27, 1995), Chirac stated "We want a policy in the former Yu-goslavia that is both clear and firm," and he subsequently called for the es-tablishment of a "rapid reaction force" (RRF) that would serve to protect the UN troops (who were themselves supposed to protect Bosnians). In short, the RRF was to have a wider mandate for the use of force, with the intention of lessening the humiliation of French peacekeepers. The RRF, however, was never deployed the way it was initially planned. By the time the RRF began its initial deployments, the United States and NATO stepped in with much more severe recourse to the use of force.

Phase 5: France's Retreat (Late Summer 1995–Present)

The summer of 1995 saw the major turning points in the war: the fall of the safe havens, heavy air strikes by NATO against the Bosnian Serbs, and the expulsion of the Croatian Serbs from Krajina. With the fall of the UN-sponsored safe havens in July and the subsequent massacre of thousands of Muslims by Bosnian Serbs, the UN's ability, legitimacy, and authority to lead peacekeeping operations in the former Yugoslavia had ended—and France's leadership role thereby diminished. In the end, on August 30, NATO planes and RRF artillery began massive bombardments of Serb positions mainly around Sarajevo, Pale, Gorazde, and Tuzla; the operation was called "Deliberate Force." The United States then stepped in (with Richard Holbrooke at the lead), to hammer through the Dayton accords, which designated NATO as the enforcer of the peace.

While France was not a member of the NATO military command, the French government was a strong supporter of the NATO interposition forces, and continued to increase its troop contributions, which had doubled (to almost 11,000) by September 1995. Although willing and able to contribute troops, politically and diplomatically, France was put on the back burner during the Dayton accords as the Russian-Serb, German-Croat, U.S.-Bosnian formula of external-internal support proved more effective. The accords were, however, signed in Paris in December 1995, as a gesture to the French government for its constant support of the peace process.

Before moving to an explanation of these shifts in France's Bosnia policy, we now briefly compare our qualitative explanation above to the quantity of statements, speeches, and declarations released by the French Ministry of Foreign Affairs over time. Figure 4.1 provides a breakdown of the total num-

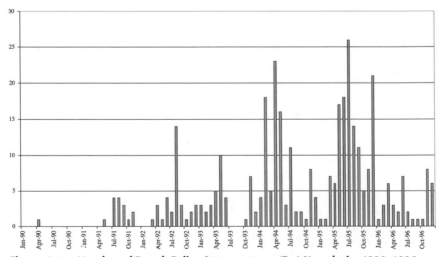

Figure 4.1.   Number of French Policy Statements on (Ex-) Yugoslavia, 1990–1996

ber of releases by the French Ministry of Foreign Affairs that include in their title one or more of the key words "Yugoslavia, former Yugoslavia, Bosnia, Serbia, Croatia, Slovenia, Sarajevo," for each month from 1990 to 1996.[13] While it is difficult to evaluate what exactly these numbers in themselves mean in terms of the content of French policy,[14] such a chronological perspective allows us to make tentative observations about the major changes that took place at specific points in time.

COMPARATIVE SURVEYS

As the figure shows, until the summer of 1992, the topic of Yugoslavia was relatively absent from the French statements. The enormous rise in August 1992, which basically corresponds with the beginning of our Phase 2, occurred after the discovery of Serb-controlled detention camps in Bosnia.[15] Although it would appear from figure 4.1 that the second phase actually began in August, not—as argued above—in late June, we feel justified in including Mitterrand's two actions described above, for two main reasons: first, they were entirely consistent with the content of the flurry of French statements in August, and second, they truly represented major turning points in French policy.

After this change in French policy and the beginning of Phase 2, the number of statements remained consistently low for the next eight months, rising somewhat in May 1993, but mainly for domestic reasons—namely that the election of a new government led the new Prime Minister Edouard Balladur and Foreign Minister Alain Juppé to seek to make their presence felt on the Yugoslav issue. As argued above, however, this slight increase in the quantity of French statements did not represent a change in French policy, which remained consistent during that time.[16]

The next major jump in French statements occurred in February 1994, which corresponds to the Sarajevo marketplace bombing discussed above. We include the month of January as the beginning of our Phase 3, even though there were relatively few statements made, because of the change in content of the French government's policy. The next jump, in April-May 1994, corresponds with NATO responses to the attack on Gorazde and France's leading role in the establishment of the contact group. The rest of 1994 can be characterized by several ups and downs in the quantity of statements released.

From the beginning of 1995 through July, one can notice a gradual crescendo of releases, which corresponds with Chirac's rise to the presidency, as well as with major changes on the ground in the former Yugoslavia. The brief rise in December 1995 corresponds with the liberation of two French pilots and with the signing of the Dayton accords in Paris. Finally, in 1996 the number of statements remained consistently low.

In short, the qualitative analysis of France's foreign policy toward the former Yugoslavia shows several clear and significant changes over time. The quantitative element shown in the tables, and explained briefly above, for the most part bolsters these findings and depicts them visually. Now, having described French foreign policy on Yugoslavia over time, our next sections attempt to explain and analyze what may have influenced it.

OVERVIEW OF FRENCH PUBLIC
OPINION ON THE FORMER YUGOSLAVIA

We turn now to French public opinion on intervention in the former Yugoslavia, which we break down into three distinct indicators: (1) the attitudes and opinions of the general public, as seen through public opinion surveys; (2) the role of the French intellectuals; and (3) media coverage.

It is standard to refer to public opinion surveys, and often to the media, as constituting public opinion, but we feel justified in incorporating the intellectuals for several reasons. Although the French intellectuals may not be representative of the general public, they are public figures whose messages can reach and influence a wide audience. Moreover, on the issue of French intervention in the former Yugoslavia, they were central to all aspects of the French national debate. As Védrine, who is himself rather critical of the intellectuals, points out, "The very French phenomenon of the 'intellectuals' gives public opinion, in our country, its own particular coloration" (Védrine 615). Finally, of our interviews with policymakers, intellectuals, and other scholars, there was not a single objection to our inclusion of intellectuals as one of the three components of public opinion.

Surveys of the Attitudes and Opinions of the General Public

Now we turn to our analysis of public opinion surveys of French attitudes on intervention in Bosnia, where we present and summarize the results of over twenty different surveys conducted between 1992 and 1996.[17] When comparing different surveys over time, in addition to ensuring that each survey was conducted by professional and nonpartisan survey organizations that followed strict sampling and questioning methods, we must pay close attention to the timing of each survey[18] and the precise wording of the questions.[19]

The Appendix presents a complete summary of all the available survey results on this issue. We have divided the long list of surveys into three categories: (a) *comparative surveys*, which show how the French results compare to those of other countries that were asked the same questions; (b) *time-series surveys*, where the same questions were asked at different points in time, thus allowing us to analyze trends in the results; and (c) *individual surveys*, usually commissioned by newspapers and magazines, which were often conducted at times of heated national debate, and which rarely use the same question wording from one survey to another.[20]

Comparative Surveys

Most of the comparative surveys were commissioned by Eurobarometer, the public opinion institute of the European Union. The results of Eurobarometer surveys conducted in June 1993 and September 1995, shown in the Appendix, illustrate that the French public was above the average for European countries on most questions relating to support for military intervention in Bosnia, but only slightly. In June 1993, for example, while the government was still firmly engaged in the second phase of "Multilateral Humanitarian Diplomacy," 58 percent of the French were for a military intervention, with 25 percent against and 17 percent unsure, compared to the European average of 55 percent for, 28 percent against, and 17 percent unsure. In September 1995, after "Chirac's Use of Force" and at the beginning of "France's Retreat" (our fourth and fifth phases), 57 percent of the French favored a military intervention "with additional capacity" (a rather vague concept), with 27 percent opposed, compared to the European average of 53 percent in favor and 38 percent opposed. While the European comparisons do not show great differences, the most striking comparison is to the United States, in a joint IFOP/Gallup survey conducted shortly after the NATO ultimatum following the Sarajevo marketplace bombing. The results show that 76 percent of French respondents favored air strikes if the ultimatum was not respected, with only 20 percent opposed, compared to 48 percent in favor and 43 percent opposed in the United States.

Overall, it is difficult to draw conclusions from these comparative surveys, other than the obvious observation that a majority of the French public appeared to be strongly in favor of military intervention, but only slightly more so than most European publics, and much more so than in the United States. This strong support for military intervention from the very beginning stands in sharp contrast to the early French policy of avoiding the use of force—a policy that eventually shifted over time in the direction of public opinion.

Time-Series Surveys

The two organizations that commissioned time-series surveys are Eurobarometer (which are also comparative) and SIRPA, the public relations institute of the French Defense Ministry. Although both sets of results are somewhat helpful, they also have extreme limitations. The main disadvantage of the Eurobarometer results is that they were conducted over a relatively short time-span (February 1994, March 1994, and June 1994—all within our third phase of "Gradual Turn toward the Threat of Force"), which prevents us from generalizing these results to the entire period of the Yugoslav conflict. The advantage, however, is that they are also comparative, and they therefore contribute to the international comparative perspective mentioned above. The only striking result of these surveys is the response to the question about launching air strikes, which shows that the French public was consistently in favor of this solution, significantly more so than fellow Europeans.

The time-series results from the surveys commissioned by SIRPA were published in their annual large-scale survey, *Baromètre: les français et la défense nationale*, which included one question on intervention in the former Yugoslavia, asked in May 1993, May 1994, June 1995, and June 1996. The problem here is with the question wording. From 1993 to 1995, the question asked was "do you approve or disapprove of the current intervention of France within the UN in the former Yugoslavia?" In 1996, the question asked was "do you approve or disapprove of the intervention of France within NATO in the former Yugoslavia?" The obvious difference is, of course, the change from the UN to NATO, which corresponds accurately to the changes on the ground, but the more subtle yet serious problem is in the first question wording, which mentions the word "current." This makes the question much more ambiguous: does it refer to one's support or opposition to French military action in general, or is it a request for a vote of confidence on the *current* government's concrete activity? As a result, it is difficult to draw firm conclusions from these time-series surveys, and impossible to provide any trustworthy graphics showing the evolution of French public opinion over time.

Individual Surveys

Now we turn to the numerous individual surveys, listed in chronological order in the Appendix, with the goal of characterizing French public opinion as accurately as possible within the limits of the surveys. The most basic yet important observation that can be made from these results is that a wide majority of the French public consistently supported French participation in a military intervention throughout the duration of the conflict. Although the question wordings were often very different, sometimes vague and/or even biased, the results showed high numbers of support for the intervention, usually between 55 percent and 70 percent.

Since a summary of all of the different question wordings would take up too much space (and since they are all available in the Appendix), we will highlight two themes that come out of the results. First, a result that seems surprising given the late-twentieth century military ethic of "zero death," the French public supported intervention even at the risk of French casualties (62 percent in December 1992 and 55 percent in February 1994—albeit with different question wordings). And we should point out that this opinion actually had a concrete basis, since sixty French soldiers died in the former Yugoslavia by

September 1996,[21] which were all very widely publicized in the French media. The support for intervention, however, remained strong.[22]

Second, at least according to the survey results, the French public's interest in the conflict was extremely high. Even before the marketplace bombing, the January 1994 BVA/SIRPA survey showed that 85 percent of the French were "concerned with the events taking place in the former Yugoslavia," and almost identical results came out of their February 1994 survey (86 percent were "concerned"). By June 1996, however, this interest had decreased significantly, although it still characterized a majority, where 55 percent were concerned, as opposed to 44 percent less concerned or unconcerned.

When interpreting such a wide array of comparative, time-series, and individual survey results, it is very important to exercise caution and skepticism, something the newspapers that commission them and publish the results seldom do. The fact is, however, that out of more than twenty major surveys, conducted by professional polling organizations following strict sampling methods, there is not a single survey result that shows less than a majority of the French public in favor of intervention in Bosnia. Significantly, while policymakers were often trying to emphasize either nonintervention or a "humanitarian" intervention, the type of intervention most frequently alluded to (whether directly or indirectly) in the survey questions was *military*. This distinction becomes especially important when we try to assess the causal impact of public opinion toward the end of this chapter.

The Role of the French Intellectuals

Although small when compared to the huge and often paralyzing public mobilization that takes place periodically in France, usually to protest domestic economic measures, French public mobilization on the issue of Bosnia was remarkable and unique. It was remarkable because of the quantity and density of networks, organizations, and associations that made the Yugoslav issue their *cause célèbre*, and it was unique in that the leaders and motivating force behind this mobilization was a small but vociferous group of Parisian intellectuals. This section briefly traces and summarizes the role of the French intellectuals on the Bosnian issue.

France has a long tradition of political engagement by diverse individuals and groups known as "the intellectuals." It is perhaps the only country where that term is used so commonly. Dating back to Emile Zola's activism in the Dreyfus Affair over a century ago and continuing well through the vibrant days of Albert Camus and Jean-Paul Sartre, an eclectic set of Parisians has seen it as their duty, individually and collectively, to speak up at the slightest sign of injustice. This has created a testy, but still mutually beneficial, relationship between them and the politicians against whom their actions have usually been aimed. It is not uncommon, for example, for a French president, in an effort to placate them or to ingratiate himself with them, to invite a group of intellectuals to lunch at the Elysée, or for other leading politicians to contact them to discuss policy matters.

While it seemed as if this tradition of intellectual resistance might have been waning since the heady days of the 1960s and 1970s, the reaction to the Yugoslav crisis proved the contrary. As early as the fall of 1991, with the Serb assaults on Dubrovnik and Vukovar, intellectuals such as André Glucksmann, Alain Finkielkraut, Bernard-Henri Lévy, Pierre Hassner, and many others started speaking out, both in written articles and then at intellectual gatherings and meetings. Although they had different theoretical assumptions, arguments, and objectives, they were united by their outrage at the atrocities that were taking place "two hours from Paris," while the French and European governments seemed to be looking the other way.[23] Although the reaction started slowly at first with individual articles, it developed into a crescendo that became even more intense with the Serb attack on Bosnia in the early spring of 1992. The flurry of articles and statements, which were extremely critical of the French government, and particularly against Mitterrand, continued unabated throughout 1993.

By early 1994, some of the intellectuals started to discuss the possibility of creating an electoral list for the European elections in May/June 1994 that would focus on Bosnia. After one or two false starts, they decided about a month before the elections to go ahead with the list, which they called "Europe Starts at Sarajevo," with the stated goal of putting Bosnia at the center of the French political debate on Europe. Their concrete goals were less clear—some in the list favored lifting the arms embargo on Bosnia, while others favored air strikes against the Bosnian Serbs. Their general idea, however, was that since these were *European* elections, this larger European issue should overtake the usual domestic ones.

In any case, the reaction to the announcement was sudden and overwhelming. Not only were the group's founders and leaders, especially Lévy and Glucksmann, instantly and incessantly interviewed on television, radio, and in newspapers and magazines,[24] but other politicians—from all parties—were then constantly asked to respond to the intellectuals. The intellectuals, meanwhile, organized large and enthusiastic meetings that sometimes even lasted through the night. Michel Rocard, the head of the Socialist list for the European elections, who was then considered a leading candidate for the French presidency after Mitterrand's term would expire the following year, attended many of their meetings, and he suddenly changed his position to one of opposing the arms embargo, thus directly challenging Mitterrand.[25]

Only two weeks before the election, the magazine *Le Point* published a survey conducted by IPSOS showing that 12 percent of respondents indicated that they would vote for the list (a very high figure considering that the center-right UDF-RPR list had 27 percent and the Socialists only 18 percent). The survey result, which was widely publicized, shocked everyone, including the intellectuals themselves. Suddenly, the intellectuals, whose stated aim was to force the other parties to address the Bosnian issue, not actually to win seats in the European Parliament, were faced with a difficult decision.

The story behind the end of the list is unclear. There was some infighting among the members, most importantly around the issue of whether or not to withdraw from the elections. In the end, they did withdraw, but only after a tight vote following an all-night meeting. Meanwhile, the ballots had already been printed with the list on them, meaning that the electorate could still vote for the list, even though it had officially been withdrawn—and the list barely received 1 percent. While this paltry electoral support may suggest that the list ended as a failure, it should not be forgotten that its organizers did succeed in their goal of bringing Bosnia to the forefront of the election campaign.[26]

Media Coverage

It is widely acknowledged by academics and policymakers that the modern media has become an extremely influential actor—capable of placing issues on the agenda, pressuring influential elites, and especially shortening the time span within which official figures can react to incidents and crises. On the other hand, one should be careful not to grant too much power and autonomy to the media, since it is also frequently the subject of manipulation by those very same elites it supposedly influences. A grand theory of the effect of the media probably cannot be formulated, since so much depends upon the issue, subject, or event at hand.[27] By carefully examining the quantity and content of media coverage on a specific issue, however, researchers can come up with persuasive accounts and hypotheses about the relationship between the media and elite policy on that particular issue.

Before getting into the specifics of French media coverage of the Bosnian conflict, it is important to explain the peculiar structure of the French media. The primary source from which most French people get their news is television; over 50 percent claim to watch the evening news (at 8 p.m.) regularly, on one of the two main channels. While newspapers are also widely read in France, the circulation of national newspapers is strikingly low when compared to other European countries. Indeed, part of the French peculiarity is that most people read regional newspapers—which also cover national and international news, although in much less detail. Within Paris, however, where the entire intellectual and policymaking apparatus is centralized, there are a variety of newspapers, which generally follow clearly defined partisan lines.[28]

This uniquely French situation presents a host of problems for social scientists seeking to use any kind of content analysis to generate results that are accurate, representative, and significant. For this chapter, we have chosen to focus primarily on television news, for several reasons: first, it is the form of news that reaches the broadest audience; second, its content is uniform throughout the country; third, our preliminary analysis of *Le Monde* coverage showed trends that were essentially similar to those of television news; and finally, we were able to benefit from and draw from a previously published study on French television coverage of the Yugoslav conflict.

Indeed, thanks to the extensive and impressive database and analysis conducted by Patrice Charaudeau, Guy Lochard, and Jean-Claude Soulages (1996), who studied the French television coverage of the war in the former Yugoslavia,[29] we can make several observations about both the quantity and content of French television on the Yugoslav crisis.

By doing searches of the key words "Yugoslavia, former Yugoslavia, Bosnia, Serbia, Croatia, Slovenia, Sarajevo," and then "cleaning up" the results by removing the small number of stories that were irrelevant to the topic (e.g., sports coverage, etc.), the authors were able to develop a consistent quantitative scale over time. Figure 4.2 shows the number of stories devoted to some aspect of the conflict that were broadcast on the evening news (8 p.m.) on the two major French TV channels, TF1 and Antenne 2, from 1990 to 1996.[30] The two most obvious and striking jumps in the amount of coverage came in August 1992, with the discovery of the camps, and then in February 1994, after the bombing of the Sarajevo marketplace. Also noteworthy is the vast amount of coverage of the French General Morillon's actions during the siege of Srebrenica in the spring of 1993, when he defied his government's orders to leave the area and return to France (Charaudeau et

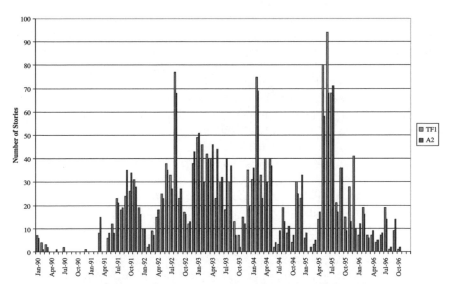

Figure 4.2.   French TV Evening News Coverage of (Ex-) Yugoslavia, 1990–1996

al., 97). Charaudeau et al. also point out the increase in coverage on a daily (not just monthly) basis with the collapse of the Yugoslav Federation from June 26 to July 2, 1991, and then especially on June 28, 1992 with Mitterrand's surprise visit to Sarajevo.[31]

Charaudeau et al. go further in their analysis, as they also consider the thematic organization of the coverage of the conflict. They reach several conclusions, two of which are relevant here: (1) the French TV coverage of the Yugoslav conflict became "Frenchisized" over time—namely, what was originally portrayed as a European problem increasingly became a "French" problem, as France became more involved in the conflict; (2) after dividing the coverage into several different categories, including "civilian," "armed conflict," "humanitarian," and "diplomatic," among others, the authors concluded that the priority of the French TV coverage, especially after 1992, was given to covering the civilian side, evoking the difficulties and losses of the civilian population, alongside the coverage of humanitarian assistance, particularly when conducted by French organizations (Charaudeau et al., 101).

This increasing emphasis on France's role in the conflict, alongside the stories and images of horrible violence and humanitarian disaster, often pressured the French government's policy, especially in the immediate aftermath of specific incidents and dramatic events on the ground.

THE INFLUENCE OF PUBLIC OPINION ON FRANCE'S BOSNIA POLICY

Having explained the different phases in the French government's foreign policy toward the former Yugoslavia, and then having described the three facets of French public opinion, we now turn to an analysis of the causal effect that the latter may have had on the former. We argue that public opinion can be influential in two different ways: first, in the form of broad and general pressures over time; and second, following specific events or incidents on the ground, where the political consensus was visibly, and sometimes significantly, shaken and adjusted.

The notion of "general pressures" is fairly straightforward. The idea behind it is that influential policymakers intentionally keep themselves abreast of public opinion; when their policies do not accord with public opinion, the latter exerts subtle yet potent pressure on them. This is a particularly modern feature of politics, given the technical capabilities of gauging public opinion, public debates, and large quantities of media coverage much more systematically and publicly. While these general pressures usually do not cause policymakers to change their policies, they certainly make them more aware of the risks they might be taking when certain policies are unpopular. Our notion of general pressures fits closely with the description of public opinion put forth by Mitterrand's close advisor Hubert Védrine: "public opinion . . . is not strictly speaking an actor, but rather a force, and, in our mediatized societies, a considerable force whose source nobody completely controls. It can be diffuse or concentrated, dormant or frenzied, spontaneous or provoked. In any case, it is always present" (Védrine, 59).

In addition to the general pressures exerted by public opinion on foreign policy over time, the occasional occurrence of specific events and incidents allows us to examine public opinion's effect more closely, relying on official documents, memoirs, and personal interviews as sources. The problem, however, is that any attempt at reconstructing the causality surrounding a specific incident becomes extremely complicated and indeterminate.

In this section, we go through our three indicators of public opinion to demonstrate that, at the key moments when French policy changed, public opinion did play a role, although not necessarily independent or direct.

Surveys of the General Public Opinion

Starting with public opinion surveys, the crucial question is whether the relative clarity and militancy of public opinion on the desirability of military intervention had any practical effect on French policy. To what extent were French policymakers aware of the opinions of the French population on this issue? Did they take them into account, and if so, how? Might the awareness of public opinion have exerted some influence on policymakers at those particular times when French policy changed?

These are particularly difficult questions to answer, especially since the crucial policymaking decisions are usually made behind closed doors, and not always for the reasons that are publicly proclaimed. Personal interviews with policymakers on this subject were not very helpful. Some responded with the predictable, but misleading, response that decisions are always made according to the "will of the people," while others proudly insisted that, on the contrary, decisions were based on the elite's special expertise and its moral conscience about what is best for the people. Both answers were vague, and neither was helpful.

There are moments, however, when more concrete evidence can be found of a government's consideration of public opinion. According to the research of Elisabeth Dupoirier, in the months leading up to the Gulf War in early 1991, for example, Mitterrand was very conscious of French public opinion on the issue, and during the month of January he ordered two surveys a week to follow the "mood" of the population.[32] These surveys were sponsored by the Service d'Information du Gouvernement—a public institute linked to the prime minister, which occasionally commissions survey questions to private survey institutes—and the results were not made public.

For the case of the former Yugoslavia, we could find no such "smoking gun" to show direct government interest in the "mood" of public opinion. Relying on more general indicators, however, we found that public opinion did exert an influence on the French government's policy on Bosnia, although certainly not in the direct way in which many political behaviorists would expect. Larger geopolitical and strategic considerations, including the positions of the other European countries and especially the United States, certainly played a pivotal role as well, but public opinion should be included as a crucial factor. As pointed out in the previous section, the French general public was a strong and consistent supporter of military intervention in Bosnia from the very beginning. The French government, on the other hand, started with a noninterventionist stance during the first few years of the conflict,[33] but then gradually moved in the direction of public opinion: nonintervention soon gave way to humanitarian intervention, which eventually turned into military intervention. By the time of Chirac's use of force in the summer of 1995, the government had caught up to public opinion.

The Intellectuals

As stated earlier, the general pressure exerted by the French intellectuals was consistent and significant. In addition to the barrage of articles and opinion pieces denouncing French government policy, the intellectuals organized many gatherings and meetings on the Yugoslav issue. They also provided nearly unrelenting pressure in support of airstrikes, as well as the lifting of the embargo on the Muslims.

In the immediate aftermath of the specific incidents and events mentioned above, the role of the French intellectuals—filtered through the media—was particularly strident, and probably somewhat influential, especially following the Sarajevo marketplace bombing. This is difficult to determine, however, given the multiplicity of factors and causes going on at the same time. It is also impossible to demonstrate quantitatively or visually, as presented in the figures above.

One incident, however, provides us with a clearer picture of how the intellectuals did have a significant and concrete impact, leading to the change from Phase 1 to Phase 2, as outlined above. The occasion was Mitterrand's June 27, 1992 speech at the Council of Europe meeting, followed by his surprise visit to the besieged Sarajevo the next day. For this event, the memoirs of some of his close confidants are quite helpful. Roland Dumas, then foreign minister, recalls that Mitterrand first told him on June 24 that he wanted to go to Belgrade or Sarajevo. Dumas' advice, which Mitterrand heeded, was to go to Sarajevo, as he told the president that "you cannot start with Belgrade. . . . The criticisms will explode. We will go visit the red tyrant, the butcher of Sarajevo. . . . I can read certain editorials even before they are written" (Dumas 1996, 365).

While on the plane to Sarajevo, according to Bernard Kouchner—then Mitterrand's special appointee for the humanitarian crisis, although also a vocal critic of Mitterrand's Bosnian policy—Kouchner asked Mitterrand, "I have often spoken to you about this appeal of the residents of Sarajevo, but what made you decide?" Mitterrand replied, "The slowness of Europe, the immobility of the Council, and the appeal from President Izetbegovic transmitted to me by Bernard-Henry Lévy" (Kouchner 1995, 39). Indeed, not long before this turning point, Mitterrand had met with Lévy, one of Bosnian President Alija Izetbegovic's clearest and loudest supporters. Might that explain the sudden change in Mitterrand's speeches, and his words at the Council of Europe meeting, where he said for the first time, "Serbia is today the aggressor, even though the origins of the conflict come from much further back"? At the very least, it played an important role. As further support for this claim, Mitterrand's visit to Sarajevo provided him with an enormous boost in popularity, something that certainly did not go unnoticed. The media, the intellectuals, and the general public alike praised his personal courage and conviction.

The election and arrival of Chirac to the Elysée provides another example of the influence of the French intellectuals, resulting in the change from Phase 3 to Phase 4. Perhaps especially because his actions coincided with the traditional "honeymoon period" of politicians taking office, Chirac benefited from an extremely high popularity and support from the general public on his handling of the hostage crisis. The French intellectuals also responded positively, as almost all of the published opinion pieces that had previously been unwaveringly critical of the French government were now hailing Chirac's *tour de force*. The result was a peculiar alliance between the gaullist Chirac and a diverse group of intellectuals, many of whom were far on the left. Chirac even met with a group of intellectuals at the Elysée shortly after taking over as president, specifically to talk about the Yugoslav crisis.[34]

We should be careful not to overstate the capacity of the French intellectuals to influence their government's Bosnia policy. Despite their pressure on Mitterrand to lift the arms embargo on the Muslims, Mitterrand never did change his position. That said, although this does indicate a weaker influence on this issue, we should not forget the aforementioned change by Michel Rocard—who at the time was a leading presidential contender—to supporting the embargo in May/June 1994, after participating in the meetings of the *Liste de Sarajevo*.

The relative influence of the intellectuals can best be explained by another role they play in French society, namely maintaining and using elite networks. Indeed, another peculiarity of French politics and society, which is no secret to anyone familiar with the centralized French system, is the importance of the networks between political elites in various positions around the center of power. Since many of these intellectuals went to the same schools, shared common experiences, and belong to a similar social status group, as the policymaking elite, it should come as no surprise that they have the ability to influence policy.

This is not to say that the intellectuals are quietly orchestrating the policies of the French government; quite the contrary, in the "normal" times of every-day politics, they are often ignored or at least not heard, since the voices are multiple and disparate, and the policy recommendations tend to be cacophonous and contradictory. In times of major crises and national debate, how-ever, the tradition of turning to the intellectuals as "experts" still remains strong. In the case of the Yugoslav issue, the mobilization of the intellectuals was remarkable because of their relative unity—in opposition to the French government, and especially against François Mitterrand himself. Although they often had different theoretical assumptions, different ideological back-grounds, and different visions of Bosnia, Europe, and the role of France, they were unified by their outrage that the French government seemed unwilling to intervene in the horrors taking place "two hours from Paris." Because of the unity and strength of their message, and also because of their privileged positions and their personal contacts, this time their voices were heard.

The Media

According to the findings of Natalie La Balme, a French scholar who has been studying the influence of public opinion on French foreign policy—and who has conducted nearly fifty interviews with French elites surrounding the presidents, prime ministers, and foreign ministers—the French policymaking elite is extremely sensitive to the media. La Balme reports that the over-whelming answer to the question "For you, what is public opinion?" is "the media" (LaBalme 1998). She also points out that Mitterrand read the national press very closely and every morning listened to political commentaries on the radio. Moreover, the press service of the Elysée provided him with daily sum-maries of the national and regional press, as well as the television news. Even in "normal" times (i.e., not times of political crisis or upheaval), French politi-cians keep a careful eye on public opinion, and particularly the media.

Aside from specific events and incidents, the media also played an impor-tant role in the day-to-day monitoring of the Yugoslav crisis, and in many ways set the agenda for potential changes in French policy. A publication is-sued by the French Parliament (Assemblée Nationale), for example, mentions that "one has to recognize the decisive influence of the media . . . as much in the decision to plan an intervention as in the way in which to carry it out."[35] This point was also confirmed repeatedly in all of our own interviews.

The most important role played by the media, however, was with three clearly identifiable specific events and incidents: first, the discovery of the camps in August 1992, which occurred soon after Mitterrand's visit to Sarajevo, and which confirmed the change in French policy from Phase 1 to Phase 2, with the recognition of the Serbs as the aggressors; second, the Sarajevo marketplace bombing in February 1994, which solidified the change from Phase 2 to Phase 3, with the gradual turn toward the threat of force; and third, the French hostage crisis in May 1995, which coincided with Chirac's inauguration as well as the use of force that characterizes the change from Phase 3 to Phase 4. After all three incidents, which were not necessarily unique in and of themselves, but rather because they happened to be filmed up close by television cameras, the policymaking establishment was shaken and France's policy was changed.

For the first incident, the television depiction of immediate and horrifying images of human misery and suffering, especially given the obvious historical significance of "concentration camps" that were "only two hours from Paris," provided an intense pressure on French policymakers to "do something" to oppose the Serb aggression. In fact, it was widely believed that Mitterrand and other Western leaders were informed of the existence of camps several months earlier, but they reacted only *after* journalist Roy Gutman's discovery and the subsequent massive media mobilization. For the second incident, the images of sixty-eight dead and over 200 injured people in a public marketplace on a Saturday morning, especially after the repeated Serb violations of the safety zone around Sarajevo, provoked a rapid and forceful reaction in the form of the NATO ultimatum against the Bosnian-Serbs with the threat of force in case of noncompliance.[36] For the third incident, the television images of French peacekeepers—showing them handcuffed to lampposts, with Bosnian Serb soldiers mocking and taunting them, in the name of publicly humiliating France—provided the spark that compelled the newly inaugurated Jacques Chirac's swift decision to create the RRF and to take decisive anti-Serb actions.[37]

What about a broader perspective on the impact of the television media on policymaking over time? Figure 4.3 presents a combination chart that compares the number of French policy statements (from figure 4.1) and the average number of television news stories (from figure 4.2).[38] Although caution should be used when interpreting combination charts that use two axes and categories, figure 4.3 does allow us to reach some tentative conclusions about the effect of the media on France's Yugoslav policy.[39] For all three of the events described earlier, which produced major turning points in French foreign policy, there seems to have been an earlier increase in television attention. Before the first major increase in policy statements in August 1992, for example, there was a noticeable increase in the TV news coverage of the issue in May, June, and July. Moreover, the rise in policy statements in May 1993 was preceded by high levels of TV coverage in January-April. Also, the upsurge in policy statements in February 1994 followed a slight rise in TV stories in December and January. Finally, the big jump in policy statements in July 1995 was slightly preceded by a higher increase in TV stories in May and June of that year. The last rise of policy statements, in December 1995—

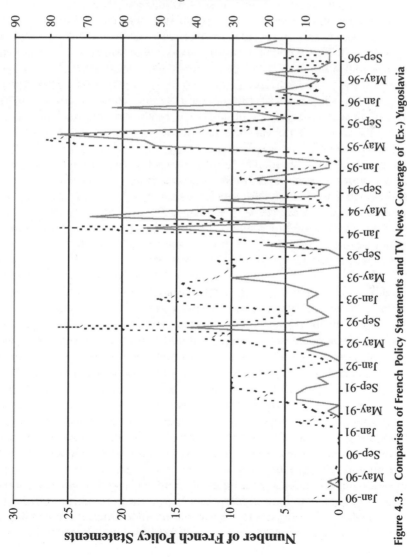

Average Number of TF1 and A2 TV Evening News Stories

Policy
Average TV

Figure 4.3. Comparison of French Policy Statements and TV News Coverage of (Ex-) Yugoslavia

corresponding with the signing of the Dayton agreement in Paris—however, was neither preceded nor accompanied by a concomitant increase in TV coverage.

In other words, although the data do not allow us to affirm definite causality, the quantitative evidence from figure 4.3 does suggest that the media was "leading" France's policy more than the other way around. This finding supports and complements our more qualitative analysis about the changes in France's policy and in particular the media's influential role in effecting such change.

The observation that the media, particularly television, tends to force policymakers to respond and sometimes to take action, leaves open the question of whether the media actually influences the *content* of the policy reaction. In an excellent and well-balanced assessment of the effect of television on foreign policy in the United States and England, Nik Gowing argues that television does frequently *set the agenda* for policymakers, by creating a sense of urgency whereby politicians must respond rapidly and seemingly effectively (Gowing 1994). Based on extensive empirical documentation and personal interviews, however, Gowing claims that television's influence on the actual specifics of the ensuing policy is quite limited and indirect. This fits our argument on the influence of the media on French policy toward Yugoslavia, both in the form of general pressures and following specific incidents. We believe that the media was essential in terms of compelling the policymakers to take a stand, reach a decision, and sometimes even change their policies on Bosnia. The actual content of the policy change, however, was more often influenced by our other two indicators, namely general public opinion and especially by the French intellectuals.

CONCLUSION

At the outset of the Yugoslav conflict, there was a disjuncture between the French state's historical ties of affinity with Yugoslavia and Serbia, on the one hand, and public opinion's outrage in response to the reports of Serb aggression, on the other. Over time, this gap between policy and public opinion closed. Throughout, public opinion remained fairly stable, while foreign policy changed slowly to line up with opinion.

We found that, at the beginning of the conflict, France's policy consisted of: (1) promotion of the continuation of a united Yugoslavia; (2) neutrality, rather than naming an aggressor; (3) negotiation through well-institutionalized international organizations (EU, WEU, and UN); (4) advocacy for humanitarian rather than military intervention and a reluctance to use force; and (5) a desire to have France at the forefront of all efforts to end to conflict. Over time, the first four of these elements eroded to give way to their opposites, mirroring the wishes of the majority of the French public, while the fifth element was consistent with public opinion since the beginning of the conflict.

We therefore return to our original question about the influence of public opinion on foreign policy. In terms of the role that public opinion plays, we suppose that much of the time, it is *not* one of the main determinants of policy. Foreign policy is more likely to shift with changes in elected and appointed officials, or with changes in the larger international context. In the case of French foreign policy in the former Yugoslavia, however, while these two factors were certainly important, public opinion appears to have been especially influential, by means of its general pressure over time, along with intense pressure following specific mediatized incidents. Whether or not this finding signals a new era of French foreign policymaking in which public opinion plays an increasingly important and autonomous role remains an open question. In any case, the findings of our case study show that the combined forces of public opinion polls, the intellectuals, and the media did significantly influence the direction and content of French foreign policy on intervention in Bosnia.

NOTES

1. See, for example, Alex Macleod and Stéphane Roussel, 1996, *Interêt National et Responsabilités Internationales: Six Etats Face au conflit en Ex-Yougoslavie*, 38, who divide French policy toward the Yugoslav conflict into three phases corresponding to precohabitation, cohabitation, and the change of president in 1995.

2. Some observers have also noted that France was interested in keeping Yugoslavia together because of its penchant for central state control. See, for example, *Unfinished Peace: Report of the International Commission on the Balkans*, 1996, 61.

3. See Beverly Crawford, "Explaining defection from international cooperation: Germany's unilateral recognition of Croatia," *World Politics* 48, no. 4 (July 1996).

4. See, for example, David Owen's *Balkan Odyssey* (1995) on this point.

5. Interview in *Frankfurter Allgemeine Zeitung*, November 29, 1991.

6. See the French Ministry of Defense document, "Nombres de militaires français dans les conflits," October 24, 1996.

7. In March of 1993, the French General Morillon became a "voluntary prisoner" in the besieged town of Srebrenica (see his *Croire et Oser*, Paris, 1993). His action was in protest against the French government's policy toward Bosnia, but did not illicit any dramatic shifts in French policy. In 1993 reports of Muslims fighting Muslims, and Croat-Muslim fighting, coupled with Serb, Muslim, and Croat refusals to sign peace agreements, complicated policymaking. The apparent response of the French government was to refrain from making changes in its policy.

8. According to Védrine, foreign policy was always mutually agreed upon between Mitterrand, Balladur, and Juppé. See Védrine, *op. cit.*, 648–49, 651, 661.

9. For example, as Balladur stated in one address: "The effort led since April 1993 has consisted of better organizing our military engagement, bringing the international community to a higher degree of coherence in its political action, namely affirming what it really wants." See Balladur, *Deux ans à Matignon*.

10. The contact group, made up of France, the United States, Russia, Britain, and Germany, was formally established on April 24, 1994.

11. The United States, however, did end enforcement of the sea ban in October, and in January 1995, the U.S. Congress voted to lift the arms embargo, which was later vetoed by Clinton.

12. See George Ross, "Chirac and France: Prisoners of the Past?," *Current History* 96 (March 1997): 100, and Ronald Tiersky, "Mitterrand's Legacies" *Foreign Affairs* (January/February 1995): 116; also see Thierry Tardy, "Le president Chirac et la Bosnie-Herzegovine: les limites d'une politique," *Relations internationales et stratégiques* 25 (1997), and Dominique Moïsi, "De Mitterrand à Chirac," *Politique Etrangère* 4 (1995–1996).

13. These documents are published in *Politique Etrangère de la France,* and most are also available on the internet site of the French Ministry of Foreign Affairs, at www.diplomatie.fr.

14. This quantitative listing is at best a rough and imperfect measurement, but it has the advantage of being able to show visually when these changes took place and how striking they were compared to the months before.

15. Since most of France is on vacation in August, this sudden flurry of statements is all the more extraordinary.

16. Unfortunately the French Ministry of Foreign Affairs did not include titles on its releases during the period from June 28, 1993 to October 18, 1993, which explains why the number of statements appears on Figure 1 during July, August, and September appears to be zero. Most likely the numbers would be between two and seven. In any case, although the quantitative standard of comparison is unfortunately lost for these three months, the important point here is that the *content* of French foreign policy toward Bosnia did not change significantly.

17. For a sophisticated discussion of the role of French public opinion in a broader context, see *L'Opinion, l'humanitaire et la guerre*, Samy Cohen, ed. (Paris: FED, 1996), especially the chapter "Ni bellicistes, ni pacifistes: les Français et l'intervention militaire extérieure," by Samy Cohen, with Natalie La Balme and Patrick Bruneteaux, 13–45. Also see Natalie La Balme, "L'influence de l'opinion publique dans la gestion des crises," in *Mitterrand et la Sortie de la Guerre Froide*, Samy Cohen, ed. (Paris: Presses Universitaires de France, 1998); and Samy Cohen, "Diplomatie et democratie," *Le Debat* (janvier-fevrier 1996).

18. For example, we should expect that a survey conducted three days after the Sarajevo marketplace bombing will produce different results than one carried out in the middle of one of the lengthy peace negotiation processes, at a point when it appeared that all sides were showing good will. Although it is nearly impossible to determine the effect of the timing of a survey, we should still take it into consideration, and exercise caution when generalizing from those results.

19. It should be obvious that variations in question wording can radically sway the results, often rendering comparisons across different surveys meaningless. On this point, see, for example, Richard Sobel, "Polling on Foreign Policy Crises: Creating a Standard Set of Questions," *The Public Perspective* (February/March 1996): 13. Sobel writes, "Generally low consistency and comparability within and between survey organizations often hinder the understanding of the complexities of events or trends over time."

20. The Appendix is organized in chronological order within each of the three categories (comparative, time-series, and individual). For easier reference, the title of each survey is indicated by the date and the institute that carried out the survey.

21. SIRPA, "Pertes Françaises en Ex-Yougoslavie," September 18, 1996.

22. For further support of the French public's support for intervention despite the risk of casualties, see Samy Cohen, with Natalie La Balme and Patrick Bruneteaux, "Ni bellicistes, ni pacifistes: les Français et l'intervention militaire extérieure," in Samy Cohen, ed., *L'Opinion, l'humanitaire et la guerre, op cit.*, 35–37.

23. The different positions may be broken down as follows: (1) *pro-Bosnian Muslim*, with the hope of saving the multicultural Bosnian dream (this position was epitomized by Bernard-Henri Lévy); (2) *pro-Croat*, with the view that Croatia belongs to the European civilization (Alain Finkielkraut); (3) *anti-Serb*, not based on a theoretical vision, but rather on the horror of Serbian war crimes (Jacques Julliard, editor of *Le Nouvel Observateur*); and (4) *anti-totalitarian* and *anti-fascist*, based more on humane and democratic principles than on an affinity for or against one particular side—although still predominantly anti-Serb (André Glucksmann, Pierre Hassner). This division is simplistic, as there were many different nuances within each position and also considerable overlap among the different positions. Despite these differences, what brought all of these positions together was their unity in opposition to a French policy that they saw as complacent, and specifically to Mitterrand's unwillingness to single out the aggressor and to enforce anti-Serb policies. It was this surprising unity that gave the intellectual opposition its strength.

24. For this reason, many policymakers have criticized the intellectuals (or at least the most visible and vocal ones) for being obsessed with media coverage. Védrine, for example, frequently refers to them as "les intellectuels médiatiques" (*op. cit.*, 637, among others). This critical view was echoed in several personal interviews with policymakers.

25. See "L'histoire secrète de la liste Sarajevo," *Globe-Hebdo*, no. 68 (May 25–31, 1994): 10–11.

26. Whenever the subject of the list came up in personal interviews with policymakers, they often pointed out quickly that the list was "ridiculous" and barely received any votes. After we reminded them of the details of the campaign and the excitement the list generated, however, the policymakers usually admitted that the list was actually very influential *during its time*.

27. For a good general account of the influence of the media, see Shanto Iyengar and Donald R. Kinder, *News That Matters* (Chicago: University of Chicago Press, 1987).

28. The three most respected and widely recognized French daily newspapers are *Le Monde* (on the center-left), *Le Figaro* (on the center-right), and *Liberation* (on the left).

29. Charaudeau, Patrice, Guy Lochard, and Jean-Claude Soulages. "La construction thématique du conflit en Ex-Yougoslavie par les journaux télévisés français (1990–1994)," *Mots* 47 (June 1996). Also see the other articles in this special issue devoted to media coverage of Yugoslavia.

30. Although their article only covered media coverage through the end of 1994, they have since been updating their research to cover up to 1996. We thank especially Jean-Claude Soulages, who kindly provided us with the 1995 and 1996 results.

31. Note that since their analysis in the published article stops with 1994, they could not cover the hostage taking in May 1995, which certainly produced an enormous jump in coverage, as shown in the Appendix.

32. See Elisabeth Dupoirier, "De la crise à la guerre du Golfe: un exemple de mobilisation de l'opinion," in Sofres, *L'Etat de l'opinion*, présenté par O. Duhamel et J. Jaffré. Paris, Ed. du Seuil, 1992.

33. Even Védrine writes about the "divorce" between general public and its political leaders (*op. cit.*, 612).

34. This was mentioned and confirmed in several personal interviews with French intellectuals.

35. See Rapport d'information n. 1950 de l'Assemblée Nationale, *La Politique d'intervention dans les conflits: éléments de doctrine pour la France*, 1995, 21 (cited by La Balme, *op. cit.*, 417).

36. In a *Good Morning America* interview on February 10, 1994, Zlatko Dizdarevic, the editor of the Sarajevo newspaper *Oslobodenje*, exclaimed "Why is there all this fuss in the West about one incident?" Indeed, for him and others in Bosnia, such deadly mortar bombings were nothing out of the "ordinary" that had grown accustomed to. The answer to Dizdarevic's question is that the reason for the fuss, in addition to the fact that this one bombing was one of the deadliest, was because the television cameras were there, instantly transmitting the gory details of it all back to their publics at home. Cited by Nik Gowing, "Real-Time Television Coverage of Armed Conflicts and Diplomatic Crises: Does it Pressure or Distort Foreign Policy Decisions," John F. Kennedy School of Government, Working Paper 94–1 (1994), 35.

37. Although several stations hesitated at first to show these images, which were actually filmed and given to them by Bosnian Serb television, the incident very quickly monopolized the news coverage for over a week. For an excellent report on how the hostage crisis came about, see Mark Danner, "Bosnia: Breaking the Machine," in the *New York Review of Books*, February 19, 1998. Note that there had been two previous hostage crises, but neither of them had this kind of television coverage, and hence did not elicit a dramatic and public French reaction.

38. Please note that since this chart has a double axis, with "Number of French Policy Statements" on the left axis (ranging from 0 to 30) and "Average Number of TF1 and A2 TV News Stories" on the right axis (ranging from 0 to 90), the graphics represented in Figure 3 should be interpreted carefully. The jumps and drops are not directly comparable in terms of actual numbers of stories, but rather in terms of the proportional increase and decrease within each of the two categories.

39. Moreover, there is some degree of intercorrelation between these two categories, since some television interviews given by leading French policymakers (e.g., president, minister of foreign affairs) are counted for both. However, as the figure makes evident, on occasion there are still significant differences in terms of the amount of attention the Yugoslav issue was given in the Foreign Ministry or in the television media.

5

Russian Decision-Making Regarding Bosnia: Indifferent Public and Feuding Elites

Eric Shiraev and Deone Terrio

"To be honest, when I was working on this problem the main thing I was trying to prevent was a national humiliation for Russia."

—Deputy Foreign Minister Vitaly Churkin on the Bosnia war
Literaturnaya gazeta no. 11 (March 16, 1994), 14

On a typical chilly October morning in 1991, one of the major Soviet daily newspapers, *Izvestia*, appeared in the news kiosks with an interview given by Andrei Kozyrev, the energetic young man who had been named Russia's foreign minister less than a year earlier (*Izvestia*, October 2, 1991, 3). In response to a question about Russia's future relationship with the West, and the United States in particular, Kozyrev predicted a strong, lasting alliance. He remarked that Russia would compete with the United States only if Russia's state interests were at stake, and discounted that struggle would re-emerge in arenas not vital to Russia's security. He said, for example, that since Russia had its own oil in Siberia, Moscow would not question U.S. actions in the Persian Gulf.

Of course, Kozyrev's confidence that the future would be characterized by stable, friendly relations between Russia and major Western powers—including the United States—was neither uncommon nor unreasonable in late 1991. The Cold War was rapidly drawing to a close and Russia's severe domestic problems made having peaceful relations with the West and the attendant opportunities to obtain aid highly desirable. As it turned out, however, support for the Yeltsin administration's Western-oriented policies was not unequivocal among Russian political elites. Moreover, support for such policies waned during the 1990s, even at the government level. A key turning point was reached in December 1995, when elections to the State Duma resulted in a large majority of seats going to opponents to "soft" foreign policies, including Russia's course in Bosnia.

Bowing to pressure from opposition legislators, Yeltsin finally removed Kozyrev and replaced him with Evgeny Primakov—a move cheered by the opposition. Kozyrev's fall signaled a new age in Russian foreign policy, which began to be shaped primarily by elite power struggles and the search for a new Russia's post-Cold War identity, and which involved a turn away from a "euphoric" foreign policy period of the early 1990s (Shiraev and Zubok 2000).

It is important to note that, as the situation above evolved, public opinion failed to become an important factor shaping foreign policy, despite Russia's struggle to develop democracy. We will demonstrate this argument at length below in relation to Russia's policy in Bosnia by showing how Russians felt about the situation in Bosnia, and then contrasting that with how elite decisions were made regarding Russia's role in Bosnia. First, we will begin with a brief summary of the context for Russian policymaking regarding Bosnia in 1991–1996.

POLICYMAKING CONTEXT

When the first reports of conflict started to flow from the former Yugoslavia in 1991, Russia was just breaking away from the U.S.S.R. and beginning to establish itself as an independent state. The period from 1991 to 1996, covering the time from the breakup of the U.S.S.R. to the first presidential elections in independent Russia, marked a time of extreme social and political turbulence. Faced with formidable problems on the domestic front, it is no surprise that Russia's leaders were preoccupied during this time with settling affairs at home. The problems of dismantling the command economy and stabilizing its new market structure were daunting enough. In addition, Russia had to be remade politically in every sense: as a state, as a nation, as a federation, as a strong and legitimate government, as well as a democracy. A primary element of political restructuring was the search for a new ideology. Elites had to find a foundation on which to rebuild their relationship with an emergent civil society—one vocal and diverse in its interests, unpracticed at democracy, and contending with privation, lawlessness, and a general sense of insecurity. Political restructuring was further complicated by the fact that democratization entailed the strengthening of opposition groups as well as criminal elements: property and power were changing hands in Russia, thus encouraging various groups to compete for emerging political and economic opportunities (Glad and Shiraev 1999).

The difficulty of Russia's domestic political problems in the post-Soviet age cannot be overstated. In the parlance of a famous long-term study of political development, Russian elites confronted the five "crises" of political development all over again, and all at once.[1] The severity of Russia's domestic political turmoil was highlighted in several instances, including the constitutional crisis of 1992–1993, Yeltsin's use of military force to disband the Supreme Soviet in September-October 1993, opposition victories in the legislative elections of 1993 and 1995, and the war in Chechnya—which officially began in December 1994 but had actually started months prior.

At the same time as Russia's leaders faced domestic problems of crisis proportions, however, they also faced gargantuan tasks in the international arena. In essence, Russia had to be remade as a world actor in a new, post-Cold War world, and forging consensus on a new foreign policy would be difficult. Not only was the domestic political context highly contentious, but also post-Soviet Russia was greatly weakened economically and militarily. Its leaders had to contend with the fact that their country was no longer one of the world's two superpowers. Also, while there were no immediate threats to Russia's security from the outside, and improved opportunities existed for obtaining Western aid, Russia's leaders were painfully anxious to avoid being treated as inferior. Specific international problems, such as the conflict in Bosnia and NATO's expansion, provided arenas for working out Russia's new international identity and foreign policy.

A further aspect of Russia's international problems was that the workshop of foreign policymaking itself had to be rebuilt. In the U.S.S.R., policymaking had been the unquestioned purview of Communist Party elites—Politburo members in particular—who had exercised decisive sway, especially over policy related to security.[2] *Perestroika* marked the beginning of serious change in Soviet foreign policymaking (Dobrynin 1996). But most of the restructuring came after Russia gained independence in 1991. Institutional reforms required that a new set of policymakers be designated and their relative powers decided. Also, in accordance with Russia's democratic aspirations, new ground rules had to be set up on how public opinion on international issues would be taken into account in foreign policy.

While the new constitution of December 1993 institutionalized the reform of foreign policymaking institutions, the practical sorting out of new arrangements continued throughout the 1990s into the new century. As this process evolved, the number of actors involved in foreign policymaking proliferated, and relations among the various elements became very contentious (Malcolm 1995, 26–28). This can be seen, in part, as a natural result of Russia's initial steps toward democratization, which transferred power over policy from party elites to representative government institutions. However, the expansion of the foreign policymaking arena and sharp struggles among politicians have also been due partially to *resistance* toward democratizing policymaking—specifically, to the president's efforts to keep decisive control over policy. In essence, Yeltsin deliberately enlarged the number of institutions involved in foreign policymaking in an effort to dilute the power of any one person or institution that might rival his own, and he played actors off each other for the same reason. Thus, while power over foreign policy decisions was more dispersed in 1991–1996 than it had been earlier, it remained concentrated in the executive branch. The dominance of the president in foreign policymaking was also formalized in the 1993 constitution.[3]

However, while the president hung on to the most power to decide foreign policy in Russia through 1996, he found it increasingly difficult to do so without taking into account the wishes of critics, especially opposition legislators. While the public at large did not figure prominently in causing the president to modify his policies (as will be shown below), legislators did gain increasing influence in foreign policymaking in the period 1991–1996 (Sherman 1995). While legislators as a whole kept a low profile in international affairs in the early post-Soviet period, the legislature started to assert itself more in 1992–1993, when members of the Supreme Soviet passed several resolutions challenging Yeltsin's foreign policy, including in countries such as Yugoslavia and some former Soviet republics. Yeltsin's obvious vexation with criticism from the legislature, culminating in his use of military force to disband the Supreme Soviet in the fall of 1993, did not daunt its successors. In fact, as opposition parties proved victorious in both the 1993 and 1995 legislative elections (which delivered the Liberal Democratic Party of Russia and the Communist Party of the Russian Federation the most seats, respectively), the legislature's voice in foreign policy matters grew stronger. Thus, the legislature (renamed the Federal Assembly in December 1993), and especially its lower house, the State Duma, became an arena in which Yeltsin's foreign as well as domestic policies were sharply criticized. In response to rising criticism, and for deeper reasons to be discussed more fully below, Yeltsin and his executive foreign policy team began gradually to reshape certain aspects of policy in limited ways (including in Bosnia) and even to change foreign policy personnel along lines more agreeable to opposition legislators. But, even as the Duma came to have more influence, it still remained an institution with less influence over foreign policy than the executive.

Thus, within the executive branch, Yeltsin and a shifting array of key appointees kept reins over the main directions of foreign policy in the 1990s. Within this circle of decision makers, Yeltsin appeared to have decisive say most of the time. As noted earlier, part of his strategy for keeping control involved proliferating the number of actors involved and causing them to compete for influence. Thus, for example, his first appointee as foreign minister, Andrei Kozyrev, was forced to compete initially for influence with Gennadi Burbulis, who was Yeltsin's hand-picked state secretary for the first year of his tenure. Burbulis, in fact, appeared to play the leading role in coordination of foreign policy matters up until the middle of 1992, not Kozyrev. Later on, two executive bodies were created to also help shape foreign policy: the Security Council and the Inter-Departmental Foreign Policy Commission. Both of these bodies clashed with the Foreign Ministry (which was, in fact, shrinking and weakening, with many experts leaving due to low salaries and declined professional opportunities) and failed to become effective coordinating institutions. In 1993, Prime Minister Viktor Chernomyrdin and Defense Minister Pavel Grachev began to play more important roles in international matters, especially in matters concerning other countries of the former U.S.S.R.—the so-called "near abroad." Thus, Kozyrev and the Foreign Ministry were kept off-guard, increasingly challenged both from within the executive branch as well as from outside it, including from within the Duma. Kozyrev, however, managed to keep Yeltsin's favor, and thus his post as foreign minister, until January 5, 1996, when his resignation was tendered. The fact that no lieutenant was allowed to amass strong sway helped Yeltsin maintain power over foreign policymaking. However, as evidenced by how Kozyrev was so strongly challenged and finally dismissed in the end, it also was true that Yeltsin's controls were whittled over time.

RUSSIAN POLICY IN FORMER YUGOSLAVIA

Before undertaking an examination of the links between public opinion and Russian policy steps in Bosnia, we will provide a brief description of the policy itself.[4] The Bosnian crisis raised one of the first serious challenges to Russia's mostly friendly relations with the West in the early 1990s. As noted previously, domestic goals of reconstruction and stabilization had pushed Moscow to end the Cold War, avoid tensions with the West, and seek extensive economic and other aid from Western sources. Domestic political considerations also dictated, however, that Moscow accept nothing less than equal status with major Western powers. Tensions obviously existed between these goals. It was difficult to demand treatment as an equal and to have a hand out for assistance at the same time. Yet, as long as no serious disagreements cropped up over how to handle international problems, and as long as Russia showed itself a stable and cooperative partner and received respect from its benefactors, it was believed that a balance between the goals could be precariously maintained. At a press conference in Paris on April 17, 1991, Yeltsin exuded early post-Cold War confidence that Russia could salvage its role as a great world power despite its relative weakness. Russia would "play a unique role as a bridge between Europe and Asia and . . . contribute towards extending the area of European cooperation, particularly in the economic field, from the Atlantic to the Pacific," he predicted (Sakwa 1996, 294).

The strength of Russia's desire to play a central role internationally was evidenced in the eagerness with which Kremlin leaders became active in UN efforts to broker peace in Bosnia (as well as elsewhere, such as in Haiti and Cambodia). Despite acute problems at home, Russian officials got involved in the Bosnian crisis right at the start, initially adopting a moderately liberal policy in the region. Playing mainly a "good citizen" role, Russia joined the Coordinating Committee of the London Conference on the Former Yugoslavia (Goble 1996; Churkin 1992). The first battalion of Russian peacekeeping forces was sent to the former Yugoslavia in March 1992. In 1993, Russia became a member of the five-country contact group on the crisis.

Through the end of 1993, Russian elites generally cooperated with the Western powers, following the UN policy in Bosnia despite mounting criticisms in the Supreme Soviet and elsewhere that, in doing so, Moscow was "betraying" Russia's traditional ally, Serbia. Ignoring such criticisms, Yeltsin's government refused to use Russia's veto power to block Security Council resolutions aimed at putting increasing pressure on Serbian President Milosevic. While efforts were made to limit sanctions against Serbia and to come up with a peace plan acceptable to the Serbs, the government ultimately supported all key UN resolutions imposing sanctions, including the 1992 imposition of economic sanctions on Belgrade. As well, Russian officials voted for Resolution No. 770 in August 1992, which allowed UN countries to use force to provide humanitarian help to Sarajevo (*Izvestia,* August 14, 1992, 5). On June 4, 1993, Russia also voted for UN Security Council Resolution No. 836, which declared Gorazde a "safe area." This resolution, adopted unanimously by the Security Council, authorized "all necessary measures, through the use of air power, in and around the safe areas" in the Republic of Bosnia and Hercegovina to support UNPROFOR in the former Yugoslavia (*The Economist,* "Pax Russiana?," February 19, 1994, 57).

Russia's initial liberal policy regarding Bosnia did reap some rewards. At first, Russian officials were treated fairly equally in terms of being included in top-level decision making. Moscow also gleaned some international prestige from playing a positive role in the crisis, most visibly in February 1994 when Vitaly Churkin, special Russian envoy to the Balkans, secured Serb agreement to a cease-fire in Sarajevo. But the approach of essentially following UN policy drew increasingly sharp opposition from the legislature, as earlier noted. Attacks in the legislature first became strong in the summer of 1992, when legislators accused Yeltsin and Kozyrev of maintaining an anti-Serb course. The Supreme Soviet passed a resolution on June 26, 1992 directing the government to work for at least an easing of sanctions against the Serbs if a moratorium in the region appeared out of reach.

As pressures for policy change mounted in the legislature, especially after the 1993 and 1995 elections, Russia began to move away from a policy that was closely aligned with the other Western powers to one that was more assertive in supporting Serbian interests, although still only in limited ways. Prominent examples include when Moscow sharply protested NATO air strikes against the Serbs in the spring of 1994. At the same time, Russian leaders still took pains to avoid endangering Russia's relations with the West, especially its friendly relationship with the Clinton administration, and continued to cooperate with other major powers to end the conflict (Pushkov 1994). This will be further discussed below.

Overall, in 1994–1996, under the pressure of the opposition, Russian official policy toward Bosnia was modified and was supposed to become more balanced between cooperating with the West and supporting the Serbs. Ultimately, Moscow's revised policy in Bosnia failed to pan out, however. Disappointment and embarrassment came to overshadow occasional successes. For example, Moscow was unable to control Serbia's leaders in Bosnia when the Serbs continued shelling Muslim positions after the February 1994 ceasefire brokered by the Russians. Most importantly, Russian government officials were faced with the fact that, despite cooperating with Western partners, they were not viewed as equal. This reality struck home especially hard in April 1994, when NATO airstrikes were launched against the Serbs near Gorazde without Russia's prior notification. The deliberate exclusion of Russia mortified the Yeltsin government (Bowker 1995). Moscow's embarrassment grew after the Serbs suffered a fatal setback in Kraina. The Croats and Bosnian Muslims were accused of using weapons in the attack that were obtained illegally, in circumvention of the international veto, and Russian leaders at home were blamed for having done nothing to prevent or punish these anti-Serbian actions (Demurin 1995).

Growing distrust of the West reached a new height in early September 1995 when NATO again conducted a bombing campaign without Russia's prior notification. The campaign lasted two weeks and included the use of Tomahawk-guided missiles in the vicinity of the town, Banja Luka. Then the UN Secretariat's approval of a secret memo relinquishing authority over the use of air power in Bosnia to NATO, which also occurred without consulting with all permanent members, further incensed Russia. This move was widely interpreted in Russia as a signal that NATO and the United States had taken over operations in Bosnia. Vladimir Lukin, chairman of the Duma's International Committee, later remarked on several occasions how the incident illustrated that some Security Council members were being treated as first-class and others as second-class.

The later years of Russia's involvement in Bosnia were not wholly without success, however. During the Russian defense minister's visit to the United States in the fall of 1995, it was announced that Moscow and Washington would each send several thousand servicemen to Bosnia to create a "special multinational operational contingent" that would not be part of NATO forces. The contingent was to be commanded by an American, General George Joulwan, the Supreme Allied Commander of Europe, and his deputy would be Colonel General Leonty Shevtsov, deputy director of the General Staff's Chief Operations Administration (*Kommersant-Daily*, October 31, 1995). Moscow's frustration was mitigated to some degree by this late agreement, which was touted as a significant political victory for the government.

Russian Peacekeeping Forces

Russia began to form its first battalion of peacekeeping forces in early 1992, which consisted of nine hundred volunteer paratroopers serving on a contract basis. The dispatch of this contingent to the former Yugoslavia was approved by the Russian Supreme Soviet on March 6, 1992. In June 1992, the UN asked Russia to send a battalion of four hundred men. The Supreme Soviet approved Yeltsin's request on this score on July 17, 1992.

Through early 1994, however, the Russian government maintained a cautious profile in the region, confining its contingent to relatively safe areas of Croatia, and steadfastly refusing to put Russian soldiers at significant risk. Media reports suggested at one point that Russian officials had even refused to follow an order from UN troop commanders directing them to send four hundred men from the Russian battalion in eastern Croatia—stationed near Vukovar—to the Bosnian capital, a significantly more dangerous area (Felgenauer 1994).

A shift in Russian policy toward larger commitments became evident in early 1994. In January, the detached Russian infantry battalion in Bosnia was strengthened to 1,200 men.

In February, the Council of the Federation (the upper chamber of the Federal Assembly) agreed to Yeltsin's proposal to send an additional three hundred Russian servicemen to the former Yugoslavia to participate in UN peacekeeping forces (Volkov 1994). By that time, Russian military contingents were performing missions with UN peacekeeping forces in Bosnia, as well as with the Commonwealth of Independent States' collective peacekeeping forces in Tajikistan, the Dnestr region, and South Ossetia.

RUSSIAN PUBLIC OPINION
ABOUT THE BOSNIA CONFLICT

Before looking at evidence about Russian public opinion regarding the conflict in Bosnia, it is important to emphasize that we found relatively little direct survey evidence on this topic. The scarcity of surveys was especially surprising because survey methods have been the favored research methodology used by social scientists in Russia in the late Soviet and post-Soviet periods. Overwhelmingly, however, surveys have tended to focus on attitudes related to domestic affairs. Moreover, surveys which explored Russian attitudes toward international affairs focused mainly on questions related to Russia's relations with neighboring states and the NATO expansion. As we will argue further below, we believe that the paucity of survey data is due to the fact that most Russians had low interest in the conflict, and researchers therefore decided not to waste time or effort conducting expensive surveys in this area.

Nevertheless, the survey data that exist on Russian public opinion about Bosnia is certainly valuable in helping us to see what average Russians thought (or did not think) about the situation at particular points in time. Furthermore, we can look to surveys that addressed other subjects, which shed light indirectly on attitudes about Bosnia. Before turning to this evidence, however, we will first try to address the question: What did ordinary Russians know about Bosnia? How much information was available to ordinary Russians about the situation in Bosnia, and what were its main sources?

People in Russia who wanted to know about events in Bosnia had plenty of information available to them. All media outlets carried news about events in Bosnia at various points, with most of the news about the situation coming through newspaper accounts. Two of the major newspapers, *Izvestia* and *Pravda* (the latter representing the views of Russian Communists) published reports on the conflict in the former Yugoslavia almost daily during particular periods. Other newspapers, too, addressed the situation regularly, offering continuing news coverage and analyses from a variety of perspectives. Television coverage, in contrast, tended to be lighter and more slanted toward supporting government policy, as the government itself or pro-government magnates at that time owned most major television stations.

In light of these facts, the low level of public interest about the Bosnia conflict cannot be attributed to lack of information. However, it is true that the most prominent information sources quoted and referred to in the media were political elites. In effect, this meant that ordinary citizens were informed about events in Bosnia mainly by being told how various elites thought about it. Even though there were sharply divergent elite views presented, coverage was still limited and slanted in this respect, and perhaps helped to convey the impression that the situation in Bosnia was an affair mainly of concern to elites. Moreover, many major newspapers, including *Argumenty i Facty*, the most popular weekly analytical newspaper, carried only minimal coverage of the subject, presumably on judgment that the topic itself was not a highly popular one. *Argumenty i Facty*, for example, according to our analysis, published only three analytical articles about the war during the five-year period from 1991 to 1996.

However, most Russians were not very interested in the information on Bosnia. In fact, it appears that Russians were generally not highly interested in most political affairs in the 1990s. While domestic politics held high public appeal in the late Soviet period when the first elections took place (1989–1990), interest sharply declined thereafter.[5] Many surveys conducted in 1986–1996 demonstrate this apolitical trend in public opinion (Glad and Shiraev 1999). Nuzgar Betaneli, director of the Institute of Sociology of Parliamentarism, estimated that only 10 to 12 percent of the Russian population fell into the politically active category (*Ogonyok*, #12,

March 1998, 6). Apparently, Russians continued to feel politically apathetic even after their first taste of political freedom in the post-Soviet age.[6]

Moreover, it appears that Russians ascribed even less importance to foreign policy issues. As Viktor Kremenyuk, deputy director of the Institute for the Study of the United States. and Canada, commented, "The average Russian thinks about his salary and prices. He's not in position to think about foreign policy" (MacWilliam, *The Moscow Times*, February 8, 1997). A survey conducted by the All-Russia Center for the Study of Public Opinion found that 72 percent of respondents attached priority to domestic problems, while only 18 percent said priority should be given to international problems. Further support comes from a New Russia Barometer III survey conducted in 1994, which asked respondents if they felt threatened by any of eight countries listed. The survey yielded a high percentage of "don't know" responses. Stephen White and other authors of the book *How Russia Votes* interpreted these results to indicate that "a large number of Russians take little or no interest in what other countries are doing" (White et al. 1997, 56). Indicative of this general disinterest in foreign affairs, many surveys showed that even the issue of NATO expansion—an issue that might be expected to have more emotional impact on Russians than the Balkan conflict due to its greater security implications— did not provoke strong reaction at the street level. In fact, despite the dire predictions put forth by public officials about the consequences of expansion and their loud protests, most Russians did not voice much anger or frustration over the prospect of NATO's enlargement.[7] In sum, this evidence showing that Russians had low interest in politics, and in international affairs in particular, suggests that they probably also had little concern for events in Bosnia.

Turning now to direct survey evidence on attitudes in Russia about Bosnia, we will start with a survey that focused on Russian attitudes about Bosnia that was conducted in early 1994 by the Centre for International Sociological Research. The timing corresponded with when the first threats of NATO air strikes against Bosnian Serbs were made. At that time, 77 percent of those surveyed said they opposed the threatened air strikes, and more than two thirds agreed with Vladimir Zhirinovsky's (leader of the Liberal Democratic Party of Russia) remarks that the strikes, if launched, would amount to an attack on Russia (the *Daily Telegraph*, February 18, 1994, 14).

In weighing the significance of this data, it is important to recognize that the survey was administered after threats were levied without Russia's agreement, and before the actual air strikes took place. This was obviously a crucial juncture in the conflict. It is not difficult to fathom why many Russians would react strongly against the threatened strikes, as did Zhirinovsky, leader of the ultra-nationalist Liberal Democratic Party of Russia. It is also worth considering, however, that those who said they shared Zhirinovsky's desire to support the Serbs may have given a more moderate response if the attacks had already taken place and Russia was faced with an immediate need to take risks to support Serbia. Thus, the strong pro-Serb reaction may have been more an emotional than a rational response, one tied to the timing of the survey more than deeply held convictions with regard to the Serbs.

Moreover, the 77 percent of respondents who said they opposed the air strikes probably included many Russians who simply desired to avoid war, and were not necessarily motivated by pro-Serb sentiments. The strong preference among average Russians to avoid war was indicated by another survey conducted immediately following the invasion of Chechnya by Russian troops. According to analysts, Russian citizens who opposed the invasion of Chechnya outnumbered those who supported it by ten to four (the *Washington Post*, December 17, 1994). While the situations in Chechnya and Bosnia were quite different, it can be surmised that most Russians wanted their government to avoid bloody conflict in both areas.

Another poll conducted in October 1992 by Romir (a Russian polling firm) suggests an important caveat to this generalization, however. According to this survey, 46 percent of respondents said Russia should send troops to the "near abroad" if the security of Russians was at stake. Another 40 percent said the Russian government should not take military action even in this case, and 14 percent expressed no opinion on the subject (the *National Journal*; Section: Opinion Outlook; Views on National Security; Vol. 25, No. 11, 654; March 13, 1993). This survey may indicate that, while many Russians had a strong general desire to avoid war, they perhaps would have been more inclined to support military action if the lives of ethnic Russians were at stake. Of course, as no Russians were directly threatened in the Bosnia conflict, this evidence offers no support to the notion that Russians would be willing to take military risks for Serbs.

Yet another survey, one conducted by the All-Russian Centre for Public Opinion Research in mid-1995, offers perspective on Russian opinions on Bosnia (Interfax news agency, Moscow, in English, 1430 gmt, September 21, 1995). This survey canvassed opinions of 1,527 respondents, and included many direct questions about the Bosnia situation. One set of questions asked respondents about which side they supported in the conflict. Nearly one third of the group (28 percent) said they did not support any side. Twenty-one percent of the respondents indicated sympathy for the Serbs. Only 2 percent indicated sympathy for Croats and Muslims.

It is important to emphasize that 28 percent (almost one third) of the respondents had no particular sympathies in the conflict at all. These respondents appear to have been completely uninterested in the conflict, for even the most casually interested person would presumably choose at least one party for which he or she held sympathy.[8] Lack of sympathy may have been the product of being uninformed or it may have resulted from being informed about the conflict but not being engaged enough to care strongly about any party. The latter case seems most likely as information about

Bosnia was widely available (as already shown), and the rate of illiteracy in Russia is very low. This generally supports our hypothesis that many Russians did not care strongly about the conflict.

It is also noteworthy that only roughly one fifth (21 percent) of the respondents professed sympathy for the Serbs in 1995. This figure sharply conflicts with the 1994 survey, which showed pro-Serb feelings to be strong in February 1994, and fits with our suggestion that the timing of the 1994 survey played into the strength of expressed pro-Serb sentiments at that point. The evidence also weakens claims by opposition elites (to be reviewed later) that the Russian populace shared their strong pro-Serb sympathies.

The 1995 survey also revealed preferences about the form the Russian government's involvement in the conflict should take. Thirty percent of respondents said they favored Russia's providing humanitarian and economic assistance. Eight percent said Russia should act jointly with the UN and NATO. Four percent indicated they supported the economic blockade imposed on the Bosnian Serbs. Only 6 percent said they wanted Russia to supply the Bosnian Serbs with armaments. These results are suggestive in several important ways. First, the number of respondents who felt most strongly allied with the Serbs—indicated in the 6 percent who wanted to give arms to Bosnian Serbs—was quite small. Recalling that 21 percent of those surveyed indicated general sympathy with the Bosnian Serbs in the conflict, we can assume that the remaining 15 percent who did not support arming them favored giving only more moderate forms of practical support. On the other extreme, we see that almost an equal percentage of respondents (4 percent) supported the economic embargo against the Serbs. This suggests that the number of Russians who felt most strongly about the conflict in either a pro- or anti-Serb fashion were in a small minority: under 10 percent of the survey population combined. In addition, neither side was predominant: the roughly equal proportion of pro- and anti-Serbian attitudes suggests their effects canceled each other out. This evidence again supports our general hypotheses that few Russians cared deeply about the conflict, and that most Russians who harbored pro-Serb sentiments could not be considered hard-core Serb sympathizers.

Secondly, of those who supported Russia's involvement in the conflict, most (30 percent of the total) favored only supplying humanitarian and economic aid. This figure is telling as well. These two types of assistance, which may include but do not necessarily imply peacekeeping missions, constitute relatively low-level, low-risk forms of involvement. Only the 6 percent who favored supplying arms to the Serbs seemed to want to make a deeper sort of commitment. The survey results failed to indicate, for example, that anyone supported putting Russian commanders in the region to give direct military advice or committing Russian troops.[9] Thus, again we see that, even among those who cared about Bosnia in one way or other, there were few who cared very strongly about the conflict.

Furthermore, the questions about forms of Russian involvement in Bosnia revealed that only 8 percent of respondents felt Russia's involvement in the conflict should be in conjunction with UN and NATO forces. Another 4 percent supported the arms embargo against the Bosnian Serbs. This combined group (12 percent of respondents) clearly manifested attitudes of interest in the conflict, support for Russia's involvement in the region, as well as pro-Western attitudes. Again, the small size of this group is meaningful. Only a small minority of people believed Russia should side with Western forces in the conflict. Presumably, most Russians who favored Russia's involvement in the conflict preferred that Moscow offer assistance at least partly independently, not fully in conjunction with the UN or NATO. For example, of the respondents who preferred giving humanitarian and economic assistance (30 percent), only 8 percent favored doing so in conjunction with the UN and NATO. Thus it would appear that most of the relatively few Russians who supported Russia's involvement in Bosnia were neither strongly pro-Serb nor strongly pro-Western, and a strong tendency existed to favor Russia's independence in determining its role in the conflict.

Finally, the majority of respondents (52 percent) failed to indicate any preferred form for Russia's involvement in the conflict. This suggests they either did not care whether Russia got involved or they had no strong opinion about the form of Russia's involvement. Both possibilities reinforce our hypothesis that most Russians were apathetic about the conflict.

In sum, what profile of Russian attitudes about Bosnia can be gleaned from the survey data reviewed above? First, most Russians were disinterested in the situation in Bosnia, as evidenced in how most survey respondents did not express strong opinions about the conflict, and those who voiced strong opinions were in small minorities. This apathy fits with the apparent fact that most Russians were focused on domestic versus international concerns generally. Second, only a minority of Russians harbored either pro-Serb or anti-Serb sentiments, and the intensity of such sentiments was limited. Third, among those who supported Russia's involvement in the conflict, most favored Russia acting in ways independent of the Western powers. In other words, there was a feeling that Russia should avoid subordinating itself to the West in its activities in the region.

General Tendencies of Russian Public Opinion

We turn now to looking at certain features of Russian political culture and mass psychology that presumably influence public opinion generally in Russia and which may help us to understand attitudes toward the Bosnia conflict in particular. We will start with the emotional nature of Russian mass psychology, a trait posited by many observers and analysts over centuries. In this view, many Russians generally tend to be guided in their behavior by spontaneous, volatile emotions rather than by rational, dispassionate decisions based on strongly held, stable convictions. An explanation for this phenomenon offered in cognitive theory is that Russians typically do not organize their perceptions in strong mental gestalts to begin with. Gavriil Popov, renowned economist and mayor of Moscow from 1990 until his resignation in 1992, drew a connection between this trait and the meaning of surveys in Russia: "Polls are created by psychologists and sociologists of Anglo-Saxon, mainly west-European mentality. . . . Here in Russia, a poll reflects not a decision of a person but his mood" (Popov 1996). Andrei Kokoshin, deputy defense minister in the 1990s and prominent social scientist, likewise emphasized the precarious nature of Russian public opinion, suggesting that a Russian man does not program his life rationally, like a German, Anglo-Saxon, or French man does. Instead, he argued, Russians are spontaneous and, therefore, may not even have opinions on particular issues (Kokoshin 1996, 3). "Emotional" and "irrational" foundations of Russian voting behavior were also commonly touted as an explanation for the dramatic reversal of public opinion during the 1996 presidential elections, when support for incumbent candidate Boris Yeltsin climbed from single digits to almost 50 percent in the three-month period prior to the first round of elections in June.

What possible connections can be made between the generally emotional nature of Russian mass psychology and Russian opinion on the conflict in Bosnia? First, we can presume that the "caring" attitudes registered by some Russians (versus the disinterested attitudes) may have been only passing emotions, not strongly held convictions. This would fit with how the survey data revealed swings over time in people's "caring" sentiments about the situation in Bosnia, including attitudes about Serbia. A large shift in pro-Serbian sentiments, for example, was evident in comparing the 1994 survey, which showed many Russians had strong pro-Serb feelings at the point when NATO air strikes were first being threatened, to the 1995 survey, which showed that those emotions had substantially ebbed. Second, we can see that, generally, Russians were not strongly stirred emotionally by events in Bosnia, and were not even strongly attached emotionally to the plight of Serbs. As we saw, the 1995 survey found only small minorities of people had either very strong pro-Serb or anti-Serb feelings. The largest of the minority groups with sympathy toward any one party was pro-Serb, but this was a relatively small proportion—again, just 21 percent—by the 1995 survey. Third, one idea that did seem to strike a chord with those who supported Russia's involvement in the conflict was the notion that Moscow should not tolerate being subordinated to UN or NATO partners. This sentiment accords with traditional Russian suspicions of the West and also corresponds to the national-chauvinistic belief that Russia is a great power deserving of equal treatment with other great world powers (Shiraev and Zubok 2000).

A second characteristic of Russian mass psychology often noted by analysts is fatalism (Kokoshin 1996). Fatalism entails beliefs that all events are inevitable, determined by destiny. Such attitudes have particular significance for political psychology, as fatalism tends to engender political passivity. Political psychologists have argued that Russian despotism depended on people's fatalistic attitudes: many individuals accepted a subject or servant status and subordinated themselves to rulers at least partly out of the sense they could not do much to shape events anyway. General pessimism about the future may similarly stem from feelings of low confidence in the ability humans (both elites and commoners) have to control the future (Gozman and Edkind 1992).

Many analysts argue that these traditional attitudes became even more pronounced in the 1990s. As one leading Russian political psychologist put it, Russians felt like a dangerous and unpredictable "political darkness" descended upon them in the 1990s, and they acted like people who suddenly become lost in underground caves (Yuriev 1992, 31, 69). The prevalence of attitudes of fatalism, apathy, and pessimism in the 1990s is strikingly confirmed in a number of surveys addressing general social attitudes. For example, a 1992 survey revealed that more than half of the respondents thought it would be irresponsible to have children with the future so uncertain (survey by Sluzhba VP, *Argumenty i Facty*, #18, 1992). A survey taken in 1995 showed that respondents who were not satisfied with their lives outnumbered those who were satisfied by a ratio of eight to one (*Segodnia*, August 2, 1995). Another survey showed, remarkably, that only 13 percent of respondents looked to the future with optimism (Shlapentokh 1996).[10]

Russia's democratic changes might conceivably have fostered the rise of different political attitudes in the 1990s: greater interest in political affairs, and a growing sense of control and optimism about the future given increased capacity to have a say in political affairs. In fact, in the early years of democratization (1989–1990), there seemed to be greater possibility that people's attitudes would change in the ways suggested. Why, then, has the trend been toward increased fatalism, apathy, and pessimism in the 1990s? One possible explanation is that democratic advances have not ultimately changed the process of policy formation—which remained essentially an elite affair, not a process shaped strongly by public opinion. This seems true, for instance, in terms of how elites made decisions regarding conflict in Bosnia. If this is the case, it makes sense that people would revert to traditional attitudes, and to even be more disgruntled for the lack of significant change.

Another factor to consider is that distrust for elites appears to have risen in Russia in the 1990s. Thus, the number of Russians who took limited comfort in believing elites would do their best to try to protect them in a world that was essentially uncontrollable appears to have shrunk. Mistrust in government institutions, apparently just slowly declining in 1989–1990, accelerated in the mid-1990s (Wyman 1997). In 1994, only 4 percent of Russians surveyed in one poll fully supported the actions of the government, and 31 percent said they believed it should resign ("Monitoring obshchestvennogo mneniya," 6, 1994, 63). In another poll, about 65 percent of respondents said their attitude toward the existing government was worse than it had been in the former U.S.S.R. Only 6 percent said their attitude was better (Grunt et al. 1996). A set of surveys conducted in 1995 and 1996 also seems to confirm popular feelings that the government was untrustworthy. According to those surveys, the number of people who believed the country was moving in the right direction fell eleven points during a two-year period, reaching a low level of 19 percent in 1996 (*Index to International Public Opinion 1995–1996*, 567–85; *Index to International Public Opinion 1993–1994*, 612–23). Another survey in 1995 found respondents put their greatest trust in the Church (which received only a 33 percent approval rating) and the military (which got a 32 percent approval rating). Least trusted were heads of banks (6 percent), parties and movements (7 percent), and the upper chamber of the national legislature, the Council of the Federation (9 percent). President Yeltsin, the legislature as a whole, and the cabinet of ministers each received just a 12 percent approval rating (Williams 1996). Lastly, a poll conducted in July 1995 revealed that 60 percent of those surveyed favored a change of leaders on the grounds that they had exhausted their potential (Boris Grushin's Vox Populi service, *Izvestia*, October 13, 1995, 6).

Further indication of popular disappointment with elites comes from data which suggests that Russians in the phase of transition have suffered serious loss of political identity. In other words, since the end of Communist Party domination, most Russians have typically not strongly identified with any single political party or group. According to various surveys, no more than 5 to 10 percent of Russians consider themselves to be members of any political association or even supporters of any specific politician, either in government or in the opposition (Shlapentokh 1996). The rapid and broad proliferation of political parties and movements, exacerbated by the widespread sense of uncertainty attendant upon the loss of the Communist Party, has conceivably been highly discomforting to many ordinary Russians, who apparently were at a loss to find trustworthy representatives in any single party.

Feelings of lowered trust for elites and lost political identity could contribute to a growing sense of fatalism. This can also help explain most Russians' apparent indifference toward the Bosnia situation. If Russians distrust their government, it makes sense they would be abject, disillusioned, and apathetic about policy in a number of arenas. As well, it would make sense for distrustful citizens to be wary of their government cooperating too closely with former adversaries such as the United States. Still, it is highly ironic that Russians during the first years of the post-communist transition had greater formal means to influence politics (such as through the vote) but were showing strong fatalistic ideas (Shlapentokh and Shiraev 2002).

Probably the most important factor to consider when trying to understand why Russians have grown more fatalistic, apathetic, and pessimistic in the 1990s comes back to the psychology of a people under duress. The severity of Russia's problems in the phase of transition cannot be overstated. The overall political and economic situation in the country in the first half of the 1990s was highly unstable, accompanied by Yeltsin's progressing illnesses and as indicated in the rise of crime, violence, political assassinations, scandals involving public officials at the highest levels. Ethnic and regional conflicts such as in Chechnya, Moldova (the Dniestr region), Ossetia, Georgia and Abkhasia, Nagorno Karabakh, Tadzikistan, and Turkmenistan also contributed to instability. On a psychological level—in part, as a result of such objective factors—burnout, disappointment, and pessimism prevailed. In these circumstances, it is not surprising that isolationist tendencies and strong self-preoccupation among people could result. It is commonly observed that, as people feel increasingly helpless to control the world around them, they may turn "inward." Many analysts have noted the rise of selfish survival instincts among Russians in the 1990s, along with an associated spurning of social good. In the darkest analysis, Russians have become largely indifferent to public issues and social values, and have become so focused on their own survival that they are reluctant to make sacrifices for the public good (Shlapentokh 1996).

The arguments mentioned earlier help us to understand better why the attention of Russians was not focused on problems in the former Yugoslavia. It is perhaps "normal" that people's everyday problems overshadowed foreign policy issues, including the distant Balkan conflict. In the summarizing words of one analyst, external threats for Russians meant little compared to the "daily attack from around every corner" within the country (Kondrashov 1996, 6).

Opinions of "Concerned Minority"

Despite the fact that most Russians were either completely detached from the conflict in Bosnia or only slightly concerned about it, however, a small minority of Russians were still engaged by the conflict and expressed strong opinions about it. This "concerned minority" included political elites—both those who supported the Russian government's policy in Bosnia and those who opposed it from many different perspectives—as well as high-profile people outside the political elite: intellectuals (including foreign policy experts), newspaper editors and journalists, military elites, top-level Church officials, popular writers, and movie directors. Opinion leaders from these groups were informed about events in Bosnia, interested in the situation, and made their attitudes about it known through various channels including parliamentary and other public debates, television and newspaper interviews, printed commentary, and scholarly journals.[11] The mix of expressed opinions created a certain "policy climate" or a predominant set of attitudes concerning how the government should act regarding the Bosnia conflict (Clinton 1979). Below we will review the main viewpoints about Bosnia expressed by members of the "concerned minority," as well as show how the Russian government came to be increasingly influenced by this policy climate even as it retained essential policy control. First, we will provide a brief overview of the evolution of public debates about Russian foreign policy in general.

Public debate in Russia about what should be the nature and direction of Russian foreign policy began in the late Soviet period, as noted earlier. In the post-Soviet period, this debate became even more highly charged emotionally and marked by struggle. A painful process of soul-searching, nostalgic yearning for the past, and extreme vexation over Russia's weaknesses was evident. Apart from these shared emotions, acute struggles emerged over how to handle pressing problems such as military conflicts within Russia and the Commonwealth of Independent States, the NATO expansion, and the conflict in Bosnia. Conflict over practical matters was colored by internal political struggles as well as real differences of opinion.

In the debates, many competing visions of future Russian foreign policy emerged. In essence, they boiled down to two broad scenarios. On one hand, there was the view that Russia should play a mainly cooperative role in Europe, helping to eliminate the vestiges of the Cold War in tandem with Western partners. In this scenario, Russia could perhaps even become integrated with Europe. On the other hand, there was the conception that Russia should take an independent stance vis-à-vis the rest of Europe, fostering its national over international identity. Those who supported this vision included people who saw Russia's future as tied primarily to Asia, not Europe. Others who subscribed to this view were motivated more by national-chauvinist sentiments, imperial interests, and anti-Western and anti-American sentiments.

The wide split between these two competing visions of the future reflected the traditional split among Russian intellectuals between Slavophiles and Westernizers (Barner-Berry 1999). Of the two groups, Westernizers were easiest to identify, as they clearly favored strong partnership between Russia and the West, and between Russia and the United States in particular. Kozyrev clearly fell into this camp, especially in his early years as foreign minister. He began his tenure by calling the West a "natural ally of Russia" (*Izvestia*, January 16, 1992). Such statements evoked anger from opposition leaders, who derided Kozyrev for his "pro-Americanism" (*Izvestia*, January 16, 1992). In the early 1990s, many major popular newspapers such as *Argumenty i Fakty*, also conveyed predominately pro-Western and pro-American attitudes.[12] It is noteworthy, however, that there was a general decline in this type of commentary later on.

Those with Slavophilic tendencies were a more varied lot. As a group, these people opposed strong ties with the West and were against coordination between Russian foreign policy and Western—especially American—foreign policies. But they were not necessarily united in their views of what Russia's main orientation should be in terms of foreign policy. Within the Slavophile category, two main sub-categories could be detected. First, there were those who could be termed essentially Eurasian in their orientation. They focused on Russia's unique geopolitical position straddling two continents, and saw Russia as destined to play a major role simultaneously in both Europe and Asia. People of this general persuasion were not clearly anti-Western in their orientation, but neither were they pro-Western. Instead, they saw Russia's destiny as unique, both oriental and occidental at once.[13]

A second brand of Slavophile-type thinking—which could be loosely termed "nationalist-chauvinist"—was more prominent to begin with and gained in strength over time. People who subscribed to this thinking were diverse, ranging from cautious patriots to right-wing fascists, from isolationists to "hawks." Despite differences among them, members of this group commonly exaggerated Russia's role in world history and international affairs, called for revision of the results of the Cold War, and claimed that the West and the United States in particular had mistreated Russia, even hatched many plots against it. National-chauvinist attitudes were evident in public discussions about the Bosnia conflict from the beginning in the summer of 1991 and became increasingly prominent over time. They grew especially strong in 1994–1996, and became dominant during the 1999 war in Kosovo. The main proponents of such views included many prominent pro-government Russian politicians, together with opposition legislators. We turn now to highlighting the public statements and policy actions that reflected this brand of thinking.

Several themes evident in Russia's public discourse about foreign policy in the 1990s could be classified as national-chauvinist. First, a hallmark theme (already noted) was that of Russia's mistreatment at the hands of the West.[14] The main example of this mistreatment touted with regard to the Bosnia conflict was that Russia was not seen as an equal partner in its dealings with Western partners in the region. The themes that Americans had concluded that Moscow was too weak to bother consulting with about affairs in Bosnia and that Russia's interests were being repeatedly ignored were evident as early as 1992–1993.[15] This theme acquired greater prominence in early 1994 when the NATO ultimatum against the Bosnian Serbs was announced. Even Mikhail Gorbachev, commonly seen in Russia as a Westernizer, said that in the Bosnian conflict Russia was "treated as a junior partner that is expected only to nod its head and support the choice made" by other countries (Gorbachev 1994, 2).

It is important to note that government elites also began to take up this theme in early 1994, marking a significant hardening of government rhetoric. In separate statements in February, for example, Yeltsin and Kozyrev both sharply rejected the NATO ultimatum and emphasized the fact that it was made without any consultations with Russia (Shapiro 1994). Yeltsin reportedly called Clinton to express his strong disapproval of the ultimatum, but Clinton allegedly did not even bother to justify and explain the American actions to the Russian president (Felgengauer 1994). Once the bombing started in April, government statements complaining that the West was not dealing fairly with Russia grew even more shrill. Commenting on the bombings, Kozyrev said at a press conference: "Trying to make such decisions without Russia is a big mistake and a big risk. I would like these words of mine to be heard and taken seriously" (*Segodnya*, April 12, 1994, 1). In a statement read at the top of the national evening TV news, Yeltsin called for an immediate summit of Russian, American, and European leaders to coordinate Bosnia policy, signaling his anger over not having been consulted before the bombings (*Chicago Tribune*, April 20, 1994). After this episode, government elites continued to evince a sense of their having been treated unfairly by Western leaders at various points, as was especially evident in 1995 when the government balked at having Russian troops put under NATO command in Bosnia. The focused and increased attention given to this topic, coinciding with manifestly growing apprehension about Russia's diminished military and economic power, seemed to indicate the awakening of old fears of encirclement and exclusion from Europe.

A corollary theme related to the ones outlined above about Russia's mistreatment at the hands of the West criticized the government for—in effect—accepting Russia's subordination to the West and forgetting Russia's own best interests (Bolshakov, March 2, 1994). In the spring of 1994, *Izvestia* commentator Stanislav Kondrashov railed against the American government's illusions of "superiority over the new Russia," and the American false belief that Russia should disregard its "national interests" in Bosnia in order to serve those of the United States. In typically tasteless post-Soviet journalistic style, Kondrashov complained that the public sense of degradation in Russia stemmed from the fact that "Russia had been spreading its legs" for the Americans (*Izvestia*, March 5, 1994, 3). Another analyst complained that the Russian government was playing a servile role in its dealings with the West: "We no longer need look with servility over our shoulders out of fear that the West will give us a 'D' for democracy or an 'F' for foreign policy behavior. We need partners, not mentors," declared Mikhail Leontiev, editor-in-chief of the newspaper *Segodnya* (Simes 1994). Other media officials blamed the United States for underestimating Russian national interests, not supporting Russia when it had done so much for peace in Bosnia, even for trying to shut Russia out of foreign markets (Pushkov 1994). *Krasnaya zvezda*, the daily publication of the Defense Ministry, emphasized that Russia should receive treatment as a great power and equal partner, not just in words but also in deeds. It was stressed that peace in Bosnia could be attained only on the basis of careful consideration of all sides, including Russia (Sidorov 1994, 1).

Not surprisingly, many commentators emphasized that Russia needed to adopt a more independent policy in the conflict, one less beholden to Western powers and supportive of Russia's own interests in the region. For example, in the spring of 1992, an article sharply critical of the Russian Foreign Ministry accused Russian foreign operations of being in "disarray," and blamed the ministry for not having a "new policy" (Survillo, *Nezavisimaya gazeta*, May 20, 1992). As early as June 1992, *Pravda* complaincd about how Russia's foreign policy had become constrained, and was not guided by "carefully checked priorities" (Bogomolov, *Pravda*, June 2, 1992, 3). The same argument was raised by two social scientists writing in *Pravda* several months later, who suggested that the most important lesson of the Yugoslav crisis was the "need to be more independent in foreign policy" and the necessity to "pay more attention to the options and interests not only of our new partners, but also of our old and time-tested friends" (Volobuev and Tyagumenko, September 16, 1992, 3). The fiercest criticism was launched against Russia's agreement to support sanctions against Serbia, which was touted as more indication of Russia's lack of an independent foreign policy (Khimenko, *Nezavisimaya gazeta*, June 9, 1992). The Russian government was accused of "one hundred per cent subordination" to the interests of the United States and the NATO bloc and of automatically following the West's decisions in the Yugoslav tragedy (Bolshakov, February 22, 1994, 3; Kondrashov, *Izvestia*, April 20, 1994, 3). The absence of independent foreign policy was emphasized by critics as late as in 1995 (Tsypko, *Ogonyok*, #25, 1995, 73).

Critical focus on the American role in Bosnia typically accompanied such statements, and was a particular highlight in Russian public debates in the field of foreign policy. Our review of 230 analytical newspaper articles on the topic showed that 196 articles contained at least some information about U.S. diplomatic and military actions in the region. Many analysts openly questioned America's altruistic motivation in the conflict. Alexander Tsypko, a former Gorbachev top advisor, asserted that Washington's desire to establish a "better relationship with the Muslim world, Turkey in particular" was at the heart of U.S. policy in the Balkans (*Ogonyok*, #25, 1995, 73). It was also often said that Washington was conducting a clearly anti-Serbian policy under the UN flag, thus minimizing cost in dollars and possible American casualties (Kondrashov, *Izvestia*, April 20, 1994, 3; Peresvet, 1995). In this vein, the UN was repeatedly accused of being a "tool of NATO" which was getting its inspiration directly from Washington (Fadeyev 1994, 3). Yeltsin himself accused European countries of allowing themselves to be dictated to from beyond the ocean in their Bosnia policies (press conference with Boris Yeltsin, Official Kremlin International News Broadcast, September 8, 1995).

Lastly, it is important to note that, throughout such commentaries, a strong nostalgia for Russia's great-power status was evident. Nostalgic references to the former Soviet Union's power were made in twenty-one publications (out of sixty examined) in pro-communist *Pravda* and *Sovetskaya Rossiya*. "How shameful for our country, how bitter for Russia, which hasn't uttered a single stern word [about Bosnia]—a word that, at one time, the world would have heard," complained Evgeny Fadeyev in *Pravda* (Fadeyev, *Pravda*, August 11, 1993). When the powerful Soviet Union and the socialist community existed, "Moscow never betrayed its comrades and allies," wrote another *Pravda* commentator (*Pravda*, March 2, 1994). The Bosnian crisis was commonly regarded as a demonstration of the arrogance of the Western community, which decided that after the breakup of the U.S.S.R. and the end of the Cold War, the West alone—without Russia's participation—would impose a new international order in which every country would carry out instructions prescribed by the West (Kuznechevsky 1994). Even in the fall of 1995, after the agreement on troop deployment was reached, it was speculated that Russian military personnel would be given "unimportant" repair and construction assignments or other secondary tasks. "This painfully touches the remains of our great-statehood conscience," noted one analyst (Kondrashov, *Izvestia*, November 21, 1995, 3).

As shown earlier, these themes correspondent with national-chauvinistic attitudes became increasingly strong in the course of Russian debates about foreign policy and the conflict in Bosnia. Most critics of the government, especially communists, vocalized the themes. However, government elites themselves also expressed ideas that were less critical of their own actions and focused instead on criticism of the West, the United States in particular. It is important to emphasize that this new stridency in government statements regarding the West and its role in Bosnia were accompanied by a real shift toward a more independent policy vis-à-vis the West as well. We will review these shifts in relationship to the conflict in Bosnia more closely below, but we must also note how the Russian intervention in Chechnya in December 1994 also fit this new policy trend. In deciding to intervene in Chechnya the Russian government showed willingness to take a step fully expected to be highly unpopular in the West. While the decision to intervene in Chechnya clearly had an internal logic, it also generally reflected the mounting desire for greater independence from the West. In this sense, the essence of the policy decision to intervene in Chechnya was nationalist in character.

THE STRENGTHENING OF PRO-SERB AND WEAKENING OF PRO-WESTERN SENTIMENTS

From the evidence reviewed earlier, it is apparent that members of the "concerned minority" varied in their opinions about what Russia's role should be in the world and in the conflict in Bosnia particularly. It is also the case, however, that while views tended to vary widely, especially initially, differences narrowed over time. Specifically, there were two related trends that were increasingly evident over time in statements by all categories of the "concerned minority." These were trends toward showing growing support for the new Yugoslav federation and the Bosnian Serbs, as well as toward showing less enthusiastic support for Western policies. Manifestations of pro-Serb attitudes ran the gamut from muted, restrained expressions of sympathy for Serbs to very strong affirmations of support. While national-chauvinists were typically the most vociferous champions of pro-Serb sentiments, others who fell into the Eurasian and even Westernizer camps also voiced sympathy for Serbs, as well as declined interest in aligning fully with Western policies. A pro-Serb orientation was, in fact, the most visible common denominator uniting members of the "concerned minority," and thus represented a major component of the policy climate regarding the war in Bosnia. We will list several examples that support the existence of these trends, focusing on the rise of pro-Serb sentiments, as well as analyze their origin and impact.

Both opposition leaders and government elites in their words and deeds evidenced pro-Serb sentiments. First, in terms of deeds, scores of politicians and public officials on both sides visited Serbia and Bosnia in the 1990s. Opposition leaders who visited the region included Vladimir Zhirinovsky and Gennadi Zyuganov, heads of the Russian Liberal Democratic Party and the Communist Party of the Russian Federation respectively. Second, the Russian government became a prime source of humanitarian help to Yugoslavia and the most active diplomatic supporter of Serbia during the embargo period (Botyanovsky 1996). Third, Russian volunteers reportedly began fighting for the Serbs as early as 1992 (*Moskovskiye novosti*, December 6, 1992, 4). Meantime, there were no reports of Russians volunteering to fight on the opposite side.

Also, many prominent politicians and government officials indicated pro-Serb sentiments in public statements, especially after the beginning of 1994 onward. Striking examples included, first, Vladimir Lukin, chairman of the State Duma's International Affairs Committee, who said after a parliamentary session on Russian foreign policy priorities in 1994 that Russia's interests would best be served by the strongest possible Serbia and Montenegro (Sidorov 1994, 3). Following the Sarajevo marketplace tragedy in February 1994, the Russian Foreign Ministry failed to echo Western media accusations that the Serbs were responsible for the massacre. Russian press commentary mainly suggested that the Muslims were to blame instead (Yushin 1994, 1, 3). Moreover, President Yeltsin defended employing a Russian military contingent near Sarajevo in 1994 on the basis of "persistent requests from the leaders of the Federal Republic of Yugoslavia and the Bosnia Serbs" (Volkov 1994, 1). Finally, it is noteworthy that there were few reported instances in which Russian public officials directly criticized Serbian leadership.[16]

What factors help to explain the growing adherence to pro-Serb attitudes in Russia in the 1990s? A simple explanation based on Russian national-chauvinism is not enough, as most people who subscribed to Westernizer and Eurasian views also exhibited pro-Serb sentiments. In attempting to discern the origins of Russian pro-Serb attitudes, then, we should turn to analyzing other factors that could be relevant.

First, we will address an explanation frequently touted by Western commentators: the so-called "cultural" factor emphasizing historic, religious, and ethnic links between Russians and Serbs (see, for example, Goble 1997, 183–85). Support for this explanation can be found in various public comments. For example, in 1992, some experts and reporters strongly emphasized "Slavic identity" and "Orthodox ties" as reasons to support the Bosnian Serbs (Schipanov 1992, 3). Symbolic of this early sentiment, Youry Bychkov wrote in *Pravda* in January 1992 that "the Serbs are wonderful and kind people, who are close to us" (*Pravda*, January 23, 1992, 5). However, comments of this type were not predominant in public opinions expressed on the subject of the Bosnia war, except in communist publications.[17] In fact, most public commentators refrained from mentioning that ties of cultural and spiritual ties should be reasons for supporting Bosnian Serbs. Moreover, there were frequent admonitions that Russia should *not* support Serbs simply on such grounds, especially in the beginning of the conflict. For example, Kozyrev cautioned in early 1992 that Orthodoxy should not be a reason for supporting the Serbs. Others who spoke out, both from inside the government and outside it, echoed this general sentiment. Many popular journalists even ridiculed suggestions that the Balkans war was religious-based, calling such arguments "myths" and downplaying notions that Russians should take the side of Serbs in the conflict as fellow Orthodox. In this vein, many commentators emphasized instead that the war was essentially materialistic in origin (Mlechin 1994). Furthermore, even those who generally supported the Serbs in Bosnia refrained from citing cultural ties as a basis for their support. For example, Aleksy II, Patriarch of the Russian Orthodox Church—who called the Serbs "suffering brothers"—was mostly neutral in his statements about the conflict, and emphasized mainly the need to end it (Shusharin 1994, 1). Even Alexander Tsypko, who had complained at one point that Orthodox Christians were regarded as "aliens" in the West, refrained from referring to common membership in the Orthodox Church as a reason for Russian support of the Serbs (*Ogonyok*, #25, 1995, 73). Cultural factors, then, do not seem to have been strong motivating factors in bringing about increased expression of pro-Serb sentiments.

A second set of factors to consider is purely political motivations. Looking at the evidence, it is undeniable that political factors were an important source of pro-Serb expressions on the part of government critics. In other words, expressing support for the Serbs was a useful tool in bashing the government's policy in Bosnia, especially in the initial stages. Of course, criticism of the government by opposition is expected in a democracy, especially when the government is making mistakes.[18] Russian missteps in handling events such as the Western ultimatum to the Bosnian Serbs in 1994, the ensuing Russian decision to send troops, the agreement on military intervention in the fall of 1995, and the Dayton negotiations all provided easy fodder for critics.

Nevertheless, the domestic political setting in Russia in the 1990s was even more conducive to opposition attacks on the government's policies and personnel. Given the newness of democracy and particular Russian political and cultural traditions, practices such as compromise, balancing of interests, and seeking consensus were weak. Instead, decisions were made primarily on the basis of power politics, where compromises were not mutual and usually regarded as a sign of vulnerability. Thus, the tendency toward infighting between politicians was deeply ingrained in Russia's new democracy. As well, in the Russian domestic political context of the 1990s, relative powers between the different branches and levels of government were still being sorted out. At the central level, the main struggle was between the executive and legislative branches. Competition over institutional powers—which was clearly evident in the struggles over the constitution in 1992–1993, the referendum of April 1993, Yeltsin's forceful disbanding of the Supreme Soviet in the fall of 1993, the legislative elections of December 1993 and December 1995, and the presidential elections of 1996—was exacerbated by the fact that, for most of 1991–1996, the central legislature was dominated by parties and groups strongly opposed to the executive government. High tension between the executive and legislative branches and stalemate over policy were thus the norm in Russian politics in the 1990s. Lastly, it was the simple truth that as Russia grappled with its major domestic transformations in the 1990s, opposition politicians were prone to criticize the government's Bosnia policy, in part, as an extension of their policy struggles in other arenas.

We turn now to highlighting how political factors, especially deep struggle at the central level of government, promoted an increasing turn toward pro-Serb sentiments as well as a weakening of pro-Western—especially pro-American—sentiments both outside and inside the government. Growing political struggle over policy in Bosnia first became evident in late 1992.[19] At the end of the year, the Bosnian Serbs leader Radovan Karadzic bragged about how his strong supporters in the Russian political opposition had said to him that "any day now Russian public opinion towards foreign policy will change in our favor, and official government policy will have to respect this" (Poggioli 1992). In December 1992, the brewing struggle over policy in Bosnia between the executive and legislative branches became evident. The Supreme Soviet overwhelmingly approved a resolution calling for a pro-Belgrade shift in policy as well as UN sanctions against all the combatants in the conflict, not just Serbia. Deputy Foreign Minister Vitaly Churkin's subsequent delivery of a clearly pro-Serbian speech at the Geneva Conference on the former Yugoslavia failed to assuage critics, as the government was accused thereafter of failing to match its words in deeds.

The struggle intensified in 1993. By then, opposition legislators in almost all areas were attacking Yeltsin's policies. Yeltsin sought to break the deepening legislative-executive stalemate by holding a referendum on April 25 asking the Russian people whether they supported Yeltsin's government, the reform process, early legislative elections and/or early presidential elections. As the referendum neared, it became clear that Yeltsin feared Russia's Bosnia policy would become hostage to the political stalemate, as he requested the postponement of any UN decision on sanctions against the conflicting sides in Bosnia until after the referendum.[20] Apparently, U.S. decision makers were sympathetic to Yeltsin's request, as the vote was postponed.[21] In the end, however, Yeltsin's victory of sorts in the referendum—which showed Russian voters supported Yeltsin and his policies more than they supported the legislature—was not enough to tame his rivals in the legislature, who continued to criticize and attack Yeltsin's policies. When the government finally decided to agree on sanctions against Yugoslavia, denunciations from opposition legislators were especially sharp.

Yeltsin ultimately disbanded the Supreme Soviet using military force in September-October 1993. Elections were held in the following December to form a new bicameral legislature named the Federal Assembly. The results were not favorable to Yeltsin or his government's policy in the former Yugoslavia. Opposition forces—in particular the ultra-nationalist Liberal Democratic Party of Russia and communists—gained sway over a small minority of reformist and pro-government deputies, especially in the more powerful lower house, the State Duma. Soon after the Duma began its sessions, it took up the topic of Bosnia upon the initiative of the Communist faction.[22] On January 21, 1994, three Duma factions (representing the Communist Party of the Russian Federation, the Liberal Democratic Party of Russia, and the Agrarian Party of Russia) presented draft statements declaring unacceptable the use of any measures involving force in the former Yugoslavia and demanding that all foreign troops be withdrawn from its territory. Russia's representatives in the UN Security Council were requested by the Duma factions to take immediate steps to implement their recommendations (Rodin 1994, 2). This constituted the harshest criticism yet leveled at the government on its Bosnia policy by legislators. Attacks on Russia's Bosnia policy in the Duma escalated at this point and even extended to harsh personal attacks on Kozyrev, including thinly veiled calls for his resignation.[23]

As strong as internal political pressures for change became, however, it was not until outside developments intervened that Russian government rhetoric and policy in Bosnia began to shift. The two external events that put major strain on Russia's policy in Bosnia were the formal proposal to expand NATO, put forth in January 1994, and NATO's threats to bomb Serbian positions in Bosnia made the following month. These developments put the Russian government in an extremely vulnerable position, making its Western-oriented foreign policies, including its liberal policy in Bosnia, look like serious mistakes. Political opposition forces as well as Russian military officials were especially outraged. In terms of the conflict in Bosnia, pressure to modify Russian policy to show more support for the Serbs intensified following NATO's air strike threats in early February. Zhirinovsky, leader of the LDPR, proclaimed that the Serbs were no longer alone, that his party would change Russia's foreign policy and send an army to help the Serbs, and even give them a new secret weapon (Gryzunov and Baturin, February 4, 1994, 4). Even moderate Westernizers, such as former acting Prime Minister Yegor Gaidar and future presidential candidate Grigory Yavlinski, joined in putting pressure on Yeltsin and Kozyrev to react to the NATO ultimatum. Finally, an overwhelming majority of Duma deputies condemned the NATO ultimatum and demanded that the Serbs be supported (Bolshakov, *Pravda*, February 22, 1994, 3).

These events were catalytic, as the government finally began to modify its stance in the Bosnia conflict in limited ways starting in February 1994. As noted earlier, government rhetoric began to shift, becoming less pro-Western and more pro-Serbian. The change in rhetorical tone was especially striking to one *Izvestia* commentator, who wrote: "For some time now, it has been difficult to determine the origin of various statements made in the field of foreign policy—Kozyrev or Zyuganov" (Yushin, *Izvestia*, March 1994, 3). Other prominent analysts also took note of the tougher line, including Viktor Kremenyuk (an interview in *Novaya yezhednevnaya gazeta*, January 15, 1994, 2).[24]

More importantly, however, the government also began to modify its policy, adopting a cautiously pro-Serb position while still working with the Western powers to end the conflict. Taking an independent stance for the first time, Yeltsin challenged the ultimatum and succeeded in thwarting NATO air strikes on Serbs in Bosnia temporarily. As NATO's deadline to the Bosnian Serbs approached, Yeltsin wrote to Slobodan Milosevic suggesting that the Serbs withdraw their heavy weapons from around Sarajevo—which would satisfy the conditions of NATO's ultimatum—while Russian troops were deployed to the city. He eventually reached an agreement with the Serbs that they completely withdraw from the designated sectors in exchange for Russian troop deployment in Bosnia. Moscow's first challenge to NATO in Bosnia seemed to please some of those who had criticized the government for being beholden to Western interests and American interests in particular. After the accord was announced, and for the only time during the course of the Bosnia conflict, the relationship between Yeltsin and the Duma regarding policy in Bosnia was somewhat positive. Some analysts even announced "the prospective emergence of a consensus" between the Duma and the Kremlin (Volkov 1994, 1).

This political truce did not last long, however. Yeltsin's face-saving agreement collapsed when the Bosnian Serbs violated the settlement agreement later in the spring of 1994. Appearing displeased, Yeltsin made an official statement that condemned Serb atrocities. This drew renewed harsh attacks from pro-Serb critics in the legislature and elsewhere, who probably saw Yeltsin's statement as a step back toward spinelessness. Thus, another stalemate of sorts on policy emerged which lasted through 1994–1995 (Yushin, April 4, 1994, 3).

During 1995, arguments emphasizing Russia's great-power status and the need for the protection of Russia's vital interests became even more loud as competition for the December elections to the State Duma heated up. NATO's proposed expansion and American dominance in Bosnia gave critics, especially the communists, great ammunition against the Yeltsin government (MacWilliam 1997, 8). In interviews given to the leading foreign policy journal *Mezhdunarodnaya Zhizn*, several leaders of Russia's main political parties, including leading liberal parties, expressed deep dissatisfaction with Russia's policy in Bosnia (*Mezhdunarodnaya Zhizn*, #4, 1995, 5–26).[25] Only Sergei Belyaev, first deputy chairman of the pro-government party Our Home Russia (*Nash Dom Rossiya*), offered a few general and cautious remarks about the importance of peace in Bosnia and the lifting of the sanctions against Yugoslavia (*Mezhdunarodnaya zhizn*, #4, 1995, 5–8).

In the fall of 1995, as internal political struggle mounted with the election campaigns and the last stage of the armed conflict in Bosnia was being played out, a further change occurred in Moscow's Bosnia policy in that main responsibility for determining Russia's conduct in Bosnia was shifted to the military. The Russian Foreign Ministry was practically excluded from negotiations in Dayton after November 21, 1995. Kozyrev openly complained that Defense Minister Grachev was conducting negotiations in Brussels alone and without even informing him (*Izvestia*, December 5, 1995, 3). It was thus left up to generals to negotiate Russia's form of involvement, the mechanism underlying the political control of Russian troops, and the channels through which Russia would interact with the NATO council (Umbach 1996). Yeltsin, meanwhile, was recuperating from his second heart attack since July in a sanitarium near Moscow. Despite his infirmity, it was widely considered that he engineered Kozyrev's downgrading as a last-ditch effort to blunt criticism of his policies and strengthen the position of his political allies before the December elections.

When the 1995 elections further strengthened opposition to the government, with the Communist Party of the Russian Federation taking most Duma seats this time, Yeltsin took another step toward accommodating his critics and dismissed Kozyrev from his post as foreign minister on January 5, 1996.

Yeltsin's new appointee for foreign minister was Yevgeny Primakov, a former candidate member of the Politburo known to be more conservative and pragmatic than Kozyrev.[26] Yeltsin's decision to sandbag Kozyrev showed the extent to which policy was being shaped in consideration of opposition forces, as Yeltsin had long resisted pressures to remove Kozyrev, and stuck with his much-maligned foreign minister for four years. Still, Kozyrev's dismissal did not substantially change the fact that the executive branch maintained essential control over foreign policy, bowing to legislative critics only at its own behest and only in relatively limited ways. But the 1995 elections, which demonstrated the growing strength of Yeltsin's critics and Zyuganov—who would contest Yeltsin in the 1996 presidential election—pushed Yeltsin to make a compromise he had strongly resisted thereto.

Thus, as can be seen, the reshaping of Russia's policy toward the former Yugoslavia still occurred "from above"—not under pressure from mass opinion, but related to domestic struggle among political elites in the executive and legislative branches. At first, in 1992–1993, Yeltsin and his team more or less ignored mounting attacks by Supreme Soviet Deputies who disdained the balanced approach and saw the government as taking an anti-Serb position. Thus, sharp criticisms from opposition politicians had virtually no effect on the Russian government's policy toward Bosnia at first. But policy began to shift noticeably after external events in early 1994 made the government's policy look weak. This, combined with how the opposition forces had been strengthened in the December 1993 legislative elections, pushed the government to begin to modify its position in the conflict. Changes escalated further as the December 1995 Duma elections approached, and especially after they delivered a strong victory for the communists. In this way, Russia's role in resolving the Bosnian conflict became a weapon in the deepening political struggle waged between Yeltsin's government and opposition forces within the three legislatures that existed between 1992 and 1996.

It remains to consider more deeply, however, why pro-Serb sentiments acquired such potency in this internal political struggle over Russia's policy in Bosnia. We argued earlier that cultural, religious, and ethnic ties between Russians and Serbs did not seem to be prime motivating factors. Also, while bashing the government's policy on Bosnia was politically expedient for opposition legislators, and somewhat easy to do given mistakes and misfortunes Russia suffered in the region, it cannot be assumed that critics of Russia's policy, including opposition legislators, took up this cause simply for political, and no other, reasons. As well, this does not fully explain why the government itself adopted changes it so strongly opposed initially. What other factors, then, may have been underneath the pro-Serb orientation adopted by critics to Yeltsin's government and then, to a lesser degree, by the government itself?

In addition to its utility as a tool of internal political struggle, Russian pro-Serbian sentiments and corresponding anti-Western views can be considered to have roots in ideological forces remnant from the past (Zubok and Ple-shakov 1996). Marxist ideology, for example, had imbued in Russians the no-tion that Western states were enemies not to be trusted. In the immediate post-Soviet context, it is not surprising that many people, especially elites, found it difficult to relinquish this idea, and thus felt insecure in partnership with the West, including in Bosnia. Some analysts even argue that the shift in Russian policy in the former Yugoslavia from an initially balanced, pro-Western stance toward a more independent, limitedly pro-Serb stance was a demonstration of the "complexes" of the post-Soviet elite, the military "four hundred" above all, who "could not exist without a foreign enemy" (Eggert 1995, 3).

Another ideological influence from deeper in the past—Russia's self-pro-claimed messianic role—also may have helped shape the policy climate toward the former Yugoslavia. Russia's long-held aspirations for great power status were finally realized in the second half of the twentieth century, only to be dramatically lost in the late Soviet period. The loss of Russia's superpower status, and the sharp diminution of means necessary to restore it, struck deep blows at Russian pride. In this context, messianism took a clearly defensive form (Shiraev and Zubok 2000). Many journalists and experts rued the loss of Russia's predominance, and decried what they viewed as instances of Russia's humiliation at the hands of the United States and other Western governments. Their statements evinced a growing and shameful sense of inferiority vis-à-vis Western countries. Some even claimed that virtually all treaties signed in the 1990s were disadvantageous to Russia, and that the end of the U.S.S.R. was a failure for Russia (Umbach 1996, 478). In terms of Bosnia, it was clear that many felt that the loss of superpower status had rendered Russia unable even to be a regional power in its traditional backyard, the Balkans.[27]

These beliefs rooted in past ideologies became increasingly evident in Rus-sian public discourse about the Bosnia conflict, as already shown, and thus presumably came to modulate the policy climate toward Bosnia to a great ex-tent. Critics of the Russian government's initially balanced policy toward the Bosnia conflict came to express more strongly views that reflected beliefs that the Western powers—and the United States especially—were suspect, that Russia had accepted for too long a subservient position vis-à-vis Western part-ners in Bosnia, that Russia deserved to play a larger role in Balkan and world affairs. Government officials themselves began to take up these themes in more muted form, and to modify policy accordingly in limited ways.

In summary, it is important to emphasize that these values likely took on added significance in the policy climate regarding Bosnia in part because of psychological factors associated with Russia's ongoing domestic transfor-mations. As noted, Russian society suffered greatly and had become badly split and fearful in the process of its transformation. How to ease the pain as-sociated with deep domestic reforms had become the focal point of the country.[28] The theme of catastrophe had become prominent in the media. In this psychological context of mass pain and fear, Russia's problems in Bosnia were probably seen by many as another sign that Russia was headed toward an economic and political catastrophe, unable to assert its interests and strengths, and that the government was failing to support Russia's traditional spirit and values. Yeltsin's policies in Bosnia probably furthered the perception that Russians were victims, and that Washington in particular, which gave support to Yeltsin's policies in Bosnia and toward Russia's "capitalization" in general—both of which caused most Russians great pain—was a major victimizer, still an enemy not to be trusted (Kremenyuk 1994, 2).[29] These sentiments, anchored in past philosophical leanings, reinforced in the psychology associated with massive and painful transformations, fed into growing pro-Serb, anti-Western sentiments in Russia.

CONCLUSION

In early 1992, two Russian political scientists predicted that the country would soon experience a social upheaval caused by material adversity and weak government. Furthermore, they predicted that people would rebel against the national humiliation caused by Russia's failed Balkan policy (Volobuev and Tyagumenko 1992). These predictions never materialized. Most people, it turned out, did not care to solve Russia's social and political problems on the barricades but preferred, instead, to dig their "own trench to hide" (Stroev 1996). Others had "no resources, no property, no knowledge or skills" in order to express their frustration in the first place (Yavlinsky, June 13, 1996). Most importantly for this study, the vast majority of Russians cared little about Russia's policy in Bosnia. At times, political elites themselves seemed to be only marginally interested in the situation in Bosnia. Strikingly, for instance, presidential assistant Yuori Ryurikov failed to mention Bosnia altogether in an article he wrote entitled "Some Discourses about Russian Foreign Policy" (*Mezhdunarodnaya zhizn*, winter 1994–1995, 15–23). Also, during the 1996 presidential campaigns, the topic of Bosnia was neglected in most major candidates' speeches, press conferences, and interviews.

At the same time, however, the critics of Russia's Bosnia policy tried to portray public opinion as very much interested in the situation in Bosnia, especially in the plight of Bosnian Serbs. Government officials also adopted this approach at times, mainly in efforts to get Western officials to confer more closely with the Russian government about policy in the region.[30] Emphasizing Russia's fragile domestic political situation, in fact, became a common tactic of the government, as officials took to warning the West about Russian "reds" and "browns"—such as Zhirinovsky, Zyuganov, Makashov, and others—who were supposedly eagerly waiting in the wings to use any "incorrect" American and NATO policy to their advantage. Thus, despite public opinion being weak on the question of Bosnia, both sides portrayed it as strong and essentially pro-Serb for their own purposes.

In many ways, the weak role that public opinion had in shaping Russia's Bosnia policy showcases that Russia in the 1990s was a developing democracy still struggling to part with old authoritarian ways. Contrary to what one would expect in an ideal democracy, the Russian public was not significantly engaged in the policymaking process, and Russian policy in Bosnia was not decided with public opinion in mind. In fact, hardly anyone outside the tiny "concerned minority," which was made up largely of political elites, tried to influence policy. The disconnect between elites and public over policy made sense as average Russians were not eager to play a policymaking role at any rate, as their everyday problems so consumed them that they did not have the energy to think about problems far away. In the end, the widespread apathy regarding Bosnia no doubt facilitated elites in being able to operate independently in policymaking.

Within the circle of elites who had a role in deciding policy, the same tendency existed as in the Soviet past for the inner circle of executive-level elites (the president in particular) to call shots mainly on their own. As a result, for the first years of the conflict, executive officials more or less unilaterally imposed policy decisions about Bosnia upon a legislature whose majority members vehemently opposed the policies. This tendency abated some after the 1993 and 1995 elections, and we saw policy reshaped in ways responsive to critics who dominated the legislature. Still, it must be recognized that the modifications in policy were belated, limited, and pushed at least initially more by unfavorable external events than internal pressures. Ultimately, the executive made changes in policy and personnel only when it was determined it politically expedient to do so. Thus, decision making about Bosnia remained essentially oligarchic even as the circle of elite players was widened and a few democratic channels for public influence over policy existed.

An oligarchic style of decision making, of course, has long been favored by Russian elites. It seems that old patterns are hard to break. The political elite of the 1990s (whether just the executive branch or all political officials combined) appears to remain convinced that they, not voters, are the ones who should decide policy—especially foreign policy, given its concern with central issues of security. The public seemed largely content to let their political leaders handle Russia's foreign policy. The attitudes of both elites and non-elites are thus conducive to oligarchic modes of decision making (especially in foreign policy), with the expected attendant policy consequences. Instead of policies reflecting the wishes of the citizenry carried out through their representatives and careful compromise among various members and branches of government, decisions were essentially controlled by the executive branch, modified to fit the wishes of critics (including within the legislature) only belatedly when the executive chose. Thus, past political traditions, more than democratization, played a strong role in shaping the formulation of Russia's policy concerning Bosnia and other foreign policy issues including the conflict in Kosovo in 1999.

That said, it must also be recognized that the case of Russian decision-making about conduct in Bosnia also illustrated that important steps toward democratization had been taken and that oligarchy had definite limits. The circle of political elites who helped decide policy was broader than in the Soviet era, and political elites were part of an elected government. There were numerous channels for unrestrained public criticism, and critics felt free to put pressure on their government to respond to their views. Furthermore, those who made up the "concerned minority"—although small in number—were a diverse crowd. The policy climate regarding the situation in Bosnia was therefore influenced not only by government elites, but also by opposition politicians and other people from many walks of life and representing practically all parts of Russia's political spectrum. As a result, a substantial body of public criticism about Russia's Bosnia policy grew between 1992 and 1996.

Finally, we did see Russian policy shift in regard to Bosnia in ways that responded to critical opinion with restraint. In particular, we saw small but significant steps taken toward convergence between Russian policy and two increasingly predominant strains of thought expressed on practically all levels of the Bosnia policy debates, even at times by government officials themselves: pro-Serb sentiments and anti-Western beliefs, of which anti-Americanism was the most strong element (Shiraev 1999). In this respect, pressure had grown for Russia to show more support for the Serbs and to act with less subordination to the West, especially Washington, and government elites slowly, and within bounds, took these steps. The evolution of Russian government rhetoric as well as policy in Bosnia, which became limitedly pro-Serbian while still sensitive to American actions, indicated that decision makers were not above being influenced by the policy climate. There were also strong independent reasons why they were susceptible to these policy shifts—as we showed, past ideological influences also predisposed these sentiments, as well as the desire to help the government gain strength in domestic political struggle—but in the end the government did not ignore or shut down critics, but instead inched towards their positions.

NOTES

1. See the Studies on Political Development published by Princeton University Press in the 1960s and 1970s. Conducted by prominent researchers associated with the Committee on Comparative Politics of the Social Science Research Center at the Center for Advanced Study in the Behavioral Sciences at Palo Alto, California, the studies were based on the premise that all states must go through five crises of political

development: the crises of identity, legitimacy, penetration, participation, and distribution. See, for example, Leonard Binder et al., *Crises and Sequences in Political Development*, 1971.

2. The extreme concentration of power over foreign policy decision making before Gorbachev can be seen in the facts that there were only three general secretaries heading the Politburo from the late 1920s until 1982, and one Politburo member—Andrei Gromyko—held the post of foreign minister for almost thirty years, from 1957 until 1985.

3. See article 86: "The president of the Russian Federation exercises leadership of the foreign policy of the Russian Federation. . . . "

4. For more detailed characterizations of this policy, see the many scholarly publications already published on Russian policy in the Balkans, such as Masker 1998; Gow 1997; and Goble 1996. In addition, there are many sources available in Russian printed media.

5. The secular decline in voter turnouts over time helps to reveal this trend. While 89.8 percent of voters voted throughout the U.S.S.R. in the Soviet Congress of People's Deputies elections of March 1989, only 77 percent of Russian voters voted in the Russian Congress of People's Deputies elections in March 1990. Thereafter, 74.7 percent of Russian voters voted in the RSFSR presidential election of June 1991, 54.8 percent voted in the Federal Assembly elections of December 1993, 64.44 percent voted in the December 1995 Duma elections, and 69.81 percent and 68.89 percent voted in the June and July 1996 rounds of the presidential election respectively. See Sakwa, 1996, and White et al., 1997.

6. Thus, most Russians today can be seen to act like people who lived under the Soviet system; i.e., they behave in the capacity of what Gabriel A. Almond and Sidney Verba termed "subjects"—those who are informed politically but do not actively participate in politics themselves—or "parochials," those who are uninformed and uninvolved politically—and not those of "citizens," who are both informed and active politically. See Almond and Verba, *The Civic Culture: Political Attitudes and Democracy in Five Nations*. Princeton, N.J.: Princeton University Press, 1963.

7. In one nationwide poll of 1600 people conducted by the Russian Center for Public Opinion and Market Research in January 1997, 41 percent of those questioned said they were against the prospective entry of former Warsaw Pact countries into NATO. But another 44 percent said they were either unsure about what NATO's expansion would mean or said it would not matter. In another poll, 73 percent of Muscovites surveyed could not express an opinion on the subject or suggested that the NATO expansion would make no difference in their lives (MacWilliam 1997).

8. This group of respondents fit the "parochial" sub-type in Almond and Verba's schema of orientation toward political participation. "Parochials" are generally uninterested in politics. See Almond and Verba 1963.

9. The survey itself apparently did not query respondents about their support for the entire range of options discussed here. This may have reflected the feeling of survey designers that deeper commitments were not supported by many Russians.

10. A more specific piece of data is revealing as well: 52 percent of respondents in a 1995 survey abstained from predicting the future course of the Russian government in Bosnia (Interfax news agency, Moscow, in English, 1430 gmt, September 21, 1995. The British Broadcasting Corporation, September 23, 1995. Text of report by Interfax

news agency). It would make sense for people to refrain from prediction if they generally felt fatalistic about the outcome, and powerless to control foreign policy outcomes in general.

11. The "concerned minority" behaved like "citizens" in Almond and Verba's schema of people's orientation toward political participation noted earlier. See Almond and Verba 1963.

12. For example, between 1990 and 1993, *Argumenty i fakty* published fifty-four articles about the United States. Thirty-two articles (59 percent) contained sympathetic, positive commentary about policies, business, and the general domestic situation in the United States. Seventeen articles (32 percent) were essentially gossip stories or reports about American celebrities. Only five stories (9 percent) contained critical commentary, which was focused on America's social problems (Shiraev, previously unpublished research).

13. Some prominent politicians, such as Supreme Soviet Chairman Ruslan Khasbulatov in 1992, expressed what could be classified as "Eurasian" leanings. (See *The Economist*, June 15–21, 1996, 19–21.) But this view was generally more popular in academic and intellectual circles than among political elites. (See Rubtsov 1995; Kara-Murza et al. 1995, 10; Gozman and Edkind 1992, 58.) This was correspondent with the fact that the concept of multipolarity generally became more prominent in Russian academic discourse in the 1990s. Many academic analysts embraced this paradigm, which emphasized that international relations had fundamentally changed from Cold War bipolarity, with many states sharing power and deserving Russia's attentions, including Asian states. (See, for example, Alexander Peresvet, *Nezavisimaya gazeta*, July 14, 1992; Vladislav Pechkurov, *Ogonyok*, #27, 1995.)

14. A review of 230 newspaper articles on Bosnia published between 1991 and 1995 revealed that this theme emerged in 191 publications. (Another 170 articles were essentially non-partisan in nature, and sixty were pro-communist.) Remarkably, major Communist newspapers differed from other sources mainly only in the types of arguments raised to explain the mistreatment (Shiraev, previously unpublished research).

15. See for example, Rodionov, *Izvestia*, June 4, 1992, 4 and Babushenko, *Nezavisimaya gazeta*, August 4, 1993. Yevgeny Ambartsumov, Chairman of the Joint Committee on International Affairs and Foreign Economic Relations of the Russian Supreme Soviet, complained that it was not obligatory for Russia to duplicate the U.S. position in all respects (*Izvestia*, June 29, 1992, 3). Andrianik Migranyan, Director of the CIS Center of the Russian Academy of Science's Institute of International, Economic and Political Research, argued that one could not fail to see that Russia's national and state interests "cannot constantly coincide with the interests of the West, let alone of the United States" (Migranyan 1992, 7).

16. Vitaly Churkin, special envoy to the Balkans, broke from this norm, however, when he called the Bosnian Serb leaders "obsessed with the madness of war" in 1994. See Eggert 1994, 3.

17. From the outset of the conflict, communist newspapers stressed that the Serbs were a "fraternal people" and that Russia policy in the former Yugoslavia was "anti-national" (Garifullina 1992, 1). A 1992 publication placed blame for the war on Islam and the Catholic Church. The Vatican, for example, was blamed for the destruction of socialism in Europe and its attempts "to push out Orthodoxy" (Volobuev

and Tyagumenko 1992). In December 1992, a group of leading historians published an open letter in *Pravda* declaring Serbs and Montenegrins to be "our blood brothers" who bled with Russians in two world wars and were linked to Russians by "age-old bonds" (*Pravda*, December 2, 1992, 1, 3). A letter published in January 1993 in two leading communist papers and signed by fifty-two politicians, writers, and scholars emphasized Russia's "Orthodox" ties with the Serbs and called the Serbs "fellow Slavs" (*Pravda*, January 21, 1993, 5; *Sovetskaya rossiya*, January 21, 1993, 5). The strength of pro-Serb sentiments among communists is ironic in that proponents of Marxism-Leninism supposedly support other groups only for reasons of class, not for cultural, religious, or ethnic reasons. But this tactic makes sense in purely political terms.

18. As was duly noted in an editorial of *The Christian Science Monitor* in 1995, "political opponents of President Clinton, Prime Minister Major, and Chancellor Kohl daily do the same." See *The Christian Science Monitor*, September 27, 1995, "The Eagle and the Bear," 20.

19. One of the earliest signs of the politicization of Moscow's Balkan policy came in the late Soviet phase, when *Izvestia* speculated that, if the August 1991 coup had been successful, policy would have turned pro-Serbian and anti-Croatian (*Izvestia*, August 30, 1991, 6; and September 12, 1991, 5).

20. As one prominent analyst put it, Yeltsin's government has become "extremely vulnerable to national pressures from below," and thus needed help from any, even unlikely, sources (Volski 1993, 22).

21. Washington reportedly slowed its efforts to secure a UN Security Council vote authorizing enforcement of the no-fly zone over Bosnia largely because it feared such an anti-Serb move would undermine Yeltsin's chances to win the crucial referendum. (See *U.S. News & World Report*, April 5, 1993). Later when the vote went forth anyway and Russia abstained from the Security Council resolution regarding the no-fly zones over Bosnia, Strobe Talbott, U.S. ambassador-at-large to the former U.S.S.R. and special adviser to the secretary of state, suggested that this was a temporizing move taken in Moscow to accommodate a substantial body of pro-Serbian public opinion in Russia. "And this body of opinion in Russian politics has greatly limited the room for maneuver that the Russian government itself has, particularly during a time of a critical showdown between the Russian president and the parliament" (See *Federal News Service*, April 19, 1993). Note that Talbott's "excuse" for Russia's abstention suggests that Russian public opinion played a large role in shaping Russia's Bosnia policy at this point. This conflicts with our arguments that pro-Serb sentiments among Russians were not very strong, and that public opinion was not an important consideration in shaping the Russian government's decisions about Bosnia.

22. This marked the first time the Duma did not discuss its own internal matters but instead focused on an international problem.

23. For example, in January 1994, the largest faction of the Duma (that of the Liberal Democratic Party of Russia) threatened that if the Ministry of Foreign Affairs failed to take a clearly "pro-Serbian" position in Bosnia within one week, the LDPR would demand the foreign minister's resignation (Rodin 1994, 2). Vladimir Zhirinovsky publicly recounted in February 1994 how he had told Prime Minister Chernomyrdin that he would not rest so long as Kozyrev remained a minister: "My mission is to remove him from the Russian government" (Baturin and Gryzunov 1994, 4).

24. The government's more "hawkish" rhetorical posture seemed to fail to appease most legislators still, however, as a majority of them indicated in a survey that they still desired Kozyrev's resignation and called for immediate corrections in Russia's policy (survey by *Mnenie* [Opinion] Service).

25. For example, Vladimir Lukin, head of the Committee for International Affairs of the State Duma and deputy chair of the influential liberal Yabloko party, outright called Russian policy in Bosnia a "fiasco" (*Mezhdunarodnaya zhizn*, #4, 1995, 24). Alexei Mitrofanov, deputy head of the Duma's International Affairs Committee and representative of the LDPR Duma faction, called NATO's involvement an "armed aggression" and called for a radical change in Russia's policy toward "the clear support of Serbia" (*Mezhdunarodnaya zhizn*, #4, 1995, 14–16). Aleksandr Shabanov and Eduard Kovalev, deputy head and head of the CPRF press center respectively, also launched sharp and emotional criticisms against Russia's foreign policy in the former Yugoslavia (*Mezhdunarodnaya zhizn*, #4, 1995, 9–12). Yuri Skokov, an ally of General Lebed and chair of the National Council of the Congress of Russia's Communities, blamed Kozyrev for what he called the "absence of foreign policy" and labeled the Balkan war and the NATO expansion "major threats" to Russia (*Mezhdunarodnaya zhizn*, #4, 1995, 12–14).

26. Primakov was later named prime minister.

27. See, for example, *The Christian Science Monitor*, September 27, 1995, "The Eagle and the Bear," 20. The theme that Russia was following along with Western policies in Bosnia to the detriment of its own best interests emerged early in the conflict and intensified thereafter. For example, in 1992, the Russian press was already full of complaints that the economic sanctions against Yugoslavia did not take Russia's best interests into account. In June 1992, five major Russian moderate newspapers carried commentary in this vein. One of the newspapers, *Izvestia*, claimed that Kozyrev had been "slapped on his nose" by the Western powers that had pushed the sanctions (Rodionov 1992, 4). *Sovetskaya rossiya* carried an article that argued that Russia's agreement to the sanctions marked a betrayal of the Serbs and a sacrifice of Russian-Serbian historic ties "for the sake of pro-American interests in Europe" (Garifullina 1992).

28. It was widely argued in numerous publications that Yeltsin's government that had pushed rapid economic reforms without sufficient modification or easing, was especially responsible for causing pain. Newspaper headlines screamed in pain blaming the reformers in the Kremlin for the "misery of millions of Russians," accusing them of committing "robbery against our national pride," describing the reforms as "national catastrophe" and "destruction, rape, deception, betrayal" (see, for example, *Literaturnaya rossiya*, December 12, 1992; *Izvestia*, July 15, 1994). Referring to the Babylon tower, some even suggested that Russia was being "punished" for its past misdeeds by receiving "freedom" in its present form (Rubtsov 1995). The theme that a fatal confrontation was at hand within the country was trumpeted by many journalists, actors, even people on the streets. It seemed that a full-blown social explosion was being nervously anticipated. Even renowned scholars discussed the possibilities of a clash. If there are no substantial changes in these three months, "an explosion will be unavoidable," commented Georgy Shakhnazarov, a top ideologist under Gorbachev, in 1996 (Shakhnazarov 1997). Boris Grushin, a Moscow sociologist who can be hardly accused of being preoccupied with fears, wrote pessimistically

that, despite democratic changes, tensions within the society kept growing (Grushin, October 8, 1994).

29. Russia's political elites themselves also began to be more leery of the effect U.S. economic "assistance" was having on their country. As early as 1992, Georgy Arbatov, perhaps the most renowned specialist on U.S.-Russia relations, noted that Russia's massive economic failure had discredited the United States in Russia. Whereas Washington had previously opposed the poorly functioning—but still working—Soviet economy, it now supported an economy that was not working at all. Arbatov further noted that many Russians believed that the West was consciously trying to turn Russia into a Third World country, to de-industrialize it, and once and for all bring it to its knees (Arbatov, *Newsday*, October 25, 1992).

30. For example, in an interview with Reuters and Cable News Network following NATO's threats of air strikes against the Bosnian Serbs, Yeltsin's special envoy to the former Yugoslavia, Vitaly Churkin, warned the West that there could be dangerous "consequences" and "repercussions" in terms of Russian public opinion and the domestic political scene if American and NATO actions in Bosnia were not decided with Russia's approval ahead of time (*Chicago Tribune*, February 11, 1994). Three months later, Deputy Prime Minister Sergei Shakhrai asserted that NATO air strikes against the Serbs had endangered the current government's domestic situation: "It wasn't so much the Serbs' positions that were bombed as it was the domestic political situation in the Russian Federation" (*Rossiiskie vesti*, April 13, 1994, 1).

6

Massacring in Front of a Blind Audience? Italian Public Opinion and Bosnia

Paolo Bellucci and Pierangelo Isernia

December 18, 1995 the first fifty soldiers of the *Garibaldi* brigade landed in Ploçe reaching Sarajevo two days later. This was the avant-garde of the Italian contingent in the *Joint Endeavour* operation. By January 1996, it will reach the number of 2,549 men, deployed in the southeast area of Bosnia-Herzegovina under the French tactical command. This deployment occurred in conformity to the Security Council resolution n.1031 of December 15, 1995 authorizing the member states to create and to deploy a multinational force (called *Ifor, Implementation Force*) under the NATO command to implement the peace agreement reached in Dayton in November and formally signed in Paris the day before. This was the first out-of-area mission since NATO's creation in 1949, the first employment of an Italian all-volunteer and all-professional force, and the first Italian military presence on the former Yugoslavia soil after World War II.[1]

The Italian decision to contribute to the NATO force in Bosnia marked the end of four years of debate among Italian politicians, experts, and bureaucrats on the opportunity to participate in the peacekeeping and later peaceenforcing operation in Bosnia. The final decision was the result of a complex game at the domestic and international level in which the willingness to play a greater role in the region faced a set of domestic and international constraints, including the uncertainty of the political élite and the stubborn and explicit opposition of the military to an Italian armed intervention in the region. The Italian policymaking process toward Bosnia has thus moved through different stages, going from a low profile of solidarity with no military commitment to a progressively more active role.

In this process public opinion played a role, being often mentioned, sometimes counted on, more rarely feared. We find several occasions in which public opinion is explicitly mentioned and at least verbally accounted for by Italian

173

politicians. However, to understand the role of public opinion in Italian foreign policy on the Bosnia issue, we have to give some preliminary attention to the nature of the Italian political system. As Cohen reminded us (1977–1978, 196) a few years ago, "the role that public opinion plays in the formulation of foreign policy in any country is inescapably related to the political system of that country." In our case, any discussion on such a role is complicated by three prevalent convictions, among scholars of Italian matters. Namely, that this country has no foreign policy, no real public opinion on security issues (or, alternatively, it is not worth the study) and that, if by chance there were both a foreign policy and a public opinion, the latter has no effect on the former. Therefore, before studying the role of public opinion in Bosnia we shall first clarify the relevance of these convictions. To this preliminary task is devoted the first section. We will then discuss the evolution of Italian foreign policymaking toward Bosnia-Herzegovina and the role public opinion played in some occasions. Thirdly, we will present and discuss the available survey materials on the attitudes of Italian public opinion on Bosnia. Finally, we will focus on the main determinants of Italian public opinion support for a military intervention in Bosnia. In the conclusion we will assess which role Italian public opinion played in the policymaking process on Bosnia.

ITALIAN FOREIGN POLICY AND PUBLIC OPINION

The role of public opinion in the Italian political system has been generally overlooked or minimized with a threefold argument on the nature of the Italian foreign policy, of Italian public opinion, and of the Italian policymaking process. First, it is commonly argued that Italy has no foreign policy (Quaroni 1967). According to several scholars (Kogan 1965; Quaroni 1967; Graziano 1968), Italy is a country in which foreign and domestic politics are so closely related that Italian foreign policy is basically a mirroring of its domestic politics (Pasquino 1974; Panebianco 1977). The argument that there is no public opinion in foreign policy has been effectively expressed by Kogan (1965, 40), quoting Sereno, in the early 1960s: "Italians like movies, soccer and girls. They are not interested in politics and even less in foreign policy." This picture was perfectly in line with both qualitative (Banfield 1958) and quantitative (Almond and Verba 1983) studies of the 1960s and it rested with us since then.[2] In other words, the lack of interest in and knowledge of international affairs makes Italian public opinion so volatile and moody as to defy any serious analysis. As to the argument that public opinion has no impact on foreign policy, it is claimed on the one hand that the fragmented and decentralized nature of our political system (e.g., Hine 1993) makes it very difficult to trace the role of any single actor in the process. As the oft-quoted answer given by Ambassador Quaroni (1967) to the question "who does the Italian foreign policy?" reminds us, none does it. On the other hand, the existence of strong parties makes them both the natural channel through which the public's demands and complaints are processed, and the main interpreters and shapers of the public mood. In this chapter, we do not intend to deal with these three arguments in detail but only to point to some counterarguments that can be opposed to them and that, overall, justify a greater attention to public opinion in Italian foreign policy.

The tight intertwining of domestic and international factors and the difficulty to disentangle their relative weight in foreign policy decisions make Italy no different from other countries. It means, above all, that any approach that focuses exclusively either on the international or the domestic factors is of no use in the Italian case. Italy is neither such a small and helpless country to be mostly driven by international pressures nor so powerful to be driven mainly by domestic considerations. More appropriate to explain Italian foreign policy are those approaches that combine explicitly international and domestic factors in their explanation of foreign policymaking. As an example, the two-level-game approach (Putnam 1988; Moravski 1993), according to which the decision makers try to manipulate simultaneously domestic and international actors, is particularly appropriate to explain the role played by foreign policy goals in Italian politics (Isernia 1996a). Italians' paramount foreign policy goal has traditionally been recognized as that of protecting the Italian political system from any internal or external demand or pressure that could threaten the purportedly precarious domestic stability and shake the present distribution of socioeconomic power. For this purpose, the Italian ruling elite, mainly entrenched around the Democratic-Christian party, pursued a twofold policy of tight, almost "servile," alliance with United States on the one hand, and of European integration at any price (Kogan 1965) on the other hand. In so doing, the Democratic-Christian party legitimized its pivotal role in ruling the country for more than forty years and delegitimized the Communist party aspiration to do the same. The ability to pursue this goal rested for many years on the ability of the Italian government to exploit the "strength of the weak" (Schelling 1980). This picture, however, does not mean a lack of foreign policy, but more appropriately it acknowledges its complexity.

As to the nature of public opinion on security and international issues, we think—contrary to those who like to cultivate an Italian "exceptionalism" in negative (e.g., Tullio-Altan 1986) that the Italian public has many things in common with other countries. In particular, (1) Italian public opinion is no different from other countries' public opinion in its level of attention, interest, and knowledge of international affairs and (2) it is not erratic or volatile in its mood toward these issues (Battistelli and Isernia 1992; Isernia 1992; Isernia 1996b; Bellucci 1998). Italians are of course worried mostly by domestic problems, in particular the economic (e.g., unemployment) and the political ones (e.g., government instability and terrorism). In this, however, they do not differ from public opinion in other countries.[3] The lack of interest in foreign policy has been mentioned (Kogan 1965; Graziano 1968) as peculiar of the Italian case. This was probably true in the early 1950 and the 1960s (to which the data mostly refer, see Willick 1969) but it is less and less true nowadays, after the dramatic cultural change produced by mass school access and secularization (Sciolla 1990). Since the 1980s the level of interest for foreign and defense issues of Italian public is similar to that of other western European countries.[4] Italians, like other western European public opinions, have only a scanty knowledge of many international issues. Between 1955 and the end of the 1980s, on average no more than 70 percent of the Italians interviewed have heard of NATO. However, Almond assessed that only 10 percent of Americans have some knowledge of international issues, and according to Converse (1964) only 5 percent of the American public can be defined as broadly "ideological" in their political reasoning.[5]

If Italian public opinion is not so abysmally different on foreign matters from public opinion in other countries, it is neither more volatile. At the aggregate level, public opinion in Italy is remarkably stable (Isernia 1996b), to a degree quite similar to that of the United States (Page and Shapiro 1992) and France (Oreglia 1997). Moreover, always at the aggregate level, Italian public opinion on foreign policy does not change erratically but in an eminently reasonable way, following the impact of international events (Battistelli and Isernia 1992).

As to the final argument, that in Italy public opinion has no impact on foreign policy, a crucial issue in this chapter, the crux of the matter is that we do not know enough to conclude either way. Admittedly, the debate on the role of public opinion on policy has been revitalized in this last decade (Jacobs and Shapiro 1994; Page 1994; Shapiro and Jacobs 1989), opening a brand new sector of interdisciplinary work and marking a "dramatic step forward" in the amount and quality of research (see Geer 1996; Jacobs 1993; Wetstein 1996). At the end of a thorough review of this literature, Jacobs and Shapiro (1994, 9) concluded that "Statistical analyses and interpretative case studies have reported (both in the United States and Western Europe) a systematic relationship between public opinion and decision making on a range of issues." However, there are two main limitations to this recent interest for the opinion-policy connection.

First, the amount, congruence, and quality of evidence available on the Western European cases is much lower than that on the American one. Almost all we know on the role of public opinion in foreign policy comes, with some exceptions (Risse-Kappen 1991; Flynn and Rattinger 1985; Sinnott and Niedermayer 1995), mostly from the United States (see Holsti 1992, 1996 and Russett 1989 for reviews), a presidential system at the pinnacle of world power. As Cohen (1977–1978) and Risse-Kappen (1991) have pointed out, the role of public opinion in pluralistic parliamentary systems may be different by the presidential system. Not only there is a lack of genuine comparative research in this field but also, to make things worse, the empirical evidence available shows very clearly that the nature of the impact of public opinion on policy is very much context dependent (Risse-Kappen 1991) and we do not know enough about its variation across political systems. European studies on these questions, even if more recent, are much less frequent, and those that are available do not always support American findings (Brooks 1985, 1987; Eichenberg 1989; Everts 1996, 1998; Flynn and Rattinger 1985; Isernia 1996b; La Balme 1998). Extending the view to a different political system makes it much more complicated to reach a unifying and neat conclusion to the question whether opinion affects policy or not.

Second, insofar as the opinion-*foreign* policy connection is concerned, as Holsti (1992) has pointed out, it might well be that the remarkable stability and effective impact of opinions on policy was an artifact of the basically stable Cold War situation. As a consequence of the end of the Cold War and the increased pace of European integration, the problem of war and peace in the Western industrialized countries has fundamentally changed. On the one hand, specific dangers at the international level have been replaced by diffuse risks entailing a variety of possible uses of the military and armed force. The thesis that democracies do not wage war on each other ("the democratic peace" argument [Russett, 1993]) may be less relevant in a situation where interstate wars have become far less likely and frequent, in contrast with forms of violent intrastate conflicts. This requires that a new look be taken at the ancient debate concerning the suitability of the democratic model concerning foreign policy in general and the use of military force in particular. This affects in particular the study of public attitudes on the use of military force. Here, a lack of comparability across nations and across time still poses severe limitations to our understanding and to our ability to generalize our findings. More specifically, more research is necessary concerning the degree of support in modern democracies for international uses of force short of war for the protection of immediate national interests. While some democratic countries, such as Israel (Arian 1995; Herman 1998), are still faced with the problem of war in its traditional form and of the use of force to protect or pursue vital national interests, for many other democracies the image and meaning of military missions have profoundly changed after the end of the Cold War. In these countries the classical concept of the defense of national and allied territory and of large-scale warfare has been pushed to the background by "crisis-management" and "peacekeeping" (Everts 1996, 1998).

With respect to Italy in particular, the research program on the opinion-policy links is still at its very beginning (Bellucci 1998; Ceri 1997; Isernia 1996b). This is so for at least three reasons. First, and in general, the nature and extent of the link between opinion and policy in the case of multiparty parliamentary democracies like Italy is generally overlooked in favor of more traditional channels like parties and interest groups. In the elitist tradition of classical political science *à la* Mosca, the bulk of attention has been devoted to parties as the main, if not unique, legitimate channel through which demands and pressures reach the political system.

Second, much of the research carried out in this field so far is inspired, as above mentioned, by the American political culture. This influence is not without consequences for this research program. First, public opinion has mainly been perceived as mass opinion (as measured by surveys). Acknowledging that the sociologist "Blumer was wrong" in his critique of survey research does not mean he was wrong all the time and in all the places. In fact, among both scholars and decisionmakers in Europe, a "sociological" and "discursive" conception of public opinion is prevalent, with both destructive (attacking survey research) and constructive implications (a more diversified conception of the nature of public opinion and its impact). Theoretically, the study of public opinion as mass opinion has overlooked the role of parties and interest groups in shaping and mediating the connection between mass opinion and foreign policy. The role of these actors is much wider in the European context than in the American one. What additional role the mass media has in this context has not yet been determined. Second, policies are clearly (in the foreign realm at least) perceived as coming from the executive and they are also empirically easily detectable because of the Great Power nature of U.S. foreign policy.

Third, the analysis of the study of a link between opinion and policy has been facilitated by the U.S. presidential political system with weak parties in Congress. Public opinion both fosters legitimacy for presidential foreign policies and is a cue for the president on where (and how far) to go, lacking strong parties. Things are quite different on parliamentary system of weak or middle powers. In these countries, on the other hand, both terms of the connection should be more broadly defined. Public opinion includes not only mass opinion, as measured by polls, but also mass media opinion (mainly elite's newspaper editorials), élite opinion (mainly parliamentary élite opinions), and finally organized opinions (like the military, etc.). On the other hand, foreign policy is for these countries often a symbolic policy area.

It is of no surprise therefore that in the late 1970s Cohen (1977–1978; 1995), comparing the Netherlands and the United States, found the opinion policy connections in these two countries profoundly different. In the United States, lacking stable and legitimate institutional links between decision makers and public opinion, there is a convergent interest on the part of both individuals and officials "to go outside the political structure of government" (Cohen 1977–1978, 204) to discover what the other is thinking. In the Netherlands, whereas well-established and legitimized channels of communication between public and government do exist, a mutual adjustment of continuous "cooptation" takes place. Cohen see manifestations on these different institutional links in the use of polling results, in the role of pressure groups in foreign policy, and in the different role mass media play vis-à-vis the government. The nature of the link is relevant also in connection to the role of surveys in foreign policy. The United States is the kingdom of polling and foreign policy is no exception. Moreover, public opinion polling is view as "the best available institutional expression" of the relationship between the citizenship and its leaders, whereas in the Netherlands polling "is not generally treated as the expression of public opinion in matters of foreign affairs" (Cohen 1977–1978, 206).[6]

Similar considerations could be put forward in regard to the Italian case. Italy is (or more appropriately was until a few years ago) a case of "dominant party government" (Katz 1987, 13) in which both "partyness" of government and party "governmentness" were considered very high (but for a different reading see Cotta and Isernia 1996).[7] A major consequence of the nature of party government is that in such a system public opinion as mass opinion has a minor role to play and, following Cohen's discovery, also the survey industry is much less developed. The major, if not unique, channel of communication of political demands was the party system (La Palombara 1964; Hine 1990), namely, in the Italian case, the major government coalition member, the Democratic-Christian party and the major opposition party, the Communist. Moreover, in the Italian political and academic culture, so imbued with historicism and idealist undertones,[8] public opinion as measured by surveys had no legitimacy in itself. That is to say, the empirical and positivist attitudes that underline the idea that "attitude can be measured" has always found a hard time in Italy.[9]

In a parliamentary, multiparty, pluralistic, and fragmented political system such as Italy a wide set of actors plays a role in shaping public policies, both domestic and international. In this connection, three factors seem relevant to explain the different impact of public opinion on public policies: the distribution of political preferences among the public, the domestic political institutions, and the bargaining strategies of national decision makers at both the national and international level.[10]

The distribution of preferences among public opinion is crucial in affecting the decision makers' room for maneuvering. Decision makers in countries in which opinion on foreign policy issues are deeply polarized along the left-right continuum have a narrower win-set (to predate a Putnam's term) than decision makers of countries in which foreign policy is a "valence issue," in which political controversy impinges on the means rather than the goals and public opinion is in basic agreements on the fundamental choices. In this regard, the East-West foreign policy cleavage has always been a fundamental source of conflict both among Italian mass public and the political élite. The European Community until the early 1960s and the Atlantic Alliance up to the 1980s have had a profoundly polarizing effect on the domestic debate. This polarization however has also been used and manipulated by Italian governments to justify the fundamentally free-riding style of the Italian foreign policy (especially on issues like NATO rearmament, military expenditures, and policy toward the oil-producing Middle East countries) (Kogan 1965; Pasquino 1974; Isernia 1996a). The progressive depolarization between PCI and DC along the traditional East-West divide during the 1980s (Putnam 1977) gave room to a wider consensus on the fundamental choices of foreign and security policy and it made both Italian foreign policy more assertive and the United States less willing to get along the Italian positions. The Italian openings toward Yugoslavia after the Osimo treaty of 1975, strengthening a process already under way after the London agreement of 1954, are part of this play in which domestic considerations marry well with international ones (Romano 1995, 24–25).

Domestic political institutions are also crucial to explain whether and how public opinion will affect public policies (Risse-Kappen 1991). In principle, and at the risk of overgeneralization, we could claim that public opinion will be heard more easily and directly in presidential rather than in parliamentary systems; in two-party parliamentary systems rather than in coalitional multi-party parliamentary systems; in political systems with weak rather than strong parties; in which regular and stable channels of communication of society's preferences are lacking or are excessively fragmented rather than in systems with consolidated and formalized channels of communications (either parties or bureaucracies); in political system in which the media play an active role of direct link to the public rather than in systems in which the media do not see them as active as a link between the government and the people (Cohen 1977–1978, 203). The Italian political system with its format of "bargained pluralism" (Heine 1995), a society in which strong and well-entrenched political subcultures divide vertically the electorate, in which channels of communication between bureaucracy and society are mainly shaped by political parties through *clientela* and *parentela* relationships (La Palombara 1964), and in which the mass media system is heavily controlled either by political or economic powers, we might venture to hypothesize that public opinion has a weaker role to play.

There is no doubt that the Italian political system is heavily fragmented and dispersed. This is true also in foreign policy. Italian governments are usually a coalition of parties and several institutional actors have a voice in formulating and a veto power in implementing Italian foreign policy: the prime minister, who is responsible for the entire cabinet and has a right to be informed of all foreign policy communications (Graziano 1968, 17); the defense, foreign and treasury ministers and the president of the Republic, just to mention the most important. Moreover, the nature of the relationships among them is not well established and in a state of continuous flux, depending on the political resource of each of these actors and of the personal skills of those who occupy these roles. At the beginning of the Italian Republic, during the De Gasperi's governments, the prime minister had a clear prevalence over all other actors, because of the electoral predominance of DC, the international prestige of De Gasperi and his role both as prime minister and secretary of DC, the major partner in the coalition. Over time, with a decreasing strength of DC *vis-à-vis* its partners and the increased factionalism within the party, the Democratic Christian prime minister has seen his role reduced while ministers were seen as feuds in continuous bargaining among themselves. The executive fragmentation has been balanced to a certain extent by a structured party system, with strong parties in regular touch with society through multiple and regular channels, having their roots in different political subcultures, vertically divided along geographical borders: the "white" catholic subculture for the DC in the northeast and the "red" socialist subculture in the Center Italy (Galli 1966). These subcultures have had at the same time a polarizing and freezing role on the Italian political culture, sharply dividing along self-contained and mutually exclusive ideologies members of each subculture and freezing the electorate along party lines. Adding to this, the prevalence, in the Italian political culture, of idealistic overtones, whether of catholic or socialist origins, it is not surprising that both among the public and the élite mass poll opinion as measured by surveys is neither the most important nor the most legitimate expression of public opinion. What is "public opinion" for the Italian elite may be different (elite media, party supporters, the Parliament, a "climate of opinion," etc.), but for sure is not mainly (or exclusively) poll opinions. This, on the other hand, does not mean that public opinion surveying is not a reliable tool to gauge the public climate. It only means that, as such, it is not naturally seen as the most legitimate expression of the public climate and consequently not carefully listened.

Third, the role of public opinion change also according to the strategies used by the central decision makers in promoting their preferred outcomes. Public opinion can be either a resource or a constraint in international and domestic bargaining. In Italy, for several years the main interest of the political parties has often been that of depoliticizing the foreign policy issues both for fear of overheating the political debate and for cultivating the image of Italian exceptional status.

Nevertheless, the impact of public opinion on policy can change over time, due to domestic and/or international causes. The collapse of the Soviet Union and the deep restructuring of the international order that followed has probably affected the Italian political system more than any other Western European country with the exception of Germany, stressing again the crucial link between internal and external dynamics on which the Italian party government was built. In part as a consequence of the disappearance of the East-West divide and in part under the growing pressure of the European integration process, Italy has known a deep change of its political élite, a redefinition of its international role, and has had a wave of radical restructuring of the political system. These changes, among other things, have affected the nature of the public policy relationships as well. To mention only two among many effects of the political transition in which Italy is nowadays immersed, the weakening and the entrance of a TV tycoon (Silvio Berlusconi) in politics has increased both the attention given to polls by politicians and the systematic use of them for political marketing. Although it is too early to conclude whether Italy is moving toward an American-style political system (Barnes 1994) or we will see a reaffirmation of party politics, we can point to at least two effects of the changed international and domestic landscape on Italian public opinion.

The first effect is a progressive depolarization of the East-West cleavage along the Left-Right continuum. The Atlantic Alliance and the general politico-military alignment with the Western world had been for decades a source of continuous cleavage for the Italian political system. No political issue was more sensitive than this in foreign policy. The support for the NATO alliance has always been a test to legitimize the governmental ability of Italian political parties and to delegitimize the governmental aspirations of the Communist one. The Communist party gradually moved from a strongly anti-American and anti-NATO stance to a gradual acceptance of the present Italian alignments. This move culminated at the party level in 1976 with the statement by the secretary general of the Communist party, Enrico Berlinguer, that he was happy to be on this side of the curtain under the NATO umbrella (Putnam 1977; 1978). However, the early 1980s crisis of détente and the new Cold War of the Reagan era put to a serious test this choice and explain why, as figure 6.1 (see Appendix) shows, the Communist electorate took more than a decade to move from an anti to a pro-NATO stance. Eventually, only by 1989, the majority of the Communist (now Democratic Left Party, PDS) electorate supports the Atlantic Alliance and by 1996 this sector of the electorate is the most favorable to a greater role of European countries in NATO (Isernia 1996b).

This radical change in terms of foreign policy attitudes goes hand in hand with a more supportive attitude toward the armed forces, an institution that has never enjoyed in the postwar period an overwhelming degree of enthusiasm among the Italian public. As an effect of the way World War II ended and the miserable performance of the military leaders after the armistice of September 8, 1943, the Italian armed forces had been almost "invisible" (Battistelli 1996) for more than forty years. Since the early 1980s with the Lebanon multinational force mission and at a greater pace after the end of the Cold War, the Italian army has been playing an increasing role in several peacekeeping operations, culminating with the multinational coordination of the Albania operation in 1997. This performance partly led and partly contributed to a change in public attitude toward the armed forces. As shown in table 6.1, public support for employing the armed forces in different roles and missions is quite

Table 6.1 Degree of support for different tasks of Italian armed forces

Tasks	11/1992	01/1994	12/1994	01/1996	07/1996
Humanitarian aid	90	93	NA	NA	NA
Natural disasters	92	97	94	95	96
Peacekeeping operations under the UN	88	85	84	83	79
Domestic order	77	81	82	83	80
National defense	70	80	76	79	71
Peace-enforcing operations under the UN	55	51	60	63	56
NATO peace-enforcing operations out of area	39	44	42	47	41
NATO peace-enforcing operations in Europe	55	62	NA	NA	NA
International terrorism	75	81	NA	NA	NA

Source: Difebarometro, various issues

Question: Nel pensare ai possibili compiti delle Forze Armate italiane negli anni'90, può indicarmi tra i seguenti, quali ritiene debbano essere svolti dalle forze armate italiane e quali no:1. Controllo frontiere per contenere gli immigrati extracomunitari, etc.

widespread. The use of the military in domestic civil tasks (like natural disasters, struggle against Mafia, etc.) is practically unanimous and military and peacekeeping missions have been highly popular for all the 1990s. More controversial is the use of Italian armed forces for NATO out-of-area missions, but still substantial pluralities would support in principle this kind of mission.

However, this willingness of Italian public opinion to see a more active foreign role for our country is very sensitive to the domestic political situation, confirming the tight connection between the domestic and the international arena. Internationalism, the attitude to see a greater Italian involvement in international affairs, is connected to the expectation of a stable internal political system. The ups and downs in the number of those who support a more active role in the international arena follow strictly the degree of turmoil and political instability in the domestic political arena. When a government is unstable, its life-expectancy is low, and uncertainty clouds the political skies, internationalism decreases. When a government enjoys a vast majority, its life expectancy is long, and no political difficulty clouds its horizon, internationalism increases. Public opinion, in other words, reacts to international events but at the same time is influenced by the domestic political turmoil in its support for a more active international role. This is an evidence that for the Italian public opinion an effective foreign policy rests on a stable and authoritative government (Bellucci 1998). This is the general context in which the Bosnia crisis took place.

ITALIAN POLICYMAKING AND BOSNIA

The Bosnia crisis occurred at a very particular time for the Italian political system, deeply affecting the reciprocal dynamic between the international and the domestic level. Yugoslavia's collapse and the Bosnia war erupted at the very moment Italy faced a double challenge, domestic and international. On the one hand, starting from 1992, Italy entered into its deepest political crisis since World War II. The collapse of the post-World War II party system, following the judicial scandals and the political and electoral turmoil it implied, meant that domestic issues absorbed almost exclusively the attention of the Italian politicians. On the other hand, Italy had to face an ever-increasing amount of demands coming from the until then "placid" international environment. The end of the Cold War by far brought about more and not less international activity for a middle-power like Italy. Italy became involved in a growing number of international crises such as the Albania's refugee flood, the Gulf War, the Maastricht Treaty negotiations, the Somalia mission, and eventually the collapse of Yugoslavia, which called for a more active and continuous Italian presence on several international bodies, taxing the already limited resources of Italian politicians. For the first time since the collapse of Fascism and the end of World War II, Italy was "alone" in making its decisions; namely the passive, slow and traditionally low profile of its foreign policy was not enough to guarantee a shield to international pressures.

No area of Italian foreign policy has been more deeply marked by the end of the Cold War than the "special relationship" with east central Europe and Yugoslavia in particular (Mastny 1995). Moreover, the dynamic of the Yugoslav crisis has had a narrowing influence on the ability of Italian foreign policy to influence both the politics in the area and the course of the events. After a first stage of creative posture that lasted approximately until 1991, Italian policy in the area became more and more reactive and low-keyed (Holmes 1993).[11] First, the failure of the European Union action—the main, if not the only, arena in which Italy can promote with success its national interests—has reduced the weight of Italian influence. Together with the declining ability of the European Union in steering the events, the growing role of the "informal" multilateral diplomacy led by the United States and, eventually, the resort to arms, Italian political influence was severely constrained. Excluded by the Contact Group until the early 1996, uncertain whether to contribute with armed forces to a military effort in which Italy was already giving a contribution in terms of logistic support and military bases, Italy chose a low profile, characterizing its contribution in terms of humanitarian aid.[12] In this context, the late 1995 decision to participate in IFOR concluded a Balkan policy that moved through two stages characterized by different policy style: solidarity and low profile in the first stage and a more protagonist, confrontational, and eventually realist in the second one.

First Phase: Solidarity and Low Profile (1991–1994)

The Yugoslav crisis interrupted a long period of Italian cooperation with an active involvement in the political evolution of Eastern European countries. As to Yugoslavia, after the settlement of October 1954 and its formalizing in the Osimo Treaty of October 1975 Italy marked a 180 degree turn in its Yugoslavia policy, from foe to friend and economic supporter.[13] In a few years, Italy became Yugoslavia's major western trading partner together with Germany. The 1980s were a period of intense attention toward Yugoslavia on the part of the Italian government. To favor the creation of a regional economic zone, in November 1978 Italy launched the regional "Alpe-Adria" initiative, associating Friuli Venezia-Giulia, Veneto, Croatia, Slovenia, Carinthia, Upper Austria and Styria and two "active observers" Bavaria and Salzburg. In time, other regions (Trentino-Alto Adige, Lombardia, Gyor-Sorpon and Vas, Burgerland) were added as members or observers. Therefore, Italy could not be a passive spectator in the Eastern evolution of the area. Both economic and political national interests were at stake. As Romano (1995, 28) stresses "Italian foreign policy could not limit itself to contemplating disorder and passively accepting its consequences. Nor could it welcome the prospect of some or all of the region's countries being drawn, in whole or in part, into the economic sphere of a new Reich such that the Alps would have become, as they were in the nightmares of Sonnino, the Italian-German border." At the beginning of the crisis, Italy made efforts at every level, bilateral, multilateral, and European, to calm the Yugoslavia crisis. At the bilateral level, Italy continued to support politically and economically the attempts by the Markovic's government to cope with the deep domestic economic crisis. In September 1989 Andreotti and De Michelis (respectively prime minister and minister of foreign affairs) signed with the Yugoslavia minister of foreign affairs, Loncar, a bilateral cooperation project "Iniziativa Adriatica" involving agriculture, communications, environment, fishing, and tourism and promising 700 million dollars to deal with the difficult economic situation. In December 1989 the Italian government signed a protocol of economic collaboration for 1000 billion Liras of investments in Yugoslavia. Still in 1991, when the Yugoslavia breakdown was clearly on its way, the Italian export support institution (SACE) granted a credit of 800 billion Liras. At the multilateral level, Italy attempted to follow through the Alpe-Adria experience, engaging Austria, Yugoslavia, and Hungary in an attempt to promote regional integration and cooperation, especially in infrastructure projects, with a view to promote Trieste and Venice as the outlet of such a vast hinterland (Romano 1995, 30–31). This project, called "Quadrangolare," rapidly enlarged to a "Pentagonale," including Czecholsovakia in 1990, an "Hexagonale" with Poland in 1991, eventually rechristened itself as the Central European Initiative in 1992, with new members as diverse as Bulgaria, Romania, and the newly independent Croatia, Slovenia, Czech Republic, Slovakia, Belarus, and

Ukraine. At the European Community level Italy was in a good position to influence the events when, following the Croatia and Slovenia declaration of independence of June 25, 1991, the Slovenia ten-day war started. When the federal parliament declared the independence declaration illegal and illegitimate and it invited the government to take all necessary measures to avoid the division of Yugoslavia, ordering the federal police and the federal army (YPA) to take the control of customs checkpoints, including those at the border with Italy, the Austrian and Italian government asked immediately for the new CSBM (Confidence and Security Building Measures) mechanism to be activated and the European Council sent a *troika*—including the Italian foreign minister Gianni De Michelis—to Belgrade. Italy was very active in this mediation effort. On July 2, the Federal Army launched an air attack on Lubjana, the EC sent an exploratory mission and the Italian member was the first to leave in advance to Lubjana.[14] On July 3, an Italian delegation, led by the general director of political affairs of the Ministry of Foreign Affairs, Ambassador Vanni d'Archirafi went to Belgrade to convince the government to stop the tanks at the border between Slovenia and Croatia. These EC efforts concluded with the EC-sponsored cease-fire in Brioni,[15] that will break down on July 14. Unfortunately, all this efforts were not able to match the pace of the events in Yugoslavia, that disintegrated itself by 1991 and Italy lost all ability of bilateral influence plunging in its domestic political transition from 1992.

As the Yugoslav crisis deepened the Italian position became more and more difficult (Holmes 1993). At the beginning of the crisis, Italy was perfectly in tune with the European Union: to facilitate the political transition of Yugoslavia, avoiding bloody and painful divisions. Until June 1991, the Italian government was strongly anti-secession and it opposed an early recognition of the Slovenia and Croatia republics. Under a set of domestic and international pressure the Italian position changed during July and August 1991, contributing to tilt the balance of forces within the European Union in favor of the pro-recognition forces. Domestically, the offensive of the presidents of the Friuli Venezia-Giulia and Trentino Alto-Adige regions, of the autonomous provinces of Trento and Bolzano and of the the Minister Bernini (a prominent DC member from Veneto) together with the pressure of the Vatican state (Romano 1995, 32) eventually convinced the Democratic Christian party to support the recognition of the two republics. The Socialist party although reluctant had no choice but to get along with it. Internationally, the adamant German decision to recognize Slovenia and Croatia even at the price of the European integration made unbearable the idea of opposing to such a process (Holmes 1993).

At the very moment the EU recognized Slovenia and Croatia and the war broke out in Bosnia, the Italian political system became embroiled in its deepest political crisis since the Second World War and the successive Italian governments (Andreotti, Amato and Ciampi) adopted on Yugoslavia a policy of solidarity, gradualism, and national low profile that will last until March 1994 and will be often acrimoniously criticized by political commentators and politicians of different parties. During the Andreotti government, Italy participated in both multilateral and bilateral undertakings. At the multilateral level, Italy was part of the Western European Union humanitarian mission and it helped to implement the joint NATO-WEU arms embargo in the Adriatic Sea. At the bilateral level, Italy recognized the new republics of Slovenia and Croatia and it signed a memorandum with the latter to guarantee Italian minorities. Since November 1991, the Italian government supported Slovene and Croat refugees in Friuli Venezia-Giulia and helped that region to cope with the impact of the Yugoslav crisis on the region's economy. The Amato government, under the experience of the Albanian refugees flood in the summer 1991, changed its refugee policy, privileging direct aid to the former-Yugoslavian territories, rather than let them in. In this frame, Italy took part in a WEU military mission to protect the flow of humanitarian aid, following the London Conference of August 26–28, 1992.

The climate changed somewhat after the shooting down, at the beginning of September 1992, of an Italian airplane flying an humanitarian mission over Bosnia.[16] Italy was not completely disappointed by the United Nations decision, in preparing Resolution n.776 which enlarged UNPROFOR to Bosnia, to exclude Italy by the peacekeeping operation there with the arguments that the common borders between Italy and former Yugoslavia and the military experiences during the Second World War made Italy not the ideal partner. There was opposition to the Italian participation also on the Yugoslav side. The Bosnian Serb leader Karadzic as well as the Slovenia and Croatia governments vetoed the Italian military contribution (see *il Corriere della Sera*, September 13, 1992). This came as a relief for the Italian minister of defense, Salvo Andò, and the Italian armed forces, worried both of the danger of such a mission and of the contemporary commitment of Italian military in Somalia.

The Ciampi government, in 1993, did not change the Italian policy of solidarity with a low profile. Italy enlarged its logistic support, making its air bases available to NATO for the operation "Deny Flight" also after the UN decision to authorize the use of air force to protect the UNPAs (United Nations Protected Areas) (UNSC Resolution n.958, November 1993) and the Atlantic Council decision in January 1994 to authorize the bombing of Serb positions under an UNPROFOR request. These Italian decisions were not without risks, as the NATO ultimatum of February 1994, in which the Bosnian Serbs were asked to withdraw their heavy weapons 20 km from Sarajevo, showed. In response to that ultimatum, among other things the Serbs threatened to hit NATO bases in Italy (see *il Corriere della Sera*, February 11, 1994).

The Italian government supported throughout this period a political solution to the Bosnian crisis and it strongly opposed an armed intervention, also because it was convinced of the low popularity of such a conflict among the

Italian public opinion. This conviction was stressed in Vienna, in January 1994, by the Italian foreign minister Andreatta (see *il Corriere della Sera*, January 8, 1994) who stated that many failures in Bosnia were due to the public opinion opposition both in Italy and in other Western countries (including the United States) to a military intervention (see *la Repubblica*, January 26, 1994). However, under the pressure of events—the killing of three journalist in Mostar, a strong Papal support for an intervention in Bosnia, and the market shelling in Sarajevo—Andreatta changed his mind and declared himself in support of a NATO intervention (see *la Repubblica*, February 6, 1994). It is interesting to point that in a later interview Andreatta smoothed the influence of public opinion on the Italian foreign policy choices (see *la Repubblica*, February 13, 1994).

As a matter of fact, the available data show (see following section and the appendix) that the general orientation of Italian public opinion was exactly the opposite of that perceived by the Italian foreign affairs minister. However, Italian officials were not alone in making this mistake. The majority of Western European countries had public opinion less reluctant than their governments to support an armed intervention in Bosnia to restore peace (Sobel 1996, 151). Italian, French, English, and German public opinion was in favor of an armed intervention since 1992. Between March 1993 and February 1994 an average 65 percent of the Italian public opinion was in support of an Italian military intervention in Bosnia to establish peace. Moreover, since 1992 the majority said that the European Community was doing "too little" to stop the fighting in Yugoslavia, and in March 1993 USIA reports that "Italian are more likely to say that their own country is doing too little than to say they are doing all they can" (USIA, ORM April 9, 1993). By December 1994 three quarters (70 percent) of Italian public opinion was favorable to the Italian armed forces participation to a NATO mission aiming at stopping the fighting in Bosnia and at establishing a lasting peace. This support changed over time, also reflecting the impact of frustrating events on the ground, but it has never decreased under 50 percent of the polled in support of an armed Italian intervention under NATO banner.

The solidarity and low profile policy had a temporary stop in March 1994, when a new debate on the opportunity to send Italian troops in Bosnia took place. The request by UN Secretary General Boutros Boutros-Ghali to increase the number of peacekeepers in Bosnia—where the military situation on the ground worsened after the shooting down of four Serb jet fighters—induced Great Britain to ask the UN Security Council for the participation of Italian and Turk troops. The Italian government was divided. Beniamino Andreatta, the minister of foreign affairs, was this time in favor while the minister of defense, Diego Fabbri, was opposed, probably under the pressure of the military chiefs of staff reluctant to involve Italian troops in Bosnia when the best trained troops available were already overcommitted in Somalia.[17]

Paradoxically, the staunchest supporters of an armed intervention were in the peace movement—already active and present in Sarajevo—whereas the parties dedicated a scanty attention to the issue, being a period of parliamentary elections. This time Slovenia and Croatia were in favor of an Italian participation. At the end, the statement by the Minister of Defense Fabbri that a UN request of troops to Italy was "not opportune" ended the political debate (see *la Repubblica*, March 8, 1994). On April 26, 1994, the United States, France, Germany, United Kingdom, and Russia formed the "Contact Group" to coordinate international effort in Bosnia and the UN approved the deployment of 6,500 troops to reinforce UNPROFOR.

Second Phase: Solidarity Is Not Enough: Looking for an Higher Profile (1994–1996)

The Italian government policy toward Bosnia changed somewhat, at least symbolically, during the Berlusconi government. The Italian foreign minister Antonio Martino (Forza Italia), during his first visit to Washington in May 1994, asked formally for the Italian admission to the Contact Group, making clear the Italian government wish to be acknowledged as an important partner in the Bosnia crisis. The explicit goal of the Berlusconi government was—as Martino stated to the Senate Foreign Affairs Committee hearing—to give Italy a greater visibility, showing "a more muscular policy after two years in which the Italian profile had been shadowed" (see *la Repubblica*, June 22, 1994). However, the decision to use Bosnia as the first stage to improve the Italian international standing was not the most appropriate. The Berlusconi government was a coalition in which one of the major partners was Alleanza Nazionale (AN). AN was the brand-new name of the extreme right-wing party MSI (Movimento Sociale Italiano) which had explicitly asked in its electoral program for a revision of the Osimo Treaty and the return to Italy of territories in Istria and Dalmatia (Bellucci 1998, 116–17). Moreover, the adversarial stance the Berlusconi's government assumed toward Slovenia's request to be associated with the European Union made Italy not the best partner to include in a negotiating role in the Contact Group. Finally, this more "protagonist" stance had its own intrinsic limits in the Italian government's reluctance to actually do more in the field. When in December 1994 the hypothesis of withdrawing UNPROFOR troops from Bosnia was discussed and NATO draw a contingency plan for the troops' withdrawal, Italy asked not to be considered in such a planning. This desire not to be involved was the result of several factors: the international hostility toward the Berlusconi government (Neal 1995), the UN reluctance to use troops of bordering countries, and also the awareness by the Italian political leaders of the limits of the Italian army in a ground operation burdened by several threats and risks.[18]

This contradictory stance of asking for more while being reluctant to bear the costs characterized also Berlusconi's successor, the Dini government, a "technical" government supported by a center-left coalition including La Lega. With the fall of Szrebrenica and Tuzla in the spring 1995 and the deterioration of UN-PROFOR position, the debate on the Bosnia crisis rekindled among the Western European countries. France and Great Britain after some debate and rumors of withdrawing decided to strengthen the UNPROFOR contingent with a Rapid Reaction Force able to withstand Serb attacks, while NATO planned a withdrawal plan for the UN forces in which Italian troops had a role this time. The Italian government however continued to have an ambivalent position. The Italian foreign minister Agnelli stated at the Chamber of Deputies that the government neither shared the extreme positions on withdrawing nor the policy of lifting the arms embargo of Bosnian Muslims, without mentioning what role the Italians troops should have. This ambivalence characterized also the positions of the main parties. The former minister Andreatta and now PPI (*Partito Popolare Italiano*) MP declared: "we must avoid that Bosnia becomes a new Vietnam; public opinion asks a military intervention but it is not ready to carry its burden" (see *Il Sole—24 Ore*, July 13, 1995). This was a slightly different version of his previous year's argument. This time, according to Andreatta, public opinion was willing to support an armed intervention, but being moody and volatile, this support was ready to dissolve as soon as the first casualties would have occurred. In the Council of Ministers meeting of July 18 devoted to defining the Italian position at the incoming London meeting of July 21 of the Contact Group enlarged to EU, UN, and NATO,[19] the government did not take a formal stance on the problem of Italian troops. As a matter of fact, the position of ministers Agnelli (Foreign Affairs) and Corcione (Defense) prevailed: no ground troops but readiness to make available Italian airplanes for the "Deny Flight" missions. According to newspapers sources, the defense minister, Domenico Corcione, former chief of the Joint Chief of Staff, stressed the danger of Serb threats to Italy and the inadequacy of Italian army for such a mission (see *il Corriere della Sera*, July 19, 1995). The decision not to decide was however criticized in several quarters. Particularly vocal was the government's major supporting party, the Democratic Party of the Left (PDS), that openly argued for the intervention.

The London Summit approved the participation of Italian airplanes to the NATO air strike and bombing missions, further enlarging the Italian commitment (at that time economically around 27 billion liras per month). In that context the participation of Italy to the Contact Group was also discussed among the members of the Contact group, without reaching an agreement on the formal admission of Italy. This exclusion opened a crisis between Italy and the United States. Invited to take part to a meeting of the Contact Group as a member of the European troika, Foreign Minister Agnelli announced to Italian newspapers that Italy had been formally admitted to the Contact group. Taken by surprise, the American embassy in Rome denied that such a formal offer had ever been done.[20] This was perceived as utterly inadequate with the Italian request for a more visible role and the government retorted informing the U.S. government that Italy "would permit no new NATO operation for the Balkans from bases in Italy" (Williams 1994, A27) and that it would withdraw the permission to land in Italian air bases for U.S. Stealth bombers. The main goal of the government was to induce the U.S. government to convince the main opponents of the Italian presence in the Contact Group, apparently France and Great Britain, to accept it as a full member.[21] When these two countries refused again to accept Italy, the United States decided to stay out of the controversy withdrawing the request of air bases for U.S. airplanes as a face-saving move (see *Il Sole—24 Ore*, September 17, 1995). The Italian government had no other choice than to accept. In the meanwhile, the same air bases became less important because the Croat-Muslim offensive and the air strikes already under way had convinced the Bosnian Serbs to accept the peace negotiations process in Dayton.

The Italian request to be involved in the Contact Group however was reiterated during the negotiations to define the multinational peace operations in Bosnia within the Dayton agreement.[22] Italy continued to be occasionally invited to join the group during 1995 in New York,[23] in connection with the Italian presidency of the Security Council. Leaving the Security Council presidency, Italy again joined formally the group in the first semester of 1996 as president of the European Union, this time participating regularly to the meetings of the contact group both in Sarajevo, New York, and in Western European capitals. In this context of a growing Italian role and of a cleared mission for the peacekeeping operation, the NATO request to participate in the IFOR mission was accepted by the Italian government, with the support of all political parties, with the only exception of the Green (Verdi) and the Communist party (Rifondazione Comunista).

The decision to send an Italian brigade in Sarajevo under the French command changed the Italian position on Bosnia. Capitalizing on the presence of Italian troops in Bosnia and on the contribution Italy gave during the first semester of 1996 to the contact group,[24] the government moved to formalize the regular presence of Italy in all of the several level of the contact group once the Italian EU presidency expired in June. On that occasion, eventually, the opposition from Western European countries was overcome and Italy became a full member.

ITALIAN PUBLIC OPINION AND BOSNIA

An Aggregate Analysis

On a comparative level, it has been argued (Sobel 1996) that the erroneous perception of the unavailability of European and American public opinion to support an armed mission in Bosnia was a source of uncertainty and ambiguity of Western powers' policy. As a matter of fact, we already noted in the previous section that the opposition of Italian public opinion to an armed intervention was used as an argument to oppose an Italian involvement in January 1994. And also during the debate whether to contribute or not to NATO plan to support UNPROFOR in summer 1995 the by then clear-cut and steady support of the public for an armed intervention was perceived by several politicians as a volatile and capricious mood and, as such, a shaky ground for a serious foreign policy commitment.

In this section we will describe, on the basis of the available data, the Italian public attitudes toward an armed intervention in Bosnia during the period 1992–1996. We will first explore the data available to see whether the support was there and how strong it was, and secondly we will examine its main determinants. The surveys discussed here (and reported more completely in the Appendix) are taken from several different sources, both Italian and foreign.[25] Unless otherwise mentioned, they come from face-to-face and telephone surveys of a representative sample of the population from age eighteen. Although data are available already at the end of 1992, only by the end of 1993 do we have questions addressing squarely the possibility of an Italian intervention.[26] Moreover, it has to be remembered that, as shown in the very case of Bosnia by Sobel (1996), support for a military intervention is very sensitive to question wording. Support for armed intervention changes depending on whether the question mentions casualties, military expenditures, the difficulties of the internal political situation of prospective hosting country. For the Italian case, however, we note that the sensitivity to question wording is higher during the first years of the war (say until 1993). As the situation on the ground gets more difficult, the indiscriminate bombing of innocents continues and a solution moves farther away, the depressing effect exerted on the degree of aggregate support by these references seem to decrease. To give just an example, in August 1993 to a severely biased question [27] asking whether the respondent was in favor of an armed intervention knowing that the peacekeeping forces would suffer casualties and heavy military expenditures, not surprisingly only 28 percent were in favor. The closest survey available, in November 1993, shows that 63 percent of the interviewed were in favor of NATO sending forces to help establish peace "if the warring parties in Bosnia are unable to reach an agreement and the fighting continues" (Doxa survey of November 2–11 for USIA, ORM December 17, 1993; see Appendix).

From the data available it emerges that Italians, as other Europeans (Sobel 1996), have always strongly supported a greater effort in the Bosnia crisis and they had had an unsatisfactory judgment of what the international community was doing. In November 1992, 67 percent of the Italians thought that both the European Community and the United States are doing too little to stop the fighting in Yugoslavia. In June 1994, 72 percent think the European Community and 70 percent that the United Nations are doing too little to stop the struggle, but only 57 percent see Italy as doing not enough. This harsh judgment on the lack of effort by the multilateral bodies is linked on the one hand to the conviction that international organizations have a real influence on the political situation in the former Yugoslavia and on the other hand to the desire to see peace reestablished in that area at (almost) any price. In February 1994, 73 percent of those interviewed by Doxa thought that if international diplomacy made a real effort it had many or some possibilities to stop the war in Bosnia. In May-June 1994 to a question on who had the role to resolve the former-Yugoslavia conflict, UN, the European Union and NATO were all mentioned by the majority in the first places. Only one country reached a similar position: the United States, with 55 percent of the interviewed thinking it had a role in solving the crisis.

As to the role the multinational force should play in Bosnia, it is clear that an active military role not only in carrying out the humanitarian intervention but also in actually ending the conflict was the most popular option. In March 1993, 92 percent of the Italians interviewed were in favor of the use of multilateral military force to protect humanitarian aid and 79 percent were in favor of such a use to impose a solution, no matter what. In June 1994, 53 percent were in favor of a "decisive military intervention for a definite solution of the present situation in Bosnia." In 1994, no more than 7 percent was on the average in favor of letting things continue and no more than an average of 34 percent in favor of withdrawing troops. For a clear two-third majority of the polled population, force should have been actually used to let the humanitarian aid's convoys to pass through.

A slightly different question, asked by Doxa on January 31, 1994 and on February 9, that is to say, immediately before and after the mortar attack of February 5, 1994 in the Sarajevo market square, which killed at least sixty-eight and wounded up to two hundred, allows us to examine the impact of an increase in the level of violence on the resolve of public opinion. The mortar attack increases of approximately 6 percentage points the share of population willing to support an armed intervention of UN troops to stop the fighting in Bosnia. On January 31, 51 percent were in favor of such an intervention and on February 9 (four days after the massacre) they were 57 percent. The data seem to indicate that the major impact of the mortar shelling was on the uncertain rather than on those opposing it. The effect of the indiscriminate killing on the support for Italian intervention is much greater among those who are already in favour of the multilateral intervention. Seventy-three percent of those in favor of an armed intervention were also supportive of the idea of sending Italian troops on January 31. The support for an Italian intervention, four days after Sarajevo's market shelling, grows up among these to

85 percent. In other words, if you support an intervention, you want Italy to be part as well.

Since March 1993, the Italian public was in favor of a military intervention by the United Nations and by the end of December 1994 this resolve was stiffened and widened. On November 1994, 54 percent of the population polled wanted to end war by any means if war were to continue until spring next year and if, following an arms embargo, war should escalate, 68 percent were against removing UN troops. The level of support increases if the question mentions explicitly that the troops are sent to implement a peace agreement. In December 1994, 77 percent of those interviewed are in favor of sending NATO troops to make a peace agreement respected. This percentage is only slightly higher than the 74 percent in favor of such an option in November 1993 with a question that had no explicit reference to peace, but only to an agreement among the warring parts. This testifies again to the steady level of support for the armed option.

The war had an effect also on the support for NATO air strikes and it shows the willingness of public opinion to get along the decision of the UN to threaten air strikes to deter attacks against the UNPAs. Between February and June 1994 no more than one third of public opinion was in support of launching air attacks. However, to a question referring to NATO air strikes on Bosnian Serb forces around Goradze, 67 percent of the population is in favor of such air strikes. This support is related to the conviction that they are effective to stop the fighting. Sixty-one percent think that NATO air strikes are more likely to lead to peace than prolonging the fight in Bosnia.

Contrary to the Gulf war, in which a villain was clearly identified and vilified, Saddam Hussein, no such a target emerged in the Bosnia crisis. Even Slobodan Milosevic, the closest candidate to such a role, was never clearly and coherently pictured like the culprit by the Italian mass media. Two surveys of August 1993 and November 1994 asked respectively against whom should we intervene and which group the respondent sympathized most. A majority of the population (42 percent) answered that we should have intervened against all and another 34 percent simply did not know. Overall, only 19 percent of the public opinion thought we should have picked up the Serbs as the major culprits. However, no group is definitely preferred in the struggle. Overall, 38 percent sympathize with none and no more than 19 percent are sympathetic with the Catholic Croats—the target of several supportive Papal statements between 1991 and 1993—and 15 percent with the Bosnian Muslims. This is probably due to the ambivalent historical position toward the parties in the Bosnia conflict. In Italy, there are historical roots of friendship both with the Serbs—especially in the left because of the struggle against Nazis during the Second World War—and the Croats for their Catholic origins.

If we move to analyze the support for the Italian intervention, we find again a remarkable stability in the support for an intervention of our armed forces. Figure 6.2 shows the overall stability of the Italian attitudes toward the idea of an Italian armed intervention. Although the early questions are worded not exactly in identical terms, the overall trend is flat and overwhelmingly positive. The only change occurs in the middle of 1995, when the gloomy situation of the UN troops taken as hostages and the patent inability of the UN to curb Serbian attacks on Sarajevo probably depressed the level of support for an intervention (figure 6.2 in the Appendix).

The data show a strong support for an armed intervention and this contradicts the image of the public by Italian political elite. But how strong was this support? As we have seen, in 1994 some politicians presented the argument that public opinion support was shaky and ready to dissolve as soon as casualties occur. We enter here in the delicate field of the willingness of public opinion to carry the burden of the consequences of their preferred choices. It has been argued forcefully that the Western public is increasingly reluctant to see its troops suffer casualties. In the Italian case, a country that has never fought a war after the end of the Second World War and whose public opinion is regularly at the last position in the willingness to sacrifice for their country, this argument seems particularly persuasive. Figure 6.3 (Appendix) shows how the support for an Italian armed intervention decreases as the level of sacrifice required increases. This trend is similar to that observed in other countries (Everts 1996) and show how the degree of support is crucially affected by the actual possibility of the use of force, the likelihood of casualties among friendly and foe troops and eventually the availability to sacrifice himself for the country. However, there are also some interesting differences among different subgroups. The support for the Italian intervention is systematically higher among the men, of age between twenty-five and fifty-four and of a center-right orientation. On the contrary, the support is lower among the women, the youngest (less than twenty-five) and the oldest (more than fifty-four) and those of left-right orientation. This negative trend however has to be framed in the appropriate context. Support for casualties is related not only to the degree of personal involvement (as in the question involved) but also to factors such as the clarity and legitimacy of the goals pursued, the sense of belonging to a multinational force, the understanding that the sufferance will last not for ever, the duration of the conflict and so on. The Gulf war and the Somalia experiences (where a dozen of Italian soldiers were killed and some more injured) point to the fact that when the goals are clear, the legitimacy of the military operation is well understood and the experience is clearly delimited temporally, Italian public opinion is willing to bear the human costs of the operation (figure 6.3 in the Appendix).

The Determinants of Support: An Individual Level Analysis

Moving from the aggregate to the individual level, we will try here to locate the variables affecting the degree of support for an Italian participation to a military mission in Bosnia, in an attempt to verify possible changes in the direction of these effects over time. We will utilize two data sets. A first data set is a monthly tracking poll starting from the beginning of the IFOR mission in January 1996 up to November 1996. It allows a precise and comparable measurement of attitude change over time although its relevance is narrowed by the short time period and by the restricted number of independent variables available. To overcome this limit, we will then look at a second source of data, Difebarometro 4,[28] a telephone survey we carried out in July 1996 and that has a richer set of background, sociological, and motivational variables.

Our level of knowledge on the reactivity of public opinion at the individual level to international crises involving directly Italy is much less wide and in-depth than our understanding of the overall evolution of Italian public opinion in foreign policy at the aggregate level. As a matter of fact, the only studies we have on this matter are those about the Gulf War (Isernia e Ammendola 1993; Ammendola 1993, Isernia 1996b). The Gulf War is not a really comparable case, given the difference among the two events, but rather is a source of hypotheses to confirm in the Bosnia crisis. Isernia (1996b) shows that in Italy, as in some other Western countries, a majority of the population (80 percent) was against an Italian armed intervention in the anti-Saddam coalition before the Gulf War started. At the end of the war those in favor have became 62 percent.[29] This change of attitude was neither part of a manipulation attempt by the media (notwithstanding the ambiguous role of the Allies in the information supply, the Italian media were quite divided on the war) nor a consequence of a well-known phenomenon like the rally-around-the-flag. Contrary to other countries, like France and the United States, in Italy the support becomes majoritarian only weeks after the war started, that is to say only when the war appeared to be a quick military campaign, with a few casualties (from the Western side), and without serious consequences both at the regional (Israel) and global (the USSR) level. The role of the media was crucial in conveying an image of the war as winnable and "clean" and of the Western coalition as technologically effective and military overwhelming.

The results show in the Gulf War case that the opposition to an Italian participation in the war was stronger among women, the oldest generations, the less educated, and the left-wing oriented. It is interesting to compare these results with those of the Bosnia crisis. Table 6.2 shows the degree of support for an Italian participation to a military mission in Bosnia among different subgroups, revealing some similarities and some differences with the Gulf War.

Table 6.2. Attitudes toward the Italian Intervention in Bosnia among Different Subgroups (Polled January–November 1996; %)

	Favor	Oppose	DK	Total	(N)
Gender					
Male	70.9	25.5	3.7	100	(3631)
Female	69.4	23.2	7.4	100	(3960)
Area					
North-West	65.8	28.7	5.5	100	(1619)
North-East	68.6	25.4	6.0	100	(1840)
Center	69.5	24.4	6.1	100	(1521)
South	74.3	20.7	5.1	100	(2611)
Age					
18–24	74.7	22.1	3.1	100	(998)
25–44	73.8	22.1	4.1	100	(3651)
45 and beyond	64.0	27.7	8.4	100	(2942)
Education					
Low School	64.5	27.3	8.2	100	(3364)
High School or University	75.6	21.3	3.1	100	(3852)
Profession					
Entrepreneur	70.8	26.4	2.8	100	(861)
Head	77.7	18.8	9.4	100	(681)
Clerks	73.1	22.7	4.2	100	(1076)
Workman	67.8	27.1	5.1	100	(1117)
Retired	59.0	31.2	9.8	100	(1117)
Housewife	68.0	22.4	9.6	100	(1362)
Student	78.2	20.1	1.7	100	(591)
Unemployed	73.2	23.2	3.5	100	(452)
Religion					
Not practicing	69.9	25.3	4.7	100	(2968)
Practicing	72.3	23.0	4.7	100	(2175)
Political Self-position					
Center-Left	73.9	22.4	3.7	100	(2550)
Center	74.0	23.4	2.5	100	(1259)
Center-Right	71.4	25.1	3.5	100	(2057)
Party Voted					
Rifondazione	71.1	25.8	3.1	100	(446)
Green	78.9	18.8	2.3	100	(133)
Pds	76.2	20.2	3.6	100	(1203)
Dini-Patto-Ad	79.7	13.9	6.3	100	(158)
P.Popolare	78.8	16.9	4.3	100	(373)
Lega	61.1	35.0	4.0	100	(452)
Fi	73.5	21.3	5.2	100	(1018)
Ccd-Cdu	80.5	15.6	3.9	100	(128)
Pannella	80.3	17.1	2.6	100	(76)
An-Fiamma	69.2	27.9	2.9	100	(964)
No answer	64.7	26.4	8.8	100	(446)
International Orientation					
Internationalist	81.6	15.3	3.1	100	(2950)
Isolationist	63.5	30.9	5.6	100	(4210)
Total	70.1	24.3	5.2	100	(7591)

Starting with the differences, a first one is the lack of any gender gap. The degree of support among women is similar to men and it is even greater than men if we exclude the "don't know" answers. Also, the political party orientation plays a minor role. Those voting for left-wing parties are more in favor of an Italian participation than those voting right-wing parties (respectively, 80 percent among the electorate of the Democratic Left party, 73 percent among FI supporters, and 69 percent among National Alliance (AN) the extreme right-wing party). Looking at the similarities, we find a greater support among the younger generations and those with a high level of education. It is interesting to note that the citizens living in the South Italy are more likely to support the Italian involvement than those living in the North-East (respectively, 74 percent versus 69 percent), probably an effect of the greater exposure of these regions to flood of immigration from former Yugoslavia. Internationalist are also more in favor of an Italian intervention than isolationist, whereas the practicing Catholic are slightly more in favor than those not practicing, following the policy of active "humanitarian intervention" stated by the Pope and the Vatican State.

These bivariate relations appear stable over the entire time period from January to November 1996. The only exceptions are religion and political orientation. As to religion, those practicing Catholics appear at the beginning to be less favorable than the others, but already in March their support increases and for the rest of the period it appears more stable than that of those who do not practice religion. Looking at the evolution among different party preferences, the Ulivo (center-left) coalition supporters appear over the entire period to be more in favor than those of the Lega, the least supporting one, with the Polo electorate in between. Right-wing voters and those supporting the center-left government (for different reasons) tend to be more likely to support the mission than the Lega voters. Lega voters are in general the least internationalist, the least enthusiastic of the use of force internationally and the most severe critic of the Prodi government and they are among the least inclined to support the mission. This explains also the wider gap in the period March-May 1996, when the acrimonious relations between the center-left coalition and the Lega were magnified by the electoral campaign first and its results later. However, once the Prodi government wins and the ruling center-left coalition is set on March, all three electorate became more sensitive to the general evolution in the domestic arena and this explains probably the synchronization of the fluctuations. The greater fluctuations among the Lega voters might also be due to the less clear position taken by this party on the Bosnia issue (Lega traditionally pays only a scant attention to international issues) and to the less politically articulated composition of its electorate.

To verify the real impact of the bivariate relations discussed so far we carried out two sets of multivariate logistic analysis. A first analysis examines a narrower set of background and attitudinal variables but includes explicitly time as an interaction factor in the regression, to examine the extent to which the variables' influence was affected in magnitude if not direction by the evolution of time.[30] For this purpose we will use the entire tracking poll data of the period January–November 1996. A second analysis will be carried out using the July 1996 Difebarometro with a wider set of attitudinal and political variables.

The results of the first regression model are reported in table 6.3. The strongest explanatory variables of the support for the Italian participation to the Bosnia mission—the direct net effects—are due to age, occupation, party preference, and internationalist attitude. As to the time factor, age, occupation, and party preference show a change of impact over the time spectrum considered. Among the youngest—those between eighteen and twenty-four years of age—the support for the mission is five times greater than those of age forty-five and older.[31] Probably the socialization experience during World War II (for the pre-1945 generation) and the Cold War (for the generation immediately after World War II) depresses the support for any military mission.[32] However, the very young are also those who show a slight inclination to increase their criticism toward the mission as time goes by. Looking at the occupational structure, middle class and housewives are the most likely to express a positive attitude toward the Italian participation to the mission. However, both these two groups have a negative trend overtime. Housewives have an average likelihood 4.6 times greater than self employed to express a positive attitude, but their support is depressed each month by a rate of 13.1 percent. An analogous trend is observed among the clerks. Their favor is 1.8 times grater than self employed, but at a monthly depreciation rate of 11.3 percent. A clear-cut difference emerges among the voters of different parties. In particular, the Ulivo voters have, on average, a probability to express a favorable position on the Italian mission 76.8 percent greater then the Polo voters. The trend coefficient for the former has a negative sign, so as to testify a slight decrease—a monthly negative 3.9 percent—in support. Finally, examining the only attitudinal variable present in the tracking poll, it is confirmed that an internationalist orientation boosts by a factor of 177.3 percent the likelihood of being in favor of the Italian participation.

The multivariate logistical regression suppress some of the potential sources of different levels of support emerging at the bivariate level. In particular, gender, education, and religiosity do not show significant differences, once controlled for other independent variables. As to gender, it is clear that being a woman, as such, does not change the likelihood of being in favor of the mission in respect to men. It is rather the kind of social relationships in which a woman in immersed that makes the difference. To be a housewife increases the support for the mission. Moreover, it could be noted that the

Table 6.3.   Attitudes toward the Italian Mission in Bosnia. Logistic regression (oppose versus favor). Time series January–November 1996—MLE

	Coefficient	S.e.
Gender		
Male (0)		
Female	0.08	0.24
Female x Time	−0.04	0.03
Area North-West (0)		
North-East	0.39	0.31
Center	0.04	0.32
South	0.25	0.29
Area x Time		
North-East	−0.04	0.04
Center	0.01	0.04
South	0.00	0.04
Age 45 and bejond (0)		
25-44	00.49***	0.28
18-24	1.66*	0.52
Age x Time		
25-44	−0.00	0.03
18-24	−0.12**	0.06
Education		
Low and intermediate (0)		
High school and University	0.16	0.25
High school and University x Time	−0.00	0.03
Occupation		
Entrepeneurs and self employed	0.45	0.51
Manager	0.86	0.55
Clerk	1.03**	0.54
Blue collar	0.40	0.50
Retired	0.33	0.55
Student	−0.31	0.60
Housewife	1.42*	0.54
Unemployed (0)		
Occupation x Time		
Entrepeneurs and self employed	−0.06	0.06
Manager	−0.09	0.07
Clerk	−0.12**	0.06
Blue collar	−0.03	0.06
Retired	−0.06	0.07
Student	0.02	0.07
Housewife	−0.14**	0.06
Religion		
Practicing (0)		
Not practicing	0.18	0.22
Not practicing x Time	−0.02	0.02

continued

Table 6.3. (*continued*)

	Coefficient	S.e.
Party voted		
Polo (0)		
Lega	−0.59**	0.25
Ulivo	0.57*	0.17
Party voted x Time		
Lega	0.05	0.03
Ulivo	−0.04**	0.02
International attitude		
Isolationist		
Internationalist	1.02*	0.23
Internationalist x Time	0.00	0.03
Time January (0)		
March	0.60**	0.23
June	1.36*	0.43
July	1.20**	0.48
September	0.89	0.61
October	1.86*	0.69
November	1.50**	0.76
Constant	−1.01**	0.53
χ^2	262.4	
Likelihood	0.000	
% classified cases	75.9	

* $p<0.01$; ** $p<0.05$; *** $p<0.10$.

gender gap—which, by the way, we also found during the Gulf war—is more likely to emerge when the international situation implies an actual use of force. On the actual use of force women tend to be less supportive than men. The Bosnia mission during 1996 had an image of a peacekeeping operation in which the actual use of military force was very remote. As to education, the coefficient is in the expected direction but is not significant. This is due to the high correlation between education and the international orientation: Isolationists are, in general, less educated than internationalists (Isernia 1996b). The latter probably captures much of the variance of the former. Finally, although not significant statistically, testifying of a lack of direct connection with our dependent variable, the sign of the coefficient for religiosity and its trend are in the predicted direction: on the average, those practicing religion have a slightly lower support for the Italian mission than those who do not practice religion. Over time, those practicing religion show a slight but steady increase in their level of support for the Bosnia mission.

Moving to a more detailed cross-sectional analysis, using Difebarometro 4 carried out in July 1996, when the support for the mission was at its peak, table 6.4 shows a richer set of bivariate relations. Some of them confirm what we found in the first bivariate analysis: the lack of a gender gap, the greater support among the youth, the educated, and the practicing catholic; the political preference, mediated by the closeness to the parties supporting the government. More interesting are the correlation with the attitudinal variables on international and defense issues that, as we said before, are nowadays the more relevant source of differences among public opinion on these issues.

Table 6.4. Attitudes toward the Italian Intervention in Bosnia among Different Subgroups (July 1996; percentage)

	Favor	Oppose	DK	Total	(N)
Gender					
Male	77,0	21,3	1,7	100	(404)
Female	76,5	19,2	4,4	100	(412)
Area					
North-West	75,6	19,2	5,2	100	(213)
North-East	75,9	20,9	3,2	100	(158)
Center	78,8	19,9	1,3	100	(156)
South	76,8	20,8	2,4	100	(289)
Commune Size					
< 10.000 inhabitants	77,9	19,1	3,0	100	(298)
10-100.000 inhabitants	77,6	19,8	2,6	100	(343)
> 100.000 inhabitants	73,1	22,9	4,0	100	(175)
Age					
18-24 years	81,4	15,9	2,7	100	(113)
25-44 years	78,8	19,2	1,9	100	(416)
45 years and beyond	71,8	23,3	4,9	100	(287)
Education					
Low School	71,4	24,3	4,3	100	(346)
High School or University Degree	80,6	17,2	2,1	100	(470)
Occupation					
Entrepreneur	77,7	22,1	0,9	100	(113)
Dependent worker	79,5	18,1	2,3	100	(386)
Retired	66,3	26,9	6,7	100	(104)
Housewife	75,2	20,0	4,8	100	(105)
Student	76,4	20,8	2,8	100	(72)
Unemployed	78,1	18,8	3,1	100	(32)
Religion					
No confession	75,7	21,3	3,0	100	(395)
Yes	78,6	18,8	2,6	100	(415)
Political Orientation					
Left	71,0	29,0		100	(62)
Center-Left	74,8	22,3	2,9	100	(103)
Center	79,5	18,0	2,5	100	(283)
Center-Right	83,8	15,1	1,1	100	(179)
Right	74,6	23,7	1,7	100	(59)

	Favor	Oppose	DK	Total	(N)
Party					
Ulivo (Center-Left)	83,6	14,5	1,8	100	(275)
Polo (Center-Right)	74,4	22,7	3,0	100	(203)
Other	64,6	32,9	2,5	100	(79)
No answer	74,9	20,5	4,6	100	(259)
Values					
Materialist	76,2	24,9	2,5	100	(241)
Mixed	82,5	15,5	2,1	100	(97)
Post-materialist	77,3	19,9	2,8	100	(423)
International Orientation					
Internationalist	85,5	12,9	1,7	100	(420)
Isolationist	67,7	28,6	3,7	100	(420)
My Country					
Parochial	63,8	32,3	3,9	100	(127)
Italy	79,1	18,6	2,3	100	(479)
World	79,9	16,1	4,0	100	(199)
Interest int.l problems					
Very much, somewhat	80,2	17,1	2,7	100	(591)
A little, nothing	67,4	29,0	3,6	100	(221)
Use of force					
Never	58,0	37,7	4,3	100	(69)
Humanitarian	74,7	22,2	3,1	100	(360)
Protect Italian interests	81,9	15,2	2,8	100	(387)
Risks Italian security					
Social and economical	77,7	20,7	1,7	100	(363)
Political and Military	76,6	19,3	4,1	100	(435)
Preferred alliance					
Nato	79,4	16,9	3,7	100	(267)
Nato-Europa	80,3	18,5	1,3	100	(314)
Neutrality	69,5	27,8	2,7	100	(187)
Support Italian participation in NATO out of area mission					
Favor	90,0	9,1	0,9	100	(339)
Oppose	67,7	28,9	3,4	100	(439)
Recruitment Armed Forces					
Volunteer	77,3	20,0	2,7	100	(401)
Mixed Volunteer Draft	76,3	21,0	2,7	100	(405)
Total	76,7	20,2	3,1	100	(816)

The value orientation, along the materialist-post materialist distinction, does not discriminate as such the support for the mission. It is probably not by chance that those with a mixed value orientation—combining a desire for order and economic security with that for self-realization and individualism—are the most favorable to the Italian mission.[33] It is of no surprise that those who have a sense of national or cosmopolitan belonging are more in favor for the mission than those who have more parochial roots.

This last result is confirmed by an analysis of the cognitive orientation of the interviewed. An interest for international issues and internationalism is related to a favorable opinion for the Italian intervention, while those who have no or little interest for international affairs and are isolationists are less in favor of such an intervention. As to the more specific defense opinions, we found a twofold effect. On the one hand, the opinions on the more domestic aspects of defense are not related to the support for the mission. The opinion on the best military recruitment system (draft, mixed or all-volunteer armed force) for Italy and the perception of the most important risks for Italian security have no connection with the support for the mission. On the other hand, the opinions on the security alliances of Italy have an important influence on the support for the IFOR mission. The attitude toward the legitimacy of the use of force, opinions about the best way to insure the Italian security, and about Italian participation to NATO mission out of area are significantly related to the support for the mission. The support for the Bosnia mission is higher among those who deem legitimate the use of force for humanitarian interventions and, even more, for those who justify it in the name of national interest; among those who support the Italian membership in NATO and the NATO mission in outer zone. The highest support for the mission is therefore coming from the most internationalist and favorable to a greater involvement of the Italian government in her politico-military alliances. It has to be seen whether this support is left untouched one controlled for demographic and political variables. For this purpose we conducted a multivariate logistical regression that, overall, seems to confirm the greater role that cognitive and attitudinal variables play in explaining the support for the mission in respect to the socio-demographic and political ones (see table 6.5).

Among the demographic variables only occupation and the geographical area of residence have a significant net direct effect: the support decreases among the independent workers and the retired, and is lower among those who live in Central Italy. On the political level, those on the right of the left-right continuum are more supportive than those on the left, but among the Ulivo voters the likelihood of being favorable is the double than among the Polo voters.[34] Among the postmaterialists, the support is lower, although those are more internationalists and the internationalists are more in favor of the mission.[35]

CONCLUSION: WHICH CONNECTIONS BETWEEN PUBLIC OPINION AND POLICY?

The data discussed in this chapter both confirm available evidences on the attitudes of European public opinion on Bosnia intervention and raise a puzzle. The data confirm what Sobel (1996, 145) found at the European

Table 6.5. Attitudes toward the Italian mission in Bosnia. Logistic regression (oppose versus favor) MLE estimate (July 1996)

	Coefficients	S.E.
Gender		
Male (0)		
Female	0.45	0.36
Area North-West (0)		
North-East	0.51	0.52
Center	−0.94**	0.48
South	−0.63	0.42
Community size		
< 10.000 inhabitants (0)		
10-100.000 inhabitants	−0.11	0.37
> 100.000 inhabitants	−0.44	0.43
Age		
18–24	0.75	0.67
25–44	−0.04	0.41
45 and beyond (0)		
Education		
Low School (0)		
High School or University Degree	0.25	0.35
Occupation		
Dependent worker (0)		
Entrepreneur	−0.80**	0.46
Retired	−1.16*	0.55
Housewife	−0.65	0.64
Student	−0.97	0.67
Unemployed	−0.31	0.77
Religion		
Not practicing (0)		
Practicing	−0.07	0.33
Political self-position		
Left (0)		
Center-Left	0.72	0.55
Center	1.03**	0.53
Center-Right	1.53**	0.67
Right	0.59	0.76
Party preference		
Other (0)		
Ulivo	1.70*	0.51
Polo	1.28**	0.50
Value orientation		
Mixed (0)		
Materialist	−0.66	0.60
Postmaterialist	−0.86***	0.57
International Orientation		
Isolationist (0)		
Internationalist	1.25*	0.34

continued

Table 6.5. *(continued)*

	Coefficients	S.E.
My country		
Italy (0)		
Parochial	−0.32	0.41
Cosmopolitan	−0.14	0.40
nterest Int.l problems		
No, a little (0)		
Enough, much	0.65***	0.36
Legittimacy use of force		
Never (0)		
Humanitarian	1.02**	0.53
Protect Italian interest	1.74*	0.56
Risks Italian security		
Socio-economic (0)		
Politico-military	−0.02	0.31
Best way to insure security		
NATO as it is (0)		
NATO-Europe	−0.67**	0.39
Neutrality	−0.50	0.43
Participation outer zone NATO mission		
Favor (0)		
Oppose	−1.72*	0.35
Recruitment Armed Force		
All volunteer (0)		
Mixed	0.26	0.31
Costant	−0.24	1.18
Model χ^2	129.9	
Likelihood	0.000	
% classified cases	84.7	

* $p<0,01$; ** $p<0,05$; *** $p<0,10$

level: "relatively strong citizen preferences, particularly for multilateral action, with relatively weak governmental policies even about employing allied forces." In the Italian case we found on the one hand a strong and quite steady support for a more active armed involvement of Italian troops in Bosnia and on the other hand an extreme reluctance of Italian government to even consider and openly discuss such an involvement. Italian public support for the idea of an Italian armed intervention in helping to solve the Bosnia crisis crystallized quite early (at the beginning of 1993 insofar as our data allow us to tell) and rested steadily in favor of it until the actual Italian troops were deployed in the frame of the Dayton agreement. This support was quite wide and stable and, more important, it crossed the entire political party spectrum, with the partial exception of the neo-Communists of Rifondazione Comunista. The only decline—in July 1995—was with all probability due more to the unsatisfactory performance of the UN on the ground than to a perceived greater danger of the situation on the ground. This support notwithstanding, in all the occasions in which the Italian government was directly or indirectly invited to consider the possibility of sending troops to Bosnia, the decision was negative.[36] This disparity between permissive general opinion and reluctant policymakers fits the Realist model of moody public and responsible élite. This outcome is also in line with another Sobel's (1996) finding: that this permissive public opinion contrast with the impression held by most governments and the media that the American and European publics are unwilling to interfere in the Bosnia conflict. More interesting and puzzling is that in at least one occasion the final Italian decision was publicly justified making explicit reference to the reluctance of public opinion to support the actual use of force and the casualties it involved, a restatement of the "body-bag hypothesis." In other words the Italian government based its decision not to intervene in Bosnia on the argument, explicitly mentioned, that public opinion was against such an intervention and that, even if favorable, the support was moody and ready to change as soon as the first casualties occurred. This is not an appropriate Realist approach, which rather tend to ignore public opinion if it is not needed. Since the data available showed on the contrary that Italian public opinion was strongly in favor of an Italian intervention, why did the Italian government used these arguments? What public opinion Italian government was reading?

In this last section, we intend to address this puzzle looking first at the nature of the public opinion-policy relationship in the Bosnia case at the aggregate level. The trend analysis offer a first possible explanation of the lack of impact of public opinion on the Italian foreign policymaking process in the Bosnia case, an explanation that brings into the picture a wider set of actors, like parties, bureaucracies, and pressure groups. Second, we will point to one actual decision, the decision not to contribute troops to UN-PROFOR, taken in January 1994 by the Italian government, to figure out what was in the Italian government officials' mind when they were talking about public opinion and whether the Italian officials were aware of the "permissive mood" of Italian mass opinion on the Bosnia intervention. In this connection, we will explore whether arguments mentioning public opinion were either brought about by a misreading of Italian public opinion (no matter who it was) in which the officials were genuinely convinced of the public opposition, or they were part of a general attempt to manipulate public opinion in order to legitimize a decision not to intervene due to other causes (e.g., the opposition of the military due to a lack of Italian military preparedness).

As mentioned earlier, to examine the role of public opinion on the Italian policymaking process, one needs to enlarge the view to a wider set of actors and roles. To start with, we can describe the Italian foreign policymaking process as the result of the interplay among four sets of actors: parties, government, bureaucracies, and public opinion, with the media as a channel of communication among parties, government, and public opinion. Of course, the process is well affected by other international and transnational actors, but we can leave them out of the picture for the moment, at least for analytical purposes.[37] Our simple model postulates one main link between government and civil society, through parties and the political party system. As we have already mentioned, in a party government model the *direct* role of public opinion is rather modest. Although the Bosnia crisis took place in the very moment in which parties were weaker in their ability to aggregate and articulate political demands coming out of the electorate, Italy had still a government in which parties played a central role and the political debate within government was mainly channeled through and shaped by party politics. This crucial set of actors—the parties—is both an actor in itself and a channel of representation. In the Italian case, in particular, parties are the main channel through which both public opinion (no matter how defined) and the bureaucracy (La Palombara 1964; Pasquino 1994) make them heard. On the other hand, the bureaucracy, through the interfacial role of the ministers, is also an actor in its own capacity *vis-à-vis* the government and the parties, especially so on very technical issues (like the monetary issues with the Bank of Italy) or on issues in which technical considerations bear on political decision (e.g., in case of use of force involving possible casualties).

Looking first at the media-parties-public opinion relationships, to establish who was reacting to whom we will examine the trends in attention expressed by media, the Parliament, and public opinion on the Bosnia issue for the period 1992–1996. Lacking a complete set of reliable and valid data on both attention and content (pro- or contra intervention) of attitudes, we used attention as a proxy of the degree of involvement of parties and public opinion in the Bosnia crisis. To measure media attention we made a simple count of the number of articles appearing monthly on the newspaper *Il Corriere della Sera* on the Bosnia issue. To assess the Parliament attention, we collected all debates taking place in either Chambers of the Italian Parliament dedicated to Bosnia and counted the number of days devoted to discussions of such an issue. We then compared these two trends with the public opinion trend in support for an Italian armed intervention in Bosnia. Figures 6.4 and 6.5 show the results, comparing the level of media attention respectively with public opinion support for Italian armed intervention and the level of Parliament's attention. They show quite clearly a closer connection between parliament and media than either parliament or media and public opinion.

The remarkable stability in public opinion support for an Italian armed intervention over the entire 1993–1996 period is in sharp contrast with the irregular trends of attention by the Parliament and the media. The media trend of attention shows an increasing attention for the issue by the press, with ups and downs related to the escalation of violence among the warring factions in Bosnia. The Parliament attention does not show a growing trend in attention, but the ups and downs match quite closely with the media oscillations. This means that media and the Italian Parliament were paying attention to Bosnia at the same time, but only the media increasingly so. The media and Parliament trends are not related to the public opinion trend, confirming that public opinion made up his mind early in the crisis and did not move from where it was during it.

The attention of parties toward the Bosnia issue was mostly determined by events on the ground, as mediated and amplified by the media, rather than by a moody and hysteric public opinion, as sometimes claimed by Italian politicians. As a matter of fact, it is surprising that even in the crucial period between the summer of 1994 and the summer of 1995 there is no remarkable change of attitudes among the public. The lowest dip in support in the summer 1995 is still a 57 percent majority in favor of the Italian intervention. It looks like parties, and the government, were rather reacting in their policy activity (be that mainly symbolically or not is another matter) to the events in Bosnia and to their perception of the attention the media were devoting to the Bosnia issue, rather than to public opinion on the one hand and to the bureaucracy, with particular reference to the military, the ones called on to implement the mission if it had been approved, on the other hand.

In this general context, it is even more puzzling to find, in at least one occasion, Italian political officials to make explicit reference to public opinion to justify the Italian dragging-feet toward a wider involvement in the Bosnia quagmire. The occasion we analyzed in detail occurred at the end of 1993, beginning of 1994. On December 23, 1993, the private TV catholic network *Telepace* interviewed Italian Foreign Minister Beniamino Andreatta. The interview was broadcasted on January 1, 1994 and press releases were sent to the major press agencies. In that interview Andreatta took a utterly straight stance against the Catholic Church argument, aired again a few days before the interview by Cardinal Sodano of the Vatican Secretariat of State, that a military intervention for humanitarian reasons, to prevent genocide and "ethnic cleansing" in foreign country, was morally legitimate. Andreatta did not criticize the moral argument as such. He acknowledged himself the moral legitimacy of such a form of intervention, but he argued that modern democracies are run by public opinion and public opinion would not support such a form of intervention. He continued, applying this line of argument to the Bosnia case, that one of the reasons why Western European governments were reluctant to be involved in Bosnia was precisely this opposition of public opinion. Using Andreatta words—as reported by the newspaper *La Repubblica* which quoted among brackets some sentences of this interview 25 days afterwards in an un-signed article titled *Ma chi vuole l'intervento?* ("Who wants to intervene?") —"Our people does not give us, neither in the United States nor in Europe, a mandate to use arms to bring justice back. This is the drama of those who are involved in the Bosnia crisis," and he continued "many responsibilities for the failures of Western countries in the Balkan issue rest on public opin-ion." In this interview, however, Andreatta did not mention explicitly nor obliquely any poll to support his argument.[38] The article appearing on the Italian newspaper *La Repubblica* on January 26, 1994 immediately after having quoted Andreatta's sentences between brackets, it wrote "To con-firm Andreatta's hypothesis, a survey carried out on a sample of eight hundred Italians by SWG (and published by *Famiglia Cristiana*). The data reveal that 61 percent of those interviewed does not want *that in the for-mer Yugoslavia war be added to war* and, therefore, it is opposed to any kind of armed intervention" (*La Repubblica*, January 26, 1994, 10). The newspaper, confirming a trend of bad and sloppy reporting of opinion polls' results, did not quote neither the date of the survey nor, even more important, the question wording. The poll's results the newspaper was making reference to were from a survey six months old. More precisely, the survey had been carried out by SWG on August, 4, 1993 and issued by *Famiglia Cristiana* a few days after. Moreover, the percentage the article was making reference to was the answer to an heavily biased question, making no reference whatsoever to the possibility of an Italian armed in-tervention. The question was "At this point in the Bosnia situation, are you in favor or oppose an armed intervention knowing that the peacekeeping forces would suffer human casualties and heavy military expenditures?"[39] Answering to this question, 61 percent of the 800 interviewed opposed, 28 percent were in favor of the intervention and 11 percent did not know. This example of polls' use by one of the most prestigious Italian newspa-pers shows the lack of any professional skills in reading, interpreting and presenting the data. Apart from the lack of any reference to exact question wording, sample type, confidence intervals, and so forth, it is remarkable that the journalist ignored explicitly the fact—he should have known—that the data he was using were six months older than Andreatta's interview and that the question wording was heavily biased in favor of a negative an-swer and, even more important, the question had no reference whatsoever to an *Italian* intervention in the conflict, so nothing could be inferred about the Italian public opinion attitudes on such a policy.

More interesting for our purposes, however, is to establish whether An-dreatta was simply misreading the public or he was intentionally manipulating the public. Was he thinking to these survey' data, inferring from them that the Italian public was opposed to the intervention—a case of misreading? Or was he reading other sources of public opinion—a case of ignorance? Or, finally, was he trying to manipulate information—with the explicit or implicit support of newspapers—in order to bring home a political argument against the supporter of an armed intervention, some of them even within the Vatican? It is hard to reach a conclusive answer on the basis of the available evidence. We do not know for sure what the Italian foreign minister had in mind when he mentioned public opinion. Had Andreatta in mind the data published by the newspaper, although he never mentioned them? Had he in mind other data never made public?[40] Or when he mentioned public opinion he was thinking to bureaucratic and expert opinions, editorialists and parliamentary opinion. Our impression is that all these actors but mass opinion were plausibly in Andreatta's mind.

First, he probably well knew the opposition of the Italian armed forces and the military experts to an Italian intervention in Bosnia. Both technical and political considerations justified the opposition to such an intervention. Italy had already had the troubling Somalia mission and the Bosnia situation was considered by experts a very difficult situation in which to conduct peace-keeping operations according to the UN rules of engagement. Moreover, to commit ground troops in the Bosnia crisis to enforce peace against the warring parties was judged a prescription for replicating the Vietnam tragedy. Second, editorialists, with some exception from the left, were in general well ready to denounce the European passivity and to concede that something had to be done right away, but they were by far more reluctant to point to what to do and even less to support openly an armed intervention by Italian forces. The general consensus was that United States was the only actor able to intervene effectively to stop the fighting, a consensus, by the way, very much in line with the public opinion mood. Third, Andreatta was probably sensing the opposition to an armed intervention within the ranks of his own party. A survey of the member of the Defense and Foreign Affairs committees of the Chamber of Deputies and the Senate carried out by Bellucci (1998) in the Spring 1994 (a few months after the Andreatta interview) had two questions on the Bosnia crisis identical to those asked to the general public respectively in December 1994 and July 1995. Tables 6.6 and 6.7 show the similarities and differences among élite and masses. Overall, public opinion and the segment of political élite specialized on foreign and defense issues seem to have a similar distribution of attitudes. Public opinion is slightly more favorable than the parliamentary élite both to a NATO mission in Bosnia and to the Italian participation in such an international mission: 77 percent of the public is in favor of a NATO contingent to make sure the peace agreement is respected whereas 72 percent of the parliamentary élite think so.

The support for the Italian participation in such a NATO mission is lower both among the élite and the public, but again public opinion is slightly more in favor of the Italian participation than the parliamentary élite (57 percent versus 51 percent). Differences however become more striking if we compare the electorate and their representatives by parties. Although the results have to be interpreted cautiously because of the reduced number of MPs, table 6.8 shows two interesting results. The first is that, as seen above, the public is systematically more likely to be in favor of the Italian participation to a Bosnia mission than the parliamentary élite across the entire political spectrum, included the communists (*Rifondazione Comunista*). Forty-three percent of the interviewed voting Rifondazione Comunista are in favor of the Italian mission whereas none of the Communist parliamentarians interviewed think so. The second result is that differences among the electorate are much less relevant than among the parliamentarians. Excluding the Rifondazione communists, there is no dramatic difference among the electorate of the different parties. Looking at the parliamentarians, we find that the differences in degree of support within the two coalitions—the Center-Left and the Center-Right—are higher than the difference between them. This is particularly so for the center-left coalition where the Catholic component (PPI) is more likely to be against the Italian intervention and the Democratic Left Party (PDS) is more likely to be in favor. Not so striking but still relevant are the differences within the Polo delle Libertà coalition, with Forza Italia less likely to support the intervention than Alleanza Nazionale. The lower popularity of the Italian armed intervention among Catholic parliamentarians could explain, at least in part, the statements of Andreatta first as minister of foreign affairs and then as parliamentarian. As a matter of fact, when Andreatta was mentioning the reluctance of public opinion to an armed intervention he could well have in mind both its electorate and his party parliamentarians rather than public opinion in general.

Table 6.6.   Attitudes toward NATO Intervention in Bosnia, 1994–1995.

	Public Opinion	Parliamentary Elite
Favor	77	72
Against	20	17
DK/Other	3	11
Total	100	100
(N)	(817)	(53)

Public Opinion, December 1994; Elite, Spring 1995

Question: Se in Bosnia si aggiungesse un accordo di pace e le Nazioni Unite richiedessero alla NATO di inviare truppe militari per assicurare il rispetto del piano di pace. Lei sarebbe favorevole o contrario ad un intervento della NATO?

Table 6.7.   Attitudes toward Italian Participation to NATO Intervention in Bosnia

	Public Opinion	Parliamentary Elite
Favor	57	51
Against	35	41
DK/Other	8	8
Total	100	100
(N)	(794)	(53)

Public Opinion, July 1995; Elite, Spring 1995

Question: Lei sarebbe favorevole ad una partecipazione delle Forze Armate italiane ad un contingente della NATO per garantire la cessazione del conflitto in Bosnia.

These reasons might explain the foreign minster ambivalence. Andreatta was in the middle between those who were opposed to the intervention and those, in the Vatican and in the left-wing parties accusing the government of doing too little to help solve the situation in Bosnia. Being probably uncertain himself (as testified by the different statements he made during those months), throwing the blame of guilty on public opinion was an elegant way for him to show how his official position (against intervention) was in tune with the general climate of opinion. The fact that public opinion can be an elusive concept, more apt to cloak rather than to clarify, difficult to test and verify, helped in this regard. Moreover, his perception was shared by newspapers. Confirming how his opposition was not totally implausible. In this specific occasion, and apparently for the entire Bosnia crisis until the Dayton agreement was signed, the Italian officials made no effort whatsoever to attempt to monitor and pulse the mood of the country in order to see what it really thought. This veil of ignorance however helped to shape a position in

Table 6.8.   Attitudes toward Italian Participation in NATO Mission in Bosnia

	Public Opinion		Parliamentary Elite		Difference Public
	For	Against	For	Against	Opinion–Elite
PdRC	43	57	–	100	+43
PDS+Other left	64	36	59	41	+5
PPI	60	40	40	60	+20
Lega Nord	56	44	50	50	+6
FI	64	36	57	43	+7
AN	71	29	70	30	−1

Public Opinion, July 1995; Elite, Spring 1995

Question: Lei sarebbe favorevole ad una partecipazione delle Forze Armate italiane ad un contingente della NATO per garantire la cessazione del conflitto in Bosnia tune with their preferred policy: not doing anything. They used public opinion as a short-cut to cloak the lack of willingness to commit troops in Bosnia. If there has been a (self-) blinded audience in this story, this has been the élite rather than the mass.

NOTES

1. The Versailles Treaty assigned Istria to Italy and during 1941 Italian troops occupied Dalmatia. After the September 8, 1943 armistice with the Allies the equivalent of two infantry divisions joined the Tito's irregulars, fighting the Germans for two years.

2. It is interesting to note that while American political science has always been inclined to explain the Italian case (and its exceptionalism) making reference to cultural variables and, specifically, the lack of civicness, Italian scholars always preferred to look at structural variables, like the party system (for a review of this literature see Sciolla 1997). A more complex view of the interplay between Italian civicness and political institutions is that of Putnam (1993).

3. Comparing the most important problem mentioned by public opinion in Italy, France, Western Germany and United States in 1983, a period in which international issues were particularly prominent on the public agenda and therefore one could expect greater attention to them, in all the four countries unemployment and inflation were top priorities, whereas fear of war and nuclear weapons lagged behind. Again, in 1992 the economic crisis and the fight against organized crime (e.g., the Mafia) were mentioned as the first national priority national by respectively the 72 percent and 71 percent of Italians interviewed, whereas only 13 percent mentioned international tension.

4. According to Willick (1969) in 1964 only 4 percent of the Italians interviewed were very interested in international issues (in Western Germany those very interested were 27 percent, in Great Britain 17 percent, and in France 12 percent) and no more than 22 percent was very much or somewhat interested. In 1983, the percentage of those very much or somewhat interested in foreign and defense issues increased to 35 percent, in line with other western European countries. As everywhere, interest for foreign policy is positively related to level of education. In 1983, 22 percent of those with a low level of education (primary school) declare an interest for international problems, whereas among those with at least a high school degree the percentage of those very much or somewhat interested in foreign and defense issues increases to 61 percent.

5. Education affects the level of knowledge as well. In 1989, 22 percent of the general public had no information whatsoever on NATO, but among those with a higher level of education this percentage declined to 2 percent. Moreover, the degree of knowledge decreases as we move from more familiar (i.e., culturally and geographically closer) and less technical issues to less familiar and more technical ones. The level of knowledge on the Warsaw Pact, the Western European Union and some of the most esoteric problems of nuclear strategy is almost minimal.

6. For a different reading of the way U.S. policymakers view and assess polls and polls' results however, see Kull, Destler and Ramsay (1997).

7. In Katz's words (1987: 45–46) partyness of government "indicates the proportion of formal government power exercised in accordance with the party government

model" and party governmentness "indicates the proportion of all social power exercised by parties within the framework of the party government model."

8. For a sobering assessment of the Italian parliamentary élite political culture compared to the British see Putnam (1973).

9. A manifestation of the extreme prudence and skepticism with which the social sciences have been accepted in Italy, is the often quoted indictment by Benedetto Croce of sociology as "inferma scienza" (invalid science), which contributed to the slow acceptance of social and political science in Italy, seen by Italian academics as "Americanate" (a mixture of naiveté and pure technical exhibitionism) rather than serious scientific undertakings.

10. These variables are those mentioned by Putnam (1988) in explaining the factors affecting the size of the national win-set and are analogous to those mentioned by Risse-Kappen's (1991) in distinguishing (following Katzenstein and Gourevitch) between nature of society, of the state and of policy networks.

11. Holmes (1993, 186) mentions Bosnia as an interesting exception in which public opinion influenced foreign policy and in the direction of greater interventionism than it is usually the case for the generally pacifist Italian public opinion. As we will see in the next section, this influence, if it was true during the first phase, will not last when the going will get though, while interventionism will last until the end.

12. This role has continued after the war. With $50 million in aid, Italy is together with Holland the main European Union contributor to Bosnian recovery. See *il Corriere della Sera*, April 14, 1996.

13. The London Memorandum of agreement of 1948 gave to Italy the territories occupied by Western allied troops at the end of the war and to Yugoslavia the area occupied by them. The Osimo treaty formalized the agreement, envisaged a plan of economic cooperation and solved the problem of the Italian community in Istria.

14. Italy was at that time the only EC country with a consulate general in Lubjana.

15. In the "Brioni statement" Slovenia and Croatia accept a three month moratorium on the independence declaration. Once the three month period has expired, Croazia and Slovenia will declare independence (October 8, 1991).

16. These were not the first Italian casualties in Yugoslavia since the collapse of the federal government. On January 7, 1992 a Serb MiG shot down an Italian helicopter of the EC monitoring and observation mission flying over Croatia, killing four Italian and one French soldier. The Italian Ministry of Foreign Affairs called the Italian ambassador for "consultations" in Roma, the Italia government asked an urgent meeting of the EC Council of Minister, which issued a declaration condemning the shot down and asked for an inquiry commission to the President of the Observatory Mission, and canceled the air flight agreement with Yugoslavia, interrupting the daily flight from Italy to Belgrade by JAT. The Federal defense Minister, General Veljko Kadijevic, resigned as a consequence of this shot down.

17. The professional troops in Italy were at that time made basically by the "Folgore" parachutists brigade. The "Garibaldi" professional brigade was not yet operational, having been financed only under the November 1993 financial law to become operative during the 1994.

18. See the interview of the Joint Chief of Staff Venturoni in *la Repubblica*, February 9, 1995.

19. The invitation was extended to all countries with troops in Bosnia and to Italy as a member of the European troika.

20. Foreign Minister Agnelli acknowledged that Italian participation in the Contact Group was at this time only consultative and intermittent in its intervention at the debate of the PDS "Festa dell'Unità" in September. See *il Corriere della Sera*, September 13, 1995.

21. An American diplomat interviewed for this research declared that the Italian government used this also as an occasion to send a strong signal to the American government to stop the violation of several rules governing the use of NATO military base in Italy perpetrated by American planes operating over Bosnia in the last months.

22. These information are based on a set of interviews Pierangelo Isernia carried out in New York, Washington and Roma with Italian and American diplomats on the Italian and American policymaking process toward Bosnia.

23. The Contact Group meets at three different levels. It meets in Sarajevo and Zagabria, at the level of the diplomatic mission there; it meets in New York, at the UN. headquarters with a larger set of countries (including Canada, Japan, Portugal and Spain), and it meets in Europe at the level of Director-General of the Political Affairs of the Ministry of Foreign Affairs of France, Germany Great Britain, Russia and the United States, plus the country having, in turn, the presidency of the European Union.

24. Interviews with American and Italian diplomats in Washington, D.C. and New York.

25. We would like here to thank the United States Information Agency, and in particular Ann Pincus, the Director of the Office of Research, Mary MacIntosh, former head of the European Branch, and Susan White for having provided to us the USIA data on Italian attitudes toward Bosnia; Reinhard Moschner and Peter Schubert of the Zentral Archive in Kohln for the Eurobarometer and Euroflash data-set.

26. Before 1992 the Eurobarometer asked several question on the attitude toward affiliation of (at that time) Yugoslavia in the European Union. These questions will not be examined here.

27. The question was the following: "A questo punto della vicenda in Bosnia, Lei sarebbe favorevole o contrario ad un intervento armato, sapendo che le forze di pace andrebbero incontro a perdite umane e a grosse spese militari?" SWG for Famiglia Cristiana, August 4, 1993. This question will be discussed again in section 5.

28. Difebarometro is a bi-annual telephone survey on defense and foreign policy issues carried out regularly since 1994 by Archivio Disarmo, a private non-profit research center, and SWG, a Trieste-based survey institute.

29. Italy participated in the Gulf war only with the Air Force and the Navy. The decision not to commit ground troops was justified in part with the lack of preparation and in part with the strong opposition of the left-wing parties and the Catholic center.

30. Time has been operationalized as a counter starting with one in January 1996 and ending with nine in November 1996. For the specifics of the sampling frame and survey design of the Difebarometro series see the appendix to Difebarometro (1996).

31. Computing the antilogarithm of the coefficient for the youngest we get an estimate of the variable's impact in probability terms on the reference level (the oldest), that can be expressed in a percentage term. In fact, [exp (1,66)-1]x 100= 425,9 percent).

32. For other analyses of the impact of cohort and political socialization on the orientation of Italian public opinion on defense issues see Bellucci (1998) and Isernia (1996b).

33. This result is in line with what another analysis (Bellucci, 1996) found that among the youth there is a negative relationship between postmaterialism and trust toward the armed forces, while among the adults the materialist are those more prone to have less trust for the military. On the connection between the military and the youth value system see Segatti (1997).

34. For the Ulivo voters this likelihood is 447.4 percent whereas among the Polo voters is 259.7 percent.

35. This result could surprise if we consider the strong relationship between post-materialism and internationalism (Inglehart 1990; Isernia 1996b). A plausible explanation is that postmaterialist are more prone "to delegate" the armed forces problems to other actors (supporting an all-volunteer forces, international organizations like NATO, etc.). For a discussion along these lines see Battistelli (1996).

36. The decisions we make reference to are the September 1992 decision to enlarge UNPROFOR to Bosnia, the January–March 1994 discussion on the United Kingdom request to involve Italian troops, the December 1994 discussion on how to help in case of UN withdrawal, the July 1995 decision on the withdrawal and the London meeting's decision to organize air strike. In all four cases, the Italian government decided not to join UN land forces in Bosnia. In July 1995 eventually the Italian government conceded airplanes for tactical air strikes and close air support.

37. Of course, international and transnational actors play a greater role in "penetrated" systems like Italy. However, their role in explaining the opinion-policy connection can be inferred, as a first approximation, by their impact on domestic actors.

38. We were unable to watch personally the tape of the interview because it had been canceled by *Telepace* short on tapes and no press release of the interview was recorded. However, we interviewed the journalist who interviewed Andreatta, Dr. Schiavazzi, and he explicitly stated that no reference was made by Andreatta to opinion polls or surveys' results. Unfortunately, it has also been impossible to locate who made the unsigned newspaper's piece on *La Repubblica*.

39. The original Italian version of the question was "*A questo punto della vicenda in Bosnia, lei sarebbe favorevole o contrario ad un intervento armato, sapendo che le forze di pace andrebbero incontro a perdite umane e a grosse spese militari?*"

40. It is hard to say whether there were surveys carried out at that time by the Italian government on Bosnia's attitudes and never released and whether, if they were, Andreatta knew. Our impression, based on the fact that some of the surveys used by the Italian government were made by us, on our careful search of possible surveys on Bosnia and on the lack of any bureaucratic or political resource systematically collecting and scrutinizing surveys' data for the foreign and defense minister, is that no secret or unknown survey exists. To our knowledge the only other survey available on foreign and defense issues at that time was one commissioned by the Italian Military Center for Strategic Studies (CeMiSS) to one of us. The field of that survey was carried out in early December and in January 1994, one of the present authors was in the process of analyzing the results. In that survey, among other things, there was a split half question to assess the bias of differently worded questions on armed intervention in foreign countries and one of the two half mentioned Bosnia. However, the data were not yet available neither when Andreatta was making the interview nor when the *La Repubblica*'s journalist wrote his piece. The report based on those data was presented to the CeMiSS in February 1994.

7

Innocence Lost: The Netherlands and the Yugoslav Conflict

Philip Everts

INTRODUCTION

In most Western countries, in the context of the post Cold War situation, the legitimacy of the use of the armed forces is no longer self-evident, even if governments decide that national interests require such use. They may still enjoy considerable freedom of action in general and in emergency situations in particular, yet a governmental decision to commit the armed forces can not be sustained for any length of time without at least parliamentary support. Parliaments will hesitate to give such support when they are not confident that public opinion at large will understand and support such a decision too.

Which are the factors shaping public opinion and what role, if it plays one at all, does it play in the political process of decision making and policy implementation?

In this chapter we shall look in more detail at one particular case, the conflicts in the former Yugoslavia, and at one specific country, the Netherlands. In this connection, I will pay particular attention to the effect of the dramatic events around Srebrenica in July 1995. At the time, the Serbian Bosnian military forced the Dutch contingent to withdraw from this town under shameful conditions. This withdrawal allowed genocidal massacres among the local Muslim population. It might be expected that this humiliating defeat would have a decisive and lasting impact on the willingness of the Dutch to continue to participate in UNPROFOR and in future risky international military operations.

THE FACTORS SHAPING PUBLIC OPINION

Through the impact of the media of communication, governments and public opinion are directly confronted today with reports of frequent domestic conflicts in other countries in which human rights are massively violated. In such cases, politicians are usually faced with considerable dilemmas. On the one hand, they are faced with strong demands, that "something be done." They may, and should, also ask themselves, however, whether the risks involved are commensurate with the values and interests at stake, and whether public opinion will not only ask for action but also continue to support it when the consequences become clear. Moreover, they may hesitate to commit themselves, feeling that others are not carrying their part of the international burden, or fearing that they may give in to the temptation of free rider behavior. This means that participation in international peace support operations is by no means self-evident or automatic.

In this connection, references are also often made to the alleged existence of a body bag syndrome, a tendency for public opinion to recoil from earlier calls to use force when the prospect of casualties appears or materializes. That there is a correlation between support for military force and casualties has been demonstrated on the basis of several historical examples (Mueller 1971; Mueller 1973; see also Mueller 1993, especially 209–10 and Mueller 1994),[1] but these outcomes and the thesis of a simple direct relationship have been contested. The nature of the war, the goals involved, and the likelihood of success seem to be relevant variables to be taken into account when explaining the evolution of public support (Burk 1995; Burk 1996; Garnham, 1994; Larson 1996; Schwarz, 1994).[2] In the case of participation of the Netherlands in UNPROFOR and other UN operations, and its aftermath, Dutch politicians and other observers, for instance, have regularly warned that casualties might lead to a sudden reversal in public support for such military operations. One might ask whether they were saying so out of democratic deference or because they were seeking an alibi for their own hesitations.

While there is considerable evidence for the effects of casualties on support for (continued) military actions, there is more, and if there is such a thing as the "body bag syndrome" it should be put into a wider context.

Compensating effects, which may occur, for instance, probably also include: the perceived success of the use of military force (there is little that is more contagious than apparently effective use of violence) as well as the combination of dehumanizing the opponent and the need to take revenge ("they did not die in vain"). These tend to contribute to a hardening of positions and a willingness to persevere in the military conflict when the effect of the well-known "rally 'round the flag" syndrome has run its course.

The Free Rider Temptation

At the same time it is also true, however, that, especially in democracies, where popular sentiments can only be neglected at certain expense, the general willingness to participate in peacekeeping operations of the UN (and other bodies) is reduced by the effect of the free rider syndrome, or the perception of such a syndrome by decision makers. In most countries only very few want their country to take the lead irrespective of what others do. This is a common phenomenon in international politics. Everybody has a stake in the production of collective goods, like international stability or the protection of human rights, and nobody can be excluded from the consumption of these goods. The good is wanted very much, but potential contributors to its production would prefer even more to get it for free, and with others carrying the burden, especially when it is to be expected that the good will be produced anyway. Consequently, everybody is waiting for others to move first, unless agreements can be made (and enforced) on what is to be considered a "reasonable share" in the collective burden. The existence of such agreements, and the conviction that one's share is not excessive, is therefore an important condition to maintain the (potential) degree of domestic support for contributing to internationalist goals, whether it is in international peacekeeping, reducing the gap between rich and poor, protecting the international environment, or preventing violations of human rights. This applies to the Netherlands as well as to other countries.

Democracies and Modern Wars

Compared to nondemocratic states, democracies are perhaps relatively well qualified to wage wars that are either, "total" with respect to war aims and to the mobilization of resources or, on the other hand, wars in which the risks are small, for example, because of the presence of escalation dominance or the weakness of the opponent. Democracies face severe problems, however, either when success is elusive or when the trade-off between costs (especially in terms of human lives) and interests is seen as unfavorable for other reasons.

Moreover, in cases that do not have to do with immediate threats, particularly individual or collective self-defense, but rather concern humanitarian intervention, peacekeeping, or collective security, a level of support in the order of two thirds (which is the level we can observe for the Netherlands for peacekeeping in general) may look impressive, but it may also turn out to be insufficient for the degree of national consensus needed for such cases of comparatively low perceived "importance."

Whatever the case, it remains a debatable point, on the one hand, which factors shape and determine public support for participation in especially high-risk military operations and for the use of armed forces, in general, and in particular whether and to what extent public opinion can or will withstand the occurrence of casualties. On the other hand, if public support is a necessary condition of engaging the armed forces in military action, it is not immediately self-evident, to say the least, in which way public opinion enters and influences the foreign policy process and government decision making.

Before we come to the specifics of the case in question I shall, first of all, briefly describe the system of political decision making in the Netherlands. Next, I pay some attention to the role of the media of communication, which are often said to play a central role in both shaping and communicating public opinion in its various manifestations. We will also have to look at more general public attitudes on the use of force and participation in military UN operations, which allow us to draw some conclusions on the general nature of public support for the use of military force and the conditions impinging on the level of support.

THE SYSTEM OF GOVERNMENT DECISION MAKING

Like most countries, the making of foreign and defense policy in the Netherlands is still highly elitist compared to domestic politics. Governments usually enjoy considerable freedom of action. There are, however, certain limitations to this freedom. Decisions like the commitment of troops to action abroad will not to be taken by the individual ministers of Defense and Foreign Affairs, but rather by the cabinet as a whole, especially given the fact that the Netherlands is always ruled by often shaky coalitions of two or more political parties. Such decisions, being essentially political, will not be taken by the military themselves, although the military leadership will have a strong say, especially on the feasibility and likelihood of success of a particular action. Objections will be taken into account, but may be overridden. When individual military leaders then voice their disagreement in public, this is usually frowned upon. For the Netherlands, decision making in NATO is also of great importance, although it has also been one of the early enthusiasts of making troops available to the UN (UNSAS system) and similar initiatives.

Given the parliamentary democratic system of government, parliament is also involved in decision making on such matters. Being a multiparty system, a considerable number of parties (around ten) are represented in the Netherlands' parliament. No single political party is ever strong enough to govern alone and this makes coalition governments the rule. Ministers can only be forced to abdicate if they lose the confidence of parliament, but given the shaky nature of most coalitions this does not occur very often, since such forced abdication could upset the coalition. Traditionally, the role of parliaments is less prominent in foreign compared to domestic affairs, but this role has grown considerably in recent decades. The experiences of recent years when (unlike the period of the Cold War when decisions on an actual use of the armed forces had to be taken at several occasions) have also constituted a learning process. While the government has over the years rejected parliament's claim that it should be consulted and give its approval before a decision to commit the forces to action is taken, it has also agreed that parliamentary approval is necessary to obtain sufficient political backing. While parliamentary disapproval is not binding per se (for this, the passing of a motion of censure forcing the minister in question to step down would be necessary), its political significance is high. This is not only a formal matter, but parliament is also seen in this respect as representing public opinion. Members of parliament are sensitive to public opinion (or their perception of it) even though they may know that issues of foreign policy are usually not salient enough to influence political preferences.

Societal support is a necessary condition to legitimize sending the military forces into action. This has been recognized and acknowledged by the Netherlands' government, when it stated in a policy document on the criteria to be applied in decisions on the use of the armed forces: "Sufficient public and societal support is an essential condition for both individual operations and commitments over a longer period of time" (Handelingen Tweede Kamer 1994–1995). This formal recognition of the role of public opinion is a new phenomenon.

THE ROLE OF THE MEDIA

The war in the former Yugoslavia differed from earlier conflicts in that the dividing lines were not easily understood and judged in general and ideological terms. It was literally new to both journalists and the public. Hence, it was more difficult for the outside world to understand and interpret the conflict and to decide what ought to be done. This meant that the public could be expected to look at the conflict relatively open-minded and not through a preconceived ideological prism. It also implied that the public was relatively more dependent than in other cases on the media as the main channel through which it was informed, and on the way these interpreted the conflicts.

Besides being an essential source of information, in this conflict too the media also played their traditional agenda-setting role. The reports about atrocities, especially on TV, were a major factor in raising the saliency of the issue from 1991 onwards and contributed to a climate in which the government increasingly perceived a pressure from the public that "something ought to be done," although it was not at all clear what this something was to be.[3]

Like all other observers, the media were ill-prepared for the task of bringing not only the facts but also for ordering and interpreting them, lacking for instance personnel with a good background training on the historical specifics of the case. Confusion rather than enlightenment was therefore the result of the information that the media provided, certainly in the initial stages of the conflict. First, there was considerable sympathy for the nationalists, because they were seen as anti-communists. It was only gradually that particular interpretations became prominent, and specifically, that Serbia began to be seen as the aggressor and the Bosnian Muslims as the most aggrieved party. Also—equally unhelpfully because of being over-ideological interpretations—the war was portrayed as a struggle between (western) Catholics and eastern Orthodox. Remarkable, because it was contrary to what one might expect in this religious interpretation, there was little anti-Muslim sentiment (which may perhaps be due to more skilful Bosnian propaganda).

While initially also the value or necessity of keeping an existing state territorially intact prevailed (there was a general fear that the former communist empire in Europe would not only disintegrate ideologically, but also fall apart politically because of the pre-existing nationality problems), gradually the media began also to stress the virtues of the right of self-determination, even if this gave rise to many new problems. Confusion increased when it became evident that plans for new territorial divisions (such as the ill-fated Vance-Owen plan) also implied an acknowledgement, even recognition, of the reprehensible policies of ethnic cleansing.

All these perspectives and resulting dilemmas were recognized, to some degree, in the media in the Netherlands, albeit that the information provided, as usual, was more focused on individual events than on structures and contextual information. This was particularly evident for news broadcasting of the CNN type, which for most people is their primary, sometimes only window onto the world and source of information. This was very effective in setting the agendas, but not very helpful in assisting people to make up their minds. The fact that except for a few area experts, even among the elites not very many were knowledgeable about Yugoslavia at the beginning of the open conflict meant that politicians, not unlike the general public, first had to cope with a backlog of information. This in turn implied a major role of the media.

This role was particularly discharged by providing platforms for experts of various qualities and persuasions and other members of the elite to present their views on the op-ed pages, by which they helped to shape the public debate.

By and large, the media failed, however, in explaining the conflict. What dominated was a story of brutal incidents, bloodshed, concentration camps and the image of a society in the grip of "age-old rivalries," a conflict where "little or nothing can be done" from the outside due to some unique Balkan viciousness.

The conflict was indeed unique, but rather through a combination of three factors: the defeat of communism, the absence of democratic alternative institutions, and nationalist exploitation of existing frustrations, be it that the violence to which this led was part of a larger European tradition.

THE IMPACT OF PUBLIC
OPINION ON DECISION MAKING

What was the impact of public opinion on government policy in the Yugoslav conflict? Usually, when we speak of the influence of public opinion we are thinking primarily of cases where governments, because of public opinion (or what they perceive public opinion to be), do something that differs from what they would rather otherwise have done (or abstain from doing something). In this they may either react to or anticipate public opinion. Usually, however, the public is either not interested or not involved, and hence governments enjoy, at least initially, a considerable freedom of action, based on a permissive consensus. In the present case the situation is somewhat different again, in the sense that public opinion was neither passive nor strongly critical of government policy. There was a strong consensus in the Netherlands, which was shared by the government, the elites, and the public at large. This does not mean that there was no discussion or no division of opinion. Indeed, there was very much of this sort, but divisions ran through rather than between parties, groups, or even individuals. It was generally felt that the international community should intervene, but it was uncertain how or what should be done and what would be the likely consequences. Military force was favored by many, but equally many were fearsome of the risks. There was a feeling of international obligations, but also a sense of futility about the efforts made and constant fear that others would give in to the "free rider syndrome." Hence, public opinion was divided, but in the sense of ambivalence rather than polarization. This was a recurrent pattern, which reappeared with varying mixtures of optimism and pessimism, of reluctance and commitments, throughout the conflict. I shall give details of this general observation below.

Four specific moments should be distinguished in this connection: (1) the decisions to restructure the armed forces after the Cold War and, as an outgrowth of this, the various decisions to become involved in the Yugoslav conflicts in 1992-1993, (2) the (initial) reactions to the Srebrenica defeat, and (3) decisions after 1995 (IFOR, SFOR). Finally, (4) attitudes on the future of peacekeeping deserve some attention.

I shall return to these four issues below and to the evolution of public opinion in general.

SUPPORT FOR THE USE OF MILITARY FORCE
AND PARTICIPATION IN UN PEACEKEEPING OPERATIONS

With the caveats expressed above on the nature and role of public opinion in mind, let us now look at the available data. In spite of the paucity of available survey data, there is little doubt that the idea of using the armed forces for furthering the purposes of the United Nations has historically and continuously enjoyed strong support and considerable goodwill in the Netherlands. This also applies to the idea of international peacekeeping operations and the participation of the Netherlands therein.[4] Other research has confirmed this.[5] In recent years about 70 percent supported the idea of participation in UN peacekeeping operations in general. Data from surveys about the cases of Lebanon (UNIFIL) (NIPO, weekly surveys, February 1979 and October 1982) and operation Desert Storm (Iraq-Kuwait) confirmed that this general support by and large also held in specific concrete cases (see Everts 1992; Everts 1993, 196–224; Everts 1996 for more details). Among the goals of such UN actions, prevention of conflict escalation into civil war drew most support, and among the motives and criteria for participation in such actions, considerations of (narrow) national interest and the proximity of the conflict drew much less support than "altruistic" ones like the protection of human rights (Schennink and Wecke 1995, 50). The Dutch seemed to be true internationalists. However, this attitude had never been really put to the test, since on those occasions when the Netherlands had been called upon to honor its general commitments, the risks involved had been small. What would happen if things were different in this connection remained to be seen.

Although still at the verbal level and in the context of the artificial setting of opinion polling, there were indications, however, that this commitment was to be taken seriously (poll by NIPO for Stichting Maatschappij en Krijgsmacht, December 1993). However, other data suggest that support for military action drops off considerably once the likelihood of casualties is raised (longitudinal survey of enemy images of Studiecentrum Vredesvraagstukken, KU Nijmegen and various others, held in 1979, 1986, 1990, and 1991; see Everts, 1996). Similar outcomes were produced in other, more recent surveys on the acceptability of military force for various purposes (van der Meulen 1993; Schenrtink and Wecke 1995, 36–40). Other outcomes suggest that while in some respects the willingness to accept force in theory seems to exceed that in practice, sometimes the opposite seems to be the case. Finally, one is struck by the fact that while in general questions among the motives justifying the use of force elements like "human rights" and "international legal order" scored much higher than for instance matters like "protecting economic interests."

Whatever the case, these outcomes suggested considerable support for the existence of a body bag syndrome, i.e., the hypothesis that support for war diminishes roughly in proportion to the number of expected or real casualties. If this effect would already occur in cases in which "national security" could be said to be involved, one would expect it to be even stronger in cases where "national interest" in the narrow sense would be less directly involved, such as operations in a UN context. The conflicts in the former

Yugoslavia and the question of the involvement of the Netherlands in military efforts to control or end these conflicts provide us with a test case.

THE CONFLICTS IN THE FORMER YUGOSLAVIA

Initially, that is at the beginning of the escalation of the conflict in the former Yugoslavia in 1991 and 1992, the Dutch were fairly skeptical of the likelihood that an international peacekeeping force would be able to keep the parties apart or bring about successful negotiations. This was in line with the way the conflict was portrayed in the media. Either because of lack of knowledge or out of disinterest, little was done to explain the detailed background of the conflict and the claims of the parties concerned. Often, the emphasis was put on the violent traditions of the Balkans. Consequently, only a minority felt that the Netherlands should commit itself, should it be asked to participate in such a peacekeeping force let alone a force that would enforce a solution.[6]

That had changed considerably by the end of 1992. While pessimism on the success of negotiations had grown too, two thirds of the population now favored military intervention in the conflict and Dutch participation in it, even when one's own soldiers would be killed as a consequence (see table 7.1). This was about double the level of one year earlier (Survey for Stichting Maatschappij en Krijgsmacht. See Maatschappij en Krijgsmacht, 1993). This was confirmed in other surveys held in August 1992 (and, shown in parentheses, in April 1993) (AVRO/NIPO surveys V-495 and T-704). Then, 63 percent (71 percent) favored intervention to bring about an end to the war in general and only 26 percent (20 percent) were against. Still more people favored intervention for humanitarian purposes only. As far as the Netherlands was concerned, it was felt by 87 percent (88 percent) that it should participate in such a military operation, while three out of four (men 85 percent [98 percent], women 66 percent [70 percent]) considered that it would be acceptable that Dutch soldiers would be killed in such an operation (Maatschappij en Krijgsmacht, 1992). It is noteworthy that in April 1993 changes had particularly occurred on the (far) left of the political spectrum. Among the adherents of the pacifist and Green party (Groen Links), who are traditionally critical of anything military, the number of proponents of intervention had increased in one year from 22 percent to 68 percent![7] With respect to the strong willingness to participate in the United Nations Bosnian action, the inherent risks were recognized but found acceptable by 57 percent.[8]

Erosion of Support for Military Action

The very large support for military action by the United Nations and participation of the Netherlands therein, which was so evident in 1993, certainly contributed to an opinion climate in which the government felt confident that it would enjoy domestic support if it would commit a relatively large Dutch contingent to UNPROFOR and so it did, with almost total parliamentary support. In doing so, it was overriding fears among the military leadership that the risks would be too great and the troops too ill-prepared for the mission.

The initial support of international intervention in Bosnia began to diminish, however, as the conflict dragged on and UNPROFOR turned out to be unable to stop it. Support eroded considerably in the course of 1994. In one year, the number of supporters of Dutch participation in UNPROFOR decreased by 14 percent (see for an overview of changes in public opinion tables 7.1 and 7.2).

At first sight, it seemed clear that the patience and endurance to continue with military operations that were seen as risky as well as militarily senseless and offering no prospect of success were diminishing rapidly to the point where it became questionable whether there was still sufficient political support for keeping the troops in Bosnia-Herzegovina especially if casualties would occur. That the public would not be willing to sustain casualties was now increasingly argued by politicians, while others stressed that this perception was the reason why other European countries were not ready to put their troops at risk in forcing an end to the war by confronting what was increasingly seen as a case of Serbian aggression.

As a matter of fact, the views on "staying" or "leaving" remained much divided, anyway up to the end of 1994, and this reflected a fundamental uncertainty at the political level concerning the question of what ought to be done with respect to the conflict, rather than a form of "cowardice" or a fear of casualties. Naturally, this state of affairs also affected the willingness to run military risks. While at the end of 1993 57 percent had felt the risks to be acceptable, this had declined to 47 percent by the end of 1994 (see table 7.2).[9] On the other hand, there were few indications yet that the Dutch public actively wanted the UN troops, including Dutchbat, the contingent from the Netherlands in Srebrenica, to be withdrawn.

By June 1995 opinions had become even more divided. On the one hand, the number of supporters of the option "leave it to the parties to solve their conflict" had increased (from 31 to 33 percent), but so had support for the option of military intervention (from 25 to 28 percent) Accordingly, the number of supporters of the third option, "to muddle through," had diminished from 30 to 20 percent (survey of NIPO for SMK, July 1995. See also Table 7.1).

Support for (continuing) participation by the Netherlands armed forces in UNPROFOR, which had already declined from 68 percent at the end of 1993 to 54 percent at the end 1994, had declined even further by the end of June 1995, to 44 percent—just after the taking of hostages among the UNPROFOR soldiers and unarmed observers (including a number of Dutch) had been ended (Maatschappij en Krijgsmacht 1995). The number of opponents to

Table 7.1. UN Operations in the Former Yugoslavia (in percent)

* Support for Participation in UNPROFOR:	08"92	04"93	12"93	05"94	12"94	06"95	07"95	08"95	12(I)"95	12(II)"95
— yes	87	88	68	—	54	44	—	62	69	71
— neither agree nor disagree	—	—	11	—	15	22	—	10	—	—
— no	8	8	14	—	26	26	—	18	12	12
— don't know/no answer	5	4	8	—	6	12	—	11	20	17
* Stay in Bosnia or leave?										
— stay	—	—	—	—	44	36	33	50	—	—
— leave	—	—	—	—	42	38	57	28	—	—
— don't know/no answer	—	—	—	—	14	26	10	23	—	—
* Options for the United Nations in Bosnia										
— continue present course with emphasis on negotiations	—	—	—	31	30	20	—	—	—	—
— withdrawal and leave it to the parties themselves	—	—	—	20	31	33	—	—	—	—
— air strikes to enforce peace	—	—	—	17	}25	28	—	—	—	—
— send ground troops to enforce peace	—	—	—	16	—	—	—	—	—	—

Sources: August 1992, April 1993: avro/nipo; December 1993, December 1994, June and December-I 1995: nipo for Stichting Maatschappij en Krijgsmacht; May 1994: international comparative survey in the European Union by Harris Research Center; July 1995: Intomart for rtl television; August 1995: nipo for Studiecentrum Vredesvraagstukken Nijmegen a.o.; December-II 1995: nos.

Table 7.2 Tolerance for Risks (casualties) with Respect to Intervention in the Former Yugoslavia (in percent)

	08/"92	12/"92	04/"93	12/"93	12/"94	06/"95	07/"95	09/"95	12/"95
Risks/casualties acceptable:									
—yes	76	66	80	57	48	34	30	55	54
—no	17	20	14	29	39	47	64	23	33
—d.k./n.a.	7	14	6	14	13	19	6	22	13

Sources: August 1992, April 1993: avro/nipo; December 1992, December 1993, December 1994, June 1995, December 1995: smk/nipo; September 1995: Telepanel/Marktonderzoek.

participation had almost doubled from the end of 1993 to the end of 1994, and stayed at that level until June 1995. At that time the number of doubters had increased, however, to a quarter of all respondents (survey of FING for SMK, July 1995). The percentage of those who considered the risks involved to be acceptable had dropped by that time to a minimum of 34 percent "acceptable" and 47 percent "unacceptable," with 19 percent not answering this question (see table 7.2). This resulted in a true reversal of opinion, which was even more prominent among women. Compared to the end of 1994, the balance had also shifted with respect to the question of "staying" or "leaving." For the first time the proponents of leaving had now gained the upper hand (38 versus 36 percent with the remainder undecided). Again, the large number of doubters is remarkable (Maatschappij en Krijgsmacht 1995). Support for staying on decreased with age. The failure of the umpteenth cease-fire in the first half of 1995, the renewal of the fighting, the Serbian hostage taking in May 1995, and the general bleak outlook for any end to the war did their bit to (further) erode the basis of public support for maintaining the Dutch troops in Bosnia. The Dutch contingent had suffered only a few casualties, mostly from accidents, and this did play only a minor role in the decrease of support.

Srebrenica

This change in climate was further reinforced by the dramatic events of July 1995 when the Bosnian Serbs forced the Netherlands' contingent Dutchbat to evacuate and surrender Srebrenica, one of the areas, which the United Nations had declared to be a "safe haven." In the course of events one Dutch soldier was killed. The Dutch were militarily not capable of mounting an effective defense (neither did they have the mandate to do so), received no air support, and were thus forced to surrender. As a consequence, thousands of Muslim inhabitants of the area were killed or disappeared.

A poll held immediately after the events, on July 11, 1995, measured the immediate impact of the events in Srebrenica (Intomart for RTL Nieuws. See NRC Handelsblad and other papers, July 12, 1995). Two thirds of all respondents now felt that the Dutch risks in Bosnia were no longer acceptable, an increase by 20 percentage points in only a few weeks. Only 29 percent thought that the risks were still acceptable. Two out of three people (64 percent) also felt that it would be unacceptable that more Dutch soldiers would die while trying to protect the Bosnian population from the violence of the war.[10] A firm majority of 57 percent felt that the government should bring the troops home as soon as possible, with only 33 percent thinking that they should stay. The embarrassment with the situation was reflected in the fact that a majority also agreed, however, that force should be used to free Dutchbat and the population of Srebrenica. Thirty-one percent disagreed.

Proponents of the use of force were to be found especially among men and younger people.

In the light of this confusion, it is not strange that opinions were, and stayed, divided on the question of whether the government had been right to withdraw Dutchbat. A plurality (of 42 percent) (but not a majority) thought that the government had taken the right decision; 31 percent had the opposite view. Again, it is remarkable how many failed to give an answer. Confusion reigned (Telepanel Marktonderzoek of the University of Amsterdam; poll held September 1–5, 1995).

To sum up the data presented above: as the war in Yugoslavia dragged on, public opinion became both more cynical and extreme (see table 7.1). It also became more polarized, with less support for UNPROFOR and more for withdrawal on the one hand, but also with increased support for strong military action on the other. Risks were increasingly felt to be unacceptable (table 7.2). Mission support and tolerance for risks/casualties clearly go hand in hand (van der Meulen and de Konink 1998). This became even more marked after the events in the first half of 1995: the taking of hostages by the Bosnian Serbians and the humiliating forced withdrawal of Dutchbat, the Netherlands contingent in Srebrenica, in the beginning of July.

NO CONFIRMATION OF THE CASUALTIES HYPOTHESIS

Even though the events in Srebrenica could be seen as the moral equivalent of casualties, it would, however, be premature to conclude that the body bag hypothesis was operative in the Netherlands in 1995. This can also be concluded from table 7.1 above and other polls taken after the events of July 1995. Indeed, very quickly, rather different and contradictory observations could be made, on the basis of a number of polls held shortly after the events described, and in the second half of 1995.

At the level of the media, the picture of the aftermath of Srebrenica was one of confusion and disappointment. There was considerable commotion and confusion at the political level in the months since the fall of Srebrenica. The debates focused on the question who had been politically responsible for the drama and which, if any, political consequences should be drawn. On the basis of these debates and press reports it was easy to conclude that the Netherlands was suffering from a terrible hangover. This, it was said, did imply that the societal basis for participation in future military operations organized or mandated by the UN was damaged or eroded, at least for the time being, perhaps permanently.

The empirical evidence at the level of mass opinion points in another direction, however. The first signs of the resilience of the public became visible in a poll held at the end of August 1995 (the poll was held shortly before the NATO air strikes began August 1995; see also Schennink and Wecke 1995). The downward trend in support for participation in military UN actions, which was so evident up to July, had now been reversed again with 62 percent supporting taking part in UNPROFOR and even more (68 percent) supporting participation in UN action in general (and only 11 percent against). This was the same high level as was previously observed. Seventy percent supported taking part in peacekeeping operations outside the Balkans. One wonders what brought about this sudden reversal. Was it the expectation that NATO would enter a new phase of "strong" action and that this action would be successful? Was it a desire for a "second chance" or for revenge? Whatever the case, the public showed a great deal of resilience. This support reached across the entire political spectrum. Even among the conservatives, which—on the whole—were most critical of taking part in UN action (again), a majority of 58 percent supported a Dutch role in ex-Yugoslavia. Similar levels of support were obtained among the supporters of the Green Left.

Support for UNPROFOR was relatively even more strong among men, the younger generations, and the better educated. Another poll held at about the same time provided additional evidence that there was (still) considerable support for humanitarian and military aid.[11]

A Resilient but Confused Public

This positive evaluation also appeared from a number of other, related questions. The answers to these questions not only revealed a positive sentiment, but also a good deal of remarkable stability. "Did the presence of Dutch troops in Srebrenica serve a useful purpose, after all?" Eighteen percent responded with "certainly," "somewhat" said 41 percent, "a little bit" was chosen by 11 percent, while only 17 percent felt that the Dutch presence had little or no value at all. When this question was repeated a few months later, in December 1995, there were hardly any changes in the pattern of answers (survey by NIPO for Stichting Maatschappij en Krijgsmacht, December 18–20, 1995).[12]

That this was true only to a very limited degree (unless one would argue, skeptically, that the hangover was only suppressed temporarily) also appears from other data.[13] This pattern was probably also shaped by the view (shared by 46 percent of all respondents) that the Bosnian Serbs were (and are) primarily responsible for the policies of "ethnic cleansing." For the critics, the view (shared by 30 percent) that the international community shares the responsibility for the events in Srebrenica and elsewhere is probably most relevant in this connection (survey by NIPO for Stichting Maatschappij en Krijgsmacht, December 18–20, 1995). In another poll 64 percent agreed with the statement that the terrible problems facing Dutchbat in Srebrenica were primarily caused by the position taken by the UN (Telepanel Marktonderzoek of the University of Amsterdam; poll held September 1–5, 1995). Faced with the question of what would have been the best course of action: to protect the population in spite of all risks, or let the safety of one's own men prevail, 19 percent preferred the first option, 33 percent the second, and 32 percent preferred to take a middle position. Clearly, feelings were confused and mixed, but in the end the safety of the troops came first.

Another question in this survey was "Has the Netherlands done enough in the question of Bosnia?" A strong majority (of 56 percent) felt that enough (or even more than enough) had been done. Only 13 percent said "not enough" and 18 percent said "absolutely too little." The others did not take a clear position on this issue (Schennink and Wecke 1995).

"Should the UN-troops stay in Bosnia despite the fall of Srebrenica and Zepa?" Fifty percent said "yes" in August 1995 and only a minority of 28 percent said "no." Twenty-two percent hesitated or did not know. That was a much higher figure than had previously been observed (survey of August 1995; Schennink and Wecke 1995, 62). On the other hand, 42 percent agreed at about the same time that "with hindsight one can say that the government was right in withdrawing Dutchbat from Srebrenica as soon as possible." Thirty-one percent, however, disagreed with this conclusion, and 27 percent had no idea or did not give a reply (Telepanel Marktonderzoek of the University of Amsterdam; poll held September 1–5, 1995). These outcomes were confirmed in general in two other surveys, held at the end of 1995, when an evaluation of the Srebrenica affair was discussed in parliament, in two other surveys (see table 7. 3).[14]

It seems that the wording of the questions had a considerable effect on the outcomes, but there can be little doubt that the conclusion that the Dutch "blue helmets" bore the responsibility for the massacres among the Bosnian Muslims was shared by only a rather small minority. Sixty-six percent disagreed with such a conclusion in its general phrasing. Almost a majority felt too that they had provided sufficient protection.[15]

A majority (53 percent) of the Dutch felt that not only the prestige and credibility of the Dutch armed forces but also that of the United Nations had suffered from the events in Bosnia. In spite of this, public opinion showed a remarkable degree of resilience. The findings of August 1995 were confirmed four months later. About 70 percent then continued to support the participation by armed forces of the Netherlands in military UN-operations (survey by NIPO for Stichting Maatschappij en Krijgsmacht, December 18–20, 1995).

Table 7.3. The events in Srebrenica (in percent)

1. "The following questions deal with the actions of the Dutch contingent in Srebrenica (Bosnia). Will you please tell me for each of the following statements whether you agree totally, partly or disagree with it?"

	agree completely	agree partly	disagree	dk/na
— The Dutch "blue helmets" in Srebrenica have provided sufficient protection to the Bosnian civilians.	47	19	18	16
— The Dutch "blue helmets" in Srebrenica share the responsibility for the disappearance of thousands of people in Srebrenica.	8	9	66	18
— The events in Srebrenica have damaged the respect for the Netherlands' armed forces.	41	15	36	7
— The events in Srebrenica have damaged the respect for the Dutch minister of defence, Voorhoeve.	34	19	37	10
— The Netherlands should contribute by providing troops for the NATO force which is going to supervise the implementation of the peace accord in Bosnia.	71	10	12	7

2. "Do you agree completely, partly or disagree with the following statements?"

	agree completely	agree partly	disagree	dk/na
— The Dutch troops should have provided more support to the local population at the fall of Srebrenica.	43	22	19	17

Source: (1) Kijk en Luisteronderzoek nos (audience survey for Netherlands' radio and television), December 1995; (2) Source: nipo for smk, December 1995

SUPPORT OF NATO INTERVENTION

The escalation of external intervention, which began at the end of August 1995 in the form of the attacks of NATO aircraft against Bosnian Serbian targets, undertaken with a general mandate of the UN, also received strong support from public opinion in the Netherlands. Three out of four respondents were in favor of the NATO actions, and only 5 percent disagreed with them. Almost as many supported the participation of the Dutch air force in the actions. Two thirds also thought the air actions had increased the chances of ending the war. It is remarkable, though, in the light of earlier outcomes suggesting quite different views (compare also table 7.1) that no less than 56 percent would now support participation by the Netherlands' armed forces in actions entailing considerable risks of casualties. Only 23 percent did not consider this acceptable and 22 percent took a neutral position on this question.[16]

Despite repeated suggestions to the contrary in the media and by political observers, the events around Srebrenica seem not to have had a strongly negative impact on the degree of support for such actions. To the degree that there was a dip in support, it was not very deep and only short-lived. Indeed, with hindsight, even stronger military action was now supported by many. At the end of August 1995, the question was asked: "With hindsight, what would have been the best position to be taken by the international community in the conflicts in the former Yugoslavia" (Schennink and Wecke 1995). Forty-six percent of those surveyed in the Netherlands now opted for large-scale military intervention, 26 percent thought that the parties should have been left to their own devices, and only 11 percent preferred the option which was actually chosen. Eighteen percent could not make a choice. The option of large-scale intervention was even more popular (55 percent) among supporters of the Green Left. This group counted also relatively less supporters of leaving the conflict to the parties themselves. In other respects there were few relevant party political differences.

Participation in IFOR

Given the restoration of the societal consensus by the end of August 1995 it came as no surprise that the decision of December 1995 to take part in IFOR, the UN-mandated and NATO-sponsored international force to supervise the implementation of the Dayton agreements, was also supported by 68 percent of the general public. Fifty-eight against 17 percent also agreed that NATO should be using force if necessary to enforce compliance with the Dayton agreements. Asked about the acceptability of casualties (dead or wounded) among the (NATO) military, 55 percent agreed to this even when the likelihood of this would be great (31 percent said "not acceptable," 14 percent gave no opinion). The same question, but mentioning Dutch soldiers specifically, produced very few differences in this respect. Again, it looks as if the Dutch, at least at the verbal level, are not free riders. The outcome mentioned above was confirmed in another survey, which even registered 71 percent support for participation in IFOR (Het aanzien van Nederland, Survey by NOS Kijk- en Luister-onderzoek for Radio-1 Journaal, Hilversum, December 15–19, 1995). Remarkably, this support was coupled, however, with considerable pessimism as to the likelihood of success.[17]

That the "readiness for sacrifice" may be considerable also with respect to "peacekeeping operations," but is mediated by political leadership and the perceived chances of success, also appears from other analyses (Cohen 1996; La Balme 1998).[18] In the case of the Netherlands the likelihood of success and the perceived chances of peace considerably lessened the impact of any fear of casualties in reducing support for the peacekeeping mission in Bosnia (Van der Meulen and De Konink 1998 and 1998a).

Mixed Attitudes

In other words, the available data suggests that four key words can characterize the views of the general public in the Netherlands with respect to the new tasks of the armed forces in general and participation in UN actions, such as UNPROFOR in particular: "idealistic," "forceful," "skeptical," and "pragmatic" (Van der Meulen 1996). The first, *idealism*, appears from the fact that while 50 percent considered the "protection of human rights" an important criterion for intervention and taking part in IFOR, only 2 percent thought so about "protecting the national interest" (survey of April 1996). The dimension of *forcefulness* shows from the increasing unwillingness (from 41 to 50 percent) to accept the view that it is not the task of IFOR to apprehend persons suspected of war crimes. *Skepticism* appears from the generally low judgment of the effectiveness of IFOR (5–8 [July 1996] 5–5) on a scale from 1–10. Only very few thought that the presence of IFOR was decisive for reestablishing peace. This was seen first and foremost as a task of the parties themselves (surveys of April and July 1996). "Should the Netherlands take part in a successor of IFOR?" was the final question (in July 1996). The answers showed a good deal of *pragmatism*: 41 percent thought that the Netherlands should participate anyway, even though the results would be limited, 12 percent said "only if the Americans also stay with ground forces," 14 percent: "as long as France and Britain continue to participate," and only 19 percent thought "not at all" (see van der Meulen 1996).

To sum up: analysis of the available data produces a considerably more complex picture than that suggested by the casualty hypothesis in its simple form.

THE EVOLUTION OF GOVERNMENT POLICY AND THE IMPACT OF PUBLIC OPINION

Let me now return to the question of the impact of public opinion on the process of governmental policy and decision making in the Netherlands. I have already stressed the coalition and consensus-based character of Dutch politics.

In the present case the Netherlands was ruled by a center-left coalition. Ironically the minister of defense was criticized most strongly by members of his own party, the liberal-conservative VVD, who increasingly questioned both the wisdom and interest of the Netherlands to (continue to) participate in the UN operation in Bosnia-Herzegovina.

After the debacle at Srebrenica the minister felt that he really ought to step down, but in the end he decided against this because he felt that this might have reinforced the misperception that the Netherlands and not Serbia or the United Nations and the other member states were to take most of the blame for the occurrence of the massacre. For most of the period concerned party political differences in or outside the ruling coalition played only a minor role, however.

I recall that four phases in the evolution of policymaking were highlighted above and I shall now look briefly at each of these.

1. Decisions concerning the armed forces and their use before 1994.

After the end of the Cold War the Netherlands' armed forces, like those in other NATO countries, were both reduced in strength and thoroughly re-structured. The new tasks and structure were outlined in a 1991 document (Prioriteitennota). Since the armed forces feared a backlash on their raison d'être there was, in principle, a certain eagerness to assume new task in a UN or other international framework. Emphasis was put on the new tasks in the realm of crisis management and peacekeeping. These served as a (new) le-gitimization of defense expenditure in a situation in which there were no im-mediate or even long-term threats to the country's security that should be met by military force. Because it was not obvious how much the country should spend on these new tasks the government agreed that the actual size of the efforts (some 10–15,000 men should be available for these tasks) was rather "a question of national ambitions." Its plans for defense restructuring gained widespread public and political support.

In the years after 1991, government and parliament in particular shared a certain eagerness to show a certain eagerness to commit the armed forces to peacekeeping operations undertaken by the UN, not only in theory but also in practice, such as UNTAC (a marine battalion in Cambodia, 1992). At an early date, the Netherlands also decided to take part in UNPROFOR-I in Croa-tia (with communication and transport units, totaling about 3,000 men, 1992) and the naval blockade of the Adriatic coast, organized by NATO and WEU. Later decisions included participation in NATO's operation Deny Flight and various other operations. However, efforts to develop more general detailed and strict criteria or guidelines on the conditions under which the forces should be used were less successful. The government wanted to retain a free hand in making decisions, but parliament wanted to have at least a major say in these matters. While it recognized that the new tasks were essential to sus-tain continued support for the armed forces, it also feared a public backlash should the forces become engaged in dangerous and ineffective operations. In this it carefully reflected the attitudes in society at large.[19]

2. The decision to take part in the military interventions in the former Yugoslavia.

Because a widely shared consensus had been formed in the country on the desirability of external intervention in the conflict, especially with respect to the three-sided civil war in Bosnia-Herzegovina, it took the government, which had been urging such concerted military action internationally for a long time already (but unsuccessfully due to the international differences of opinion), not very much effort to decide to take part in UNPROFOR-II with some considerable contingents (adding 1,000 men to the about 2,200 already engaged in the former Yugoslavia) when this operation was decided upon in 1993. This decision was preceded by extensive discussions in the media.[20] It was a major change since the new operation in Bosnia was put under chapter 7 of the UN charter, which meant that, in principle, force could be employed more easily to enforce the UN mandate. Though not uncritically, parliament showed itself on balance as eager as the government, if not more, to take part in this operation, and there was little political opposition to the decision, even from the, traditionally antimilitarist left side of the political spectrum.

If the dispatch of the troops was still controversial, this was due to opposition among the military, voiced by some among the military leadership and by outside military commentators. Part of the criticism was initially that the (professional) military had not joined the armed forces for tasks other than defense of the immediate national interest (the territorial and political integrity of the country) and should not be exposed to severe risks against their will. Rather quickly, though, this type of criticism became subdued.

Others, however, argued either that the restructuring of the armed forces was not yet ready and that, for instance, units with conscripts could not be employed,[21] or that the troops were not properly equipped or trained. While the Netherlands also sent other units, much of the discussion on participation of the Netherlands in what would become UNPROFOR coincided with and focused on debates on the role and use in Bosnia of the newly formed airmobile brigade. This brigade, decided upon in the immediate post-Cold War situation, was intended for crisis management operations, but was, as some said, neither trained for nor equipped for the kind of operations it would have to carry out in Yugoslavia to this purpose (being too lightly armed), and these critics feared the consequences. Others again argued that the air mobile brigade might be an expensive gadget but should now be given the chance to prove its worth.

The situation was said to require heavier armor (despite the "peacekeeping" character of UNPROFOR) and armored infantry. One general, stating what others merely though, wrote: "It is to be expected that also the airmobile battalion will incur casualties, in which case the majority of the population will cease to support the dispatch of the troops" (Major General A. S. J. van Vuren, in *Rotterdams Dagblad*, December 9, 1993.) Yet, all of this criticism was finally overridden by the politicians.

One observer, commenting on the decision-making process in this case and particularly on the eagerness of the ministers concerned to contribute to UNPROFOR, concluded: "The ministers had it easy in a certain sense. The

Second Chamber fully supported the efforts of the armed forces in the area of peacekeeping. In this it was urged on by public opinion which was in majority in favor of strong and forceful action in former Yugoslavia, and in going along with this the Second Chamber has contributed to the creation and maintenance of public support for the changed tasks and structure of the armed forces. The new 'intervention policy' was supported from right to left. Even the Green Left party (in 1993) voted for the first time—against its tradition—in favor of the defense budget" (Wecke 1994).

3. The events in Srebrenica and their aftermath.

In the course of 1994 and particularly the first half of 1995 many began to question the wisdom of a continued military presence in Bosnia. Doubts increased with each failed cease-fire agreement and when members of UN-PROFOR were taken as hostages for Serbian misbehavior. In the Netherlands politicians (especially from the conservative VVD party) began to urge the government to reconsider its position or even to urge withdrawal from the Srebrenica enclave. The government felt, however, that Dutch forces should stay until replacement could be found (Wecke and Cras 1995). This took considerable time. Fear of becoming embroiled in hostilities and risky situations also increased as the situation in Bosnia further deteriorated.

The attack on and fall of Srebrenica should not have come as the surprise it was, but anyway the shock of the events was considerable. The sense of failure and humiliation was widespread, both among the public and the politicians. Though it seemed clear that militarily little else could have been done, because air strikes would clearly have exposed one's own forces to (Bosnian) Serbian reprisals, it was a shock to realize what the consequences were of putting the safety of the troops first. Yet, this was the political condition under which they had been sent to Bosnia, and governments realized the constraints of public opinion in this respect.

The moral and political uneasiness increased even more after the media and some among the military had turned the reception of the withdrawn and defeated Dutchbat into a heroes' welcome party.

It was understandable that these events led to intense societal and political debates and to discussions between parliament and the government. Especially these discussions were long drawn out, because, among other reasons, it took time to put together a debriefing report while the media kept discovering new and often unpleasant facts. These did affect public opinion and did not increase confidence in the government's defense that the Netherlands and Dutchbat could not be blamed for the events.[22] Parliament, which could not press the issue too much, having been strongly in favor of the dispatch of Dutchbat in neglect of military warnings, largely accepted the government's defense. The Netherlands accepted, with some relief, the

chance to participate in the international Rapid Reaction Force around Sera-
jevo and the NATO air strikes that began in August 1995.

By this time, as was mentioned before, the societal basis for supporting
military actions in the framework of the UN had been completely restored,
and it showed itself strong enough to allow the government to accept new
commitments, when the question of participation in IFOR (the NATO-led
international Implementation Force) arrived on the political agenda in December 1995. IFOR would supervise the implementation of the military aspects of the Dayton agreements, which brought about an end to the fighting
in Bosnia. In spite of the many doubts that one could have considering both
the mandate and the tasks of this force, it was decided by the government to
participate in IFOR and this decision was supported by a very large majority
in parliament, despite some misgivings and doubts on the basis of the earlier
experience. Public opinion fully supported this decision.

4. The future of peacekeeping.

Above, it has been shown that, in spite of lack of success and the dramatic
experience of the defeat of Dutchbat and the massacre at Srebrenica
notwithstanding, support for the use of the armed forces in peace support
operations did not only enjoy considerable public support, but will probably
also enjoy this in the future.

Public opinion, however, is not a static and immutable factor, which
comes into being and changes on its own alone. The willingness to sustain
casualties, for example, is also not a constant. It has been argued that the
steadfastness of political leaders may create or help to sustain public support, and that politicians are too timid in this respect (Everts 1998. See also
van der Meulen 1994; van der Meulen 1995; Parsons 1995, 242–43).

Structured and Organized Public Opinion:
The Role of the Peace Movement

The available data reinforce the general observation that (unstructured)
public opinion at the mass level is at best a raw indicator. It is not an actor-
in-its own right nor an independent variable that can be treated in isolation
from the general political context. Moreover, to understand its political impact, it is important if not essential to look not only at the content, but also
at the saliency of attitudes. Both are equally relevant dimensions of attitudes.
In order to be politically relevant it has to be mobilized, expressed, and organized into a meaningful and visible format, in the form of structured and
organized public opinion, for instance through the activities of political parties or other societal actors (Everts 1983).

One of these is the peace movement, which in the Netherlands had acquired a certain measure of renown in the 1980s during the struggle over nuclear weapons.

It was understandable, therefore, that when the wars in the former Yugoslavia escalated and the media showed the viciousness of the conflicts, people began to ask "where is the peace movement?" and even began to blame it for its apparent inactivity.

However, the peace movement in the Netherlands was as divided on the Yugoslav conflicts as the rest of society, with some sticking to a commitment to nonviolent resolution and others pleading for military intervention, if only out of despair. As the violence grew simple pleas for "peace through negotiations" were clearly no longer sufficient and the agony increased when it became evident that the price of peace might be the equally despicable acceptance of the results of ethnic cleansing.

While the peace movement did not organize demonstrations and the like (since it largely shared the government's assessment of the possibilities of external action), it would be a mistake, however, to think that the international peace movement was absent or inactive. Through its international networks it undertook strong and concerted efforts, for instance to foster contacts and cooperation among local peace groups in Yugoslavia. In 1991 a peace crusade, of four hundred persons from thirteen countries, supported by a resolution of the European Parliament went from Slovenia through Croatia to Sarajevo showing the strength of domestic opposition to the war and the like.

In the Netherlands the peace movement helped to press successfully in three cases: (1) the admission of (more) refugees in 1992; (2) the decisions on international military intervention in 1993; and (3) the idea of the creation of safe havens, and the controversial idea of turning Bosnia-Herzegovina into a UN protectorate (there was considerable political sympathy for this proposal but it interfered with the Vance-Owen plan for the [temporary] division of Bosnia, and it would require a much greater military presence than the countries concerned were willing to provide at the time].

Caveat Lector

In all of this we should remind ourselves again to be careful in interpreting the data, however. To the extent that these conclusions are based on opinion polls where respondents are faced with hypothetical cases, the validity of the findings may be called into question. Interview situations may and probably will differ considerably from real life situations in this respect.

As an aside (but not, as I shall argue below, an irrelevant aside) one should note, ever, that in terms of political relevance, real attitudes are less important than how public opinion is perceived. Thus, a recent study of foreign policy, which the Netherlands government commissioned, argues (without presenting any evidence, one should add): "In most (UN)-member countries public opinion is not willing to sacrifice the lives of their 'own' soldiers for the sake of international principles in countries where war is endemic. At least this is how opinion is perceived by politicians." (emphasis added, Ph.P.E.) (Wetenschappelijke Raad voor het Regeringsbeleid 1995, 89).

SOME CONCLUDING GENERAL OBSERVATIONS

The available data on the case in question suggest, first of all, that with respect to the possible use of military force there is little reason for concern about the often alleged "emotionality" of the general public, its inconsistency, and its susceptibility to sudden impulses and shifts. This undermines the argument that the public's judgment cannot be relied upon in international affairs, especially in the specific case of gruesome civil wars and conflicts in which human rights are violated on a large scale, and where, it is said, the public demands of their governments that they should act and intervene ("do something"), whatever it may be, while on the other hand it would recoil equally unreflectedly as soon as the going gets tough and casualties occur. To listen to this, it is said, would make it impossible to initiate and maintain a consistent and, if need be, a robust security policy.

There are, it is true, sometimes indications of such inconsistencies and of a certain capriciousness, but the perceived success and sensibility of a particular (military) action as well as credible political leadership appear to be important intervening variables, which determine whether public opinion turns out to be stable or volatile, a reliable guide, or a force to be mistrusted, and whether it presents an obstacle or a condition of a sensible and effective foreign and military policy.

Secondly, the resilience of Dutch attitudes, which was so visible after the fiasco of Srebrenica in the second half of 1995 may have been reinforced by the possibility that the humiliating withdrawal from Srebrenica not only led to a temporary but short-lived hangover but also contributed to a stronger "we-feeling" and to a desire for a second chance to prove oneself.

The Lessons from Yugoslavia for the Future

We have seen that there was, certainly at the beginning, considerable support for the government's decision to share in the military operations in the former Yugoslavia. After the events of 1995 this support was fully restored, be it that both elites and the public would want to put stricter limits to the occasions and conditions under which the forces should be committed to action. What does this mean for the future?

Whether support for participation in risky UN operations will be forth-coming and stable or fail to materialize depends strongly on the credibility and persuasiveness of political leadership. The persuasiveness of and degree of unanimity among the decision makers are equally relevant factors and undoubtedly influence the stamina of the general public. Politicians may re-fer to public opinion as the reason why certain desirable steps cannot be taken, but an appeal to this is often suspect and public opinion does not usu-ally provide a perfect alibi for failing in one's duties.

Committed and credible government action may not only create support for what are indeed risky operations and it may also compensate for the downward pressures caused by casualties in such military operations (or the fear of such casualties)—at least partly, at least temporarily. Parsons (1995, 242–43) was probably correct in concluding after an analysis of the UN peacekeeping operations of the past: "I shall always believe that the governments concerned underestimated the steadfastness of their own electorates, and that the excessive timidity was unnecessary." Inept govern-ment policies may destroy such support as there was.

SOME NORMATIVE CONCLUSIONS

From a political, normative perspective it is worrisome that especially those wars and uses of force, which seem least difficult to justify today in terms of the humanitarian interests involved and because of the support of the "international community" (however elusive that concept may be), seem to fall into the second category mentioned above. In these cases, the free rider temptation rears its head too, and the public may always ask why we (or, for the military: why they) should be the ones to "mourir pour Danzig."

It is common today to explain the perceived present-day lack of support for risky humanitarian or collective security operations in the well-to-do democracies of the West from general feelings of disinterest, even callous-ness and from a false sense of being secure from bloodshed and anarchy in the zone of "democratic peace." It is relatively easy to plead ignorance about complicated conflicts in "faraway countries" and to be fatalistic about them.

There is certainly a degree of truth in this argument, but it does not seem to be the whole story. True, indifference and lack of care are not uncommon. Also, the ideological certainties that allow us to draw sharp lines between "good" and "bad" and the concomitant Cold War distinctions between "them" and "us" may have gone. Yet, there is also the pervasive stream of constant information in the mass media, which fosters and increases feelings of concern and heightens our sensitivity. If people fail to act upon this con-cern, it may be less due to indifference than to a sense of impotence and powerlessness, to the apparent failure of available international institutions (especially in countries, which, unlike the United States, never have the option "to go it alone").

Shame, compassion, and genuine concern are also important elements in the reactions of many people. On the one hand, sensitivity seems to have increased due to increased communication, but so has a sense of fatalism and skepticism about what can be accomplished by outsiders, let alone by the use of international military force. This feeling is combined with a growing moral abhorrence of violence, which grows easily in societies that have more to lose than to win.

This frustration is also a probable consequence of the perceived impotence of existing international institutions, the United Nations in particular, but also of the cynicism of political leaders. President Bush's plea for a New International Order has turned out since 1991 to what it perhaps always was: an empty slogan. Politicians in the West have tried to make a victory and vindication of their policies out of what were essentially moral and political defeats of democratic and ethical values of vast proportions, as was and is the case in the former Yugoslavia and elsewhere. Their cynicism in this respect is striking.

For others, a genuine sense of disappointment with respect to the success of earlier efforts in the field of economic, social, and political development should be added as causes of their disbelief in the possibilities of successful intervention. The perceived intractability of the problems of underdevelopment and of the conflicts that are connected to them as well as the pervasiveness of intrastate and communal violence quite easily lead to a sense of powerlessness and to a disbelief in the possibility of ending, let alone solving, the conflicts in question by outside military intervention. Moreover, to the extent that solutions or possible ways of action are suggested, one is struck by the lack of consensus concerning such solutions. In such situations, it is tempting to give in to prejudices and to stress the "age-old" origins of these conflicts ("ancient ethnic hatreds"), the fact that "violence has always been endemic," to argue that "these people are irrational and irresponsible," in short: to conclude that "there is nothing one can do about it." All of this is to justify one's inaction.

That particular public sentiment, fostered by politicians and journalists alike, rather than an unwillingness to make sacrifices, specifically to accept casualties or the risk of them, per se, seems to provide a much better explanation of the present situation. That situation is characterized by a considerable reluctance of democratic nations to commit their troops to risky military operations for causes beyond immediate and direct self-interest and a confused public opinion. That opinion, for example in the Netherlands, is shaped by a combination of a good deal of genuine concern, a strong commitment to the United Nations, to human rights, and (in principle) to concomitant action to protect these rights and further peace and justice and an abhorrence of violence and of the risks involved in such action as may be necessary. The gaps in people's minds between these contradictory elements can only be bridged by providing convincing explanations, that is better theories of what is happening in the world and insights as to which actions can and cannot be expected to work and, on the other hand, by providing political leadership including a willingness to take responsibility for such things as need to be done, even though one's immediate popularity may suffer.

No Alibi for Inactivity

The combined appeal to the body bag syndrome and the free rider dilemma, however, provides politicians with an apparently perfect moral and political alibi to abstain from doing what is necessary. Thus, the lack of public support may turn out to be the consequence and not the cause of governmental inaction and moral failure. In this connection, one is struck by the facile way in which the body bag argument is used by politicians and in the media. There is a tendency to parrot one another and to anticipate situations, which may indeed be caused by such talk.

Frequent statements of politicians and observers about a to-be-expected body bag effect on public support may be turn out be self-fulfilling prophecies. If politicians use this argument, it will often be because they seek an alibi to escape from their own, in themselves quite reasonable, hesitations. This has become particularly evident in the case of IFOR/SFOR in Bosnia-Herzegovina and the political unwillingness to run risks, as might be involved when one would actively try to get hold of suspected war criminals. Given the temptations of an appeal to "public opinion" there may and will be other cases in the future.

NOTES

· 1. An illustrative example from the United States is the following: in one poll (*USA Today*/CNN/Gallup poll, October 1995) American support for peacemaking in Bosnia fell dramatically when the hypothetical casualties did rise. Americans favored the mission by more than a two-to-one margin if no Americans were killed and opposed the mission by nearly the same margin if twenty-five Americans were killed (the *New York Times*, "Soldiering, With No Enemy," October 29, 1995, E4).

2. Kull (1995, 57) argues that American casualties in the Gulf War—be it a relatively small number—had no noticeable effect on the degree of public support for the war. For a discussion of the evidence from the Netherlands, see van der Meulen and de Konink (1998).

3. Likewise, new news reports of atrocities and allegations of misbehavior of soldiers in 1995 led to a renewal of political debate in 1998 and forced the government—which had hoped that the matter had been put to rest by ordering a scientific review of the whole Srebrenica affair—into action again.

4. Collections of data of older research are Roschar (red.), 1975 and Vaneker and Everts (red.), (1985). See also Everts 1992.

5. The most important source for this conclusion is a survey by NIPO for Studiecentrum Vredesvraagstukken, Nijmegen and Stichting Maatschappij en Krijgsmacht, August 21–24, 1995. See also Schennink and Wecke 1995, 21–34.

6. Poll by NIPO for Stichting Maatschappij en Krijgsmacht of late 1991. See Maatschappij en Krijgsmacht, 1992. See for more and other data on the Yugoslav conflict Jaarboek Vrede en Veiligheid 1993, 187–88 and idem, 1994, 211–14. See for other analyses van der Meulen 1995a.

7. Other surveys in 1993, however, showed a somewhat lower degree of support, but still a clear majority of the respondents (Jaarboek Vrede en Veiligheid 1993, 187–89).

8. This figure had, however, decreased in comparison to a few months earlier. Survey by NIPO for Stichting Maatschappij en Krijgsmacht, December 1993.

9. Incidentally, the disappointment in connection to UNPROFOR had had little impact yet at the end of 1994 on the willingness to participate in actions by the United Nations in general. The number of supporters of taking part in such actions had only declined from 72 to 69 percent "(strongly) in agreement." (Data for end 1994 cited from Maatschappij en Krijgsmacht 1995.)

10. Text of the question: "Last weekend a Dutch soldier died in Bosnia. Do you think that the efforts of the UN in Bosnia to protect the civilian population can justify the risk of more casualties among the Dutch military?"

11. This survey was held by NIPO (August 21–25, 1995) for broadcasting organization Studio RKK, September 5, 1995, and was executed by Studiecentrum Vredesvraagstukken, University of Nijmegen and Stichting Maatschappij en Krijgsmacht.

12. However, another repetition, in July 1996, showed a slightly more pessimistic public, a decrease from 61 to 50 percent saying the effort had been certainly or somewhat useful (Survey for Stichting Maatschappij en Krijgsmacht, July 1996). See also van der Meulen 1996.

13. It is true that there have been repeated revivals of the Srebrenica debate in the Netherlands. One example was 1998 when new press reports about atrocities in Srebrenica and possible misbehavior of Dutch soldiers at the time appeared and new evidence emerged too about alleged withholding of incriminating information by the authorities in the Ministry of Defence. While this debate also involved the question of the wisdom of Dutch policies at the time, it appears to have only marginally affected the willingness to partake in future international military operations. In spite of its commitments to the UN the Dutch government was among those strongly pleading for military action against Serbia even without a formal mandate of the Security Council. Another example was 2002 when the long-expected report from the Netherlands' Institute for War Documentation (NIOD) was finally made public. The institute had been charged by the government to make a historical reconstruction of the developments and decisions leading up the Srebrenica debacle. While rejecting the conclusion that the Netherlands' contingent could have prevented the massacre, the report was very critical with respect to other aspects such as the amount of wishful thinking involved in the original decisions and the complicity of the armed forces in covering up what had happened in the aftermath of the events. Without waiting for the eventual outcome of the parliamentary debate on this report the cabinet, under the premiership of Wim Kok, decided to resign shortly before the incumbent general elections in May 2002.

14. The sources of these findings are: Het aanzien van Nederland, Survey by NOS Kijk- en Luisteronderzoek for Radio 1 Journaal, Hilversum, December 15–19, 1995 and survey by NIPO for Stichting Maatschappij en Krijgsmacht, December 18–20, 1995.

15. See note 14.

16. Source: see note 13.

17. For examples see Jaarboek Vrede en Veiligheid 1995, 216–18.

18. The French should not be seen as trigger-happy, however. They support military engagement "à la francaise" with limited means "which favors a dissuasive attitude to that of confrontations, appeasement to escalation, and which tries to limit casualties" (Cohen [réd.], 1996, 42).

19. See for more detailed surveys of these developments Everts and Koole 1995 and Everts 1998a.

20. See for an overview of the debates de Boode 1993.

21. Parliament had adopted a motion that conscripts could not be forced to take part in operations outside the NATO area, such as in UN peacekeeping. Conscription (or more precisely the actual drafting of men of military age) was not terminated until 1996.

22. See for an overview of the debates in the media de Boode 1995.

8

German Public Opinion and the Crisis in Bosnia

Karin Johnston

The major foreign policy question in the 1990s was the question of Germany's new international responsibilities and its relationship to the use of German military force. The German public faced a series of hard questions: did its changed circumstances demand that Germany accept more international responsibility—more commensurate with its new status—and did those responsibilities include a larger German military role in the world? Prior to the onset of hostilities in Bosnia, and in keeping with a deep-seated cultural anti-militarism, the German public was resistant not only to a greater international role, but to any use of German military force other than self-defense. Confronted with scenarios involving the potential involvement of German forces, public opinion during the Bosnian conflict was fluid and at times contradictory, revealing the degree to which the public struggled with the issues of out-of-area missions, peacekeeping and peacemaking, and the role of the UN and NATO. By the end of the crisis in December 1995, however, the German public had come to support in principle the need for German military engagement outside of its territorial borders, but always within a multilateral context and with strong preferences for humanitarian and "soft power" tasks coupled with a clear rejection of German participation in combat operations.

German public opinion and government policy on the use of force shifted dramatically over the course of the Bosnian crisis. In the period immediately after the fall of the Berlin Wall, the German public and large segments of the political elite registered strong opposition to any German military role in the growing crisis in Yugoslavia, reflecting attitudes on the use of force evident since the early years of the Federal Republic. Under external pressure to assume greater international responsibility, the conservative parties supported a broader military role for the *Bundeswehr* (German armed forces) as part of this expanded responsibility, while the parties on the political left either rejected any military role save for self-defense or supported a very narrowly defined role. These differences led to constitutional challenges on the issue of the use of force. In 1994, the Federal Constitutional Court in Karlsruhe ruled that German participation in out-of-area operations was permissible, and by December 1995 the German *Bundestag* approved by a wide margin the deployment of German forces in Bosnia to assist in the implementation of the Dayton Accords. Every political party save the PDS, the former East German communist party, had at some point shifted its position relative to out-of-area deployments.

Opinion polls in late 1995 revealed that most Germans supported the government's decision.[1] It is evident that public attitudes did have an impact on the policymaking process, but that public opinion was only one of many variables that shaped the parameters of the policy choices available to policymakers. External pressures and domestic institutional and societal factors all were important elements in the shift in attitudes and policy towards the use of German military forces.

This chapter will examine the relationship between public opinion and foreign policy in the Federal Republic of Germany during the Bosnian crisis in order to shed light on how these attitudes shifted, leading to the decision, after decades of resistance, to commit German military forces outside of its borders. The first section will discuss the relationship between public opinion and foreign policy in the German case. The second section will examine public opinion data to determine the public's response to the growing conflict. The third section will place the development of events and the divisions within and among the political parties within the context of the German public's reactions. The argument presented here is that in the case of Germany, it is critical to set the context within which public attitudes on the use of force developed, since understanding how and in what direction public attitudes shifted is very much a function of where attitudes on the use of force stood on the eve of German unification.

PUBLIC OPINION AND FOREIGN POLICY

Public opinion is the product of a complicated synthesis of social and political processes, contextual factors, and the act of public discourse and communication. Views have differed on whether public opinion matters, and if it does matter, what the impact on the policymaking process is. Most of the literature on the opinion-policy nexus, much of it in the context of U.S. public opinion and foreign policy, falls into one of two categories: either elite-driven (top-down) or public-driven (bottom-up).

The conventional wisdom that has dominated the discourse on public opinion and foreign policy is an elite-driven model. The public is viewed as uninterested in world affairs, fickle, volatile, unstable, given to mood swings, and thus too easily manipulated. Attitudes were seen as so incoherent and unstructured that they were deemed "non-opinions." This pessimistic view of the public is consistent with realist assertions about public opinion, particularly with regard to foreign policy. Classical realism rejects any notion of public opinion affecting the policymaking process. The professed need for secrecy, the high level of technical expertise required, and the complexity of issues and diplomatic relations are reasons given for leaving foreign and security policy in the hands of a small group of highly qualified policymakers. As Ole Holsti writes, the motivation for much of the earlier work on public attitudes was based on elite concerns that the ignorance and inconstancy of the public would severely constrain foreign policy, since for them the public was too parochial in its interests and incapable of attaining the knowledge base to make rational decisions (Holsti 1996, 35).

By the 1970s, as researchers began to look more closely at public opinion and its impact on the policymaking process, there was increasing evidence that the top-down analysis was flawed. Some studies revealed a more bottom-up dynamic, where public attitudes were shown to have an impact on policy and where policy changes followed shifts in public opinion. The aggregate data collected by Page and Shapiro, for example, showed that this was true for half of the cases they studied. Their study of trends in collective public opinion showed that, contrary to conventional wisdom, American policy preferences are rational, stable, coherent, and meaningful, based on the values held by the public and the information at their disposal.[2] Though the public's knowledge of policy issues remains low, the public possesses deeply held values on which they base their assessments of those issues, which serve to stabilize the political system by setting the boundaries of political discourse (Rogers 2000). It is thus not unreasonable for public attitudes to inform the process of determining public policy decisions.

But while the top-down and bottom-up terminology seems to imply a linear relationship between the public and the policy process, this is misleading. The relationship is one of reciprocity between public opinion and policymaking. As Jacobs and Shapiro have observed: "It is not the case that policymakers' relationship with the mass public simply involves either shaping or responding to public opinion. Rather, responsiveness and direction often coexist; they are not mutually exclusively alternatives."[3] Case studies have shown that public opinion can constrain or even push strong policy positions, and that policy leaders have responded to such pressures. There is also evidence to show that governments have implemented policies despite public opposition. Nevertheless, scholars have warned against a definitive ruling on causality; empirical evidence does show patterns of correlation in the opinion-policy linkage, but the evidence remains circumstantial at best.[4]

Importantly, in terms of the public's response, the view that foreign policy is fundamentally different from domestic policy has not been substantiated. There are differences, to be sure, but they are differences in the degree of salience, with foreign policy often less salient to the public, and in the interpretation assigned to an international event (e.g., serious threat to national security). Once an issue emerges, however, public opinion will stabilize and respond to events in ways that are stable and meaningful.[5] External events, then, are important in shaping the public's response.

German Public Opinion and Foreign Policy

While fewer case studies of European countries have been conducted, not all of their conclusions support the findings outlined in American case studies.[6] European scholars have drawn distinctions between the American presidential system and the European parliamentary system, arguing for the need to study public opinion within the organizational structures and groups of actors in which it operates. For example, while the directional emphasis in some of the U.S. case studies appears to argue for a more direct impact of public opinion on policymaking,[7] European scholars contend that the impact in parliamentary systems is necessarily more indirect because of the structural differences in the political systems. The American presidential system is characterized by weak party institutions and a strong executive branch. The system is also highly fragmented, and this fragmentation creates a greater number of access points for political actors and for public opinion to enter more directly into the policymaking process. This is not to say that the impact on policy itself is more direct, but only to point out that the fragmentation and permeability is greater in the American system (Risse-Kappen 1991). Parliamentary systems, on the other hand, have stronger parties and weaker executive powers. In such a system, the impact of public opinion appears more indirect, and the parties play a much more central role as an interpreter and channel for public attitudes on policy issues.

As more data across countries was collected, more comparative work was possible. Thomas Risse-Kappen examined the relationship between public opinion and foreign policy in four countries (Japan, Germany, United States, and France) and found that one could not assume the effect of public opinion on foreign policy was similar for all countries. His research showed not only that the impact of public opinion on foreign policy was neither top-down nor bottom-up but a mix of the two, but that one could not understand foreign policy decisions without examining the intervening variable of domestic social and political structures. Three factors were important: political institutions, structure of society, and policy networks. For Germany, factors in the German political system important in the decision-making process were: a corporatist structure, with more executive control over foreign policy; comparatively strong social organizations with less fragmentation; and a party system that forms the link between social actors and the political elite. In the German case, an important conduit for public opinion to influence foreign policy are the political parties; they are the link between society and the political system because they integrate divergent societal demands: "[p]ublic influence on central decision makers is mediated by political parties and constrained by the structure of the political system" (Risse-Kappen 1991, 493).

In applying his model to two case studies, that of the end of the Cold War and the Gulf War, Risse-Kappen showed that domestic political and social structures were important in shaping policy decisions; the party system facilitated the development of a societal consensus, and elite coalition-building accommodated public opinion and public influence, though the impact of public opinion consequently was less direct than was observed in the U.S. case. His conclusion on German public opinion and its impact on foreign policy: public opinion did matter but its impact was indirect; that the primary role public opinion has in the German corporatist system is to influence the coalition-building among the elite; that this support by mass public opinion is important for societal actors to influence policy outcomes; and that because of the process of coalition-building and consensual politics, the impact of public opinion may actually last longer than in other political systems. Thus, the impact of German public opinion is indirect, with attitudes mediated by the party system that in turn leads to a policy consensus that encompasses both public and elite opinion.

In situations in which salience is high and conflict within the political elite is great, the avenues for public opinion to diverge from the elite are amplified. Again, there is reasonable evidence to support the view that when there is division within the political elite on a policy direction, public opinion can carry more weight in the policy debate. Thus, when the process of consensus-building is impaired and the outcome unclear, public opinion has more room to shape parameters within which policy choices develop.[8] This dynamic of elite opinion divergence and public opinion shaping the contours of the foreign policy debate was evident during the debates on *Ostpolitik* in the late 1960s and early 1970s. Though the conservative CDU/CSU parties bitterly fought the Social Democrats' policy of *Ostpolitik* (it did not officially embrace the policy until 1980), public support for détente continued to rise throughout the 1970s, and this public support was crucial in shifting the weight in the political coalition-building process towards a consensus on détente and *Ostpolitik* in the country. This social consensus, in turn, was absorbed into the policy networks of the party system and became one of the main pillars of German foreign policy. By 1980, 74 percent of West Germans supported the continuation of détente (Berger 1996).

Finally, societal factors are relevant in understanding German public attitudes on foreign and security policy, particularly the political-military culture of postwar West Germany, defined as the set of cultural beliefs and values that are a society's points of reference on issues of defense, national security, the military as an institution, and the use of force in international relations. Of particular importance in shaping attitudes on the use of force is Germany's relationship with its history of militarism and aggression during the Nazi regime. As a result of their historical experience and anti-military political culture, Germans have a highly ambivalent relationship to the question of force, and there has long been a profound reluctance by policymakers as well as the public to contemplate the use of force for anything other than for purposes of territorial defense.[9] The attitudes on use of force and what was later termed Germany's "culture of reticence" or "culture of restraint" were shaped by the political and ideological battles in the early years of the Federal Republic, when the work of the Western allies to demilitarize and democratize German society helped institutionalize anti-military sentiment. In the 1950s, the German public reacted strongly against the growing pressure to rearm Germany, but in that charged Cold War climate public opposition gave way to the exigencies of *Staatsraison*, and the Federal Republic was rearmed and integrated into NATO. With the thaw in East-West relations in the 1960s and 1970s, the German public embraced the policy of *Ostpolitik*, pushing the political parties closer towards a consensus on détente. And by the 1980s, with the Euromissile debate and the strong role the public played at that time, it was evident that the public was increasingly capable of shaping the political discourse. Thus, from the very early years of the Federal Republic, issues relating to the use of force were characterized by a struggle between differing external and domestic interests and pressures.

Thus, the argument here is that the relationship between public opinion and foreign policymaking in Germany is influenced by the interaction of three factors: external events, domestic institutional structures (party system), and the political culture (civilian power, historical memory). As Thomas Berger argues, changes in public and elite attitudes on defense reflected actual shifts in policy. These shifts were influenced by changes in the international environment, but the change in policy was not implemented until the necessary public support existed (Berger 1996). Changes in policy were tempered by the public's aversion to the use of force as a tool of policy, thereby shaping the parameters of the debate on German foreign and security policy.

This historical legacy has led to self-imposed constraints on force (e.g., rejection of nuclear, chemical, and biological weapons) and a commitment to a foreign policy reflective of its role as a civilian power—a foreign policy approach that "promotes multilateralism, institution-building and supranational integration and tries to constrain the use of force in international relations through national and international norms" (Maul 1999, 1). This deeply skeptical view of the utility of military force was shared among elements of the political elite as well as the public at large, and it was this attitude on the use of force that was challenged by the end of the Cold War and the onset of the crisis in the former Yugoslavia.

SETTING THINGS IN MOTION

The Gulf War

The Gulf War—which began only months before the onset of breakup in Yugoslavia—forced open the debate on the use of military force and Germany's role in the world, but it found the Germans singularly unprepared to take up the issue. The German public, in the aftermath of the collapse of the Soviet threat and the Warsaw Pact, did not see the need for a new, expanded military role for Germany. The Cold War had ended, the Soviet threat was gone, and a peace dividend had been declared. Concerns shifted to the domestic political needs of unifying Germany, but the unification of Germany and its changed international circumstances forced open fundamental questions about German foreign and security policy: what would be Germany's new role in the world? Should it assume more international responsibilities, and if so, should this expanded role include a military dimension? If the decision were made to expand Germany's military role, did this mean that German troops could be deployed in areas outside of NATO, even globally? The Gulf War had the effect of pulling these still relatively abstract questions directly into Germany's first real test case of its international commitments in the post-cold war world. The first question the Germans faced was whether or not a united Germany should take on more responsibility in the world, and if so, whether that responsibility included accepting a greater military role.

When Iraq invaded Kuwait in August 1990, external and internal pressures began to push the Bonn government in different directions. Germany's allies, particularly the United States, expected the Germans to fully participate in the coalition being organized against Saddam Hussein and did press for Germany to contribute some military forces. Domestically, however, the German leadership was caught up in its own political drama of negotiating the final chapters of the Two-Plus-Four Treaty that would bring unification and full sovereignty to Germany. The focus and overriding concern of the Kohl government was to secure unification; attending to the Gulf crisis took a much lower priority. In addition, the attention of the public and the political parties was riveted on the first all-German elections in postwar history, which were scheduled for October 3, 1990. Finally, there was disagreement on whether the Constitution (the Basic Law, or *Grundgesetz*) allowed for German troops to be deployed outside of the NATO area. While legal scholars argued that there was no prohibition in the Constitution against the commitment of German troops outside its borders, the German government held that such operations were unconstitutional.

Shortly after the Iraqi invasion, Kohl remarked that Germany was prepared to assume its international responsibilities and would do its part in international peacekeeping efforts, and he added that he would consider sending German troops to the Gulf without first resolving the issue of constitutionality of such an action. Foreign Minister Hans-Dietrich Genscher and the FDP party objected to such an act without first obtaining an amendment to the constitution (*Washington Post*, August 17, 1990). The SPD rejected any expansion of Germany's military role beyond participation in UN peacekeeping operations or the use of such forces for purely humanitarian purposes. The Green party was opposed to any use of German force outside its borders. Because of the political battle that would certainly ensue, the government decided to delay the debate on constitutionality until after the October elections, which the CDU/CSU won. Kohl was sworn in as the first chancellor of a united Germany on January 17, 1991, the same day that Desert Storm began.

The military intervention revived the emotions and scenes experienced in Germany in the early 1980s during the Euromissile debate, with large antiwar demonstrations and peace marches. Germany's allies were dismayed by the protests and by Bonn's initial lukewarm support of the military intervention. Its allies, particularly the United States, expected Germany to actively participate in the Gulf intervention, but the German leadership rejected out of hand any German military involvement and even appeared reluctant to contribute more financially until directly asked.[10] As a result, German-American relations suffered a serious setback. The United States had looked to the Gulf crisis as a test case on Germany's commitment to its growing international responsibilities and in the end felt the Germans had failed that test.[11] Germany's NATO allies were particularly disturbed by Germany's publicly stated reluctance to come to the defense of its ally Turkey if Iraq attacked Turkey for its decision to allow the use of its southern bases to launch bombing raids against Iraq—a scenario many believed did fall under Article V of the Washington Treaty, that an attack against one NATO member constituted an attack against all.[12]

The Germans worked hard to repair the damage caused by their handling of the crisis. Nevertheless, though the government continued to refuse to send any combat troops on constitutional grounds, it agreed to provide logistical and financial support, military hardware, and cash payments that in the end totaled DM 11.4 billion (Fact Sheet, 1991). The Germans were roundly criticized for their "checkbook diplomacy," since many critics believed the constitutional argument a convenient excuse for Germany not to live up to its international responsibilities and not to assume the same risks others were assuming in defense of what was arguably in the interests of all countries, including Germany.[13] This criticism was especially difficult to deflect when news surfaced of

German companies having contributed to the buildup of Iraq's chemical weapons capabilities, possibly even to the development of weapons of mass destruction. This, coupled with the prospect of Saddam Hussein using such chemical weapons on Israel, galvanized the Bonn government. Aid was sent to Israel, air defense units to Turkey, naval ships to the Mediterranean, and personnel to assist with humanitarian aid shipments to Kurdish refugees—but no combat troops (Germroth, David, and Hudson 1992).

In April 1991, with CDU electoral losses in Kohl's home state of Rhineland-Pfalz and SPD electoral gains that brought the upper house of parliament (*Bundesrat*) under its control, Kohl's political position had weakened. The government's intention to resolve the issue of constitutionality on out-of-area deployments thus would not be resolved anytime soon. Kohl and the CDU continued to believe that the only way for Germany to become a "normal" state was to show it could wield power responsibly, and this meant particularly the wielding of military power. Because of this view, Kohl turned to a more incremental approach, deciding that sending troops on humanitarian missions that were uncontroversial (Germany had participated in dozens of humanitarian operations since the 1960s) could eventually ease Germany into the kind of expanded global role that he advocated. By doing so, the German public would become accustomed to such military actions and eventually see them as a "normal" extension of German foreign and security policy.

Public Reactions to the Gulf War

The Gulf War was the catalyst that brought all of the issues on the use of military force in German foreign policy to the surface. On the eve of the Gulf war, attitudes continued to reflect skepticism about the use of force and of Germany's role in the world, coupled with uncertainty and a real fear of an impending war. The German public strongly disagreed with the view that other states should simply "come to terms with" the occupation of Kuwait, but uncertainties surfaced when asked what to do if all non-military "peaceful" efforts fail to force a withdrawal of Iraq from Kuwait. Only 35 percent agreed that military means should then be used; 44 percent felt the occupation of Kuwait should be accepted because war should be avoided at all costs; and 21 percent were undecided. Nevertheless, 75 percent thought it was good that the United States and others had sent troops to the region, though a strong majority of 77 percent rejected sending German troops to the Gulf region. One out of three Germans continued to feel that Germany should never be allowed to deploy out-of-area; a bare majority (50 percent) did not want Germany to take on more international responsibility at all (Allensbacher Jahrbuch 1984–1992).

From September through December 1990, the mood continued to be one of non-involvement on any level and no significant support for increased global responsibilities. In three surveys conducted between September 1990 and December 1991, Allensbach notes that the number of Germans who did not want Germany to take on more responsibility increased from 50 percent to 60 percent in the West and to 57 percent in the East. On the eve of the first all-German elections in October 1990, a majority of Germans (75 percent) wanted Germany to "stay out" and not "interfere in" international conflicts; in this question there was little regional variation.[14] Even the issue of providing financial assistance in lieu of troop support was contentious. In September 1990, only a bare majority of respondents (52 percent) felt Germany should contribute financially in lieu of military support, and almost a third (31 percent) disagreed that Germany should at least help financially since the other states "are also defending our interests."[15] But Germans felt it was a good thing that the UN had sent troops to the region, though two-thirds of Germans opposed sending German troops to the Gulf (only 17 percent approved).[16]

The American-led intervention generated strong protests and street demonstrations against the United States, but while the antiwar demonstrators captured the news headlines, the survey data showed they were not representative of the German public at large. Once the intervention had begun in early 1991, three out of four West Germans agreed with the military action of the allied forces, but of those who did support the military action in the Gulf, 60 percent of them would not have approved had German troops participated. Only 53 percent of East Germans supported the military intervention.[17] Another poll question from January revealed that 81 percent of Germans approved of the military action against Iraq but opposed sending Bundeswehr troops to the area.[18]

Majorities (56 percent) in East and West Germany supported the government's handling of the Gulf crisis,[19] but only the West Germans were prepared to shoulder more financial costs than before (54 percent), as compared to the East Germans (18 percent).[20] The East Germans' opposition to increasing Germany's share of the costs is not surprising, given the economic uncertainties they faced in the wake of unification and the structural adjustments it necessitated. Finally, when asked whether they would consider changing the constitution to allow for out-of-area deployments, majorities in West Germany (66 percent) and East Germany (86 percent) said no.[21] Since the German public was not prepared to condone German military participation in out-of-area operations, it is not surprising that they also were unwilling to consider changing the constitution to allow for such contingencies.

Short of sending combat troops, however, the German public was willing to support the use of German military forces in a variety of nondirect military support functions (e.g., humanitarian aid, patrolling perimeters, technical and logistical support).[22] The German public—at least in the West—supported the government's decision to send German naval personnel to assist in mine-sweeping operations (81 percent). The operation was deemed a humanitarian aid operation, which may explain why public support for the mission was high.[23]

On the issue of Turkey, the German public also was reluctant to come to the assistance of its NATO ally. In February 1991, a bare majority (52 percent) in West Germany agreed Germany should help if Turkey were attacked; 39 percent said the Germans should stay out of it (East Germany: 44 percent and 47 percent, respectively).[24] Though pressured by other countries to take a much more active and direct role in the fighting, the German public was not prepared to do so. At a time when domestic political factors topped the political agenda, with the realization of the enormous costs of reconstructing East Germany along with the billions of dollars promised to the Soviet Union to expedite the pullout of its troops from the former GDR beginning to sink in, this issue was clearly beyond what the German public was willing to support. Though the German public believed the war was the right thing to do, when asked if Germans had a moral obligation to support the American action, only a plurality in West Germany (47 percent) and just under a third (32 percent) of East Germans agreed. Strong majorities still clung to the view that territorial defense remained the most important responsibility of the German armed forces (West Germany, 89 percent; East Germany, 84 percent).

The Germans were unsettled by the demands to contribute combat military forces, since they were so clearly at odds not only with their own deep-seated aversion to the use of military force but also with competing voices raised in fear of an unrestrained, aggressive German state. The government found it difficult to find a balance between the external pressures exerted by its allies to take a more active role in the conflict and the domestic political sensitivities to the political opposition and public demonstrations against the Gulf War. Chancellor Kohl expressed what many Germans were feeling when he commented that "many critics demanded, not too long ago, that the Germans keep quiet in military matters. . . . I want to say it very simply: first the Germans were accused of not taking off their combat boots and now they are accused of not putting them on" (*This Week in Germany*, February 22, 1991, 1).

Recognition of Croatia and Slovenia

The next crisis was not long in coming. The conflict in the former Yugoslavia began to build in the summer of 1991, when tensions within the Yugoslav Federation led to Croatia and Slovenia declaring their independence. Pressure had been building since April 1990, when the pro-nationalist Croatian Democratic Union refused to grant rights to the Serb minority. The German political leadership was initially reluctant to support independence; it wanted the Yugoslav state to remain intact, as did the EC. However, all hopes for a diplomatic solution faded when Croatia and Slovenia declared independence on June 25, 1991 and the Serbian government responded with force. With the onset of hostilities, the German elite abandoned its previous position and began to lobby the EC to accept recognition of the two states; two weeks after the declarations of independence, all major German parties had announced their support for recognition.

Politbarometer surveys in the fall of 1991 revealed that a strong majority of East and West Germans (77–78 percent on average from August-September through December) supported Slovenia and Croatia's declaration of independence, paralleling the parties' position supporting self-determination.[25] The Germans felt very strongly that they did not have the right to reject the self-determination efforts of the Slovenians and Croatians given their own recent experience, though they were reluctant to get involved. Factors other than the support for the principle of self-determination also appear to have been relevant: the public's impression that the EU and other involved actors failed to stop the conflict and the growing number of reports about Serbian atrocities against the Croatians.

The recognition episode is important for a number of reasons, but of relevance here was the assertion that pressure from the public, the Croatian immigrant community in Germany, and the media pushed the German leadership to commit to a policy of early recognition. The evidence does not support the view that public opinion drove the political elite to shift its support towards independence. Public support for recognition grew only after the party elite had publicly stated its position and after the continued failure of the EC to stop the conflict had eroded public confidence in the EC's ability to keep Yugoslavia together. An important determinant in the recognition episode for the elite and the public was the principle of self-determination. Both had drawn parallels between Germany's application of the rights of self-determination in its drive for unification with the self-determination of the Croatians and Slovenians.

However, a consensus position was reached quickly because the SPD was sensitive to the fact that its own ambivalent position on Germany's self-determination in the months following the fall of the Berlin Wall in November 1989 had resulted in its resounding defeat in the all-German elections in October 1990. Thus, in the end, the government's decision was not pushed neither by external pressures nor by internal pressures emanating from the public, interest groups, or the media. Rather, it was a result of the dynamics of German domestic politics, i.e., a combination of the power of the norm of self-determination with the effects of elite "bandwagoning" (Crawford 1996). The party elites had been able to reach a quick consensus on independence, a view shared by the public who quickly moved to support the self-determination efforts of the Croatians and Slovenians. Contrary to expectations, however, the decision did not stop the conflict from growing; indeed, Germany was blamed for the crisis spiraling out of control and for touching off the war in Bosnia.

The Bosnian Crisis

External events and the domestic political debate about German foreign policy in the post-Cold War era pushed the issue of military power to the forefront of the political debate. The trend during the Bosnian crisis turned towards a more activist international role, one that did not necessarily reject out of hand the use of military force but saw the application of armed force severely constrained. Several broad patterns in public attitudes are discernible. Whatever the considerations about the types of military missions that were acceptable—humanitarian, traditional peacekeeping, peace-enforcing, or out-of-area missions—the threshold the German public was unwilling to cross was that of the use of combat troops. There was generally consistent support for humanitarian aid missions, and support for traditional peacekeeping missions grew gradually. But public support for peace-enforcing missions, or scenarios that implied some kind of military intervention, was much weaker. The German public showed support for the principles of peacekeeping and conflict reduction, but they were unwilling to support actual German participation in such operations. This dichotomy of support of abstract principles but rejection of specific scenarios involving German troops was a pattern evident throughout this period. On the issue of UN versus NATO missions, the German public was more supportive of UN-mandated missions than of NATO-led missions, though this support for UN operations declined if the mission strayed from traditional "blue-helmet" peacekeeping toward some type of military intervention. Finally, attitudes of East Germans and West Germans were quite different; on almost any question relating to the use of force and German military engagement, East Germans were consistently less supportive, sometimes diametrically opposed to those of their Western counterparts. Thus, while support among West Germans for German participation in peacekeeping missions gradually rose from the early to the mid-1990s to a slight majority, this was not true for East Germans.

Also reflected in the data is the public's strong commitment to multilateralism and for non-military tools of reducing conflict: a commitment to multilateral cooperation and to the use of non-military tools of policy, such as negotiations and diplomacy, and the view that force is acceptable only as a tool of last resort. If the political culture strongly emphasizes the use of non-military means of conflict prevention and reduction—force as last resort—then it is arguable that such attitudes will color views on the parameters set in the use of military force. For example, two-thirds of West Germans and four-fifths of East Germans agreed with the view that all disputes could be resolved through negotiations.[26] Reflecting the commitment to multilateral cooperation and conflict resolution, a strong majority of East and West Germans felt that the both the UN and the EU should take more responsibility in solving conflicts.

Public Opinion on the Bosnian Crisis

Though initially resistant, the German public came to accept the view that the Federal Republic should assume a greater degree of international responsibility. Whether this willingness included expanding the role for its armed forces was another issue, though it was clear the public remained opposed to any missions that involved the use of combat troops. Short of this, however, were questions concerning other types of missions: humanitarian aid efforts, peacekeeping, peace-enforcing, or out-of-area missions. Of these, the German public was most supportive of humanitarian aid missions. With regard to peacekeeping operations, support for German involvement in traditional "blue helmet" UN peacekeeping operations gradually increased. The German public was less comfortable with the UN undertaking a mission that was not a traditional peacekeeping operation, such as peace-enforcing or actual military intervention. With regard to support for NATO operations in the Bosnian crisis, the German public was less supportive of NATO missions than of UN missions, more supportive if the mission was humanitarian, significantly less supportive if the NATO mission involved military intervention and the deployment of combat troops. Attitudes were fluid and at times contradictory, but the public's aversion to German participation in combat operations remained a threshold the public was unwilling to cross. This remained true throughout the Bosnian crisis.

EXPLAINING DIFFERENCES
BETWEEN EAST AND WEST GERMANS

One of the most persistent patterns in the data during the period 1990–1995 is the difference in attitudes between East and West Germans on defense and security issues. German respondents living in the former GDR generally did not want Germany to assume greater international responsibilities. Though supportive of humanitarian aid missions, support was not as strong as in the West. East Germans held much stronger views opposing German participation in any military action, even traditional peacekeeping operations. Those East Germans who were supportive of peacekeeping operations preferred the task to be assigned to the UN, rather than to NATO. Few studies have been conducted to examine the reasons for the persistent gap between East and West Germans on issues relating to German military force, and more research is needed, but a few tentative points can be made here.

First, issues about German military force inevitably are tied to NATO. The East Germans show consistently lower support for NATO than the West Germans.[27] The East Germans have an entirely separate historical and emotional relationship to NATO; consequently, their image of NATO is decidedly different. Their own experience of military alliances was decidedly different and may have made them more wary of supporting a military alliance in which they see fewer advantages than do the West Germans. Part of the explanation may also be their own experience with the East German military establishment—that the East Germans saw their own forces as an instrument of the Soviets, and perhaps as an instrument of their own government directed against the GDR's population. In the absence of any shared historical experience, it is not surprising that there is more ambivalence about NATO and about the seemingly dominant role of the United States in NATO.

What all Germans do share—what has become part of the historical consciousness for both East and West—is a deep skepticism about the utility of force: *nie wieder Krieg* (never again war) was a sentiment voiced by Germans on both sides of the Cold War divide. This translated into the strong sentiment among Germans that the *Bundeswehr* should be used solely for territorial defense and for humanitarian purposes but never as a projection of German national interests. Thus, the answer to what kind of role Germany should assume is one that does not necessarily uphold a vision of a globalized German foreign policy.

International Responsibility

In the early 1990s, the German public was uncomfortable with the Federal Republic assuming a greater share of international responsibility; some polls showed majority support for assuming greater responsibility already in 1990–1991, while others reported less than majority support (particularly among East Germans). But in general, from 1991 onward, the data show a gradual increase in support among Germans for taking on more responsibility in the world.[28]

The data also show that the debate on Germany's expanded responsibilities was often couched in the language of German history and Germany's moral obligations because of its history. This theme was applied in arguing both sides of the issue: because of the Germans' history, Germans had a moral obligation to participate in peacekeeping operations and share in the responsibility of upholding peace; conversely, precisely because of the Germans' history, Germans had a moral obligation not to participate in any military operations outside its borders. An example from the Gulf War is illustrative:

Question: Two people are talking to one another about the kinds of lessons the Germans should draw from their history. Which would you agree with?

One says: When one sees all of the pain and grief caused by the world war, we Germans should have learned, never take part in war again.

The other says: I see that differently. German history shows us how dangerous a dictator can be. If nothing else will work, then a dictator must be fought. (Allensbacher Jahrbuch 1984–1992, February 1991, 1088)

In three surveys conducted by Allensbach from September 1990 to December 1991, respondents were asked: "Should Germany assume more responsibility in the world, or should we hold back or restrain ourselves (*zurückhalten*)?" Both East and West Germans opposed Germany assuming more responsibility, and the numbers increased over that time period, with respondents favoring restraint increasing from 50 to 60 percent in the West and from 49 to 57 in the East. By 1993, polls were showing a majority of Germans (54 percent of West Germans, 50 percent of East Germans) agreeing that a united Germany should assume a greater share of responsibility in the world.[29] By 1995, 55 percent of West Germans still agreed, while only 45 percent of East Germans still agreed that Germany should take on more responsibility in resolving international conflicts.[30]

Realist arguments outlining the necessity of German involvement for reasons of state or for national interest were not as persuasive to the German public as were questions that raised the issue of moral responsibility. As the Bosnian conflict progressed, and more atrocities came to light, Germans struggled with conflicting norms: the strong views against the use of military force versus the strong support for international human rights, and a reluctance to interfere in the affairs of other countries. Asked in 1992 whether one should interfere in the internal affairs of another country when human rights and international law were being violated, the West Germans were split, while strong majorities in East Germany opposed any such intervention (Asmus 1992).

But as the data show, ethnic cleansing and other atrocities seen in news broadcasts eroded "the moral legitimacy of pacifism" (Janning 1996, 33) and contributed to a shift in attitudes towards an acceptance in principle for military interventions in clearly defined circumstances (such as genocide) within a collective security context. This shift was particularly evident in the political left. The inability of the international community to stop the conflict in Bosnia, and to stop the deliberate targeting of civilian populations, helped shift public attitudes on peacekeeping, but there still remained a threshold of acceptability for the circumstances in which German forces could be deployed.

Humanitarian Support

By 1992–1993, more Germans felt the Federal Republic should assume a greater international responsibility, but what that meant in terms of assuming new military roles was not clear. The difficult question was what kinds of military roles and missions would be acceptable. The public's skepticism vis-à-vis the utility of force was reflected in preferences for non-military instruments of policy, which translated into support for humanitarian aid and logistical and medical support, while almost no support existed for combat-related missions. Thus, "soft security" tasks such as humanitarian aid efforts received more support than the "hard security" tasks of deploying military forces in a combat environment.[31] Asked in 1994 to rank what they thought should be Germany's foreign policy goals, the Germans placed soft power tasks such as humanitarian aid efforts, economic sanctions, and UN peacekeeping before more traditional hard power tasks such as participation in NATO-led military interventions and UN-sanctioned military interventions "such as the Gulf War" (Asmus 1992). Revealing in this context was a comment made in a German focus group in 1990 that arguably points to a psychological division of labor in the minds of Germans, in which the Europeans conduct soft power tasks while the hard power tasks are left to the Americans. Asked about the dichotomy between the German willingness to take on more international responsibility yet refusing to take on more military missions, a young participant responded: "War—that is something we leave to the Americans."[32]

Peacekeeping: Principles and Scenarios

The increasing military involvement of the United States, the EU, and the UN in the Bosnian conflict pushed the issue of mission types beyond simply humanitarian aid. The gray area lay between the commitment to humanitarian relief efforts and combat operations, particularly out-of-area operations. Between these two points lay questions about German participation in traditional UN blue helmet operations, UN peacemaking or peace-enforcing operations, and NATO-led missions.

On the issue of how to respond militarily to the deepening conflict in Bosnia, German public opinion responded at different levels and remained fluid through much of the Bosnian crisis. When asked in the abstract whether they would support Germany participating in UN peacekeeping or "blue helmet" missions, support was strong, particularly if the mission were geared towards humanitarian goals. However, asked specifically whether they would support sending German troops to participate in operations, public support declined dramatically. This also was true for elite opinion; the more specific the scenario, the greater the opposition to German participation. This tendency to support abstract principles but reject specific scenarios involving German forces was evident already during the Gulf War, as it was mentioned earlier.

An illustration of this dichotomy relative to the Bosnian conflict can be seen in a series of poll questions in the 1994 Politbarometer Survey Report. Taking just the West Germans in 1994 alone, there is a gradual shift from an abstract willingness to shoulder more international responsibility to rejection of specific scenarios involving the use of German armed forces. West Germans supported the view that: Germany should take on more international responsibility (60 percent); the UN should intervene more forcefully in Bosnia (59 percent); and the EU should take more responsibility in resolving international conflicts (81 percent). However, West Germans did *not* want the *Bundeswehr* to send troops as part of the UN protection forces (54 percent); to use Tornado combat aircraft to participate in air strikes to safeguard UN protection forces (54 percent); and to participate in out-of-area operations with allies (52 percent).[33]

Germans were more comfortable supporting UN-mandated missions rather than NATO-led missions, but they were not particularly supportive if the question implied the mission would be out-of-area, or if it hinted at some type of direct military engagement.[34] In March 1992, 45 percent of West Germans (but only 26 percent of all East Germans) supported the view that Germans must finally participate in UN "blue-helmet" peacekeeping operations because "we can no longer shirk our responsibilities and leave it to others, but 37 percent of all Germans still felt that "considering our history, Germans should not participate in UN peacekeeping missions."[35]

Asked in August 1992 how the *Bundeswehr* should participate in the military operations in Yugoslavia—as part of a UN combat troop, only in the form of UN peacekeeping forces, i.e., blue helmets, or not participate at all—50 percent of West Germans (40 percent of East Germans) favored participation as part of a UN peacekeeping operation, 28 percent of West Germans (42 percent of East Germans) felt the *Bundeswehr* should not participate at all, and only 12 percent of West Germans (8 percent of East Germans) favored the *Bundeswehr* participating in a combat operation.[36] But by early to mid-1993, public opinion had reached a level where an increasing number of Germans supported the *Bundeswehr* participating in non-combat peacekeeping operations, even if that meant out-of-area. An April 1993 question showed majority support in East and West Germany and across the political spectrum.

Thus, support declined when the UN mission was posed as something other than humanitarian, such as peace-enforcing, or when the question implied some kind of military intervention for the UN force. A survey conducted in April 1993 revealed that while 64 percent of all Germans agreed the *Bundeswehr* should be able to participate in blue helmet missions, in instances where "peace must be made first" (i.e., implying the presence of combat troops in a peacemaking operation), 54 percent of all Germans did not want the *Bundeswehr* participating even if the operation were under UN auspices. Asked bluntly whether they supported *Bundeswehr* participation in combat operations under UN command, majorities in the West (51 percent) and the East (64 percent) were opposed.

As the conflict continued into 1993 with no end in sight—peace accords had been negotiated and abandoned, cease-fires negotiated and broken—it was clear that public opinion in Germany, as well as in most of Europe and the United States, revealed a public increasingly frustrated by the inability of the international community to stop the conflict.[37] A plurality of Germans did feel as if something had to be done to stop the hostilities in Bosnia, even if that meant sending more troops. But unlike other Europeans, Germans were not supportive of their own country's military engagement in Bosnia. Support for Bundeswehr participation continued to lag if the mission implied some form of military intervention. In a USIA poll conducted in March/April 1993, only a plurality of respondents supported the view that the UN should authorize a multinational peacekeeping force to intervene militarily in Bosnia (USIA Briefing Paper July 20, 1993, 1). In May 1993, German support for a possible military intervention in Bosnia had risen to 53 percent in the West but only to 36 percent in the East. The specific question of German participation in such a military intervention, however, continued to gain little support from either East or West Germans—less than a third in the West (31 percent) and less than a quarter (21 percent) in the East.[38]

As NATO was drawn into the conflict in Bosnia, surveys showed less support for NATO operations than for UN operations, even if the NATO-led mission were humanitarian or more traditionally peacekeeping. A December 17, 1993 USIA survey showed that West Germans favored sending NATO peacekeeping forces to Bosnia, though the East Germans did not. Asked whether NATO should send in troops to help establish peace if the fighting continued—the question was phrased "What if the warring parties in Bosnia are unable to reach an agreement and the fighting continues; should NATO send forces to help establish peace, or should NATO not become involved?"—a plurality of 48 percent in the West and a majority of 64 percent in the East did not want German troops involved; only 44 percent in the West and 27 percent in the East supported involvement. Not surprisingly, CDU supporters were more likely to support such a *Bundeswehr* mission (45 percent) than were the Greens (32 percent) or the PDS (13 percent), but even CDU supporters were essentially divided on the issue.[39] There was thus a great deal of uncertainty and resistance to German participation in any military intervention to stop the war in Bosnia and force a peaceful settlement on the parties, whether that mission was led by the UN or by NATO, and there was much more skepticism among the East Germans than the West Germans.[40]

The ferocity of the Serbian campaign against the Bosnian Muslims, the ethnic cleansing, the massacre in the Sarajevo marketplace in February 1994, and the perception that the international institutions involved were ineffective in stopping the fighting began to change attitudes about the acceptability of the use of force and of German participation in operations involving the application of force. Though only West Germans were surveyed by the Politbarometer on the NATO ultimatum on Sarajevo, a majority of respondents felt that since the threat of NATO air strikes produced a cease-fire in Sarajevo, this threat should be used to force a cease-fire in other parts of

Bosnia. This majority support was seen across the political spectrum, from CDU/CSU (86 percent) to Green sympathizers (75 percent). If it were to come to a general cease-fire in the former Yugoslavia and the UN sent peace-keeping forces to secure the cease-fire, a majority of West Germans would support German troops participating in such a force (58 percent). When the Serbs marched on Gorazde, nearly two-thirds of West Germans (65 percent) felt the UN should militarily defend the declared safe havens against any Serbian attack, while just over one-quarter (26 percent) believed the UN should pull back (Politbarometer monatliche Umfrage, February 1994).

Asked whether the *Bundeswehr* should participate in air strikes to safeguard the UN protection zones by sending Tornado combat fighters, a majority of 54 percent of West Germans surveyed were opposed, nor did they want German troops participating in UN protection forces in Bosnia (54 percent against). But while the German public rejected the notion of German aircraft participating in air strikes, it was willing to consider using Tornadoes to protect humanitarian aid flights to Bosnia. Though there was a majority in the aggregate (56 percent for all of Germany), the breakdown shows the familiar pattern of majority support among the West Germans (61 percent) and majority opposition among East Germans (60 percent). Thus, differently worded questions about the use of Tornado combat fighters—this time to protect humanitarian aid flights to Bosnia—emphasizes once more the support for soft power tasks.[41]

The gradual shift in support of German participation in peacekeeping missions outside of NATO area became more pronounced as the war heated up in 1995. After a significantly more powerful NATO airstrikes in May, the Bosnian Serbs took hundreds of UN peacekeepers hostage, releasing them only gradually. The Serbs renewed their bombing campaign against Sarajevo, NATO airstrikes continued, hundreds of UN peacekeepers were taken hostage, and the safe haven of Srebrenica fell to the Bosnian Serbs. In surveys conducted between January and July 1995, respondents were asked whether the UN should intervene militarily more strongly or not. In January, while a majority of West Germans (54 percent) were in favor, slightly over one in five (22 percent) responded that things should stay the same, rather than intervening more or pulling out. In East Germany, a plurality of 41 percent favored the UN intervening more strongly; 37 percent remained opposed.[42] On June 6, the Kohl cabinet announced its decision to participate in the NATO-led action to re-deploy UNPROFOR troops, and the *Bundestag* approved the motion to send German troops to protect the UN forces, an unprecedented decision. After the government decision, West German support for intervening more strongly decreased slightly (52 percent), while those supporting a complete pullout increased almost to one-third. By June, just under a third of East Germans felt Germany should intervene more strongly; 50 percent wanted the German forces to withdraw immediately.[43] Thus, there remained under the surface more undercurrents of unease and reluctance to condone more military actions in Bosnia.

September 1995 saw a two-week bombing campaign by NATO, to enforce an ultimatum to the Bosnian Serbs to stop the bombing of Sarajevo. German fighters flew photo reconnaissance flights over Bosnia. Surveys showed a majority of Germans in East and West supporting the view that the military action in Bosnia was right (West: 67 percent; East: 51 percent). In a very generally worded question, 58 percent of West Germans, but only 42 percent of East Germans, supported the participation of German military combat fighters in UN and NATO military actions (Politbarometer monatliche Umfrage, September 1995).

In October 1995, asked whether they were prepared to support German participation were NATO to send ground troops to oversee a cease-fire, 52 percent of West Germans said yes, while 57 percent of East Germans said no. By November, with the Dayton Accords under negotiation, there were majorities in both East and West Germany in support of UN and NATO military actions in Bosnia.[44] Prior to the German government's decision on November 28 to contribute German troops to IFOR, a majority of West Germans from the CDU/CSU, SPD and the Greens felt it was appropriate for the German government to send 4000 *Bundeswehr* soldiers to assist in monitoring of a cease-fire in the former Yugoslavia, while half of East Germans still opposed the mission. On December 6, the German *Bundestag* met to vote on the government's decision, and the motion was passed by an overwhelming majority of *Bundestag* members (543 to 107). Sixty-nine percent of West Germans supported the decision, while a slight majority of 53 percent of East Germans voiced their support. Thus, by the end of the Bosnian conflict, opinion polls showed that majorities in East and West Germany supported sending German troops to Bosnia.

That a settlement existed in the form of a signed agreement may well have bolstered support.

CONSTITUTIONALITY AND PARTY DIVISIONS

The major domestic political debate in the 1990s focused on the constitutionality of German participation in peacekeeping and out-of-area missions. There was no consensus on whether the Constitution permitted out-of-area missions or whether a constitutional amendment was required. The political party elite was deeply divided on the issue, and the reluctance of the German public to accept a greater military role for its armed forces meant that the public would continue to question the terms of German military engagement and shape the parameters of policy choices.

The constitutionality issue was not new. Although the *Bundeswehr* had taken part in humanitarian assistance operations since the 1960s, prior to unification in 1990 it had participated on a bilateral level, but not as part of any UN peacekeeping mission outside its borders.[45] The reasons lay in the unique Cold War circumstances of Germany's division and in concerns that any German military contribution might endanger its policy of *Ostpolitik*, with potentially serious reverberations in its relationship with the Soviet Union and Eastern Europe. For these reasons, in 1981 then Chancellor Helmut Schmidt and Foreign Minister Hans-Dietrich Genscher took the position that the constitution did not permit German participation in military operations outside of NATO territory. Thus what became the accepted constitutional interpretation rejected the notion of German participation in any military operation save that of territorial defense. This position was formalized by a Federal Security Council decision in 1982 and later affirmed by the Kohl government.[46] There was, however, no consensus among constitutional scholars that such a restriction, in fact, existed.

The debate focused on the validity of the prevailing but more restrictive interpretation of the Constitution. The question revolved primarily around two articles. Article 24 allows for the Federal Republic to enter into a system of mutual collective security. Article 87(a), added as an amendment to the constitution in 1956 after the establishment of the *Bundeswehr*, declares that Germany's armed forces are to be used solely for the defense of the country.[47] The contours of the political debate divided around whether one emphasized the broader collective security arrangement of Article 24 or the restrictive defense-only arrangement of Article 87(a). It was on this issue that the divisions within the political elite were most evident.

The CDU/CSU government's position favored the broader interpretation of Article 24. At the onset of the Gulf War, however, Kohl had announced his intention to allow the participation of German military forces. This revealed that he was willing to abandon the prevailing interpretation, but faced with the deeply held aversion to the use of force, both within the public and within much of the political elite, and swimming against the strong tide of long-standing policy practice on the use of force, Kohl had to back down. But one of the most important reasons for the CDU's position was that a united Germany must shoulder more responsibility in the international community, and this required a credible German foreign policy. Indeed, Germany's experience in the Gulf War was a painful reminder of the need for this. But in order for Germany to do this—to have a seat at the table and be able to influence decisions—it must be like all other "normal" countries in its ability to choose from a range of options that includes the application of military force.

Some conservative elements of the CDU/CSU argued that Germany should have no restrictions on the use of its forces, and many party members believed there should be no restrictions placed on the type of mission or the institutional venue—be it peacekeeping or peacemaking, NATO, WEU, or the UN. Such restrictions, it was believed, would prevent Germany from fulfilling its growing international responsibilities. This viewpoint also implied that the prevailing interpretation no longer fit Germany's changed circumstances. Thus, either a consensus on a new constitutional interpretation had to be found, or a constitutional amendment more reflective of Germany's new role was required.

Many CDU/CSU members and constitutional scholars believed the constitution already allowed for out-of-area deployments, thereby obviating the need for a constitutional amendment. But there was strong disagreement on this between the CDU/CSU and its coalition partner, the FDP, which rejected the view that the constitutional restriction was a question of interpretation and insisted that a constitutional amendment was absolutely necessary to clarify the circumstances under which the use of German military force would be permissible. The FDP was not opposed to German participation in out-of-area deployments per se, but it sought a much more restrictive amendment that would limit German participation to blue-helmet peacekeeping operations only. In the end, the view that prevailed was that a clarifying amendment was politically desirable (Duffield 1999).

The SPD initially held to the more narrow interpretation of Article 87(a), supporting the prevailing interpretation that the constitution restricted the use of German armed forces to territorial defense only (thus rejecting German participation in any out-of-area mission, including peacekeeping). This position was strongly defended by the rank and file members of the party. But a small group of members, aware of how Germany's new position had changed the political context, began to argue that this highly restrictive stance was increasingly indefensible because it risked isolating the SPD both domestically and internationally. By May 1991, after a particularly difficult internal debate which split the rank-and-file members, the party agreed to support a constitutional amendment that allowed German participation, but only in UN-mandated blue helmet operations (Duffield 1999, 185). The SPD thus held to a more narrow interpretation of the conditions under which German military force could be applied.

The Green party in the early 1990s remained adamant in its opposition to any expansion of German military power. But as the targeted violence against civilians escalated, many in the party leadership began to see the issue as human rights violations and moved towards a position of using force under very restricted conditions and circumstances, such as genocide. In 1993, the party's regional board supported a move to allow German participation to prevent aggression such as genocide, but the Federal Board rejected the motion (Smith 1996). It was not until 1994–1995 that this position of allowing the use of German armed forces under restricted circumstances was accepted by the majority of Green party members. In the summer of 1995, Joschka Fischer created a storm of protest by calling for an end to the party's pacifism and urging party members to support military intervention (*Die Zeit,* 18 Aug 95; FT 2). In the end, concluded a Green party leader, it was "the humanitarian justification that tipped the balance of public opinion in favor of the air strikes—the prevention of large scale ethnic cleansing as

well as Foreign Minister Fischer's active role in the search for a political solution and the integration of Russia into this solution." [48] The PDS remained
unequivocal in its opposition to the use of any military force, the only party
that did not shift its position during the Bosnian conflict.

By 1991, then, the CDU/CSU, the FDP, and the SPD had agreed on the necessity of a constitutional amendment, which required a two-thirds majority
vote in the *Bundestag* and in the *Bundesrat*, but they could not break
through the fundamental differences between the parties to agree on the
provisions of the amendment. The SPD, and to an extent the FDP, insisted on
a narrow range of options on the use of force, which the CDU/CSU felt
would ensure that Germany would not, in the end, be able to fulfill its international commitments. The debate was stalled.

In a way, this impasse led Kohl to consider approaching the problem of constitutionality from a different angle. He decided the way to build the necessary
domestic and political support for German out-of-area operations was through
a gradual, step-by-step acclimation by committing small contingents of forces
to multilateral humanitarian aid operations even before the constitutionality
question was resolved. The Kohl cabinet began implementing this incremental strategy by sending German minesweepers to the Persian Gulf in 1991 (under WEU auspices) and continued with deployments that delivered humanitarian aid to Iraqi Kurds in 1991, medical assistance to Cambodia in 1992
(under UN auspices), and AWACS planes to monitor the trade embargo in the
Adriatic in 1992 (under NATO auspices).[49] But the act of committing small
numbers of troops for humanitarian, non-military operations prior to any resolution of the constitutional issue not only brought intense resistance from the
opposition SPD and Green parties but from its own FDP coalition partner.

It was the CDU/CSU's application of this strategy to Bosnia that brought the
use of force issue to a head and prompted both the opposition SPD and its
own coalition partner to challenge its actions in court on the grounds of un-
constitutionality. The political struggle within the elite on peacekeeping and
out-of-area operations was fought through three separate cases brought before the Constitutional Court in Karlsruhe. Of the three, two related directly to
the war in Bosnia, the third to the deployment of German troops to Somalia.[50]

The war in Bosnia had begun in earnest after the Bosnians declared independence in April 1992 and the Serbs intervened militarily. As the conflict intensified, the UNSC approved the stationing of 14,000 peacekeeping troops in
various crisis areas of the former Yugoslavia. In May 1992, NATO and the
WEU agreed to support the UN's efforts by first monitoring and then eventually enforcing a naval embargo in the Adriatic aimed against Serbia. On July
15, 1992 the Kohl government announced its intention to participate in the
monitoring of the embargo by sending German AWACS crews, a decision that
precipitated the first Constitutional Court challenge. The government's ra-
tionale was based on the following assertions: the deployment did not violate

the constitution because there was no intention to use force; the forces would be deployed in NATO territory (over the Adriatic); the German contribution would be strictly one of intelligence-gathering; and that German participation was necessary on the grounds of alliance reliability and credibility.

The Social Democrats denounced the action, contending the mission could in no way be defined as "humanitarian" and thus violated the constitution (Smith 1996). When it failed to garner enough votes in an emergency session of the *Bundestag* to stop the deployment, the SPD filed suit in the Constitutional Court on August 9, 1992 on the grounds that the Kohl government had overstepped its authority by failing to consult with the *Bundestag* before the troops had been committed. Nevertheless, despite the request for an injunction, by November 1992 German troops were participating in the naval blockade, albeit with restrictions. The constitutionality of this decision would not be decided until the summer of 1994.

By the end of 1992, the German political parties were no closer to finding common ground, and the next constitutional challenge not only exposed the divisions among the parties, but exposed the division between the coalition partners themselves. The case began to develop in November 1992, when the UNSC issued a flight ban over Bosnia and NATO AWACs planes were dispatched to monitor the "no-fly zone." Germany military personnel had been sent to assist in monitoring the ban, but some 465 violations of the no-fly zone between November 1992 and March 1993 moved the UNSC to consider a resolution to enforce the no-fly zone.[51] The coalition government was split over the impending enforcement resolution. The CDU argued that since the German flight personnel constituted a third of the AWACS crews, it was imperative for the success of the mission that the Germans crews remain in place. The FDP demanded they be pulled out immediately because enforcing the no-fly zone crossed the "no combat" threshold, since crews would provide information to fighter planes that would then shoot down any violators.

What followed was what many later described as either a clever compromise or a political farce. Because the coalition was internally divided, the CDU/CSU and FDP agreed on a compromise: once the UN passed its resolution to enforce the ban on the no-fly zone, the CDU would vote to comply with the resolution and the FDP would respond by filing suit in the Constitutional Court for a temporary injunction—the government thus, in essence, suing itself and handing over to the court the messy job of resolving the deployment issue. The UNSC resolution was passed on March 31, 1993; two days later, on April 2, the Kohl cabinet announced its decision to assist in the enforcement mission. The FDP—joined by the SPD—filed suit, requesting an injunction to halt the deployment on the grounds that, again, the *Bundestag's* right of consultation had been violated.[52] By April 8, 1993 the Constitutional Court announced its decision to deny the motion for injunction, giving the green light for German deployment of AWACS as part of NATO's enforcement operation. The court's decision was a decidedly political one: it ruled that withdrawing the German AWACS personnel would seriously compromise the success of the operation. The court's decision, however, did not speak directly to the constitutionality of out-of-area deployments. That decision would have to wait for more than a year.

In April 1994, the Constitutional Court was prepared to hear oral arguments on the first case. On July 12, 1994, the court handed down its decision, ruling that the constitution did allow for German armed forces to participate in military missions beyond its borders, but that the government must seek parliamentary approval for each *Bundeswehr* mission. Three key norms set by the Constitutional Court were that military actions must take place within a multilateral context, they must be undertaken within the context of collective security arrangements, and they must be approved by a simple majority of the *Bundestag* (Maul 1999).

The Constitutional Court's decision essentially supported the Kohl government's position—in particular, the CDU/CSU's position—on the issue of out-of-area deployments and peacekeeping operations, allowing for the full range of actions and institutional venues (UN, NATO, WEU) the government had wanted. More importantly, though the Constitutional Court's decision held that there were no constitutional restrictions on German participation in any type of peacekeeping operation—traditional blue helmet peacekeeping, peacemaking, or peace enforcing, or whether it was UN-mandated or NATO-led—there was a limit to the kinds of options the policy elite could consider. Thus, while the court gave the government the authority to choose deployments across the operational continuum, from non-military support to full combat support, the reality of German political-military culture and German public opinion was that the public still would not contemplate the use of German troops in a combat situation.

In the wake of the Constitutional Court decision, Defense Minister Rühe outlined a framework to guide any future decision-making on out-of-area deployments. First, there must be a "compelling reason" for approving the deployment. Second, the deployment would be limited to the European theater and not beyond. Third, it would be implemented only within a multilateral context. Finally, there must be strong public support for such a mission. Decisions would still be made on a case-by-case basis, and the deployment would still require the support of the *Bundestag*. What was clear, then, was that the decision would not significantly alter Germany's foreign and security policy.

CONCLUSION

Even before the country had united, Germany faced growing pressure to extend its international responsibilities, including considerations for using military force. After unification, Germans gradually accepted the realities of the post-Cold War environment and a larger role in the world. They were supportive of humanitarian aid efforts, showing a strong preference for this as well as other soft power tasks. Though there was a gradual acceptance of German armed forces participating in missions beyond territorial defense, the outside limit of that acceptance for the German public was any scenario involving the participation of German troops. The German public's consistent rejection of German participation in combat missions was not tested by *Bundeswehr* participation in Kosovo peacekeeping after June 1999, and remains unbreached by any government action up to this writing.

Short of combat, however, the German public found it just as difficult as their political leadership to come to some kind of resolution on the acceptability of intermediate roles. The question of what kinds of missions the public would accept inevitably drew the discourse towards specific scenarios involving UN peacekeeping and NATO out-of-area operations. The uncertainties (or ambivalence towards peacekeeping and out-of-area questions) were reflected in the poll data in which Germans were supportive of peacekeeping missions in principle, but when faced with a specific scenario requiring German participation, public support declined dramatically.

Central to the debate on the future of German foreign and security policy after German reunification, particularly during the Bosnian war, was the issue of peacekeeping missions and out-of-area deployments. The major disagreements focused on the types of missions the *Bundeswehr* should assume and how such missions were to be undertaken. The conservative Kohl government wanted Germany to assume more international responsibilities, and within that, to assume expanded military role in the world. But while there had been external pressure, particularly from the United States, for Germany to take on a greater military role, there was stiff opposition not only from the left—SPD, Greens, PDS—but from its own coalition partner, the FDP. Kohl's reading of the general public was that there also was no support for the more expanded military role without restrictions or conditions, as a small group in his party insisted on. As a consequence, Kohl concluded that the most appropriate strategy to take was one in which his government would gradually acclimate the public by committing very small contingents of German military personnel in out-of-area missions conducted within a multilateral framework. Getting the public accustomed to such deployments would dissipate the opposition to the expansion of the roles the Bundeswehr would take. But his tactics met with resistance both from his FDP coalition partner and the opposition parties. The constitutionality of some of these deployments were challenged in court. The Constitutional Court's landmark decision of July 12, 1994 determined that such deployments were allowed but required parliamentary approval.

Thus, German participation in missions outside of NATO in defense of humanitarian has become an accepted part of German security policy. By the end of the Bosnian war, German public opinion had accepted the idea of a more active international role for the Federal Republic and had accepted a broader set of missions for the German armed forces. This support extended across the political spectrum, from the conservative CDU/CSU to the Green party, though there was still significantly less support by PDS members both for a greater international role and for any expanded use of force by the *Bundeswehr*). The pattern of majority support for *Bundeswehr* participation in principle but lesser support for specific missions remained. Thus, while the German public had come a long way since the Gulf War in 1990, cultural and political restraints continued to impact the parameters of potential policy decisions.

NOTES

1. Poll data used for this chapter: Politbarometer 1977–1999. Forschungsgruppe Wahlen e.V., Zentralarchiv für Empirische Sozialforschung an der Universität Köln. CD; Institut für Demoskopie Allensbach, USIA.

2. Benjamin I. Page and Robert Y. Shapiro, *The Rational Public: Fifty Years of Trends in Americans' Policy Preferences* (Chicago: University of Chicago Press, 1992), 14.

3. Lawrence R. Jacobs and Robert Y. Shapiro, "Presidential Manipulation of Polls and Public Opinion: the Nixon Administration and the Pollsters," *Political Science Quarterly*, vol. 110, no. 4 (1995). http://epn.org/psq/psnixo.html. See also section on "Public Opinion and Policymaking," coedited with Lawrence R. Jacobs, in Carroll J. Glynn, Susan Herbst, Garrett J. O'Keefe, and Robert Y. Shapiro, *Public Opinion* (Boulder, Colo.: Westview Press, 1999), 299–336.

4. Robert Y. Shapiro and Lawrence R. Jacobs, "Public Opinion-Foreign Policy Linkage: U.S. Presidents and Public Opinion," Paper presented at Conference on Public Opinion, the Mass Media, and European Foreign Policy. Italian Academy for Advanced Study in America, New York, November 19–20, 1998, 8–10; Thomas Risse-Kappen, "Anti-Nuclear and Pro-Détente? The Transformation of the West German Security Debate," in Hans Rattinger and Don Munton, eds., *Debating National Security: The Public Dimension* (Frankfurt/Main: Peter Lang), 271.

5. Page and Shapiro, *Rational Public*, 14, 47. See also Thomas W. Graham, "Public Opinion and U.S. Foreign Policy Decision Making," in David Deese, ed., *The New Politics of American Foreign Policy* (New York: St. Martin's Press, 1993), 191–215.

6. See, for example, Richard Eichenberg, *Public Opinion and National Security in Western Europe* (Ithaca: Cornell University Press, 1989); and Gregory Flynn and Hans Rattinger, eds., *The Public and Atlantic Defense* (London: Rowman & Allanheld, 1985). See also Richard Sinnott, "European Public Opinion and Security Policy," Chaillot Paper 28 (Institute for Security Studies, WEU, Paris, July 1997). www.weu.int/institute/chaillot/chai28e.htm.

7. Graham, for example, argues that the impact of public opinion can be substantial and direct, depending on the phase of the policymaking process in question. See Graham, "Public Opinion and U.S. Foreign Policy Decision Making," 196. Graham concludes that the uniqueness of the American political system raises doubts that his model can be applied to other countries.

8. Jeffrey A. Karp, Holli A. Sometko, and Klaus Schoenbach, "Campaigns, Media Exposure and Support for European Integration: How Party Positions Influence Political Attitudes," Paper presented at the American Political Science Association Conference, August 30–September 3, 2000, Washington, D.C. See also Risse-Kappen, "Anti-nuclear and Pro-détente: The Transformation of the West German Security Debate," in Hans Rattinger and Don Munton, eds., *Debating National Security: The Public Dimension* (Frankfurt am Main: Peter Lang, 1991), 274–76.

9. For discussions on collective memory and historical memory, see Andrei S. Markovits and Simon Reich, *The German Predicament: Memory and Power in the New Europe* (Ithaca: Cornell University Press, 1997); and Thomas Banchoff, *The German Problem Transformed: Institutions, Politics, and Foreign Policy, 1945-1995* (Ann Arbor: University of Michigan Press, 1999).

10. There were differences between the publics as well. To compare publics, 79.1 percent of West Germans and 86.5 percent of East Germans believed Germany's financial and material support was sufficient, but only 42.5 percent of Americans shared this view. There were also great differences in role expectations. Fifty-two percent of Americans thought Germany should have sent troops to the Gulf, while only 14.9 percent of West Germans and 5.9 percent of East Germans thought the same. Brigitte Fassbender, "Germany's Military Role in the World," CRS Report for Congress, August 25, 1992, 3.

11. Marc Fischer, "Germany Reluctant to Defend Turkey if Iraq Retaliates," *Washington Post*, January 22, 1991; Marc Fischer, "Germany Pledges $5.5. Billion More Toward Gulf War," *Washington Post*, January 30, 1991; Christoph Bertram, "Die Deutschen im Zwielicht: In den Wirren der Golfkrise hat die Bonner Staatskunst versagt," *Die Zeit*, February 8, 1991; Ronald D. Asmus, "Fragen unter Freunden: Der Golfkonflikt hat zu einer schweren Vertrauenskrise zwischen Bonn und Washington geführt," *Die Zeit*, February 22, 1991, 4.

12. There was great disagreement among the political parties on this count. See Beverly Crawford and Jost Halfmann, "Domestic Politics and International Change: Germany's Role in Europe's Security Future." Some SPD members argued that NATO was not obligated to come to the defense of Turkey because the United States was waging war from Turkish soil, which did not constitute an Article V scenario. FDP politician, Otto Graf von Lambsdorff, said his party was convinced that a missile attack on Turkish territory did not require a NATO response, since a defense of Turkey could take place only in the event that Iraq mounted a ground attack. See Marc Fisher, "Germany Reluctant to Defend Turkey if Iraq Retaliates," *Washington Post*, January 22, 1991, A20; Ronald D. Asmus, *Germany and America: Crisis of Confidence* (Santa Monica: Rand, February 1991), P7703.

13. See, for example, Stephen Kinzler, "Kohl Draws Rising Charges of an Insufficient War Role," *New York Times*, January 26, 1991; Jim Hoagland, "Germany: Timidity in a Time of Crisis," *Washington Post*, January 29, 1991, A19; Alan Sked, "Cheap Excuses: Germany and the Gulf Crisis," *The National Interest* (Summer 1991): 51–60.

14. Polled in November 1990, three out of four Germans in the East and the West felt Germany should stay out of rather than interfere in international conflicts. Süddeutsche Zeitung/Infratest poll, quoted in This Week in Germany, January 11, 1991 (German Information Center, New York), 2.

15. Allensbacher Jahrbuch 1984–1992, 1086. A Politbarometer poll conducted in August 1990 showed a bare majority of West German respondents (51 percent) unwilling to contribute financially to the costs of the military action. See *Politbarometer* ZA-No. 1920, Survey Report 1990, Forschungsgruppe Wahlen, e.V., Zentralarchiv für Emprische Sozialforschung an der Üniversität zu Köln, V 238, p. 186. For data on the Gulf War, see 182–86.

16. Politbarometer, Wahlstudie 1990, ZA Nr. 1920, September 1990, V233, 183. The Politbarometer Wahlstudie data cited are unweighted.

17. For West Germans, see Politbarometer ZA-No. 2102, Survey Report 1990, V163, 136; for East Germans, see Politbarometer ZA-No. 2114, Survey Report 1991, V168, 142.

18. Oskar Hoffmann, *Deutsche Blauhelme*, p. 77; and Wolfgang Schlör, 76.

19. Fifty-six percent in both East and West Germany. For West Germans, see ZA-2102, V179, 145; for East Germans, see ZA-2114, V169, 142.

20. Fifty-three percent of West Germans were in favor of increasing Germany's financial contribution to the war, but an overwhelming 82 percent of East Germans were opposed. For West Germans, see ZA 2102, V173, 142; for East Germans, see ZA-2114, V177, 146.

21. Politbarometer ZA-No. 1920, Survey Report 1990, Forschungsgruppe Wahlen, e.V., Zentralarchiv für Empirische Sozialforschung an der Üniversität zu Köln, Variables 235–38, 184–86.

22. EMNID poll conducted January 1991, quoted in Oskar Hoffmann, *Deutsche Blauhelme bei UN-Missionen: Politische Hintergründe und rechtliche Aspekte* (Bonn: Verlag Bonn Aktuell), 78.

23. Politbarometer Survey Report 1991, ZA-2102, V170, 140.

24. Allensbacher Jahrbuch 1984–1992, 1084. Support was greatest among CDU voters (65 percent), least among the Greens (33 percent). See also Politbarometer question: "If the Gulf war spreads to Turkey, should German soldiers stationed there come to the defense of Turkey?" Fifty-four percent of West Germans agreed Germany should do so; 71 percent of East Germans disagreed. See Politbarometer Survey Reports; for West Germans, see ZA- V169, 139; for East Germans, see V174, 144.

25. Politbarometer Survey Reports: for West Germans, ZA-2102, V150, 128; for East Germans, ZA-2114, V227, 170.

26. Christian Holst, "Public Attitudes and Elite Attitudes toward a New Foreign Policy Consensus?" in Klaus-Dieter Eberwein and Karl Kaiser, eds., *Germany's New Foreign Policy: Decision-making in an Interdependent World* (Houndsmill: Macmillian, 2001), 256. In his study, Holst argues that the pronounced differences in attitudes regarding military force have to do with differing assessments of the state's ability to bring about peace; the commencement of hostilities implies the breakdown of the political process and the mechanisms designed to prevent such conflict.

27. Support among West Germans, while still in the majority, nevertheless had declined in the latter half of the 1980s and in the early 1990s before returning in the mid-1990s to the strong levels of support seen in the early 1980s. East German support in the early 1990s was quite low, but it did gradually rise in the mid-1990s to move above 50 percent, though it never reached the levels seen in West Germany. One study found confirmation of a convergence of attitudes between East and West Germans based on the observation that the levels of support for NATO had risen both in East and West Germany. But this conclusion is premature, since rising levels of support for NATO doesn't

necessarily mean attitudes are converging. Looking only at attitudes on NATO is too narrow and ignores the gap on a host of other issues related to the use of force. It also seems to suggest that the reasons East and West Germans support NATO are similar, when they may not be similar at all. See Hans-Joachim Veen and Carsten Zelle, "National Identity and Political Priorities in Eastern and Western Germany," *German Politics*, vol. 4, no. 1 (April 1995), 1–26. Here, 7–8, 16.

28. For example, Allensbach surveys in 1990–1991 show less than majority support for Germany assuming a greater international role, and an EMNID poll in 1990 found a majority of Germans felt Germany should stay out of international conflicts. However, Ronald D. Asmus reports that in a Rand poll conducted in 1990, 51 percent of Germans supported a greater international role for the Federal Republic. By 1994, this support had increased to 62 percent. Support was greatest among CDU, SPD, and FDP members; only half of the Greens and a third of the PDS members shared this view. See Asmus, *Germany's Geopolitical Maturation: Public Opinion and Security Policy in 1994* (Santa Monica: Rand, 1995), 39–41.

29. Politbarometer, monatliche repräsentative Umfrage, February 1993, Forschungsgruppe Wahlen e.V., Mannheim.

30. Politbarometer, monatliche Umfrage, April 1995. See also Ronald D. Asmus, *Germany's Geopolitical Maturation: Public Opinion and Security Policy in 1994* (Santa Monica: Rand, 1994), MR-608-FNF/OSD/A/AF, 38.

31. A Rand poll conducted in 1992 showed majority support for humanitarian missions, economic sanctions and traditional peacekeeping operations, but not for combat missions. See Ronald D. Asmus, "Germany in Transition," 1992, 34. See also Asmus, *Europa-Archiv*, 1992, 206; and Asmus, *Germany's Geopolitical Maturation*, 39–45, particularly figure 5.5 and 5.6, 41 and 42, respectively.

32. Ronald D. Asmus, *German Strategy and Opinion After the Wall, 1990–1993* (Santa Monica: Rand, 1994), MR-444-FNF/ODS/A/AF, 61. See also the focus group discussions summarized in Asmus, *Germany in Transition: National Self-Confidence and International Reticence* (Santa Monica: Rand, 1992), N-3522-AF, 49–54.

33. Politbarometer Survey Report 1994, ZA–2546, 170–71, V211–V216.

34. The reasons for this differing view on NATO and the UN may be that NATO is viewed as a defense alliance, and that more often than not it is seen as dominated and led by the Americans. NATO thus is seen not as an impartial observer or participant, while the UN is viewed as a neutral, mediating authority that people look to for resolving international conflicts. My thanks to Detlef Puhl for this observation.

35. Allensbacher Jahrbuch, 1988–1992, question from March 1992, 1094.

36. Allensbach Jahrbuch, 1988–1992, March 1992, 1094–1095.

37. USIA data show this: by a two-to-one margin, European publics said that multilateral institutions had been ineffective in resolving the conflict. See USIA Briefing Paper, "Opinion Roundup: The UN Peacekeeping Role in Bosnia and Somalia," July 20, 1993, 1.

38. Politbarometer monatliche Umfrage, May 1993. The February 1993 Politbarometer reported that German participation in a possible military action by the UN in the former Yugoslavia was supported by half of West Germans and 34 percent of East Germans. In May, West German support had decreased to 47 percent. Once the issue of military operations enters the picture, even if the UN is the designated actor, support weakens.

39. USIA Opinion Research Memorandum, "European Security Views on the Eve of the NATO Summit," December 17, 1993, 13 and 40 (table 11). Generally, European public support for peace-enforcing was less than the support for peacekeeping, as was the case in Germany.

40. There also was more skepticism among the public relative to the political elite. An Allensbach question in September 1995 asked whether the respondents supported sending NATO troops to Bosnia. Fifty-six percent of West Germans would have welcomed such an action, while only 31 percent of East Germans shared that view. Elite support for such an operation was high in both parts of the country: 94 percent among West German elites, 84 percent among East German elites. This is also true for attitudes on combat troops; only one half of West Germans and one quarter of East Germans would welcome German participation in a NATO combat troop deployment in Bosnia; 92 percent of West German elites and 83 percent of East German elites would have supported this. See Allensbacher Jahrbuch, 1993–1997, September 1995, 1147.

41. Politbarometer Survey Report 1994, ZA–2546, 170, V211, V212. Also, Politbarometer Survey Report 1994, for West Germans, see ZA-2765, 129, V145, and for East Germans, see ZA–2777, 145, V165.

42. Again, European publics for some time had supported stronger military intervention in Bosnia, though the elites were far less willing to do so. While majorities in West Germany also supported intervention (though at lower levels than other Europeans), only a plurality of East Germans supported military intervention. See Richard Sobel, "U.S. and European Attitudes toward Intervention in the Former Yugoslavia: *Mourir pour la Bosnie?*" in Richard H. Ullman, ed., *The World and Yugoslavia's Wars* (New York: Council on Foreign Relations, 1996), 153–54.

43. Politbarometer Survey Report 1995; for the West Germans, see ZA–2765, 126, V140; for East Germans, see ZA–2777, 142, V160.

44. Politbarometer Wahlstudie: West German data: ZA–Nr. 2765, V142, 128; East German data: ZA–Nr. 2777, V162, 144.

45. See "Humanitäre Einsätze (1960–1979), web site of the German *Bundeswehr.* http://www.bundeswehr.de/im_einsatz/humanitaer/chronik/human1960.html.

46. See Ronald D. Asmus *Germany's Contribution to Peacekeeping: Issues and Outlook* (Santa Monica: Rand, 1995), MR-602-OSD, 15; FAZ 29 July 94; John S. Duffield, *World Power Forsaken: Political Culture, International Institutions, and German Security Policy After Unification* (Stanford: Stanford University Press, 1998), 176; Elizabeth Pond, "Germany Finds its Niche as a Regional Power," *Washington Quarterly* 19, no. 1 (winter 1996): 25–43.

47. Carl-Christoph Schweitzer, "Defence policy and the Armed Forces," *Politics and Government in Germany, 1944–1994: Basic Documents* (Oxford: Berghahn Books, 1995), 150–51. See also Paul Stares, *Allied Rights and Legal Constraints on German Military Power* (Washington, D.C.: Brookings Institution, 1990), 12–13. The defensive nature of German military power was also underscored by Article 26 of the constitution, which states that preparing for aggressive war is unconstitutional.

48. Speech by Ralf Fücks, President, Heinrich Böll Foundation, "What's new about the Berlin Republic?" given on December 14, 1999 at the Goethe Institute, Washington, D.C., p. 5.

49. See Bundeswehr web site. See also Pond, 34; Peter Schmidt, "German Strategic Options," in Emil Kirchner, James Sperling, Christoph Bluth, eds., *The Future of European Security* (Brookfield, Vt.: Dartmouth, 1995), 32.

50. In April 1993 UN Secretary General Boutrous-Ghali formally requested that Germany contribute troops to the humanitarian efforts under way in Somalia. The SPD, not convinced that the mission would remain a humanitarian operation, again filed suit on June 15, 1993, demanding another injunction be imposed until the issue of constitutionality was decided. On June 21, 1993, the court ruled that the *Bundeswehr* could continue with its mission to Somalia. However, the ruling was restricted to the Somalia mission and did not resolve the constitutionality question. Support for Somalia was based on the fact that it was presented as a humanitarian mission, with West Germans supporting the mission (52 percent) and East Germans opposed (61 percent). See Politbarometer monatliche Frage, February 1993.

51. See the United Nations website on UNPROFOR: http://www.un.org/Depts/dpko/co_mission/unprofor.html, the Background Text section, "Bosnia-Herzegovina 'No-Fly Zone' Enforcement," paragraph 2.

52. The FDP, as noted, felt the constitution must be amended, and it demanded that a decision on the constitutionality of such an action had to be made. The CDU/CSU, however, took the view that the constitution needed no revision in order to support the deployment. Thus, in a pre-arranged compromise, the FDP joined by the SPD filed suit against the government on the same day the cabinet announced its decision. See discussion in Duffield, 197; Michael Smith, *Frankfurter Allgemeine Zeitung*, April 1, 1993, 57–58; *Washington Post*, April 3, 1993.

9

Public Opinion and the Bosnia Crisis: A Conclusion

Eric Shiraev and Richard Sobel

Few items in the study of democratic policymaking are more debated and less tested than the relationship between mass public opinion and foreign policy. Policymakers in democratic societies tend to be aware of their countries' public opinion—although to very different degrees. By and large, there is substantial correspondence between policy and public opinion. Moreover, policymakers also tend not to act against an overwhelming public consensus (see Risse-Kappen 1991; Shapiro and Jacobs 2000). Despite recent advances in studying "opinion-policy correlation" based on various national cases (see works of La Balme, Everts, Belucci, Isernia, Sobel, Wybrow, Richman, Shapiro and Jacobs, and others), there have been few attempts to study these links from a comparative perspective (see, for example, Shapiro, Nacos, and Insernia 2000). This volume combines various national cases to shed light on one of the most fascinating and dynamic elements of contemporary democracy.

In studying national cases, a comparativist must wrestle with divergent variables and unlike research approaches. While de-emphasizing the obstacles can be an effective analytical maneuver, this method does not conceal well-known difficulties of the comparative approach about the validity of broad generalizations. This final analytical chapter is an attempt to conceptualize the empirical evidence in the national cases according to a multilevel approach for comparative study of opinion-policy relationship. This approach facilitates a more comprehensive evaluation of opinion-policy links from a comparative perspective that directs attention to issues that are sometimes overlooked in national cases.

The examination of the cases here in this book and elsewhere provides growing evidence of the existence of complex "mediating" variables between public opinion and policymaking (Sobel 1998; Isernia 1998; Everts

1996; Page and Shapiro 1992; Hinckley 1992; Bartels 1991; Wittkopf 1990; and Page and Shapiro 1983). Though the results of opinion polls reach top decision makers, public opinion does not "convert" itself necessarily into foreign policy. Polling may affect what issue policy executives push to the top of their political agenda; nevertheless, policymaking plays from a different script (Shapiro et al. 2000; Wybrow in this volume). Just because the public maintains a strong and stable opinion about a specific foreign policy issue does not mean the influence of public opinion on policy is obvious and direct (Risse-Kappen 1991).

The impact of public opinion on policy is context-dependent and conditioned by mediating variables. To illustrate, Vengroff, Carriere, and O'Reilly describe in this book (chapter 1) variables such as the context of the international problem under consideration; the nature of the proposed policy; the effectiveness of the communication among elites; elite awareness of the public opinion and the perceived level of public support for the policy; and structure and timing of decision making. Other experts refer to at least three factors that mediate the impact of public opinion on policy: (1) the distribution of political preferences among the public; (2) the structure of domestic political institutions; and (3) the bargaining strategies of national decision makers at both national and international levels (see Putnam 1988; Risse-Kappen 1991; and Bellucci and Isernia in this volume).

Public opinion's influence on foreign policy is also mediated by a relatively stable system of values developed through socialization (Page 1994). For instance, most people in democratic countries would rather support peacekeeping actions than interventions directed at political changes in other nations (Jentleson 1992). The composition of the parliamentary system, political views of elected officials, salience of presidential leadership, effectiveness of elite communication, and elite perception of the public opinion are also critical mediating factors in our understanding of opinion-policy interaction (Powlick 1991; Jentleson 1992; and Graham 1986). Domestic factors can mediate the impact of international developments on policymaking (Putnam 1988; Moravski 1993). A country's general political context, including media coverage of international events, mediates between attitudes and policy (Everts 1983; Everts here; Howard and Howard here). In short, understanding the opinion policy links requires one to undertake the investigation of the context in which the links are established.

The terms "policy climate" and "climate of opinion" (Clinton 1975; Bellucci and Isernia in this volume) help in understanding the mediating variables between policy and public opinion. The policy climate consists of a set of beliefs about what the country and the government should or should not do on the international level and, in particular, in case of an international conflict. This is the prevailing sentiment among policymakers and those individuals capable of influencing the direction of foreign policy through their roles as security and defense executives, analysts, problem definers, "gate keepers," "watchdogs," and "experts and commentators" (Page and Shapiro 1988, 243). These political elites constitute the "concerned minority" of the nation, or the "citizens" (Almond and Verba 1963). In both parliamentary and public debates, statements, televised interviews, printed publications, and via other channels of communication, the "attentive public" voices opinions about their country's foreign policy and some international developments. The media in these circumstances, speaking on behalf of the people, become not only a conductor but also a source of foreign policy attitudes. Therefore, some public officials may intentionally or unintentionally confuse the sources of attitudes by not distinguishing between mass opinion identified through polling and the policy climate. For instance, Bellucci and Isernia suggested in their chapter that policymakers sometimes refer to public opinion when, in fact, they talk about their fellow party members or other parliamentarians.

Some examples illustrate the connection between policy climate and policy. In Canada, from the beginning of the Bosnia conflict, the policy climate that was predominant among officials favored intervention. As a result, Ottawa, securing a political consensus between the government and general public, took the lead in asking the United Nations to intervene and promised clearly to contribute personnel and equipment to any United Nation's mission (Keating and Gammer 1993, 730). France has a long tradition—as it was shown in the chapter 4—of political pressure originating in the intellectual leaders who historically have been engaged in raising concerns about injustice in the country and abroad. The Italian policy climate regarding Bosnia took shape in a complex set of domestic constraints including the uncertainty of the attitudes of the political elite and prime minister, and the stubborn opposition of the military to any armed intervention.

Policy climate has its own internal dynamics. Policy climate can be salient and non-salient; it can be assertive or non-assertive, becoming at times more susceptible to pressure under the influence of general public and less susceptible when the public doesn't care much about foreign policy. Each country's policy climate at different times can have different impacts on policy making. In Italy, for instance, the climate evolved the Italian policy toward Bosnia through different stages (Bellucci and Isernia in the chapter 6). Russian policy climate toward Bosnia also evolved from neutral into aggressively negative with increasing salience of anti-American and anti-NATO attitudes (see also Shiraev and Zubok 2000). In France, for example, because of the relative unity and strength in the voices contributing to policy climate, and because of the privileged positions and personal contacts of the French "intellectuals," the policy climate became a consistent and significant pressure factor on the government.

Policy climate does not always resemble mass opinion—people's attitudes measured through polling. For example, in the Canadian and Dutch cases described in this book, one should notice a close proximity of mass opinion measured in many surveys and each country's policy climate. On the other hand, Russia's policy climate during the conflict in Bosnia was substantially different from what the majority of generally indifferent people had in mind regarding Bosnia.

Let us suppose that policy climate is empirically testable. Assuming this, we introduce the following frame of reference that should clarify further analyses of policy climate as a mediator between opinion and policy. Each country's particular policy climate originates in and is linked to a set of political, ideological, and situational conditions. These variables may be examined from several dimensions or axes (see table 9. 1). Each axis refers to a different domain of information that may help the researcher in ana-

Table 9.1. A Multiaxial Assessment of Policy Climate in Mediating Opinion-Policy Connections

Basic socioeconomic and political factors affecting the opinion-policy links:

Axis 1. Political institutions and communications. The edifice of political institutions and political communications that mediate the opinion-policy links. These generally include: the type of republic, that is, parliamentary or presidential; formal distribution of roles among foreign policy institutions; frequency of national and local elections; the design and ownership of the media; basic socioeconomic conditions; and the level of institutionalization of opinion polls by the government.

Axis 2. Political landscape. The specific political landscapes in which particular foreign policy debates take place and how they reflect specific political interests pursued by the government and its opposition. Special areas of attention include existing government coalitions with other parties; debates and internal struggle within the government; political struggle between the ruling party and other political forces; domestic and international political issues relevant to election campaigns; and decision makers' anticipation of public reaction to various foreign policy-related issues in their attempts to either boost or maintain their popularity.

Basic cultural and psychological factors affecting opinion-policy links:

Axis 3. General sociocultural variables. The fundamental values and effects of socialization, including religious, moral, and major psychological predispositions that can influence particular foreign policy attitudes. Special areas of attention include isolationist or interventionist values; religious beliefs; historic experience; and general stereotypes and prejudice toward particular foreign policy, policy actors, or groups.

Axis 4. Contextual and situational factors. These determine the quality of information that both the public and policymakers receive. Special areas of attention include salience of the considered foreign policy issue; perceptions of public opinion by policymakers; framing, priming, and agenda-setting of the designated foreign-policy issues conducted by the media; presence or absence of specific media effects, i.e., particular media coverage that evokes specific reactions in people, including their opinions; and individual characteristics of decision makers as political leaders.

lyzing opinion-policy links. Theoretically, when one attempts to create certain empirical categories, all the variables, within such categories, are expected to be homogeneous, there are clear boundaries among the categories, and the categories are mutually exclusive. However, this rarely occurs in practice.

Let us now examine the proposed dimensions of opinion-policy links, using the evidence provided in the book's chapters (see table 9.2).

Table 9.2. A Comparative Analysis of Policy Climate in National Cases

	Political Institutions and Communications	*Political Landscape*	*Sociocultural Factors and Values*	*Contextual Factors and Media Perceptions*
CANADA	Parliamentary republic; coalition-based cabinet; prime minister conducts foreign policy	Strong multi-partisan consensus about peace-keeping mission in Bosnia	Strong interventionist and peace-keeping values	Serbs are the aggressors; victims should be helped; peace can be established through strength
FRANCE	Presidential republic; multiparty system; president conducts foreign policy	Moderate consensus about peace-keeping mission in Bosnia; pressure from "intellectuals"	Mixed and uncertain attitudes changing to interventionism	All ethnic groups are responsible; Serbs are the aggressors; victims should be helped; peace can be established through strength
GREAT BRITAIN	*De facto* parliamentary republic; coalition-based government; prime minister conducts foreign policy	Moderate multi-partisan consensus about peace-keeping mission in Bosnia	Moderate interventionist and peace-keeping values	Serbs are the aggressors; victims should be helped; peace can be established through strength
ITALY	Parliamentary republic; coalition-based government;	Weak multi-partisan agreement; competition	Mixture of interventionist and isolationist attitudes	Serbs are the aggressors; victims should be helped;

continued

Table 9.2.   (*continued*)

	Political Institutions and Communications	Political Landscape	Sociocultural Factors and Values	Contextual Factors and Media Perceptions
	prime minister conducts foreign policy	among influential groups		peace can be established through strength
HOLLAND	Parliamentary republic; coalition-based government; prime minister conducts foreign policy	Strong multi-partisan consensus about peace-keeping mission in Bosnia	Strong interventionist and peace-keeping values	Serbs are the aggressors; victims should be helped; peace can be established through strength
RUSSIA	Presidential republic; multi-party system; president conducts foreign policy	Continuous struggle between legislature and cabinet about policy in Bosnia	Anti-Western and pro-Serb sentiment, mixture of isolationist and interventionist attitudes	All ethnic groups are responsible; Serbs should be helped; isolationism; peace can be established through strength
USA	Presidential republic; de facto two-party system; president conducts foreign policy	Weak multi-partisan agreement about peace-keeping mission in Bosnia	Mixture of interventionist and isolationist attitudes	Serbs are aggressors; victims should be helped; peace can be established through strength
GERMANY	Parliamentary republic; coalition-based cabinet; chancellor is in charge of foreign policy	Moderate multi-partisan consensus about peace-keeping mission in Bosnia	Moderate interventionist and peace-keeping values	Serbs are the aggressors; victims should be helped; peace can be established through strength

POLITICAL INSTITUTIONS AND COMMUNICATIONS

The role public opinion plays in the shaping of any country's foreign policy is indispensably linked to the country's political system (Cohen 1977–1978, 196). On this level, one should assess how the country's existing political, democratic institutions mediate the links between public opinion and foreign policy. Political systems—which include a wide set of actors including political parties, bureaucracies, and pressure groups—may or may not transmit opinions into the policy process, so that public opinion may or may not act as a "catalyst" to foreign policy operations. In some cases, such as Russia, the lack of democratic alternative institutions during the period of transition was a weighty factor that affected policy climate. Therefore, the major and persuasive conductor of public opinion about both domestic and international events was the lower house of the Russian parliament, the Duma.

Different national governments may have dissimilar traditions of soliciting and considering public opinion as a factor in foreign policymaking, which is called "institutionalization" of polling. Therefore, in analyzing opinion-policy links one should determine whether and to what extent polling becomes institutionalized by the government. For instance, in the Italian political and academic culture—imbued with historicism and idealist undertones—public opinion as measured by surveys was long considered as having little legitimacy in itself. That is to say, the empirical and positivist attitudes that underline the idea that "attitude can be measured" have been often discarded in Italy (Bellucci and Isernia in this volume). In British parliamentary debates, results of opinion polls about international developments were discussed continuously. On the contrary, polls were practically unmentioned in Russian parliamentary debates (Shiraev and Terrio in this volume). In short, a comparison of the United States to some other democratic and transitional systems, for instance, shows how different the governments' approaches to mass polling can be.

Obviously, voters can exert the control over policy through reward and punishment in elections and government shake-ups. During the war in Bosnia, the United States and France changed their presidents, Russia reelected one, and Italy changed three of its prime ministers. However, different types of democracy create unlike frameworks of relationships between the branches of the government. Bellucci and Isernia (in this volume) suggest that public opinion should influence policy more directly in two-party parliamentary settings than in coalition-based multiparty assemblages. Stronger parties should be "stronger" conductors of public opinion than weaker ones. Also, national systems with consolidated and established channels of communications—involving parties, interest groups, bureaucracies, and the media—ought to provide better conditions for public opinion expression than in the systems with fragmented communications. In the

United States, the links between opinion and policy develop within the presidential political system with relatively weak parties. Party factions are relatively weak in the Senate and stronger in the House of Representatives. In comparison, the role of political parties and party factions is more salient in other countries, such as Italy and France.

In parliamentary and presidential systems where executive power is based on the strength of the parliamentary majority, foreign policy is often influenced and directed by internal political considerations. Typically, the head of the government tries to avoid taking policy steps that could undermine the ruling parliamentary majority. To exemplify, in the French system, the president lacking a majority in the parliament is forced to appoint a prime minister from an opposing party and then try to find a formula to work together. Thus in "cohabitatio'" the president becomes somewhat responsive to the views of the prime minister and foreign minister. In the Italian political system, the channels of communication between the highest foreign policy executives and society are shaped mainly by political parties and the mass media that are also heavily controlled by political groups.

Yet, foreign policy is perceived by most as coming from an executive office. The highest foreign policy executives appear to be more independent in their activities than their counterparts in parliamentary systems. Nevertheless, one should acknowledge that the formal roles inherited by the chief government executives vary from country to country. French presidents, for example, depend on the national "intellectuals" to a greater extent than American presidents would. In the Netherlands, important foreign policy decisions will not be taken by the minister of foreign affairs, but rather by the cabinet as a whole. The Netherlands and Germany are typically ruled by often shaky coalitions of two or more political parties and no single party is strong enough to govern alone. Foreign and defense ministers can only be forced to abdicate if they lose the confidence of parliament. Italian governments are usually based on a coalition of parties, and institutional actors have a voice in formulating and a veto power in implementing Italian foreign policy. The nature of the relationships among them is not well established and depends on the political resources of each of these actors and of the personal skills of those who occupy these roles.

In Great Britain, even though the prime minister may enjoy support of his or her party in the Parliament, foreign policy is an arena of historic competition—not unique to Britain though—among Foreign Office, Joint Intelligence Committee, and foreign policy advisers to the prime minister. Bob Wybrow, for example (chapter 2), mentions the resistance of many British prime ministers to the Foreign Office as an institution who sought their "own," independent advice. Russian presidents—both Yeltsin and later Putin—preserve a traditional view that any compromises between the government and the opposition weaken the president. On the other hand, in the

Canadian political system, the dominant theme is a pluralist conception of the origins of politics, the spirit of compromise and negotiation that characterizes domestic politics and spills over into foreign policy.

One interesting issue raised by the authors of the French chapter is the importance of the connections and networks between political elites in various positions around the center of power. Because many influential opinion leaders went to the same schools, shared common experiences, and belong to a similar social-status group, as the policymaking elite, the opinion leaders have the ability to influence policy. Another aspect of policy climate is the existing practices of coordination or rather lack of such between a country's foreign and military departments. According to some existing practices, military policy can be operated relatively separately from foreign policy, with its own norms, guidelines, and accountability. In the Italian case, the military were strong and determined in their intentions to stay away from a military involvement in Bosnia. In 1995, the negotiations about the deployment of Russian troops to Bosnia were conducted by Russian generals, whereas the foreign ministry was virtually cut off. Moreover, the surprising 1999 deployment of the first Russian contingent in Kosovo—during the civil war in this province—was also ordered by top military commanders, and the Kremlin did not inform the foreign ministry of this extraordinary and risky development (see interview with Russian prime minister in *Newsweek*, July 26, 1999).

Political Competition

Political parties and interest groups influence the ways public opinion affects foreign policy. Internal political developments can make public opinion either more or less salient in the eyes of policymakers. Policymakers in democracies are perhaps relatively well qualified to conduct policies for which the risks are small, in part because of the weakness of the domestic political opponent (Everts 1996). Politicians face severe problems, however, either when success is elusive or when the trade-off between costs (especially in terms of human lives) and interests is seen as unfavorable. Mistakes cost the decision maker politically. On the whole, in Bosnia, many governments aimed at conducting a relatively "play-it-safe," low-risk, and low-cost foreign policy line.

Both national and local elections provide mechanisms for determining the ways foreign policy executives pay attention to or manipulate public opinion. When opinion polls reflect people's concerns about an international event, it may or may not be noticed by elected officials. However, when the potential voter expresses his or her dissatisfaction with how the government or ruling party handles a foreign policy issue, such opinions are likely to become more salient to those who represent the government or the ruling party or parliamentary faction, as Wybrow showed in this volume. It is important to determine, however, the importance of a particular election campaign for the average voter. For example, despite the fact that the war in Bosnia became an issue during the European parliamentary elections, the relative insignificance of the elections helped the French president to resist the demands of public opinion about particular decisive actions in Bosnia. On the other hand, a constitutional referendum in Russia in 1993 was crucial for Yeltsin's political survival and this made him ask the western allies not to undertake any actions against the Serbs who were supported by Russia's media and public opinion (Shiraev and Terrio in this volume).

The desire to be elected or reelected creates pressing incentives in politicians to be responsive to public opinion in order to avoid falling too far out of line with the median voter. Moreover, in the United States and in other democracies, foreign policy actions can be naturally linked to each other. Bellucci and Isernia imply that Italian foreign policy is so closely related to the country's domestic policy to the point that the former basically mirrors the latter. That is, parliamentary approval of certain government policies may be based on yielding to the opposition in some other policy areas. When a government is unstable and is not able to rely on a shaky party coalition in the parliament, internationalism in foreign policy—because of it potential high risk and cost—should decrease despite the pressure of public opinion (Isernia 1998; Bellucci and Isernia in this volume). As the Russian case also suggests, while many Russians had a general desire to avoid war, and almost one third of Russians did not support any side involved in the conflict, the Russian policy climate around the Bosnia situation shaped up in a distinct way. That is, under persistent pressure from the Duma, the administration was forced to start building up a Russian policy of resistance to the West, and the United States in particular. As a result of victories of opposition parties—primarily of nationalistic and communist orientations—in both the 1993 and the 1995 legislative elections, President Yeltsin and his executive foreign policy team began to reshape their Bosnia policy and change personnel along lines more conducive to opposition legislators. Not public opinion per se, but rather perceptions of public opinion by policymakers reflected through the mirrors of their political calculations, were the main driving horses of the carriage of Russia's Balkan policies.

As a matter of political survival, public officials try to anticipate public approval and objections. Assumptions about a positive public reaction to a proposed action or policy contribute to a "permissive" policy climate, whereas anticipation of criticism may contribute to a "non-permissive" climate. Political opposition would not challenge foreign policy decisions if the public support of such actions were going to be overwhelming. On the contrary, the opposition would be more likely to challenge the government if the public reaction is negative, split, or just anticipated to be negative or split. As an example, the announcement of the French president meant to exclude any participation of new draftees into the Gulf War combat operations was designed mostly to appease domestic public opinion. The avoidance of public disapproval was one of the reasons why France began its participation in the military operations on Somalia in 1992 (La Balme 1998). The same internal considerations of potentially low domestic support, perhaps, held the Clinton administration and the German chancellor away from making any definite commitments to the use of ground troops in Kosovo in the spring of 1999. Policymakers pay attention to whether there is likely to be sufficient political support for their actions especially if casualties occur. They quickly distance themselves from unfortunate events—like a tragedy in Srebrenica in the context of the Dutch policy—by criticizing the United Nations for a set of mistakes (see Everts in chapter 7).

As the British case most likely shows, domestic political affiliations affect people's responses to opinion polls' questions, in their willingness to support the government's action, assessments of particular foreign policy steps, and overall approval of elected officials. In Italy, for example, those on the right were more supportive of intervention than those on the left. By the time of the crisis in Bosnia, the majority of the Democratic Left Party (former communists and political adversaries of NATO) supported the Atlantic Alliance and the Italian greater role in NATO (Isernia 1998). In Russia, the left held an isolationist attitude in the early 1990s, but became increasingly hawkish by the mid-1990s as soon as they gained political weight in the parliament. In Canada, support for peacekeeping was expressed across party and regional lines. Similarly, virtually all of the leading parties supported the international mediation role for Canada's armed forces in one form or another. However, in 1994, the newly elected Liberals began to act more decisively regarding Bosnia, perhaps trying to distance themselves from their predecessors—the Conservatives. In the Netherlands there was little political opposition to the military solution of the Bosnia dilemma, even from the traditionally antimilitarist left side of the political spectrum (a trend that was repeated clearly during the Kosovo crisis later in the 1990s). For most of the period political differences within or outside the Dutch ruling coalition played only a minor role.

Sending troops abroad might have looked problematic in the context of particular domestic political tribulations and "bad experiences" in some previous military engagements. Any nation—like the United States and the former Soviet Union—that once sent its troops abroad and took casualties may develop its own Vietnam or Afghan "syndrome." Success or failure in previous wars and military engagements may also become either a stimulating or restraining factor in making decisions about new peacekeeping operations. Many armed engagements of the post-Cold War period—all of a different nature though—in Northern Ireland, Chechnya, Somalia, or Afghanistan in 2001, could have been such "stumbling blocs" for Great Britain, Russia, the United States, France, or Italy. The ghost of World War II was powerful enough in Germany to influence decisions about sending German soldiers abroad. Great Britain had a relatively positive experience with the Falkland mission during a brief conflict with Argentina, whereas Russian military contingents were performing peacekeeping missions and taking casualties with the UN forces in Tajikistan, and with the collective peacekeeping forces in the Dnestr region and South Ossetia.

To summarize, on one hand, foreign policy issues, and especially mistakes or anticipation of mistakes in foreign policy—negatively evaluated in opinion polls—are used by the opposition to put pressure on the government responsible for the mistakes to undertake particular actions. In all national cases presented in the book, political pressures initiated by the opposition in order to influence the governments to take action were common. Not only political rivals, but also concerned citizens, as is shown in the French case, could become influential sources of criticism. On the other hand, the government can use specific foreign policy-related issues to strengthen present political standings and electoral chances in the future. Immediate electoral concerns may affect specific foreign policy decisions.

Sociocultural Factors and People's Values

Each country's policy climate taps into a unique political consciousness that consists of values and beliefs—shared by most individuals and communicated among citizens in the form of relatively stable mental representations. These attitudes grow out of cultural, ideological, and religious commitments characteristic to the people of a particular country and are not necessarily based on a cost-benefit calculus. For example, fundamental religious and cultural values—and the Bosnian, Iraqi, and Kosovo crises of the 1990s provide evidence in support of this suggestion—may become absolutely essential in how public sees particular figures, foreign policies, or foreign political regimes. A terrorist and villain in the eyes of the majority of American public may be perceived as a hero and freedom fighter in other nations. Ethnic "cleansing" may be justified and explained in some countries' media (in Russia and Greece, for instance, in relation to the Kosovo conflict) as an inevitable byproduct of a civil war. The "southern," "center," and "northern" subcultures in Italy have long had a polarizing and freezing role on Italian political culture.

Public opinion may reflect some stable and fundamental values that do not change under the pressure of new facts, challenging these values. Thus, since World War II the public in the United States has had a generally activist, not isolationist, orientation toward foreign policy. The Vietnam War split American public opinion along a two-dimensional spectrum (Hinckley 1992). Likewise, the war in Kosovo has put an end to the Russian public's predominant isolationist attitudes of the 1990s toward international conflicts.

Some researchers (see Vengroff et al.; Howard and Howard in this volume) while discussing national cultures, mention a set of values shared by a majority of the population. Specifically, these values include stable national attitudes such as moral responsibility to assist suffering and seemingly help-less people (Martin and Fortmann 1995) the attitudes that become a core set of beliefs determining people's views on international events.

Public opinion is not necessarily capricious, erratic, or volatile. It tends to be relatively stable partly because of the general lack of public interest in for-eign policy and the fear of casualties in cases of possible military conflicts. In the mid-1990s, no less than 56 percent of Dutch people supported participation by the Netherlands' armed forces in actions entailing consider-able risks of casualties. A consistent majority of the French public appeared to favor military intervention. In Italy, public opinion was also strong in sup-port of an armed Italian intervention in Bosnia under the NATO banner.

At the beginning, the war in Bosnia was a *terra incognita* to both journal-ists and the public. The situation differed from other conflicts of the Cold War period, in the sense that the dividing lines between the competing sides were not easily understood in general and ideological terms. Hence, it was not easy for the outside world to interpret the conflict and decide what ought to be done. Thus the public became relatively dependent on the media and government in its attempts to make sense of the ongoing events in the for-mer Yugoslavia. A preconceived and convenient ideological "Cold War" prism, an ideological gestalt for interpretation of international events and distinctions between "them" and "us," was no longer available. However, to a certain degree, this "Cold War" schema—portraying the war as a battlefield between the "evil" authoritarian forces and "noble" freedom fighters—was reinvented in the war in Bosnia. As a result, the Bosnian Serbs were con-stantly portrayed in the Western media as villains.

There is a fairly stable belief system regarding peacekeeping operations in some countries and yet not in others. In general, as Everts shows in chapter 7, questions about the motives justifying the use of force such as "human rights" and "international legal order" scored much higher than matters like "protect-ing economic interests." In Great Britain, polls indicated a significant increase in the people's willingness to perceive their country as a world power. Peace-keeping continued to serve as one of the cornerstones of Canadian foreign policy. Postmaterialist values enhanced the development of a specific self-im-age, a coherent worldview, and a set of distinctly Canadian instrumental val-ues, such as altruism, concerns for environment, human rights, and individual freedom. Canadian foreign policy in Bosnia was congruent with Canadian po-litical culture and sense of identity in spite of their own internal conflict of Quebec separatism that threatened to tear the nation in two (Carriere, O'Reilly, and Vengroff in this volume). Such a global desire to be a major actor in re-solving the conflict was evident in the Canadian, German, and Dutch cases. It permeated the views of elites and the general citizenry, the media, and the content of foreign policy debates across party and ethnic lines.

However, postmaterialist values alone do not explain the complexity of contemporary foreign policy attitudes. Surprisingly, for example, these values and internationalism were found to be negatively correlated in Italian respondents. Though public support for the use of the military in civil tasks and peacekeeping missions have been highly popular among Italians in the 1990s, it was due, most likely, to fundamental idealistic assumptions of catholic or socialist origins (Bellucci and Isernia in this volume). On the other hand, the validity of the "postmaterialist" hypothesis in interpreting the congruence of public and elite opinion is enhanced by the Russian case. That is, economic hardship and material insecurity were strongly correlated with isolationism and apathy (Shiraev 1999a). As a challenge to some rational actor models of political behavior, the Russian case suggests how important it is to consider "ideological values" in interpreting motivations in foreign policy. To illustrate, while no immediate threats to Russia's security existed from the outside, and while the ending of the Cold War had brought increased opportunities for obtaining Western aid, Russia's leaders consistently underemphasized the importance of such help and were painfully concerned instead about not letting Russia be treated as an inferior partner compared to other leading international powers (Goble 1996).

The war in Bosnia cracked the ideological commitments of the so-called peace movement, with some individuals sticking to a nonviolent resolution of the conflict and others pleading for military intervention—and both sides pleading their cases in the name of peace. It is remarkable how in 1999, many European pacifists and German "greens" in particular became unified in their support for military strikes against Serbia (see chapter 8). It remains to be seen whether an embarrassing inaction in the Bosnian war caused a cognitive dissonance between a desire to stop the bloodshed and the lack of will power required for action. According to the psychological theory (Festinger 1957) a mismatch between a person's intentions and behavior create unpleasant psychological pressures and urges the person to act in order to reduce the dissonance. Such dissonance resulted in moral guilt among certain opinion leaders and politicians and prepared some psychological foundation for the development of strong interventionist attitudes and readiness to act in case of the Kosovo crisis a few years later.

Not only pacifist values but also fatalistic assumptions about the nature of all ethnic conflicts conveyed by the European and North American press penetrated public opinion. At the beginning of the escalation of the conflict in the former Yugoslavia, the Dutch were skeptical of the likelihood that an international peacekeeping force would be able to keep the conflicting parties apart. As Everts implies, the emphasis was put on the violent and vicious traditions of all civil wars. Most Russians and many Americans also were skeptical about the conflict. Many French and Russian commentators hinted at the complicated nature of civil wars. Skepticism was also a consequence of the perceived impotence of international institutions and an empty plea of the U.S. president Bush in 1991 for a new international order. On a psychological level, as Philip Everts suggests, it was relatively easy to plead ignorance about complicated conflicts in "faraway countries" and to be fatalistic about them.

Contrary to the developments during the Gulf War in 1991 or during the anti-terrorist actions in Afghanistan in 2001, in which a villain was clearly identified and vilified, no such target emerged immediately in the Bosnia crisis. Both French and Russian governments, for example, refused to name the aggressor in the beginning of the conflict (the French position changed later, but Russian's remained undaunted) and did not support the partition of Yugoslavia. The Italian media never clearly and coherently pictured the Serb leaders Karadzhic and Milosevic as evil. Moreover, arguments about the historic nature of this particular conflict, anti-Nazi actions of the Serbs during World War II, Slavic and Orthodox roots of Serbs and Russians, and historical ties of affinity with Yugoslavia and Serbia lessened the simplicity of the situation (Ullman 1996; La Balme 1998). In Russia, a pro-Serbian sentiment was partially intensified under the influence of a broader anti-Western prejudice growing since the early 1990s as a byproduct of the search for the country's post-Cold War identity (Shiraev 1999b; Sidorov 1994, 3). Gradually, nationalistic and chauvinistic attitudes— evident in public discussions about Russia's role in the Bosnia conflict from the beginning of the conflict in the summer of 1991—became increasingly prominent over time, grew especially strong in 1994–1996, and later became dominant during the 1999 war in Kosovo. Russian leaders desired to see the restoration of the great empire status and were ready to use any opportunity to challenge U.S. interests in the Balkans.

On the other hand, in the countries studied—and the German, Russian, and Dutch cases showed this trend clearly despite some substantial differences between these two countries' policies in the region—setbacks in diplomatic fields and failed attempts to end the conflict in Bosnia led to a sense of humiliation and defeat among opinion leaders in both countries and contributed to strong compelling will for action in Bosnia.

Contextual Factors

Contextual factors such as framing, priming, and agenda-setting—all related to the distribution of information—determine the quantity and quality of information exchanged between the policymakers and the public. These factors communicated by the media and by policymakers through the media determine the salience of a particular foreign policy issue (Paletz 1999, 141–43). For example, at the beginning of the conflict in the former Yugoslavia, few opinion leaders and citizens were knowledgeable about what was going on in the region. The media, providing opportunities for experts of various qualities and persuasions to present their views, helped to shape public debates on the role of foreign countries in the conflict settlement. In effect, some ordinary citizens were informed about events in Bosnia only by reading and listening to various experts and accepting what they conveyed about the war. Bob Wybrow refers to the "bad press" received by the Serbs in British media as a factor contributing to low support of the Bosnian Serbs in opinion polls in 1993. Similarly, the "good press" about the Serbs in most Russian newspapers contributed to relatively pro-Serbian attitudes of the public. Geographic proximity to a region of conflict affects the way a conflict is perceived and seen as a threat to national interests. The "proximity" factor appears in the German, French, Russian, U.S., and Italian cases.

Public awareness about the war in Bosnia—especially in the beginning of the conflict—was relatively low: less than one in ten in Canada named Bosnia as part of the country's peacekeeping activities in the early 1990s. People express their concerns, however, when something substantial touches their emotions. In the broad sense, as suggested by Wybrow in this volume, without the media, the Bosnian tragedy would have faded from people's minds after the first few months of fighting. Coverage of the Sarajevo market massacre in 1994—and followed unanimous calls for action—serves as an example of how quickly a consensus about the necessity of an intervention between governments and public could be reached.

The examination of opinion-policy should also take into consideration the level of unity or disagreement among the elites—including the media—regarding particular foreign policy issues. Coverage of foreign policy in the media is crucial to the formation of a specific policy climate and achievement of a relative agreement between the public and government officials. The Italian government, by way of illustration, at a crucial stage of the war was divided: the minister of foreign affairs was in favor of a military intervention while the minister of defense was opposed to it. The Russian parliament took an anti-NATO stand in Bosnia, whereas the administration tried to balance its approach to the situation. In the Netherlands, the parliamentary opposition demanded from the cabinet a more assertive stand regarding the conflict. The dispatch of the troops found opposition among the Dutch military, voiced by the military leadership and outside military commentators, who referred to national interests, unfinished restructuring of the military, and lack of experience of conscripts.

If the consensus in opinions is predetermined by a political alliance among the officials, the policy climate will be strong and relatively stable. If the government officials are bound by only party coalitions in the parliament (for example, in Italy, Israel, Russia, or Germany), the policy climate will be very unstable and gullible. Moreover, a leader's personal commitment, his or her ability and skills necessary to frame the issue at hand in a desirable way, may also act upon opinion-policy links. La Balme (1998) shows, for example, how Mitterand's personal opposition to war helped him to argue against a military involvement in the Balkans and, on the contrary, how American commitment to the Operation Restore Hope in Somalia affected his decision to finally make a commitment in that region.

The strength of the opinion-policy links can be determined by several communication effects that influence a country's policy climate. These effects are defined as specific schemes of news coverage that determine and shaping people's political preferences and choices (Ansolabehere et al. 1993). Even though it is assumed that the effects share cross-national similarities, this requires additional empirical research. Obviously, each of these phenomena should be examined within national political and cultural contexts. Let us discuss one common denominator of the media effects—their formative role in creating either a "permissive" or a "non-permissive" political climate regarding the country's intervention in Bosnia.

The Free-Rider Effect

Philip Everts notes that few people want their country to take steps irrespective of what other nations do. The existence of an understanding about other countries' commitment is therefore an important condition of domestic support for participating in international peacekeeping. As long as there is no clear commitment for intervention from other countries, a wait-and-see attitude among policymakers and ordinary people becomes prevalent. This situation serves as a restraining factor on the government despite pressures of public opinion. As soon as one or several countries begin to act or show a strong commitment to intervene, a permissive set of attitudes begins to develop in support of the trend (Sobel 1996; Shiraev 2000). Both governments and the public may also hesitate when feeling that other governments are not carrying their part of the international burden. The debates around the Bosnia crisis were mostly directed at the United States. Specifically, the wait-and-see attitude in European governments was influenced by their preference for a more active role for the United States. In Russia, on the other hand, perceptions of the United States' active role in the Balkans induced attitudes and actions of resistance to the growing American influence.

The Victim Effect

People can remain relatively indifferent to a foreign conflict if it gets little media coverage. As soon as gruesome images of civilian suffering and casualties start to appear in the media, attitudes tend to change and the pressures "to do something about it" grow. Shame, compassion, and genuine concern are also important elements in the reactions of many people (Everts; Howard and Howard in this volume). Meanwhile, sensitivity seems to increase due to more communication. Learning more about civilian casualties and starvation, most

Europeans indicated in the opinion polls that they didn't want to let these things continue. The wicked mortar attack on a Sarajevo market in February 1994 that killed sixty-eight people, and the subsequent frightful video images of it distributed around the world brought public opinion together with opinion leaders and policymakers to a consensus about the necessity of taking decisive steps to stop the conflict. Britain's Channel 4 announced at one time that it was to devote fifteen hours of prime-time television to heighten public awareness of the war in Bosnia and the suffering it had caused (Wybrow in this volume). In the Netherlands, the media continued to play their traditional agenda-setting role. Television and newspaper reports about atrocities were a major factor in raising the saliency of the issue from 1991 onwards, and contributed to a climate in which the government increasingly perceived pressures from the public as demanding that something ought to be done in Bosnia. Contrary to other countries, in Russia the Serbs were presented as victims and President Yeltsin defended employing a Russian military contingent near Sarajevo on the basis of persistent requests from the Bosnian Serbs (Volkov 1994, 1). It is also remarkable that the Russian foreign ministry refused to accept the Western media's accusations that the Serbs were responsible for the Sarajevo market tragedy. Instead, clear suggestions were made in the Russian press that the Muslims themselves could have been behind the massacre (Yushin 1994, 1, 3).

The Rally-Around-the-Flag Effect

In democratic countries, before a foreign military operation is announced, political opposition to this operation may be strong. However, when the troops are being deployed or have already been deployed, most people tend to support the government and the nation's commander-in-chief. The effect can be enhanced if the country's national interests appear to be threatened or violated. For example, detention by Bosnian Serbs of several French peacekeepers in May 1995 led to a dramatic change in French policy. In Italy, the climate changed in 1992 after the shooting down of an Italian airplane flying a humanitarian mission over Bosnia. With a popular executive leader in office, this effect can become significant in determining the strength of public and elite support. For example, the French president's visit to Sarajevo provided him with an enormous boost in popularity. Moreover, policymakers can "spin" the issue by using their popularity to promote some designated policy steps. As an example, France's most vociferous policy shift did correspond, as Howard and Howard suggest, with the election of Jacques Chirac to the presidency in 1995. Chirac's foreign policy initiatives were designed to be impressive, especially in the early months following his election. Actions themselves may boost public support. As Everts implies, whether public support for participation in risky peacekeeping is forthcoming and stable, or fails to materialize, depends partly on the credibility, unanimity, and persuasiveness of political leadership. Foreign policy decision makers are able to frame issues through the media in terms designed both to generate popular support for a particular policy and to strengthen people's pre-existing attitudes. For instance, government elites successfully "framed" the issue of Canada's intervention in the former Yugoslavia as one that is peacekeeping, not interventionist, knowing that the public since the 1950s had continuously preferred the former over the latter.

The Body-Bag Effect

Support for war diminishes roughly in logarithmic proportion to the number of expected casualties. People express their concerns about a particular type of an intervention, whether it is a peacekeeping mission or military operation with an increased risk of taking casualties. In the Netherlands, a change in opinion climate toward isolationism was reinforced by the dramatic events of July 1995 when the Bosnian Serbs forced the Dutch military contingent to surrender Srebrenica. (In 2002, the Dutch government announced its resignation, bending to pressure after a report blamed political leaders in part for failing to prevent the Serb massacre of Muslims during the 1995 withdrawal from Srebrenica.) Even the anticipation of casualties can affect public opinion. Politicians thus may refer to public opinion as the reason for which certain policies cannot be implemented. The Italian government maintained an attitude that public support of a military action would change as soon as the first Italian casualties occurred. In January 1996 in Great Britain, the proportion wanting to pull the troops out if they suffered serious casualties was at a high 43 percent level. Assumptions that the public would not be willing to sustain casualties tomorrow even though people support military intervention today was commonly argued by politicians and opinion leaders in every examined case. Public opinion, however, is not static. The unwillingness to sustain casualties is not a constant. It has been argued that the steadfastness of political leaders may create or help to sustain public support (Everts 1996; Sobel 1996; see also van der Meulen, 1994; van der Meulen, 1995; Parsons 1995, 242–43). Even though sixty French soldiers died in the former Yugoslavia by September 1996, the support for intervention remained strong. In spite of some early humiliations, threats to the lives of Canadian troops, a lack of clarity regarding their role, and significant budget cuts for the Canadian armed forces, Canadian public opinion was continuously supportive of a peacekeeping action.

The Likely Success Effect

Support for the use of force increases if a quick and victorious outcome is anticipated at a minimal cost. Depending on the situation posed to them, the

European public was generally in favor of each country's troops being used in Bosnia, particularly when they appeared to be operating in a relatively safe environment where they were providing help and protecting the civilians (Sobel 1996). As Everts explained it, the perceived success of a particular military action appear to be an important intervening variable, determining whether public opinion turns out to be stable or volatile, and whether it presents an obstacle or a condition of effective foreign and military policy. The air campaigns in Bosnia in 1995, in Kosovo in the spring of 1999, and in Afghanistan in 2001, a virtual reality seen by millions on their television screens, have enhanced a perception in some viewers that wars can be easily won from the air. This belief, expressed in opinion polls, may encourage some future political leaders to undertake reckless military actions supported by enthusiastic—but unfortunately misled about the nature and consequences of air war—public opinion. The combined appeal to the described earlier "body bag" and "free rider" effects provides policymakers with a moral and political reasoning—as Wybrow noted—for inaction in the international arena. Anticipation or perception of the "victim," the "likely success," and the "rally-around-the-flag" effects creates a policy climate favorable for implementing the decision to act. In sum, the support for military action drops considerably once the likelihood of casualties becomes apparent. However, the high probability of success and the perceived chances of peace, dehumanization of the opponent, and the need to take revenge, all considerably lessened the impact on policy climate and public opinion that the fear of casualties would have had. These tend to contribute to a hardening of people's positions and a willingness to persevere in the military conflict.

CONCLUSION

To summarize the empirical evidence presented here, we use a multi-axial approach for a comparative study of opinion-policy links. According to this approach, each country's particular policy climate—within which foreign policy decisions are made—is originated by and linked to a set of empirically testable variables. These diverse variables may be examined from several dimensions that refer to specific socioeconomic, political, cultural, and psychological conditions of a country. The use of this approach should help facilitate a more comprehensive evaluation of the relations between public opinion and foreign policy from a comparative perspective and direct attention to conditions that may be unintentionally overlooked in examining of national cases.

First, public opinion is interpreted from a particular standpoint; public opinion "exists" in someone's perception and should be evaluated within a particular ideological and political context. From the pollster's standpoint, public opinion about Bosnia in Europe, Canada, and the United States, in general, was characterized by a combination of concerns about the tragic situation, a relatively strong commitment to the United Nations, and human rights. There was an expressed commitment to taking coordinated—but not unilateral—actions to protect these rights and further peace, justice, as well as a growing antipathy toward ethnic violence. People were aware of the risks inevitable in military operations. On the other hand, public support increased when there was an anticipated success of certain foreign policy. The book displays that from the policymaker's standpoint, public opinion was either strong (Canada) or weak (Russia), based on core values (the Netherlands, Germany) or more immediate concerns (the United States), conveyed directly by the people (Germany), opinion leaders (France), or via political parties (Italy)—it all depends on the context within which the opinion polls were taken and analyzed.

Second, guided by their own beliefs and motivations, policymakers may follow public opinion (1) because of their democratic commitment, religious, and ideological values, or (2) because by initiating a policy they want to make political investment that brings future electoral votes. If policymakers are pressured by strong demands for action, they might question whether the risks involved in the implementation of such actions are equivalent to the values and interests they intend to defend, and whether public opinion will continue to support their policy when the first casualties are taken. The decisions that persons make and opinions that people express about their country's participation in an international military operation are both logical calculations and moral choices, no matter where these topics are discussed or decisions are made—at a kitchen table or in the Oval Office. A level of public support of 55 or 60 percent may look impressive for a journalist or any other observer; however, it can be insufficient for a politician who makes his or her decision on a larger number of variables than the public usually does. Politicians themselves—when asked about the role public opinion plays in their foreign policy decisions—typically tell researchers about the complexity and controversy surrounding opinion-policy connections. Some public officials imply that political decisions are always made according to the will of the people. For instance, George Stephanopoulos, former long-term adviser to president Clinton, suggested in an interview that no foreign policy should be implemented without support of public opinion (Stephanopoulos 1999). Others, as the authors of this volume repeatedly show, often feel insulated from public pressures and imply that public opinion has no direct effect on foreign policy. They insist that their decisions were based on the elite's special expertise and its moral conscience about what is best for the people. It is no surprise that the corridor between opinion and policy resembles a multilevel highway intersection, not a narrow one-way street. The links are interactive and reciprocal rather than unidirectional and linear.

Third, public indifference has its bearing on foreign policy. As Everts brings to mind, if the public is not interested in a foreign policy issue or passive in expressing its opinion, this gives governments considerable freedom of action. However, the public may develop relatively stable and strong attitudes in particular situations when the victims are easily identifiable, for example in cases of terrorism or civil wars and conflicts in which human rights are violated on a large scale. Knowing that they are supported or they are under pressure, policymakers have fewer foreign policy choices to consider except of military actions. Public opinion dynamics during the war in Bosnia in the early and mid-1990s, during the 1999 conflict in Kosovo, and during the anti-terrorism campaign in 2001 mainly support this assumption. Even though a governmental decision to commit the armed forces can be sustained in most countries for some time without parliamentary support, such a legislative approval was also needed. Parliaments, however, hesitate to give such support when they are not confident that public opinion at large will demonstrate understanding and support of the government's actions (Everts; Shiraev and Terrio; Bellucci and Isernia in this volume).

Fourth, the cases present the comparative evidence that government policy is more likely to change in response to a shift in public opinion than vice versa, and to shift in the direction preferred by the public, thus supporting what Graham (1986) and Page and Shapiro (1983) have suggested about U.S. foreign policy. All in all, the cases presented in the book show that public opinion pressures do not per se cause policymakers to change their policies; however, the pressures create a difficult dilemma between the risks they might be taking—if certain policies are unpopular—or the benefits they could gain when they appeal to voters. Public opinion was a relatively consistent supporter of intervention in Bosnia from the beginning of the conflict. The governments, with the exception of Canada and the Netherlands, started with a noninterventionist stance during the first few years of the war, but gradually moved in the direction of public opinion: nonintervention soon gave way to humanitarian intervention, which eventually turned into military intervention. However, public opinion was not always steady, becoming at times less certain about a military action in Bosnia. Fear of casualties, growing pessimism about the ability to bring an ethnic conflict to an end, the lack of clear objectives for peacekeeping missions caused fluctuations in public support for the countries' involvement into the conflict. Fortunately for the peace process, such fluctuations did not change the governments' policies that eventually led to the long-term military intervention. Since a commitment is made, the public support for the military action grows, especially if (1) the perceived success of the operation is evident, (2) fear of casualties is low, and (3) other countries become active participants of the intervention.

And finally, summarizing the empirical evidence presented in the book, and using a multi-axial approach for a comparative study of opinion-policy links, one can make critical assessments and suggestions about some current and future tendencies in public opinion's influence on foreign policy. For instance, the end of the Cold War has decreased the "visibility" of foreign policy because the "evil empire" has disappeared thus demolishing the old foreign policy assumptions and making foreign policy attitudes less accessible in people's minds. The more difficult it is for people to explain foreign affairs, the less pressure is applied to influence policy. Moreover, with the disappearance—though prematurely proclaimed—of the "Cold War frame" in international relations, both policymakers and the media have a chance to frame international news in new ways and by doing this influence public opinion in a way they desire. If there is no clear ideological view about who the enemy really is, the public will tend to pay attention to opinion leaders who can name, define, and explain new dangers in contemporary world. Therefore, often motivated by specific political interests and election concerns, playing on people's fears and anxiety—especially related to international terrorism—public officials can accumulate considerable strength in framing the foreign policy agenda. On one hand, they may face the public that is more detached from foreign policy issues, has less information and fewer attitudinal predispositions (or beliefs about what is "right" and what is "wrong") than it had in the 1980s. On the other hand, the developments after September 11, 2001, may consolidate public opinion and make it less critical to a variety of actions undertaken by governments, especially in the name of the fight against international terrorism.

It is possible that with the growing complexity of international events, while making judgments about foreign politics, the public in democratic countries perhaps will be more dependent on an immediate struggle of ideas among elites—expressed via the media—than on people's own stable ideological commitments. In this context, the role of the leader's persuasive skills—his or her ability to persuade or "spin" an issue for policy-justification purposes—as well as the potential impact of the media will inevitably increase.

This book offers some explanations as well as sets forth testable hypotheses about opinion-policy linkages in international relations. These new hypotheses should encourage researchers to examine not only public support for or objection to particular policies per se but also the policy climate and a variety of contextual factors that influence decision making. The approach for the multiaxial analysis of the opinion-policy links supported by the evidence presented in this volume allows us to remain optimistic about the direction of future research.

Appendix

FOR CHAPTER 4

Table 4.1. June 1993

Question: In the framework of a common foreign and defense policy, the European Community should intervene militarily in former Yugoslavia, in order to reestablish peace.

	Bel	Den	Fr	Ger	Gr	It	Neth	Sp	UK	EC12
For	58%	39%	**59%**	44%	32%	64%	62%	60%	60%	55%
Against	24%	47%	**25%**	38%	50%	21%	24%	19%	24%	28%
DK	18%	14%	**17%**	17%	18%	14%	14%	21%	16%	17%

Source: Eurobarometer 39

Table 4.2. February 7–11, 1994
(survey compares U.S. and French results)

Question: NATO has just issued an ultimatum to the Serbs to lift the siege of Sarajevo within 10 days. If this ultimatum is not respected, would you favor or oppose an aerial military intervention by NATO in which France [the U.S.] would participate . . . ?

	France	U.S.
Favor	76%	48%
Oppose	20%	43%
DK	4%	9%

continued

Table 4.2.　(continued)

Question: In your opinion would attacks against Serbian forces be effective or not in stopping the Serbian attacks on Sarajevo . . . ?

	France	U.S.
Yes	60%	42%
No	31%	47%
DK	9%	11%

Question: Do you approve or disapprove of the way in which the crisis in ex-Yugoslavia has been handled by the President and the government . . . ?

	France	U.S.
Approve	41%	37%
Disapprove	52%	37%
DK	7%	26%

Source: IFOP/Gallup France for Le Journal du Dimanche; Gallup USA for CNN/USA Today

Table 4.3. February, March, and June 1994

Question: The European Community (European Union), United Nations and NATO are involved in former Yugoslavia. Are you for or against the following possible actions being taken by them concerning the conflict between Serbs, Muslims and Croats in Bosnia?

a. Let things as they go now
b. Withdraw all troops
e. Lift the arms embargo against Bosnia
f. Fight when necessary to get humanitarian convoys through
g. To launch air strikes (air attacks)

(options c and d omitted)

	February 1994				March 1994				June 1994			
	France		*EC12*		*France*		*EC12*		*France*		*EC12*	
	+	−	+	−	+	−	+	−	+	−	+	−
a.	8	89	12	82	15	80	16	78	11	84	14	78
b.	23	72	31	62	27	68	30	63	31	62	31	60
e.	32	58	33	54	30	59	31	55	36	54	32	52
f.	90	7	75	20	89	7	76	17	85	10	71	21
g.	53	41	37	55	58	33	46	45	48	46	37	52

Source: Flash Eurobarometers 24, 25, and 29

Table 4.4. September 1995

Question: The European Union, the United Nations and NATO are involved in former Yugoslavia, in the conflict between Serbs, Bosnians and Croats. Do you think that these organizations should or should not . . . ?

a. Let the parties at war settle the conflict amongst themselves
b. Lift the arms embargo against Bosnia
d. Carry on with diplomatic negotiations
e. Keep the UN troops [Casques Bleus] in place, but for humanitarian purposes only
f. Intervene militarily with additional capacity

(option c omitted)

	Bel		Den		Fr		Ger		Gr		It		Neth		Sp		UK		EC 15	
	+	–	+	–	+	–	+	–	+	–	+	–	+	–	+	–	+	–	+	–
a.	44	47	39	53	33	63	36	58	58	33	28	64	29	65	36	53	43	50	6	57
b.	45	42	46	44	40	51	42	48	37	42	42	47	43	47	44	35	39	47	41	46
d.	79	15	78	17	83	15	84	13	91	6	81	14	85	13	83	9	81	17	83	13
e.	60	33	64	32	70	29	66	28	81	9	72	25	61	35	73	21	73	25	70	26
f.	57	35	38	53	57	27	49	44	10	84	59	33	58	37	42	45	55	35	53	38

Source: Europinion 6

TIME-SERIES SURVEYS

May 1993, May 1994, June 1995, June 1996

Questions:
Do you approve or disapprove of the current intervention of France within
the UN in the former Yugoslavia? (asked in 1993, 1994, and 1995)
Do you approve or disapprove of the intervention of France within NATO in
the former Yugoslavia? (asked in 1996)

	May 1993	May 1994	June 1995	June 1996
Approve	69%	62%	52%	54%
Disapprove	21%	25%	35%	28%
DK	10%	13%	13%	18%

Source: SIRPA, Baromètre: les français et la défense nationale (1993–1996)

(Also see Eurobarometer results above)

INDIVIDUAL SURVEYS

August 10, 1992

Question: Do you favor or oppose that, within the framework of the UN,
France participate in a military intervention in Bosnia-Herzegovina (ex-
Yugoslavia)?

Favor	61%
Oppose	33%
DK	6%

Source: IFOP for VSD

December 10-12, 1992

Question: Since the UN is intervening militarily in Somalia, some think it
should also do so in ex-Yugoslavia. Which of the following two opinions do
you agree with more?

France should participate in a military intervention because it is intolerable to let such a civil war take place in Europe without reacting	67%

France should not participate in a military intervention because it would be too risky for our soldiers	23%
DK	10%

Question: If your child or someone in your family were called to serve in a military intervention in Sarajevo, what would be your reaction?

You would be worried but you would understand the necessity of this operation	62%
Your worries would be such that you would not want him to go	30%
DK	8%

Source: CSA for La Vie

December 28–30, 1992

Question: Concerning the situation in the former Yugoslavia, are you personally in favor or opposed to the use of military force to . . . (Is that strongly or somewhat?)

	Total in favor	Total opposed	DK
Protect the delivery of humanitarian aid in the former Yugoslavia	76%	16%	8%
Enforce a cease-fire	70%	21%	9%
Separate the warring parties	61%	27%	12%
Impose a solution	52%	38%	10%

Question: Are you personally in favor or opposed to France using its military forces to . . . (Is that strongly or somewhat?)

	Total in favor	Total opposed	DK
Protect the delivery of humanitarian aid in the former Yugoslavia	71%	22%	7%
Enforce a cease-fire	64%	27%	9%
Separate the warring parties	53%	36%	11%
Impose a solution	48%	42%	10%

Source: IFOP for Le Parisien

April 15-16, 1993

*Question: Do you personally approve or disapprove of the actions of Général
Morillon in Bosnia?*

Approve	73%
Disapprove	11%
DK	16%

*Question: Do you think that Général Morillon should continue his mission
in Bosnia until the end of his mandate in June, or should he be called back
to France right away?*

Continue until June	68%
Be called back to France	15%
DK	17%

*Question: Concerning the actions of the French government in ex-Yu-
goslavia, would you say that . . .*

It is doing everything in its power to stop the fighting in ex-Yugoslavia	31%
It is not making enough efforts to stop the fighting in ex-Yugoslavia	52%
This is not its role (spontaneous response)	5%
DK	12%

*Question: Do you think that the events in ex-Yugoslavia constitute a threat
to peace in Europe?*

Yes	75%
No	20%
DK	5%

Source: IFOP for VSD

January 7–8, 1994

Question: In the upcoming months, do you think that the confrontations in Bosnia and Sarajevo will remain a localized conflict, or will they degenerate into a conflict in all of Europe?

The confrontations in Bosnia and Sarajevo will remain a localized conflict	56%
The confrontations in Bosnia and Sarajevo will degenerate into a conflict in all of Europe	29%
DK	15%

Question: Would you personally want France to participate in a genuine military intervention in Bosnia?

Yes	53%
No	38%
DK	9%

Question: Do you think that a genuine military intervention by the UN would result in ending the war or, on the contrary, make the conflict degenerate?

It would result in ending the war	48%
It would make the conflict degenerate	33%
DK	19%

Source: SOFRES for France Télévision

January 8–9, 1994

Question: Do you feel very concerned, somewhat concerned, somewhat unconcerned, or not at all concerned with the events taking place in the former Yugoslavia?

Very concerned	39%
Somewhat concerned	46% (Total concerned = 85%)
Somewhat unconcerned	8%
Not at all concerned	6% (Total unconcerned = 14%)
DK	1%

Question: Does the presence of military forces under the command of the UN in ex-Yugoslavia seem very useful, somewhat useful, somewhat useless, or completely useless for reestablishing peace?

Very useful	25%
Somewhat useful	37% (Total useful = 62%)
Somewhat useless	22%
Completely useless	12% (Total useless = 34%)
DK	4%

Question: If the UN intervenes militarily, would you be entirely in favor, somewhat in favor, somewhat opposed, or completely opposed to brutal military actions, for example air strikes, knowing the risks that it entails for our soldiers?

Entirely in favor	14%
Somewhat in favor	30% (Total in favor = 44%)
Somewhat opposed	20%
Completely opposed	31% (Total opposed = 51%)
DK	5%

Question: Do you think the UN should:

Continue humanitarian aid in ex-Yugoslavia, without intervening directly in the conflicts	34%
Accentuate military action	47%
Leave ex-Yugoslavia next spring	12%
DK	7%

Question: There exists today an embargo that forbids the different warring parties from acquiring weapons. Are you entirely in favor, somewhat in favor, somewhat opposed, or completely opposed to the elimination of this embargo?

Entirely in favor	13%
Somewhat in favor	15% (Total in favor = 28%)
Somewhat opposed	16%
Completely opposed	49% (Total opposed = 65%)
DK	7%

Source: BVA for SIRPA

February 8–9, 1994

Question: Should the French "Blue Helmets" remain or be withdrawn from Bosnia?

Remain	58%
Be withdrawn	28%
DK	14%

Question: Should NATO bomb the Serb units that are installed around Sarajevo?

Yes	54%
No	29%
DK	17%

Question: Should French soldiers participate in air strikes if NATO decides to bomb the Serb units that are installed around Sarajevo?

Yes	70%
No	21%
DK	9%

Question: Should the French authorities accept the risk of military losses in the fighting taking place in ex-Yugoslavia?

Yes	55%
No	35%
DK	10%

Source: IPSOS for Le Point

February 18–19, 1994

Question: Do you feel very concerned, somewhat concerned, somewhat unconcerned, or not at all concerned with the events taking place in the former Yugoslavia?

Very concerned	31%
Somewhat concerned	55% (Total concerned = 86%)
Somewhat unconcerned	7%
Not at all concerned	7% (Total unconcerned = 14%)
DK	0%

Question: France now has 7000 men stationed in ex-Yugoslavia within the framework of the UN. Do you think that in current conditions, this French presence should be:

Reinforced	27%
Maintained	51%
Diminished	18%
DK	4%

Question: NATO recently issued an ultimatum to the different warring parties in ex-Yugoslavia, demanding that they withdraw their heavy weapons that are located within 20 km from the center of Sarajevo. This ultimatum will expire on February 20, that is on Sunday evening. In case of non-compliance with the conditions set by NATO, are you personally entirely in favor, somewhat in favor, somewhat opposed, or completely opposed to an aerial military intervention by NATO in ex-Yugoslavia?

Entirely in favor	30%
Somewhat in favor	41% (Total 71% in favor)
Somewhat opposed	15%
Completely opposed	9% (Total 24% opposed)
DK	5%

Question: And are you entirely in favor, somewhat in favor, somewhat opposed, or completely opposed to ground operations by NATO in ex-Yugoslavia?

Entirely in favor	18%
Somewhat in favor	37% (Total 55% in favor)
Somewhat opposed	25%
Completely opposed	15% (Total 40% opposed)
DK	5%

Question: And are you entirely in favor, somewhat in favor, somewhat opposed, or completely opposed to France's participation in air strikes in ex-Yugoslavia?

Entirely in favor	26%
Somewhat in favor	42% (Total 68% in favor)
Somewhat opposed	16%
Completely opposed	13% (Total 29% opposed)
DK	3%

Question: And are you entirely in favor, somewhat in favor, somewhat opposed, or completely opposed to France's participation in ground operations in ex-Yugoslavia?

Entirely in favor	18%
Somewhat in favor	35% (Total 53% in favor)
Somewhat opposed	24%
Completely opposed	19% (Total 43% opposed)
DK	4%

Source: BVA for SIRPA

May 19–20, 1994

Question: Concerning the current crisis in Bosnia, would you personally be in favor or opposed to France's military intervention (alone or with its partners) on behalf of the Boniacs?

1. Alone, in the event that the Europeans and Americans refused . . .

Entirely in favor	7%	
Somewhat in favor	13%	Total in favor = 20%
Somewhat opposed	31%	
Completely opposed	46%	Total opposed = 77%
DK	3%	

2. Within the framework of a common European and American intervention . . .

Entirely in favor	27%	
Somewhat in favor	41%	Total in favor = 68%
Somewhat opposed	15%	
Completely opposed	14%	Total opposed = 29%
DK	3%	

Source: IFOP for Globe Hebdo

June 24, 1996

Question: Today do you feel very concerned, somewhat concerned, somewhat unconcerned, or not at all concerned with the events in the former Yugoslavia?

Very concerned	14%	
Somewhat concerned	41%	(Total concerned = 55%)
Somewhat unconcerned	31%	
Not at all concerned	13%	(Total unconcerned = 44%)
DK	1%	

Question: Do you view the presence of French soldiers in ex-Yugoslavia today as very indispensable, somewhat indispensable, not very indispensable, or not at all indispensable?

Very indispensable	13%	
Somewhat indispensable	37%	(Total indispensable = 50%)
Not very indispensable	27%	
Not at all indispensable	15%	(Total not indispensable = 42%)
DK	8%	

Question: Do you think their mission in ex-Yugoslavia is very useful, somewhat useful, somewhat useless, or completely useless?

Very useful	19%	
Somewhat useful	41%	(Total useful = 60%)
Somewhat useless	23%	
Completely useless	12%	(Total useless = 35%)
DK	5%	

Question: Would you be very much in favor, somewhat in favor, somewhat opposed, or completely opposed to an extension of their mission in ex-Yugoslavia after December 20, the end of the application of the Dayton accord concerning the reestablishment of peace?

Very much in favor	12%	
Somewhat in favor	26%	(Total 38% in favor)
Somewhat opposed	26%	
Completely opposed	27%	(Total 53% opposed)
DK	9%	

Source: IPSOS for SIRPA

FOR CHAPTER 6

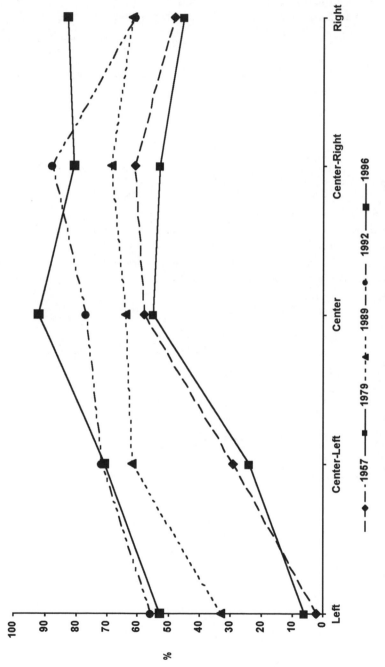

Figure 6.1. Support for NATO by Party Preference in Different Years (% of those in favor of NATO)

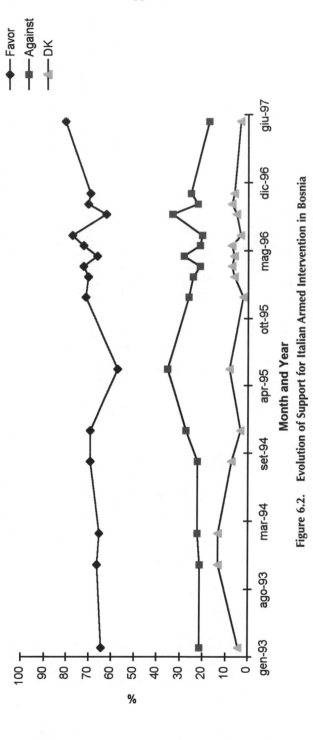

Figure 6.2.   Evolution of Support for Italian Armed Intervention in Bosnia

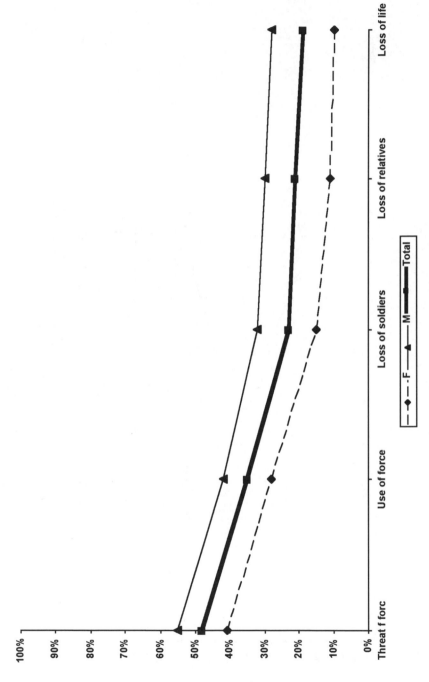

Figure 6.3.   Support for Italian Participation under Different Conditions by Gender

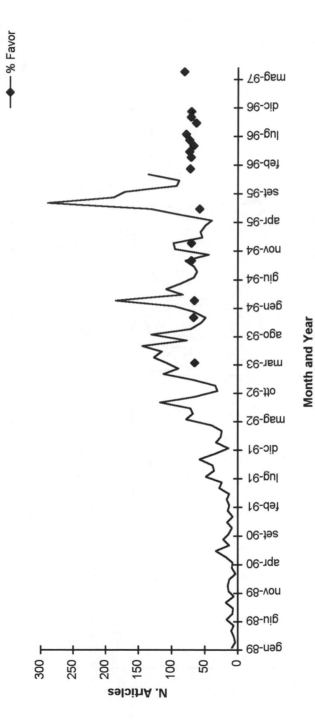

Month and Year

Figure 6.4. Evolution of Media Attention and Public Favor

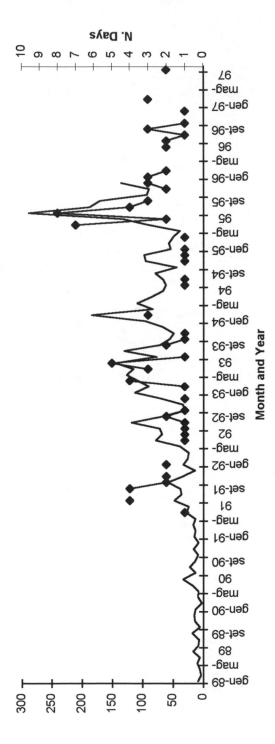

Figure 6.5. Evolution of Media and Parliamentary Attention

——— N. Articles ——◆— N. Days in Parliament

References

Aldrich, J. H., J. L. Sullivan, and E. Borgida. 1989. "Foreign Affairs and Issue Voting: Do Presidential Candidates Waltz before a Blind Audience?" *American Political Science Review* 83: 123–42.

Allensbacher Jahrbuch der Demoskopie, 1984–1992. Vol. 9, Institut für Demoskopie Allensbach.

Almond, Gabriel A. 1960. *The American People and Foreign Policy.* New York: Praeger.

Almond, Gabriel, and Sidney Verba. 1963. *The Civic Culture: Political Attitudes and Democracy in Five Nations.* Princeton, N.J.: Princeton University Press.

Almond, Gabriel A. 1950. *The American People and Foreign Policy.* New York: Harcourt, Brace.

Almond, Mark. 1994. *Europe's Backyard War: The War in the Balkans.* New York: Heinemann.

Alston, Jon, Theresa Morris, and Arnold Vedlitz. 1996. "Comparing Canadian and American Values: New Evidence from National Surveys." *American Review of Canadian Studies* 26: 301–14.

Ammendola, Teresa. 1993. "Opinione pubblica e politica militare in Italia." *Rivista Trimestrale di Scienza dell'Amministrazione* 3–4: 277–99.

Ansolabehere, Stephen, Behr Roy, and Iyengar Shanto. 1993. *The Media Game: American Politics in the Television Age.* Boston: Allyn and Bacon.

Arbatov, Georgy. 1992. "Rescue Russia, or Else!" *Newsday* (October 25).

Asher, Arian. 1995. *Security Threatened: Surveying Israeli Opinion on Peace and War.* Cambridge: Cambridge University Press.

Asmus, Ronald D. 1992. *Germany in Transition: National Self-Confidence and International Reticence.* Santa Monica, Calif.: Rand. N-3522-AF, 34.

Atkinson, Rick, and John Pomfret. 1995. "NATO Hits Bosnian Serbs with Massive Air Raid." *Washington Post,* August 30, 1995, A1.

Axworthy, Lloyd. 1997. "Canada and Human Security: The Need for Leadership." *International Journal* 52: 183–96.

Banfield, Edward C. 1958. *The Moral Basis of a Backward Society.* Chicago: Free Press.

Barnes, Samuel H. 1994. "L'elettorato italiano e la teoria della democratizzazione." In M. Caciagli, F. Cazzola, L. Morlino, and S. Passigli, eds. *L'Italia fra crisi e transizione.* Bari: Laterza.

Bartels, L. M. 1991. "Constituency Opinion and Congressional Policy-Making: The Reagan Defense Buildup." *American Political Science Review* 85: 457–74.

Battistelli, Fabrizio. 1996. *Soldati. Sociologia dei militari italiani nell'era del peacekeeping.* Milano: Angeli.

Battistelli, Fabrizio, and Pierangelo Isernia. 1992. "Dove gli angeli non osano mettere piede: opinione pubblica e politica internazionale in Italia." *Teoria Politica* 7, no. 1, 81–119.

Baturin, Andrei, and Sergei Gryzunov. 1994. "A Dance with a broom, as performed by Zhirinovsky." Russian News Agency *Novosti*, special to *Izvestia* (February 1): 4.

Bausin, Alexei. 1995. "Who Should Decide Europe's Future?" *Vek* 46: 4.

Beal, R. S., and R. H. Hinckley. 1984. "Presidential Decision Making and Opinion Polls." *Annals of the American Academy of Political and Social Science* 474: 72–84.

Bellucci, Paolo. 1996. "Opinione pubblica giovanile e difesa." In F. Battistelli, ed. *Giovani e Forze Armate: Aspetti sociologici della condizione giovanile e della comunicazione istituzionale.* Milano: Angeli.

Bellucci, Paolo. 1998. *Difesa, politica e società: La politica militare italiana tra obiezione di coscienza e professionalizzazione delle Forze Armate.* Milano: Angeli.

Berger, Thomas. 1996. "Norms, Identity, and National Security in Germany and Japan." In Peter Katzenstein, ed. *The Culture of National Security: Norms and Identity in World Politics.* New York: Columbia University Press.

Blanchette, Arthur, ed. 1994. *Canadian Foreign Policy 1977–1992.* Ottawa: Carleton University Press. Canadian Broadcasting Corporation (CBC) *Canada on Record: Part Eight (8. Suez).*

Bolshakov, Vladimir. 1994. "In the Name of the 'New Order.'" *Pravda* (March 2): 6.

———. 1994. "Yugoslavia: Tense Waiting—Russia Could Not Have Acted Otherwise." *Pravda* (February 22): 3.

Boode, S. de. 1993. "Meningen in de media: Het debat over militair ingrijpen in Bosnië/Joegoslavië." *Transaktie* 22, no. 4: 362–68.

Boode, S. de 1995. "Het debat na Srebrenica." *Transaktie* 24, no. 4: 509–15.

Botyanovsky, Alexander. 1996. "Bosnian Knott." *Mezhdunarodnaya Zhizn* 1: 80–86.

Brand, Joel. 1994. "NATO Patrols Return to Skies Over Bosnia: Serbs Renege on Pledge to Release 402 UN Peacekeepers Detained in Bihac Pocket." *Washington Post,* December 4, A41.

Brooks, Joel. 1985. "Democratic Frustration in the Anglo-American polities: A Quantification of Inconsistency between Mass Public Opinion and Public Policy." *Western Political Science Quarterly* 38 (June): 250–61.

———. 1987. "The opinion-policy nexus in France: do institutions and ideology make a difference?" *Journal of Politics* 49, May: 465–480.

Bryce, James. 1888. *The American Commonwealth.*

Burbyga, Nikolai. 1994. "Russia's Peacekeeping Forces in action." *Izvestia* (March 23): 2.

Burk, J. 1995. "Public Support for Peacekeeping in Lebanon and Somalia." Paper presented at the conference of the Inter-university Seminar on Armed Forces and Society, Baltimore (October 22–25).

Burk, J. 1996. "The Casualties Hypothesis and Public Support for Peacekeeping." Paper prepared for the Seminar on Public Opinion, Democracy, and Security Policy, Certosa di Pontignano, Siena (October 7–10).

Canadian International Development Agency. 1995. "Canadians' Opinions on Canadian Foreign Policy, Defense Policy and International Development Assistance." www.acdicida.gc.ca/cida_ind.nsf.

Carment, David. 1996. "Rethinking Peacekeeping: The Bosnia and Somalia Experience." In Fen Hampson and Maureen Molot, eds. *Canada among Nations 1996: Big Enough to be Heard.* Ottawa: Carleton University Press.

Ceri, Paolo, ed. 1997. *Politica e sondaggi.* Torino: Rosenberg and Sellier.

Charaudeau, Patrice, Guy Lochard, and Jean-Claude Soulages. 1996. "La construction thématique du conflit en Ex-Yougoslavie par les journaux télévisés français 1990–1994." In *Mots* 47.

Churkin, Vitaly. 1992. An interview to *Izvestia.* Interview by N. Yermolovich. *Izvestia* (December 15): 6.

Clark, Joe. 1997. "The First International Country." *International Journal* 52: 539–45.

Clinton, Richard. 1975. "Politics and Survival." *World Affairs* 138, no. 2 (Fall): 108–27.

Cohen, Bernard C. 1995. *Democracies and Foreign Policy: Public Participation in the United States and the Netherlands.* University of Wisconsin Press.

———. 1973. *The Public's Impact on Foreign Policy.* Boston: Little, Brown and Co.

———. 1977–1978. "Political Systems, Public Opinion, and Foreign Policy: The United States and the Netherlands." *International Journal* 33, no. 1: 195–216.

Cohen, S., ed. 1996. *L'Opinion, l'humanitaire et la guerre: une perspective comparative.* Paris: Fondation pour les Etudes de Défense.

Comfort, Nicholas. 1993. *Brewer's Politics.* London: Cassell.

Comments on President Bill Clinton's Visit to Moscow. *Novaya Yezhednevnaya gazeta* (January 15): 2.

Commonwealth Relations Office (CRO). 1956. Files. London: Public Record Office.

Converse, Philip E. 1964. "The Nature of Belief Systems in Mass Publics." In David E. Apter, ed. *Ideologies and Discontent.* New York: Free Press.

Cooper, Andrew F. 1997. *Canadian Foreign Policy: Old Habits and New Directions.* Scarborough, Ontario: Prentice Hall Allyn.

Cotta, Maurizio, and Pierangelo Isernia, eds. 1996. *Il gigante dai piedi d'argilla. La crisi del regime partitocratico in Italia.* Bologna: Il Mulino.

Cradock, Percy. 1997. *In Pursuit of British Interests: Some Reflections on Foreign Policy under Margaret Thatcher and John Major.* London: John Murray.

Crawford, Beverly. 1996. "Explaining Defection from International Cooperation: Germany's Unilateral Recognition of Croatia." *World Politics* 48, no. 4: 482–521.

Crisis and Pearson the Peacemaker. CBC Radio Broadcast, September 28, 1979. Ottawa: National Archives of Canada.

Dancocks, Daniel G. 1989. *Welcome to Flanders Fields, the First Canadian Battle of the Great War: Ypres, 1915.* Toronto: McClelland & Stewart.

Demurin, Mikhail. 1995. "Press briefing by foreign ministry vice spokesman Mikhail Demurin, May 23, 1995," *Official Kremlin International News Broadcast.*

Department of Foreign Affairs and International Trade. 1996. "Canada and the Former Yugoslavia." www.dfait-maeci.gc.ca/geo/europe/yugo-cda.htm.

Department of Foreign Affairs and International Trade. 1996. "Canada's contribution to the OSC's Mission in Support of the Dayton Peace Agreement." www. dfait-maeci.gc.ca/geo/europe/dayton.htm.

Dobrynin, Anatoly. 1997. *Sugubo Doveritelno [Very Confidentially]*. Avtor: Moscow.

Duffield, John. 1999. *World Power Forsaken: Political Culture, International Institutions, and German Security Policy after Unification*. Stanford: Stanford University Press.

Dumas, Roland. 1996. *Le Fil et la Pelote*. Paris: Plon.

Efron, Sonni. 1994. "Russia Moves to Encircle Capital of Rebel State." *Los Angeles Times*, December 12, A1.

Eggert, Konstantin. 1994. "Defeat in Bosnia, United Russia and the West." *Izvestia* (April 30): 3.

———. 1995. "A 'Great-Power' Foreign Policy Is Too Expensive." *Izvestia* (December 16): 3.

Eichenberg, Richard C. 1989. *Public Opinion and National Security in Western Europe*. London: MacMillan.

English, John. 1989. *Shadow of Heaven: The Life of Lester Pearson*. Vol. 1. Toronto: Lester & Orpen Dennys.

———. 1993. *The Worldly Years: The Life of Lester Pearson*. Vol. 2. Toronto: Vintage Books.

Everts, Philip. 1996. "Public Support for the Military UN-Operation in the Netherlands: The Case of Bosnia-Herzegovina. A New Look at the 'Body-Bag Hypothesis.'" Paper presented at the Conference "Democracy, Public Opinion, and the Policy of Defense," Certosa di Pontignano, Siena (October 7–10).

———. 1998. "Public Opinion and Decisions on the Use of Military Force in Democratic Societies." Paper presented in the Workshop "Democracy, Public Opinion, and the Use of Force in a Changing International Environment." Joint sessions of workshops, European Consortium for Political Research, University of Warwick (March 23–28).

Everts, Ph. 1983. *Public Opinion, the Churches and Foreign Policy: Studies of Domestic Factors in the Foreign Policy of the Netherlands*. Leiden: Institute for International Studies.

———. 1992. *Wat denken 'de mensen in het land'? Ontwikkelingen in de publieke opinie over problemen van buitenlandse en defensiepolitiek, 1983–1992*, Cahier 55, Studiecentrum voor Vredesvraagstukken, Nijmegen.

———. 1993. "Support for War: Public Opinion on the Gulf War, 1990–1991." In J. Balasz and H. Wiberg, eds. *Peace Research for the 1990's*. Budapest: Akademiai Kiado.

———. 1996. "The 'body bag hypothesis' as alibi. Public support for UN military operations in the Netherlands: the case of Bosnia-Hercegovina." *Politics, Groups, and the Individual* 6, no. 1: 75–84.

———. 1998. "Public opinion and decisions on the use of military force in democratic societies." Paper prepared for presentation in the Workshop "Democracy, Public Opinion, and the Use of Force in a Changing International Environment," Joint Sessions of the European Consortium for Political Research, University of Warwick (March 23–28).

———. 1998a. "Les Pays-Bas, Innocence Perdue." In P. Buffotot, ed., *La défenseen Europe. Les adaptations de l'après-guerre froide*. Paris: La Documentation Francaise.

Everts, Ph. P., and R. A. Koole. 1995. "Un atlantisme de plus en plus pragmatique." In P. Buffotot, ed., *La défense en Europe. De la guerre du Golfe au conflit yougoslave*. Paris: La Documentation Francaise.

Everts, Philip. 1983. *Public Opinion, the Churches, and Foreign Policy. Studies of Domestic Factors in the Foreign Policy of the Netherlands*. Leiden: Institute for International Studies.

Fact Sheet. 1991. German Information Center. New York (February 21).

Fadeyev, Yevgeny. 1994. "Bosnia: NATO Begins and . . . " *Pravda* (March 3): 3.

Felgengauer, Pavel. 1994. "Balkans: UN Command tries to send Russian 'blue helmets' to Bosnia." *Sevodnya* (February 16): 1.

———. 1994. "Someone Else's War." *Sevodnya* (April 12): 1.

Festinger, Leon. 1957. *A Theory of Cognitive Dissonance*. Stanford, Calif.: Stanford University Press.

Flynn, Gregory H., and Hans Rattinger, eds. 1985. *The Public and Atlantic Defense*. Totowa, N.J.: Rowman & Allanheld.

Foyle, Douglas C. 1997. "Public Opinion and Foreign Policy: Elite Beliefs as a Mediating Variable." *International Studies Quarterly* 41: 141–69.

Galli, Giorgio. 1966. *Il bipartitismo imperfetto. Comunisti e democristiani in Italia*. Bologna: Il Mulino.

Gallup Canada Poll. 1994. January 27.

Gallup Canada Poll. 1995. January, June, September, and December.

Gallup, George, and Saul Forbes Rae. 1940. *The Pulse of Democracy*. New York: Simon & Schuster.

Gallup, George. 1976. *The Sophisticated Poll Watcher's Guide*. Princeton, N.J.: Princeton Opinion Press.

Gamson, William. 1989. "News as Framing." *American Behavioral Scientist* 33: 157–61.

Garifullina, N. 1992. "Who betrays his brothers." *Sovetskaya Rossya* (June 6): 1

Garnham, D. 1994. *War Casualties and Public Opinion: A Cross-National Replication*. Paper presented at the International Studies Association Annual Conference, Washington, D.C. (March).

Geer, John G. 1996. *From Tea Leaves to Opinion Polls*. New York: Columbia University Press.

Gelb, Leslie. 1992. "False Humanitarianism." *New York Times*, August 6, A15.

Germroth, David, and Rebecca Hudson. 1992. "German-American Relations and the Post-Cold War World." *Aussenpolitik* 1: 33–42.

Glenny, Misha. 1992. *The Fall of Yugoslavia*. New York: Penguin Books.

Goble, Paul. 1996. "Dangerous Liaisons: Moscow, the Former Yugoslavia, and the West." In Richard Ullman, ed. *The World and Yugoslavia Wars*. New York: Council on Foreign Relations.

Gorbachev, Mikhail. 1994. "It Is Dangerous When Russia Is Treated as a Junior Partner." *Nezavisimaya Gazeta* (February 22): 2.

Gornostaev, Dmitry. 1994. "Two Bears before 1996." *Nezavisimaya Gazeta* 10 (November): 1.

Gourevitch, Peter. 1978. "The Second Image Reversed: The International Source of Domestic Politics." *International Organization* 32: 881–911.

Gowing, Nik. 1994. "Real-Time Television Coverage of Armed Conflicts and Diplomatic Crises: Does It Pressure or Distort Foreign Policy Decisions." John F. Kennedy School of Government, Working Paper 94–1, 35.

Graham, T. W. 1986. *Public Attitudes toward Active Defense: ABM and Star Wars, 1945–1985*. Cambridge, Mass.: Center for International Studies, MIT Press.

Granatstein, J. L. 1974. "Canada and Peacekeeping: Image and Reality." *The Canadian Forum* (August): 14–19.

———. 1982. *The Ottawa Men: The Civil Service Mandarins, 1935–1957*. Toronto: Oxford University Press.

Granatstein, J. L., and Robert Bothwell. 1990. *Pirouette: Pierre Trudeau and Canadian Foreign Policy*. Toronto: University of Toronto Press.

Graziano, Luigi. 1968. *La politica estera italiana nel dopoguerra*. Milano: Marsilio.

Gromyko, Anatoly. 1997. *Andrei Gromyko: V Labirintakh Kremlia [Andrei Gromyko: In the Labyrinth of the Kremlin]*. Moscow: IPO Avtor.

Gryzunov, S., and V. Baturin. 1994. "An Editorial." *Nezavisimaya gazeta*, February 4, 4.

Handelingen, Tweede Kamer. 1994–1995. Betrokkenheid van het parlement bij de uitzending van militaire eenheden [Notitie Toetsingskader. Letter of the ministers of Foreign Affairs and Defense to the Second Chamber of Parliament]. 28 June 1995, 23 591, n. 5.

Hansard, *House of Commons Debates* (Canada) 1994. 133, 1, 35th Parliament, September 21.

Hansard, *House of Commons Debates* (Canada) 1994. 133, 1, 35th Parliament, January 25.

Hansard, *House of Commons Debates* (Canada) 1995. 133, 1, 35th Parliament, May 29.

Hansard, *House of Commons Debates* (Canada) 1995. 133, 1, 35th Parliament, March 29.

Hartley, T., and B. Russett. 1992. "Public Opinion and the Common Defense: Who Governs Military Spending in the United States?" *American Political Science Review* 86: 361–87.

Hayes, Geoffrey. 1997. "Canada as a Middle Power: The Case of Peacekeeping." In Andrew F. Cooper, ed. *Niche Diplomacy: Middle Powers after the Cold War*. New York: St. Martin's Press.

Hearst, David. 1995. "Bear's Sore Heart." *The Guardian* (London) September 14, 17.

Helman, Gerald B., and Steven R. Ratner. 1992–1993. "Saving Failed States." *Foreign Policy* 89: 3–20.

Herman, Tamar. 1998. "After Oslo: Israelis' perceptions of peace and the use of force." Paper presented in the Workshop "Democracy, Public Opinion, and the Use of Force in a Changing International Environment," Joint Sessions of Workshops, European Consortium for Political Research, University of Warwick (March 23–28).

Hilliker, John. 1990. *Canada's Department of External Affairs*. Vol. 1. Montreal: McGill-Queens University Press.

Hillmer, Norman. 1992. "The Canadian Diplomatic Tradition." In J. L. Granatstein, ed. *Towards a New World: Readings in the History of Canadian Foreign Policy*. Toronto: Copp Clark Pitman Ltd.

Hinckley, R. H. 1992. *People, Polls, and Policymakers: American Public Opinion and National Security*. New York: Lexington Books.

Hine, David. 1993. *Governing Italy. The Politics of Bargained Pluralism*. Oxford: Oxford University Press.

Holbrooke, R. 1998. *To End a War*. New York: Random House.

Holmes, John. 1993. "La politica estera italiana." In S. Hellman and G. Pasquino, eds. *Politica in Italia. I fatti dell'anno e le interpretazioni*. Bologna: Il Mulino.

Holmes, John W. 1970. *The Better Part of Valour: Essays on Canadian Diplomacy*. Toronto: McClelland & Stewart Ltd.

———. 1982. *The Shaping of Peace: Canada and the Search for World Order 1943–1957*. Vol. 2. Toronto: University of Toronto Press.

———. 1992. "Most Safely in the Middle." In J. L. Granatstein, ed. *Towards a New World: Readings in the History of Canadian Foreign Policy*. Toronto: Copp Clark Pitman.

Holsti, Ole. 1992. "Public Opinion and Foreign Policy: Challenges to the Almond-Lippmann Consensus." *International Studies Quarterly* 36, no. 4: 439–66.

———. 1996. *Public Opinion and Foreign Policy*. Ann Arbor: University of Michigan Press.

Hosking, Geoffrey. 1997. *Russia: People and Empire, 1952–1917*. Cambridge: Harvard University Press.

Hughes, Barry B. 1978. *The Domestic Context of American Foreign Policy*. San Francisco: W. H. Freeman.

Inglehart, Ronald. 1990. *Culture Shift in Advanced Industrial Society*. Princeton, N.J.: Princeton University Press.

———. 1991. *World Values Survey*. Ann Arbor, Mich.: Institute for Social Research.

———. 1997. *Modernization and Postmodernization: Cultural, Economic, and Political Change in 43 Societies*. Princeton, N.J.: Princeton University Press.

Inglehart, Ronald, Neal Nevitte, and Miguel Basanez. 1996. *The North American Trajectory*. New York: Aldine de Gruyter.

International Security Review. 1993. The Royal United Services Institute for Defense Studies.

Isernia, Pierangelo. 1992. "Opinione pubblica e politica di difesa in Italia." In C. M. Santoro, ed. *L'Elmo di Scipio: Il Nuovo modelo di difesa*. Bologna: Il Mulino.

Isernia, Pierangelo. 1996a. "Bandiera e risorse: La politica estera italiana negli anni ottanta." In M. Cotta and P. Isernia, eds. *Il gigante dai piedi d'argilla: La crisi del regime partitocratico in Italia*. Bologna: Il Mulino.

Isernia, Pierangelo. 1996b. *Dove gli angeli non mettono piede: Opinione pubblica e politiche di sicurezza in Italia*. Milano: Angeli.

Isernia, Pierangelo. 1998. "Italian Public Opinion and Foreign Policy." Paper delivered at an international conference "Public Opinion, Mass Media, and Foreign Policy," Columbia University (November 19–20).

Isernia, Pierangelo, and Teresa Ammendola. 1993. "I nuovi compiti delle Forze Armate e l'opinione pubblica." Paper presented at the Conference Le metodologie qualitative nella sociologia dell'organizzazione: modelli e applicazioni nell'organizzazione militare, Università di Roma "La Sapienza" (May 18–19).

Iyengar, Shanto. 1997. "Framing Responsibility for Political Issues: The Case of Poverty." In Yengar Shanto and Richard Reeves, eds. *Do the Media Govern Politicians, Voters and Reporters in America?* Beverly Hills, Calif.: Sage Publications.

Jaarboek Vrede en Veiligheid 1993. 1993. Nijmegen: Studiecentrum Vredesvraagstukken.

Jaarboek Vrede en Veiligheid 1994. 1994. Nijmegen: Studiecentrum Vredesvraagstukken.

Jaarboek Vrede en Veiligheid. 1995. 1995. Nijmegen: Studiecentrum Vredesvraagstukken.

Jacobs, Lawrence R. 1993. *The Health of Nations: Public Opinion and the Making of American and British Health Policy.* Ithaca: Cornell University Press.

Jacobs, Lawrence, and Robert Y. Shapiro. 1994. "Studying Substantive Democracy." *PS: Political Science and Politics* 27, no. 1 (March): 9–17.

Janning, J. 1996. "A German Europe—A European Germany? On the Debate over Germany's Foreign Policy." *International Affairs* 72, no. 1: 33.

Jenkins, Simon, and Sloman, Anne. 1985. *With Respect, Ambassador.* British Broadcasting Corporation.

Jentleson, Bruce. 1992. "The Pretty Prudent Public: Post Post-Vietnam American Opinion on the Use of Military Force." *International Studies Quarterly* 36: 49–72.

Johnson's Russia List #32705, May 1999 davidjohnson@erols.com.

Katz, Richard S. 1986. "Party Government: A Rationalistic Conception." In F. G. Castles and R. Wildenmann, eds. *Vision and Realities of Party Government.* New York: De Gruyter.

Katz, Richard S., ed. 1987. *Party Government: European and American Experiences.* Berlin: de Gruyter.

Keating, Tom, and Nicholas Gammer. 1993. "'The New Look' in Canada's Foreign Policy." *International Journal* 48: 720–48.

Kegley, Charles W. Jr., and Eugene R. Wittkopf. 1987. *American Foreign Policy: Pattern and Process.* 3rd ed. New York: St. Martin's Press.

Kelley, Jack. 1994. "Clinton's Moscow Welcome Uncertain: Frustrated Russians Cool to the USA." *USA TODAY,* January 12, 1A.

Kissinger, Henry. 1994. *Diplomacy.* New York: Simon & Schuster.

Kogan, Norman. 1965. *La politica estera italiana.* Milano: Lerici.

Kokoshin, Andrei. 1996. An interview to Argumenty i Facty, #25, 3.

Kondrashov, Stanislav. 1994. "Toward Partnership without Illusions through Bosnia and 'Ames Affair.'" *Izvestia* (March 5): 3.

———. 1994. "Who Was Forced to Do Something against His Own Interests in Goradze, and How Did That Happen?" *Izvestia* (April 20): 3.

———. 1995. "Russia Can Go Cheap in Bosnia and in General?" *Izvestia* (November 21): 3.

———. 1995. "Who Are Russian Voters more Dissatisfied With—Clinton or Yeltsin?" *Izvestia* (October 13): 6.

Kortunov, Sergei. 1998. "Is the Cold War Really Over?" *International Affairs* 5: 147.

Kouchner, Bernard. 1995. *Ce que je crois.* Paris: Grasset.

Kremenyuk, Viktor. 1994. "Deputy Director of the Russian Academy of Sciences' Institute of the U.S. and Canada Comments on President Bill Clinton's Visit to Moscow." *Novaya Yezhednevnaya Gazeta* (January 15): 2.

Kull, Steven, I. M. Destler, and Clay Ramsay. 1997. "The Foreign Policy Gap: How Policymakers Misread the Public." A Report by the Center for International and Security Studies at the University of Maryland and the Program on International Policy Attitudes, University of Maryland.

Kull, Steven. 1995. "Misreading the Public Mood." *Bulletin of the Atomic Scientists* 51, no. 2: 55–59.

Kull, Steven, and I. M. Destler. 1999. *Misreading the Public: The Myth of a New Isolationism*. Washington, D.C.: Brookings Institution Press.

Kull, Steven, I. M. Destler, and Clay Ramsay. 1997. *The Foreign Policy Gap: How Policymakers Misread the Public*. Program on International Policy Attitudes, Center for International and Strategic Studies at the University of Maryland.

Kuznechevsky, Vladimir. 1994. "The UN Peace Plan in Yugoslavia Ends in Disaster." *Rossiiskaya Gazeta* (April 19).

Kyle, Keith. 1991. *Suez*. New York: St. Martin's Press.

La Balme, N. 1998. "The Public's Influence on France's Decision to Use Force." Paper presented in the Workshop "Democracy, Public Opinion, and the Use of Force in a Changing International Environment." Joint sessions of workshops, European Consortium for Political Research, University of Warwick, March 23–28, 1998.

La Balme, Natalie. 1998. "L'influence de l'opinion publique dans la gestion des crises." In Samy Cohen, ed. *Mitterrand et la Sortie de la Guerre Froide*. Paris: Presses Universitaires de France.

———. 2000. *Raison d'état or Raison Populaire?* [The Influence of Public Opinion on France's Bosnia Policy]. In R. Shapiro, B. Nacos, and P. Isernia, eds. *Decision-Making in the Glass House*. Boulder: Rowman & Littlefield.

La Palombara, Joseph. 1964. *Interest Groups in Italian Politics*. Princeton, N.J.: Princeton University Press.

Lapitsky, Vladimir. 1999. "Bayonets and Placards?" *Rossiyskaya Gazeta* (March 27).

Larson, E. 1996. *Casualties and Consensus: The Historical Role of Casualties in Domestic Support for U.S. Military Operations*. Rand Report.

Levy, David. 1997. *Tools of Critical Thinking*. Boston: Allyn and Bacon.

Lippmann, Walter. 1955. *Essays in the Public Philosophy*. Boston: Little, Brown.

Lipset, Seymour M. 1990. *Continental Divide*. New York: Routledge.

Lloyd, John. 1999. "East-West: New Cold War in the Making." *Financial Times*. April 12, 1.

Maatschappij en Krijgsmacht 14. 1992. 1: 14–18. "Zonder de Sovjet-Unie."

Maatschappij en Krijgsmacht 15. 1993. 1: 2–6.

Maatschappij en Krijgsmacht 17. 1995. 1: 3–8.

Mackay, R. A. 1992. "The Canadian Doctrine of the Middle Powers." In J. L. Granatstein, ed. *Towards a New World: Readings in the History of Canadian Foreign Policy*. Toronto: Copp Clark Pitman Ltd.

MacKenzie, Jean. 1995. "High-Profile President Looks Like a Candidate." *The Moscow Times*. October 20.

MacWilliam, Ian. 1997. "Bread Impresses Russians More Than NATO." *The Moscow Times*. February 8.

Malcolm, Neil. 1995. "Russian Foreign Policy Decision-making." In Peter Sherman, ed. *Russian Foreign Policy Since 1990*. Boulder, Colo.: Westview Press.

Martin, Pierre, and Michel Fortmann. 1995. "Canadian Public Opinion and Peacekeeping in a Turbulent World." *International Journal* 50: 370–400.

Masker, John Scott. 1998. "Signs of a Democratized Foreign Policy? Russian Politics, Public Opinion, and the Bosnian Crisis." *World Affairs* 160 (spring): 179–92.

Mastanduno, Michael. 1989. "Toward a Realist Theory of State Action." *International Studies Quarterly* 33: 457–74.

Mastny, Vojtech, ed. 1995. *Italy and East Central Europe: Dimension of the Regional Relationship.* Boulder, Colo.: Westview Press.

Maull, Hanns. 1999. "Germany and the Use of Force: Still a Civilian Power?" *Trierer Arbeitspapiere zur Internationalen Politik*, no. 2 (November): 2.

McNaught, Kenneth. 1988. "Canada's European Ambiance." Paper presented at the annual meeting of the Italian Association for Canadian Studies, Sicily. Cited in Lipset, 1990, 220–21.

Meulen, J. van der. 1993. "Het verlangen naar de ideale oorlog." *Maatschappij en Krijgsmacht* 15, no. 4 (August): 3–8.

———. 1994. "Veiligheid hier en daar." *Maatschappij en Krijgsmacht* 16 (February): 2–8.

———. 1995. "Einde missie?" *Maatschappij en Krijgsmacht* 17, no. 4 (February): 2–8.

———. 1995a. "Publieke opinies over de krijgsmacht." *Maatschappij en Krijgsmacht* 17, no. 1: 3–8.

———. 1996. "P.O. Kroniek 1." *Maatschappij en Krijgsmacht* 18, no. 3/4: 3–7.

Meulen, J. van der, and M. de Konink. 1998. "Zero-Dead? Testing the 'Casualty Hypothesis': Dutch Public Opinion and Peacekeeping in Bosnia." Paper presented at ECPR joint sessions of workshops, Warwick.

———. 1998a. "Nooit meer sneuvelen? Precisering van de slachtofferhypothese." *Transaktie* 27, no. 2: 191–208.

Migranyan, Andranik. 1992. "Real and Illusory Guidelines in Foreign Policy." *Rossiyskaya Gazeta* (August 4): 7.

Mikheyev, Vladimir. 1994. "The NATO Ultimatum Threatening Bombing in Bosnia Gets No Support in Moscow." *Izvestia* (February 11): 1.

Mlechin, Leonid. 1994. "A Strategy of Deterrence May Be the Last Chance to Achieve Peace in Bosnia." *Izvestia* (February 16): 3.

———. 1994. "Moscow Is Making a Mistake by Shunning Joint Actions with the West in Bosnia." *Izvestia* (April 23): 1, 3.

Monroe, A. D. 1979. "Consistency between Public Preferences and National Policy Decision." *American Politics Quarterly* 7: 3–19.

Moravcski, A. 1993. "Introduction: Integrating International and Domestic Theories of International Bargaining." In P. B. Evans, H. K. Jacobson, and R. D. Putnam, eds. *Double-Edged Diplomacy: International Bargaining and Domestic Politics.* Berkeley: University of California Press.

Morgenthau, H. J. 1973. *Politics among Nations.* 5th ed. New York: Alfred A. Knopf.

Mueller, J. E. 1971. "Trends in Popular Support for the Wars in Korea and Vietnam." *American Political Science Review* 65, no. 2.

———. 1973. *War, Presidents and Public Opinion.* New York: John Wiley.

———. 1993. *American Public Opinion and the Gulf War.* In S. A. Renshon, ed. *The Political Psychology of the Gulf War: Leaders, Publics, and the Process of Conflict.* Pittsburgh: University of Pittsburgh Press.

———. 1994. *Policy and Opinion in the Gulf War.* Chicago: University of Chicago Press.

Neal, Pernila M. 1995. "La 'nuova' politica estera italiana." In P. Ignazi and R. S. Katz, eds. *Politica in Italia. I fatti dell'anno e le interpretazioni.* Bologna: Il Mulino.

Nelson, Thomas, Zoe Oxley, and Rosalee Clawson. 1997. "Toward a Psychology of Framing Effects." *Political Behavior* 19, no. 3: 221–46.

Nevitte, Neal. 1996. *The Decline of Deference*. Peterborough, Ontario: Broadview.

Nossal, Kim Richard. 1989. *The Politics of Canadian Foreign Policy*. 2nd ed. Scarborough, Ontario: Prentice-Hall Canada.

Oreglia, Simona. 1997. *L'opinione pubblica e la politica estera: un'analisi del pubblico francese in prospettiva comparata*. MA thesis. Università di Siena.

O'Reilly, Marc J. 1997. "Following Ike? Explaining Canadian-U.S. Cooperation during the 1956 Suez Crisis." *The Journal of Commonwealth & Comparative Politics* 35, no. 3: 75–107.

Owen, David. 1995. *Balkan Odyssey*. New York: Harcourt Brace.

Page, Benjamin I. 1994. "Democratic Responsiveness? Untangling the Links between Public Opinion and Policy." *PS: Political Science and Politics* 27, no.1 (March): 25–29.

Page, Benjamin I., and Robert Y. Shapiro. 1983. "Effects of Public Opinion on Policy." *American Political Science Review* 77: 175–90.

———. 1984. "Presidents as Opinion Leaders: Some New Evidence." *Policy Studies Journal* 12: 649–61.

———. 1988. "Foreign Policy and the Rational Public." *Journal of Conflict Resolution* 32: 211–47.

———. 1992. *The Rational Public: Fifty Years of Trends in American Policy Preferences*. Chicago: University of Chicago Press.

Paletz, David. 1999. *The Media in American Politics*. New York: Longman.

Panebianco, Angelo. 1977. "La politica estera italiana: Un modello interpretativo." *Il Mulino* 26: 845–79.

Parsons, A. 1995. *From Cold War to Hot Peace: UN Interventions, 1947–1994*. London: Michael Joseph.

Pasquino, Gianfranco. 1974. "Pesi internazionali e contrappesi nazionali." In F. L. Cavazza and S. R. Graubard, eds. *Il caso italiano*. Milano, Garzanti.

Payerhin, Marek, and David Hubert. 1998. "Rhetorically Speaking: Elites and the Public in the Making of Foreign Policy." Paper presented at the 1998 meeting of the New England Political Science Association, Worchester, Mass.

Pearson, Geoffrey A. H. 1993. *Seize the Day: Lester B. Pearson and Crisis Diplomacy*. Ottawa: Carleton University Press.

Pearson, Lester B. 1951. "The Development of Canadian Foreign Policy." *Foreign Affairs* 30, no. 1: 17–30.

———. 1957. "Force for UN." *Foreign Affairs* 35, no. 3: 395–404.

———. 1972. *Mike: The Memoirs of the Right Honourable Lester B. Pearson*. Vol. 1. Toronto: University of Toronto Press.

Peresvet, Alexander. 1995. "Peacekeeper in the Helmet." *Ogonyok*, no. 31 (July).

Poggioli, Silvia. 1992. A Report on National Public Radio. December 25. A transcript.

Popov, Gavriil. 1996. An interview to *Argumenty i Facty*, no. 8: 3.

Powlick, P. J. 1991. "The Attitudinal Bases for Responsiveness to Public Opinion among Foreign Policy Officials." *Journal of Conflict Resolution* 35: 611–41.

Pushkov, Alexei. 1994. "Russia and America: The Honeymoon's Over. Part Three." *Moscow News* (January 10).

Putnam, Robert D. 1973. *The Beliefs of Politicians: Ideology, Conflict, and Democracy in Britain and Italy*. New Haven, Conn.: Yale University Press.

———. 1977. "Italian Foreign Policy: The Emergent Consensus." In H. R. Penniman, ed. *Italy at the Polls: The Parliamentary Elections in 1976*. Washington, D.C.: American Enterprise Institute.

———. 1978. "Interdependence and the Italian Communists." *International Organization* 32, no. 2: 301–49.

———. 1988. "Diplomacy and Domestic Politics: The Logic of Two-Level Games." *International Organization* 42, no. 3: 427–60.

———. 1993. *Making Democracy Work*. Princeton, N.J.: Princeton University Press.

Quaroni, Pietro. 1967. "Chi è che fa la politica estera in Italia." In M. Bonanni, ed. *La politica estera della repubblica italiana*. Milano: Comunità.

Radio Ekho Moskvy. May 3, 1999.

Reid, Angus. 1997. "International Views on Canada—Canada's Foreign Affairs and Policy." www.angusreid.com/cdnwrld/world_b/sld019.htm.

Richman, Alvin. 1996. "The Polls—Trends: American Support for International Involvement: General and Specific Components of Post-Cold War Changes." *Public Opinion Quarterly* 60 (summer): 305–21.

Rieff, David. 1986. *Slaughterhouse: Bosnia and the Failure of the West*. New York: Touchstone Books.

Risse-Kappen, Thomas. 1991. "Public Opinion, Domestic Structures and Foreign Policy in Liberal Democracies." *World Politics* 43, no. 4: 479–512.

Rodgers, Regina. 2000. "Playing Their Part: Public Opinion in American Democracy." *Public Perspective* (March/April): 24–26.

Rodin, Ivan. 1993. "Foreign Ministry Doesn't Like Three Factions' Draft." *Nezavisimaya Gazeta* (January 22): 2.

Rodionov, Boris. 1992. "UN Sanctions against Yugoslavia didn't take into Consideration Russia's Interests." *Izvestia* (June 4): 4.

Romano, Sergio. 1995. "East Central Europe in Post-World War I Italian Diplomacy." In Vojtech Mastny, ed. *Italy and East Central Europe: Dimension of the Regional Relationship*. Boulder, Colo.: Westview Press.

Roschar, F. M., ed. 1975. *Buitenlandse politiek in de Nederlandse publieke opinie, 1960–1975*. Den Haag: Nederlands Instituut voor Vredesvraagstukken.

Rosenau, James N. 1961. *Public Opinion and Foreign Policy: An Operational Formulation*. New York: Random House.

Rosner, Gabriella. 1963. *The United Nations Emergency Force*. New York: Columbia University Press.

———. 1989. "Democracy, Public Opinion, and Nuclear Weapons." In Philip E. Tetlock, Jo L. Husbands, Robert Jervis, Paul C. Stern, and Charles Tilly, eds. *Behavior, Society and Nuclear War*. Vol. 1. New York: Oxford University Press.

———. 1990. *Controlling the Sword: The Democratic Governance of National Security*. Cambridge: Harvard University Press.

———. 1993. *Grasping the Democratic Peace: Principles for a Post-Cold War World*. Princeton, N.J.: Princeton University Press.

Sallot, Jeff. 1997. "Neighborhood Watch." *Globe and Mail* (Toronto). April 26, D1, D9.

Schelling, Thomas C. 1980. *The Strategy of Conflict*. Cambridge: Harvard University Press.

Schennink, B., and Wecke, L. 1995. *Draagvlak voor de vn-vredesoperaties en de vn na Srebrenica*. Paper presented at conference "Vijftig jaar vn-vredesoperaties Nijmegen" (October 23).

Schlesinger, Arthur Jr. 1995. "New Isolationists Weaken America." *New York Times.* June 11, sec. 4, 15.

Schneider, Howard. 1997. "Canada's Global Clout Grows as its Army Shrinks." *Washington Post,* December 3, A1, A39.

Schwarz, B. 1994. *Casualties, Public Opinion and U.S. Military Intervention: Implications for U.S. Regional Deterrence Strategies.* Santa Monica, Calif.: Rand Corporation.

Sciolla, Loredana. 1990. "Identità e mutamento culturale nell'Italia di oggi." In Vincenzo Cesareo, ed. *La cultura dell'Italia contemporanea. Trasformazione dei modelli di comportamento e identità sociale.* Torino: Fondazione G. Agnelli.

Sciolla, Loredana. 1997. *Italiani. Stereotipi di casa nostra.* Bologna: Il Mulino.

Segatti, Paolo. 1997. "Gli orientamenti dei giovani in Italia e in Europa." In R. Cartocci and A. M. L. Parisi, eds. *Difesa della patria e interesse nazionale nella scuola.* Milano: Angeli.

Seldon, Anthony, and Lewis Baston. 1997. *Major: A Political Life.* London: Weidenfeld & Nicolson.

Shapiro, Margaret. 1994. "Yeltsin Scoring Points at Home With Bid to Block NATO Airstrikes; Moscow Sees President Reasserting Russian Diplomacy in Sarajevo." *Washington Post,* February 19, A19.

Shapiro, Robert Y., and Lawrence R. Jacobs. 2000. "Who Leads and Who Follows? U.S. Presidents, Public Opinion, and Foreign Policy." In Brigitte L. Nacos, Robert Y. Shapiro, and Pierangelo Isernia, eds. *Decision-Making in the Glass House.* Lanham, Md.: Rowman & Littlefield.

———. 1989. "The Relationship between Public Opinion and Public Policy: A Review." In Samuel Long, ed. *Political Behavior Annual.* Vol. 2. Boulder, Colo.: Westview Press.

Shchipanov, Michail. 1992. "Don't We Need Serbia?" *Kuranty,* no. 97 (May 20): 3.

Sherman, Peter. 1995. "Russian Policy toward the United States." In Peter Sherman, ed. *Russian Foreign Policy Since 1990.* Boulder, Colo.: Westview Press.

Shiraev, E. 1999a. "Attitudinal Changes During the Transition." In Betty Glad and Eric Shiraev, eds. *The Russian Transformation.* New York: St. Martin's.

———. 1999b. "The Post Soviet Orientations toward the United States and the West." In Betty Glad and Eric Shiraev, eds. *The Russian Transformation.* New York: St. Martin's.

Shiraev, E., and Zubok, V. (2000). "Against the West: Anti-Western Attitudes as a Mediating Factor in Russia's Opinion-Policy Linkages 1991–1999." In Brigitte L. Nacos, Robert Y. Shapiro, and Pierangelo Isernia, eds. *Decision-Making in the Glass House.* Lanham, Md.: Rowman & Littlefield.

Shlapentokh, V. 1996. Russia: "Privatization and Illegalization of Social and Political Life." *The Washington Quarterly* 19 (Winter): 65–85.

Shlapentokh, V., and Shiraev, E., eds. 2002. *Fears in Post-Communist Societies.* New York: Palgrave.

Shusharin, Dmitry. 1994. "Aleksy II Opposes Sanctions But Refrains from Expressing Direct Support for Serbia." *Sevodnya* (May 17): 1.

Sidorov, Sergei. 1994. "Russia's Position is Clear: No NATO Air Strikes Against the Bosnian Serbs." *Krasnaya Zvezda* (February 19): 1.

Sidorov, Sergei. 1994. "Yugoslavia: Moscow Opposes Air Strikes on Bosnia." *Krasnaya Zvezda* (January 25): 3.

Simes, Dimitri. 1994. "The Imperial Consensus; From Czars to Reformers, Why Russia Keeps Returning to the Dream of Empire." *Washington Post*, December 25.

Sinnott, Richard, and Oskar Niedermayer. 1995. *Public Opinion and Internationalized Governance*. Oxford: Oxford University Press.

Smirnov, Andrey. 1997. "Paradoxes of Post-Soviet Perceptions." *Segodnya* (September 20): 1–4.

Smith, Denis. 1988. *Diplomacy of Fear: Canada and the Cold War 1941–1948*. Toronto: University of Toronto Press.

Smith, Michael. 1996. "Sending the Bundeswehr to the Balkans: The Domestic Politics of Reflexive Multilateralism." *German Politics and Society* 14 (Winter): 59.

Sobel, Richard. 1993. *Public Opinion in U.S. Foreign Policy: The Controversy over Contra Aid*. Lanham, Md.: Rowman & Littlefield.

———. 1996. "U.S. and European Attitudes toward Intervention in the Former Yugoslavia: *Mourir pour la Bosnie?*" Washington, D.C.: Council on Foreign Relations.

———. 1998. "Portraying American Public Opinion toward the Bosnian Crisis." *Press/Politics* 3, no. 2: 16–33.

———. 1998. "Peacekeeping in Bosnia and Public Opinion in Comparative Perspective." Paper delivered at an international conference, "Public Opinion, Mass Media, and Foreign Policy," Columbia University, November 19–20.

Solzhenitsyn, Alexander. 1998. *Rossiia v obvale [Russia in the ruins]*. Moscow: Russkii Put.

St. Laurent, Louis. 1970. "The Foundations of Canadian Policy in World Affairs." In R. A. Mackay, ed. *Canadian Foreign Policy 1945–1954: Selected Speeches and Documents*. Toronto: McClelland & Stewart.

Stairs, Denis. 1977–1978. "Public Opinion and External Affairs: Reflections on the Domestication of Canadian Foreign Policy." *International Journal* 33: 128–49.

———. 1982. "The Political Culture of Canadian Foreign Policy." *Canadian Journal of Political Science* 15, no. 4: 667–90.

———. 1989. "The Diplomacy of Constraint." In Norman Hillmer, ed. *Partners Nevertheless: Canadian-American Relations in the Twentieth Century*. Toronto: Copp Clark Pitman.

Stephanopolous, George. 1999. Telephone interview. WJFK, J. Gordon Liddy Radio Show. March 22, 2:10 p.m.

Telen, Lyudmila. 1992. "Yugoslavia: The Russians have already come." *Moscovskie Novosti* (December 6): 4.

This Week in Germany. 1991. February 22.

Thordarson, Bruce. 1974. *Lester Pearson: Diplomat and Politician*. Toronto: Oxford University Press.

Tullio-Altan, Carlo. 1986. *La nostra Italia. Arretratezza culturale, clientelismo, trasformismo e ribellione dall'Unità ad oggi*. Milano: Feltrinelli.

Ullman, Richard. 1996. "The World and Yugoslavia's Wars." In Richard Ullman, ed. *The World and Yugoslavia Wars*. New York: Council on Foreign Relations.

van der Meulen, J. 1994. "Veiligheid hier en daar." *Maatschappij en Krijgsmacht* 16, no. 1.

———. 1995, "Publieke opinies over de krijgsmacht." *Maatschappij en Krijgsmacht* 17, no. 1: 3–8.

Vaneker, Ch. H. J., and Ph. P. Everts, eds. 1985. *Buitenlandse politiek in de Nederlandse publieke opinie, 1975–1984*. Den Haag: Clingendael.

Védrine, Hubert. 1996. *Les mondes de François Mitterrand*. Paris: Fayard.

Vengroff, Richard. 1996. "Canadian Public Opinion on Free Trade." In Subash Jain and David Ralston, eds. *Proceedings of the Colloquim on the North American Free Trade Agreement*. Storrs, Conn.: CIBER.

Volkov, Dmitry. 1994. "Russia's attitude toward NATO is Getting Colder." *Sevodnya* (February 26): 1.

Volobuev, Pavel, and Lyudmila Tyagumenko. 1992. "It Makes a Difference to Russia." *Pravda* (February 27): 1, 3.

Volski, Dmitry. 1993. "Eastern Europe—Counterbalance to Russia?" *New Times*, no. 21, 22.

Von Riekhoff, Harald. 1977–1978. "The Impact of Prime Minister Trudeau on Foreign Policy." *International Journal* 33: 267–86.

Wecke, L. 1994. "Lotgevallen van de Nederlandse krijgsmacht." In *Jaarboek Vrede en Veiligheid 1994*. Nijmegen: Studiecentrum Vredesvraagstukken.

Wecke, L., and M. Cras. 1995. "Lotgevallen van de Nederlandse Krijgsmacht." In *Jaarboek Vrede en Veiligheid 1995*. Nijmegen: Studiecentrum Vredesvraagstukken.

Weir, Fred. 1999. A column from *Hindustan Times* (April 8).

Wetenschappelijke Raad voor het Regeringsbeleid. 1995. "Stabiliteit en Veiligheid in Europa. Het veranderende krachtenveld voor het buitenlands beleid.'" Rapport 48. Den Haag: SDU.

Wetstein, Matthew E. 1996. *Abortion Rates in the United States: The Influence of Opinion and Policy*. Albany, N.Y.: SUNY Press.

Weymouth, Lally. 1992. "Milosevic's Next Target." *Washington Post*, November 23, A21.

White, S., R. Rose, and I. McAllister. 1997. *How Russia Votes*. Chatham: Chatham House Publishers.

Williams, Daniel. 1995. "Italy Seeks Bigger Role on Diplomatic Stage." *Washington Post*, October 11, A27.

Willick, Daniel H. 1969. "Public Interest in International Affairs: A Cross-National Study." *Social Science Quarterly* 50, no. 2: 272–85.

Winter, James. 1992. *Common Cents: Media Portrayal of the Gulf War and Other Events*. Montreal: Black Rose Books.

Winter, James, eds. 1990. *The Silent Revolution: Media, Democracy, and the Free Trade Debate*. Ottawa: Actexpress.

Wittkopf, Eugene. 1990. *Faces of Internationalism*. Durham, N.C.: Duke University Press.

Wittkopf, Eugene. 1986. "On the Foreign Policy Beliefs of the American People: A Critique." *International Studies Quarterly* 30: 425–46.

Yastrzhembski, Sergei. 1993. Official Kremlin International News Broadcast. Press Briefing by the Russian Federation Foreign Ministry Spokesman (January 12).

Yeric, Jerry, and John Todd. 1996. *Public Opinion: The Visible Politics*. Itasca, Ill.: F.E. Peacock Publishers.

Yushin, Maxim. 1994. "Moscow Is Calling for Restraint." *Izvestia* (February 8): 1, 3.

———. 1994. "President Yeltsin Issues an Ultimatum to the Bosnian Serbs." *Izvestia* (April 21): 3.

———. 1994. "Relations between Russia and the U.S. are going through the Most Serious Crisis in Recent Years." *Izvestia* (March 12): 3.

Zaller, John, and Dennis Chui. 1996. "Government's Little Helpers: U.S. Press Coverage of Foreign Policy Crises, 1945–1991." *Political Communication* 13: 385–405.

Index

About the Contributors

Eric Shiraev is an author, coauthor, and coeditor of five books, including two college textbooks: *The Russian Transformation* (St. Martin's Press, 1999), *Anti-Americanism in Russia: From Stalin to Putin* (Palgrave, 2001), *The Accent of Success* (Prentice Hall, 2001), *Fears in Post-Communist Societies* (Palgrave, 2002), and *Introduction to Cross-Cultural Psychology* (Allyn & Bacon, 2001). He is coauthor of a college textbook on public opinion scheduled to be released in 2003. He now teaches political science at George Mason University and serves as a Research Associate at the Institute for European, Russian, and Eurasian Studies at George Washington University.

Richard Sobel is author of *The Impact of Public Opinion on U.S. Foreign Policy Since Vietnam: Constraining the Colossus* (Oxford University Press, 2001), *Public Opinion in U.S. Foreign Policy: The Controversy Over Contra Aid*, and numerous articles. He is coauthor of a college textbook on public opinion scheduled to be released in 2003. He is a Senior Research Associate at the Roper Center for Public Opinion Research at University of Connecticut, Storrs and has been researching public opinion and policy issues at Harvard University since 1996.

Erin Carrière was awarded a Ph.D. with concentrations in Comparative Politics and Survey Research from the University of Connecticut in 2001, and is currently working as an analyst of European public opinion at the Department of State, Office of Research. She has a particular interest in the relationship between opinion and policy, which she now investigates on a daily basis.

Marc O'Reilly, a graduate of the University of Connecticut, is an Assistant Professor of Political Science at Heidelberg College. He has published articles on Canadian foreign policy in the Journal of Commonwealth & Comparative Politics and the American Review of Canadian Studies. His other research interests include U.S. foreign policy and Middle Eastern politics.

Richard Vengroff is Head of the Department of Political Science at the University of Connecticut. He is the author or coauthor of seven books and over seventy scholarly articles and book chapters. His current research centers on electoral systems and electoral reform cross-nationally.

Robert J. Wybrow worked for the British Gallup Company for forty-one years, twenty-five of which were spent in charge of Gallup's polling activities. He holds a Diploma in Sociology from the University of London and has written many books and papers, as well as lecturing in Oxford and Paris, on British public opinion.

Steven Kull is the Director of the Program on International Policy Attitudes, a joint program of the Center on Policy Attitudes and the Center for International and Security Studies at the University of Maryland, and a member of the faculty at the University's School of Public Affairs. A political psychologist specializing in the study of public and elite attitudes on public policy issues, he has conducted numerous nationwide polls and focus groups. He is regularly interviewed by the media, and frequently briefs government officials in the United States and Europe—and officials of NATO and the UN—on the U.S. public. He is the author of several books, including *Misreading the Public: The Myth of a New Isolationism* coauthored with I. M. Destler (Brookings Institution Press, 1999). He is a member of the Council on Foreign Relations and the American Association for Public Opinion Research.

Clay Ramsay has been Research Director of the Program on International Policy Attitudes (a joint program of the Center on Policy Attitudes and the Center for International and Strategic Studies at the University of Maryland) since 1999, and Senior Fellow since 1993. He has coauthored numerous reports and articles on the Program's work, including *The Foreign Policy Gap: How Policymakers Misread the Public* with Steven Kull and I. M. Destler (1997), and is currently working on the on-line reference "Americans and the World" website <www.americans-world.org>.

Marc Morjé Howard is an Assistant Professor in the Department of Government and Politics at the University of Maryland. He is the author of *The Weakness of Civil Society in Post-Communist Europe* (Cambridge University Press, 2003). His research interests include such topics as democratization, civil society, citizenship, right-wing extremism, ethnicity, democratic performance, and public opinion, focusing on both Eastern and Western Europe.

Lise Morjé Howard is an Assistant Professor in the Department of Government at Wesleyan University. Her research interests span the fields of international security and international organization, focusing on peacekeeping, civil wars, comparative foreign policy, the Balkans, and Africa. She is currently working on a book entitled, *UN Peacekeeping in Civil Wars: Success, Failure, and Organizational Learning.*

Philip Everts is Director of the Institute for International Studies, Leiden University, Holland. His research focuses on problems of European security, the role of domestic factors in the making of foreign policy, and on public opinion on international affairs. He is the author of *Democracy and Military Force* (Palgrave, 2002).

Paolo Bellucci is Professor of Political Science at the Università degli Studi del Molise at Isernia. He is cofounder and member of the Board of the Italian National Election Study (Itanes) and Research Associate at the Istituto Cattaneo, Bologna. He is currently investigating the Italian political elite's response to European integration and the transformation of Italian mass attitudes toward politics. His most recent work is *The Return of Berlusconi*, edited with M. Bull (Berghahn Books, 2002).

Pierangelo Isernia is Professor of Political Science at the University of Siena, Italy. His main research interests are public opinion and foreign policy in Western Europe, international crises, and comparative foreign policy. He has recently edited a book with Philip Everts, *Public Opinion and the International Use of Force* (Routledge, 2001) and he is now completing—with Philip Everts—a book on the Kosovo War and public opinion.

Deone Terrio received a Ph.D. in Government from Cornell University in 1994. Her interests are Russian politics, comparative politics, international relations, and political theory. She taught in the Political Science Department at Oregon State University from 1990 to 1999.

Karin Johnston is Research Associate at the American Institute for Contemporary German Studies, Johns Hopkins University. She served as the Assistant Director of the Program on International Policy Attitudes at the Center for International and Security Studies at the University of Maryland, and

Program Coordinator at the Institute for Global Chinese Affairs, also at the University of Maryland. A former recipient of the Robert Bosch Foundation Fellowship, she is currently pursuing a Ph.D. in Political Science at the University of Maryland on the use of force in German foreign policy.